# Lecture Notes in Computer Science

Vol. 117: Fundamentals of Computation Theory. Proceedings, 1981. Edited by F. Gécseg. XI, 471 pages. 1981.

Vol. 118: Mathematical Foundations of Computer Science 1981. Proceedings, 1981. Edited by J. Gruska and M. Chytil. XI, 589 pages. 1981.

Vol. 119: G. Hirst, Anaphora in Natural Language Understanding: A Survey. XIII, 128 pages. 1981.

Vol. 120: L. B. Rall, Automatic Differentiation: Techniques and Applications. VIII, 165 pages. 1981.

Vol. 121: Z. Zlatev, J. Wasniewski, and K. Schaumburg, Y12M Solution of Large and Sparse Systems of Linear Algebraic Equations. IX, 128 pages. 1981.

Vol. 122: Algorithms in Modern Mathematics and Computer Science. Proceedings, 1979. Edited by A. P. Ershov and D. E. Knuth. XI, 487 pages. 1981.

Vol. 123: Trends in Information Processing Systems. Proceedings, 1981. Edited by A. J. W. Duijvestijn and P. C. Lockemann. XI, 349 pages. 1981.

Vol. 124: W. Polak, Compiler Specification and Verification. XIII, 269 pages. 1981.

Vol. 125: Logic of Programs. Proceedings, 1979. Edited by E. Engeler. V, 245 pages. 1981.

Vol. 126: Microcomputer System Design. Proceedings, 1981. Edited by M. J. Flynn, N. R. Harris, and D. P. McCarthy. VII, 397 pages. 1982.

Voll. 127: Y.Wallach, Alternating Sequential/Parallel Processing. X, 329 pages. 1982.

Vol. 128: P. Branquart, G. Louis, P. Wodon, An Analytical Description of CHILL, the CCITT High Level Language. VI, 277 pages. 1982.

Vol. 129: B. T. Hailpern, Verifying Concurrent Processes Using Temporal Logic. VIII, 208 pages. 1982.

Vol. 130: R. Goldblatt, Axiomatising the Logic of Computer Programming. XI, 304 pages. 1982.

Vol. 131: Logics of Programs. Proceedings, 1981. Edited by D. Kozen. VI, 429 pages. 1982.

Vol. 132: Data Base Design Techniques I: Requirements and Logical Structures. Proceedings, 1978. Edited by S.B. Yao, S.B. Navathe, J.L. Weldon, and T.L. Kunii. V, 227 pages. 1982.

Vol. 133: Data Base Design Techniques II: Proceedings, 1979. Edited by S.B. Yao and T.L. Kunii. V, 229–399 pages. 1982.

Vol. 134: Program Specification. Proceedings, 1981. Edited by J. Staunstrup. IV, 426 pages. 1982.

Vol. 135: R.L. Constable, S.D. Johnson, and C.D. Eichenlaub, An Introduction to the PL/CV2 Programming Logic. X, 292 pages. 1982.

Vol. 136: Ch. M. Hoffmann, Group-Theoretic Algorithms and Graph Isomorphism. VIII, 311 pages. 1982.

Vol. 137: International Symposium on Programming. Proceedings, 1982. Edited by M. Dezani-Ciancaglini and M. Montanari. VI, 406 pages. 1982.

Vol. 138: 6th Conference on Automated Deduction. Proceedings, 1982. Edited by D.W. Loveland. VII, 389 pages. 1982.

Vol. 139: J. Uhl, S. Drossopoulou, G. Persch, G. Goos, M. Dausmann, G. Winterstein, W. Kirchgässner, An Attribute Grammar for the Semantic Analysis of Ada. IX, 511 pages. 1982.

Vol. 140: Automata, Languages and programming. Edited by M. Nielsen and E.M. Schmidt. VII, 614 pages. 1982.

Vol. 141: U. Kastens, B. Hutt, E. Zimmermann, GAG: A Practical Compiler Generator. IV, 156 pages. 1982.

Vol. 142: Problems and Methodologies in Mathematical Software Production. Proceedings, 1980. Edited by P.C. Messina and A. Murli. VII, 271 pages. 1982.

Vol. 143: Operating Systems Engineering. Proceedings, 1980. Edited by M. Maekawa and L.A. Belady. VII, 465 pages. 1982.

Vol. 144: Computer Algebra. Proceedings, 1982. Edited by J. Calmet. XIV, 301 pages. 1982.

Vol. 145: Theoretical Computer Science. Proceedings, 1983. Edited by A.B. Cremers and H.P. Kriegel. X, 367 pages. 1982.

Vol. 146: Research and Development in Information Retrieval. Proceedings, 1982. Edited by G. Salton and H.-J. Schneider. IX, 311 pages. 1983.

Vol. 147: RIMS Symposia on Software Science and Engineering. Proceedings, 1982. Edited by E. Goto, I. Nakata, K. Furukawa, R. Nakajima, and A. Yonezawa. V. 232 pages. 1983.

Vol. 148: Logics of Programs and Their Applications. Proceedings, 1980. Edited by A. Salwicki. VI, 324 pages. 1983.

Vol. 149: Cryptography. Proceedings, 1982. Edited by T. Beth. VIII, 402 pages. 1983.

Vol. 150: Enduser Systems and Their Human Factors. Proceedings, 1983. Edited by A. Blaser and M. Zoeppritz. III, 138 pages. 1983.

Vol. 151: R. Piloty, M. Barbacci, D. Borrione, D. Dietmeyer, F. Hill, and P. Skelly, CONLAN Report. XII, 174 pages. 1983.

Vol. 152: Specification and Design of Software Systems. Proceedings, 1982. Edited by E. Knuth and E. J. Neuhold. V, 152 pages. 1983.

Vol. 153: Graph-Grammars and Their Application to Computer Science. Proceedings, 1982. Edited by H. Ehrig, M. Nagl, and G. Rozenberg. VII, 452 pages. 1983.

Vol. 154: Automata, Languages and Programming. Proceedings, 1983. Edited by J. Díaz. VIII, 734 pages. 1983.

Vol. 155: The Programming Language Ada. Reference Manual. Approved 17 February 1983. American National Standards Institute, Inc. ANSI/MIL-STD-1815A-1983. IX, 331 pages. 1983.

Vol. 156: M.H. Overmars, The Design of Dynamic Data Structures. VII, 181 pages. 1983.

Vol. 157: O. Østerby, Z. Zlatev, Direct Methods for Sparse Matrices. VIII, 127 pages. 1983.

Vol. 158: Foundations of Computation Theory. Proceedings, 1983. Edited by M. Karpinski, XI, 517 pages. 1983.

Vol. 159: CAAP'83. Proceedings, 1983. Edited by G. Ausiello and M. Protasi. VI, 416 pages. 1983.

Vol. 160: The IOTA Programming System. Edited by R. Nakajima and T. Yuasa. VII, 217 pages. 1983.

Vol. 161: DIANA, An Intermediate Language for Ada. Edited by G. Goos, W.A. Wulf, A. Evans, Jr. and K.J. Butler. VII, 201 pages. 1983.

Vol. 162: Computer Algebra. Proceedings, 1983. Edited by J.A. van Hulzen. XIII, 305 pages. 1983.

Vol. 163: VLSI Engineering. Proceedings. Edited by T.L. Kunii. VIII, 308 pages. 1984.

Vol. 164: Logics of Programs. Proceedings, 1983. Edited by E. Clarke and D. Kozen. VI, 528 pages. 1984.

Vol. 165: T.F. Coleman, Large Sparse Numerical Optimization. V, 105 pages. 1984.

Vol. 166: STACS 84. Symposium of Theoretical Aspects of Computer Science. Proceedings, 1984. Edited by M. Fontet and K. Mehlhorn. VI, 338 pages. 1984.

# Lecture Notes in Computer Science

Edited by G. Goos and J. Hartmanis

219


# Advances in Cryptology – EUROCRYPT '85

Proceedings of a Workshop on the
Theory and Application of Cryptographic Techniques
Linz, Austria, April 1985

Edited by Franz Pichler


Springer-Verlag
Berlin Heidelberg New York Tokyo

**Editor**

Franz Pichler
Institute of Systems Science
Department of Systems Theory and Information Engineering
Johannes Kepler University Linz
A-4040 Linz, Austria

**Workshop Organizers**

F. Pichler, Chairman
T. Beth, Program Chairman
H. Beker, Program
D.E. Denning, Program
R. Eier, Program
E. Henze, Program
T. Herlestam, Program
O. Horak, Program
I. Ingemarsson, Program
J.L. Massey, Program
Ch. Müller-Schloer, Program
A. Odlyzko, Program
W.L. Price, Program
R. Rivest, Program
G.J. Simmons, Program
E. Draxler, Registration

The Workshop was sponsored by
International Association for Cryptologic Research (IACR)
Austrian Computer Society (OCG)
Austrian Society for Cybernetic Studies (ÖSGK)
Ministry of Science and Research, Vienna, Austria
Johannes Kepler University Linz

CR Subject Classifications (1985): E.3

ISBN 3-540-16468-5 Springer-Verlag Berlin Heidelberg New York Tokyo
ISBN 0-387-16468-5 Springer-Verlag New York Heidelberg Berlin Tokyo


Printed in Germany

Printing and binding: Beltz Offsetdruck, Hemsbach/Bergstr.
2145/3140-543210

## Preface

The storage, routing and transmission of information, either in the form of digital data or of analog signals, plays a central role in modern society. To ensure that such information is protected from access by unauthorized persons is an important new challenge. The development of the theory and practical techniques needed to meet this challenge is the goal of current cryptological research. This research is highly varied and multidisciplinary. It is concerned with fundamental problems in mathematics and theoretical computer science as well as with the engineering aspects of complex information systems. Cryptology today ranks among the most active and interesting areas of research in both science and engineering.

EUROCRYPT '85 maintained the tradition of the three previous workshops in this series (Paris 1984, Udine 1983, Burg Feuerstein 1982) with its emphasis on recent developments in cryptology, but also made a concerted effort to encompass more traditional topics in cryptology such as shift-register theory and system theory. The many papers on these topics in this volume are witness to the success of this effort.

I am grateful to the speakers and to the authors of the papers in this volume for their contributions to EUROCRYPT '85, and to the Program Committee headed by Professor Thomas Beth, University of London, now University of Karlsruhe, for its labors in putting together a provocative and interesting program. My thanks go also to all the sponsors of EUROCRYPT '85, with a special "Dankeschön" to the International Association for Cryptologic Research for its indispensable support. I hope that this volume, with its cross-section of current research in cryptology, will extend the reach of EUROCRYPT '85 and be a stimulation to its readers of their own research in cryptology.

Franz Pichler
Chairman
EUROCRYPT '85

EUROCRYPT '85 - **Afterthoughts**

Thomas Beth, Program Chairman

Having served as Program Chairman for EUROCRYPT 85, held at Linz (Austria) I think this is a suitable place to compare my a posteriori impressions of this 4th European Meeting on Cryptography with the a priori expectations, most of which - with some modifications of course - made me initially organise the first of these meetings at Burg Feuerstein.
As the field of cryptography is by nature an interdisciplinary one it has proved to be a successful policy to arrange these meetings around a skeleton of survey lectures. This is a fruitful tradition, from which everyone - users and designers, practitioners and theoreticians, speakers and participants have gained largely.

To make a skeleton walk, however, one needs a bit more than a strong backbone.

In these past few years we have witnessed some breakthroughs in cryptography, especially in the field of analysis, e.g. breaking the Merkle-Hellman-Scheme, towards which Ingemarson and Shamir took the first steps at Burg Feuerstein leading to the final general method presented by Brickell at Linz.
Other improvements, e.g. in the question of discrete logarithms by Blake, Mullin, Vanstone, Coppersmith and Odlyzko were equally impressive.

The regular appearance of many other "crypto schemes" and their immediate analysis shows, however, that we are still rather far away from a general theory. Even if we consider this problem optimistically, in my view it is clear that such a general theory would have to incorporate results on

- Complexity
- Protocols
- General Systems

which I count amongst the most difficult fields of research at present.

From research in complexity we urgently need results on lower bounds which would be the basis for an approach to a general theory of data security. The need for such a development has become especially obvious in the area of developing sequential ciphers. After the last few years successful work on designing PN-generators of large linear equivalent, it has now become apparent that other evaluation principles have to be applied. While the work by Yao, Blum, Micali and Goldwasser has shown theoretical instances as to how to proceed, the first two practical analytical results are those presented by Siegenthaler and Rueppel at Linz.
What we are lacking at present are PN-generation methods that are fast, easily implemented and secure in the light of the approaches above.
We are also still urgently waiting for fast implementation of exponentiation algorithms as needed for the RSA-System or the Diffie-Helman Scheme.
With respect to public key systems it should meanwhile have become clear that, although more such systems are strongly sought after, the imitations of the original RSA idea by means of different permutations over possibly different semi-simple algebras is of not much impact, - unless reliable security estimates i.e. lower bounds can be achieved.

The need for these estimates is not only a question of great urgency in the very topic of encryption but also in a general approach towards secure systems. On the one hand the readily proposed rather futuristic general systems models, though intellectually stimulating, are largely pending on the availability of suitable encryption schemes. There is no need to refer again to the inherent dangers of systems based on common sense rather than theorems. On the other hand one has to recognize the ideas coming from non-secrecy cryptography as described by Simmons in his survey lecture on authentication.

Equally important are the engineering aspects as described by Davies and Price in their survey lecture. But again, qualitatively and quantitatively sufficient systems analysis tools are missing.

These tools, if they were available, would be of immediate application in the design of Hierarchical Key Distribution Systems as they are urgently needed in large networks as ISDN, but possibly also in the evaluation of Software Protection Systems. Although some first systems have been presented in Linz, it is my conviction that we are far away from a system that is secure beyond the designed man-machine interface, it has been designed for.
This leads us to the question of new technology in cryptography:

Except for a paper on proposed analog encryption schemes, by Davida, no progress can be reported. Concerning the technology of smart cards improvements w.r.t. to their memory size and mechanical stability have been reported. But the heavy criticism uttered by Simmons and myself at the EUROCRYPT '84 is still valid as the British solution by socalled intelligent token is still in its experimental phase.
I would furthermore have liked to see speculative papers for instance on optical scrambling or encryption for soliton transmission systems, to name a few. Expecially the optical solitons on glass fibres could provide a feasible solution for a socalled quantum crypto system i.e. a system which would detect "information theft".

Coming down to earth again, I would like to point out the large efforts taken internationally towards standardisation. The report by Price on the state of a proposed standard for public key encryption had been followed with great interest.

But with the process of accepting DES as ISO standard being in a rather mature state, I would like to draw the attention to the fact, that when DES was conceived more than a decade ago, it was planned to be a standard for the next 10 to 15 years. It is therefore a surprise to me that in view of the latest releases of computer hardware, there was no general effort made or proposed towards a replacement of DES or should I say "DES Ersatz"?

Remark of the editor: These notes have already appeared immediately after the conference in IACR NEWSLETTER, June 1985

## CONTENTS

### SECTION I: HISTORY OF CRYPTOGRAPHY



### SECTION II: PUBLIC KEY CRYPTOGRAPHY

## SECTION III: SECRET KEY CRYPTOGRAPHY



## SECTION IV: SHIFTREGISTER SEQUENCES AND RELATED TOPICS

## SECTION V: CRYPTOGRAPHIC SYSTEMS AND APPLICATIONS



---

# SECTION I

# HISTORY OF CRYPTOGRAPHY

# THE CONTRIBUTION OF E.B. FLEISSNER AND A. FIGL FOR TODAY'S CRYPTOGRAPHY

Otto J. Horak
Armed Forces ADP Agency (HDVA)
A-1070 Vienna, Austria

About two and a half thousands of years ago the antique philosopher HERACLIT has stated that "The war is the father of all things". He was right also for cryptography till to the recent past. Now since some decades business and computer application are perhaps a stronger propulsion for cryptography than military and diplomatic requirements. Therefore on should not wonder that the central figures mentioned here living near the turn of this century were both officers.
Eduard B. FLEISSNER with the full name Eduard Freiherr(baron) von FLEISSNER von WOSTROWITZ, son of an Austrian cavalry captain was born on January 25, 1825 in Lemberg, today capital of Ukrainian Soviet Socialist Republic, at his time part of the Austrian Monarchy. After his education as officer in the famous Theresian Military Academy in Wiener Neustadt (50 km south of Vienna), founded 1752 by the empress Maria Theresia and still even now the academy for Austria officers, he became second lieutenant of the Imperial-Royal Austrian Army in 1843. He advanced continuously, was finally appointed commander of a school for brigade commanders in 1870 and additionally division commander in 1872. In 1874 he retired and moved in 1880 to Vienna where he died on April 29, 1888.

During his work as commander of different military units and especially as teacher on the school for brigade commanders he came in contact with cryptographic means and measures. After his retirement he finished his book on cryptography described later for which he has felt an urgent requirement and which has been published 1881 in Vienna entitled "Handbuch der Kryptographie" (Manual of Cryptography) /1/ (Figure 1). Figure 2 shows the first page of FLEISSNER's personnel file kept in the Austrian Public Record Office/War Record Office (Staatsarchiv/Kriegsarchiv) /2/.

Andreas FIGL was born in Vienna on June 22, 1873 fifteen years before FLEISSNER died. He got his officers education in the cadet school in Trieste, also in the Austrian Monarchy at his time and became lieutenant in 1893. On January 1, 1910 he retired as captain because of defective vision on one eye. Figure 3 shows the first page of his personnel file from this time /2/. One and a half years later he became recommissioned for special services in 1911 and started his career as deciphering officer and cipher specialist. At this time the General Staff of the Austro-Hungarian Army was just establishing a Cryptoanalytic Bureau in the so called Evidenzbüro, an intelligence office, where FIGL was appointed head of this Cryptoanalytic Bureau. After some years at the front during World War I where he was again working in cipher services he became head of the Supreme Army Command Cipher Group from January 1917 till to the end of World War I with an continuous advancement to lieutenant colonel of the Imperial-Royal Austrian Army. After the end of World War I he worked in the new built Staatsamt für Heerwesen (State Agency for Armed Forces Affairs) and advanced 1920 to a colonel. Some time later he changed to civil service in the Federal Police Direction and finally in the Bundeskanzleramt (Federal Chancellor Agency) also responsible for Foreign Affairs where he was working in the cipher group till up to his retirement in July 1937. Nearly ninety-five years old he died on November 11, 1967 in Salzburg, Austria, where he spent the years after his retirement. Soon after World War I new needs for basic cryptographic literature arose. Because FLEISSNER's Book, which fulfilled this task in the past, was sold out FIGL decided to write also a book on cryptography. Entitled "Systeme des Chiffrierens" (Systems of Ciphering) this book was published 1926 in Graz, Austria /3/ (Figure 4).

What are now the contributions of FLEISSNER and FIGL for today's cryptography? The main contributions were their work itself which finds visible expression in the books containing all experience they have collected during their services. Having a look to bibliographies of cryptography like Galland /4/ or Shulman /5/ for the last decades of the $19^{th}$ and the first of $20^{th}$ century there are not to find so much comprehensive manuals like these from FLEISSNER and FIGL. Both books have some in common especially their most impressive quality namely the clear and systematic way in which the authors have mentioned all matter and particular systems as well as they have worked out the difference between ciphering, deciphering and decrypting (unauthorized deciphering) today known as cryptography and cryptoanalysis respectively. Furthermore both authors have announced a second volume of their books but non was ever published. This second volume should mention the area of cryptoanalysis and there FLEISSNER and FIGL found their boundaries, boundaries not in knowledge but in political and military environment. Their time was not yet ready for public scientific cryptoanalysis.

Looking to FLEISSNER's book, about one hundred years old, it is very surprising that his preface translated in today's colloquial language is still true (Figure 5). For example in the first break

> "By the introduction of Post-Correspondence-Cards and the circumstance that encrypted telegrams are allowed in private traffic cryptography or the art of ciphering and deciphering, till now science for few classes, has won significance and interest also for a broader public"

it needs only to exchange the expressions "Post-Correspondence-Cards" and "encrypted telegrams" perhaps by "Credit Cards" and "data communications" respectively and this paragraph will fit for a book on cryptography of the 80s in this century.

Similar is true for the third break where FLEISSNER says that knowledge on cryptography generally is insufficient despite frequent application also in public authorities and professions which should be familiar with cryptography. Therefore they often use cipher methods useless for protecting the secret.

FLEISSNER divided his book in three parts:

I. General on cryptography and preferenced methods,
II. A new grille/transposition cipher (Patronen-Geheimschrift),
III. The art of unauthorized deciphering (cryptanalysis).

The first and third part give a detailed overview on means and methods in these areas based on the knowledge of that time. From the viewpoint of today the second part with the proposed new transposition cipher called "Patronen- Geheimschrift" (Stencil Cipher) is of interest. As "Patrone" (stencil) is to understand a square of cardboard with holes in such an arrangement that by turning 90 degrees around the center to the four possible positions the holes are never on the same place (figure 6). The four sides - proposed with a length of fifteen fields - are designated with 1 to 4 or A to D and on the reverse surface with 5 to 8 or E to H respectively. The character of the cryptogramm in the center hole shows surface and side for starting the encipherment and decipherment. Some complications for security reasons are also described. In the introduction of part II FLEISSNER schedules nine advantages of his new cipher and in number five especially, that this cipher

> "is of extreme security like best other cipher methods only. Science and art are not able to find the key except by a favourable accident what is possible for any cipher".

Furthermore he emphasized the huge variety of possible keys: As known today FLEISSNER is wrong with his new cipher twofold. First the variety depends very on the length of square sides and is additionally limited by the strong regularity necessary to allow turning the square around the center. A further limitation is given with respect to equivalent and weak keys. Second key and cipher device is nearly the same and therefore this "Patrone" has to be kept secret, a condition which hurts very hard the cryptologic axiom that a cipher device must not be secret.

In modesty FLEISSNER stated in his preface that he has written the book as layman for laymen and users and not for specialists. Not so speaks FIGL. Self-confident he believed that a new comprehensive book on cryptography is necessary because all available literature was some decades old, incomplete and unsystematic. Therefore his intention was to collect all his knowledge and practical experience gained in the years of his cryptographic occupation and form it with a strong systematic and scientific structure to a book.

The structure of his book looks like follows:

- Introduction
  - Visible and invisible secret writings,
  - Boundaries and structure of the matter,
  - Special terms,
  - Literature,
- Part I: Letter-Methods
  - Transpositions,
  - Substitutions,
  - Mechanical Methods,
  - Screening,
  - Hiding of writings,
- Part II: Syllable- and Word-Methods
  - Special methods,
  - Key tables (command tables),
  - Book methods.

It is to say that FIGL has not only structured the content very strong he has also worked out all details extremely deep and systematic. Many ancient and at his time more or less well-known methods are described with scientific precision together with their advantages, disadvantages and week points. FIGL described for example already the Enigma cipher machine and in this connection he stated that not the cipher device but only the cipher key is the real cryptographic secret, an axiom hurted by FLEISSNER's "Patronen-Geheimschrift".

Despite the fact that FIGL's book is no longer up-to-date it is cited often also in recent literature because of its fundamental character. Therefore it is not astonishing that the question for his second volume is asked. As already mentioned earlier neither FIGL's nor FLEISSNER's announced second volume were published. Maybe for FLEISSNER the time was to short because he died seven years after publishing the first volume or there was no interest for a second volume on "The Patronen-Geheimschrift (grille/transposition cipher) as word cipher and cryptoanalysis in foreign languages". In case of FIGL the reason is obvious and well documented: The edition of the second volume has been interdicted officially by the same agency where FIGL was working as government official. In 1926 as his book has been published he was with the cipher group in the department for foreign affairs of the Federal Chancellor Agency and he dedicated one copy of his book to the head of this cipher group with a personal inscription. The reaction was horror. The reason is to find in the way of thinking on secrecy at this time. Some of the methods described by FIGL with its advantages and weaknesses were obviously still in governmental use. Now they are reacting like an oistrich: they rather wanted to keep a week method secret hoping that nobody will detect the weakness than to look for a secure new method. So they were shocked that now the weakness was public. But it was impossible to bring the started arrow back, i.e. to eliminate the already published first volume. Therefore after a contact with the Federal Ministry for Armed Forces Affairs (Bundesministerium für Heerwesen) it was decided to interdict at least the publication of the announced second volume entitled "Systeme des Dechiffrierens" (Cryptoanalysis of Systems). It is known that the second volume was already prepared for printing and that the publisher has been indemnified for the lost copyright. Figure 7 shows the first page of this official document /6/. Furthermore it is said that a typed manuscript should exist based on FIGL's manuscript, written, rearranged and supplemented in some points by a pupil of FIGL.

Concluding the matter mentioned previously it is to ask what can be learned from the work of FLEISSNER and FIGL and the outcome they have initiated with their books. There are three main points worthy to note here:

1. DON'T THINK CRYPTOGRAPHIC NEEDS AND REQUIREMENT ARE KNOWN, UNDERSTOOD AND ACCEPTED EVERYWHERE.

   The remarks in FLEISSNER's preface and the interdiction of FIGL's second volume should illustrate this clear enough.

2. DON'T OVERESTIMATE THE SECURITY OF YOUR OWN SYSTEM.

   FLEISSNER's "Patronen-Geheimschrift" is a splendid negative example. Studying FIGL's book one can find a lot of similar grille ciphers and can be sure that his second volume would have shown a solution.

3. LOOK CAREFULLY WHAT IS TO KEEP SECRET FOR SECURITY REASONS AND WHAT NOT.

   Here again two examples are to count. First FLEISSNER's "Patrone" (stencil): it must not be secret because it is not only a key it is also a cipher device, second the already mentioned interdiction of FIGL's second volume. Week cipher methods will not become more secure if they will kept secret.

Remembering this points in all situations the work of FLEISSNER and FIGL is not wasted and their contribution for today's cryptography will bear fruits.

## References

/1/ FLEISSNER v. WOSTROWITZ Eduard B.
Handbuch der Kryptographie
Seidel & Sohn, Vienna, 1881

/2/ Record files kept in Österreichisches Staatsarchiv/Kriegsarchiv (Austrian Public Record Office/War Record Office), Vienna

/3/ FIGL A.
Systeme des Chiffrierens
Mosers Buchhandlung (J. Meyerhoff), Graz, 1926

/4/ GALLAND Joseph S.
An Historical and Analytical Bibliography of the Literature of Cryptology
Northwestern University, Evanston, 1945

/5/ SHULMAN David
An Annoted Bibliography of Cryptography
Garland Publishing, Inc., New York & London, 1976

/6/ Österreichisches Staatsarchiv/Kriegsarchiv
Number A 49635-1/26

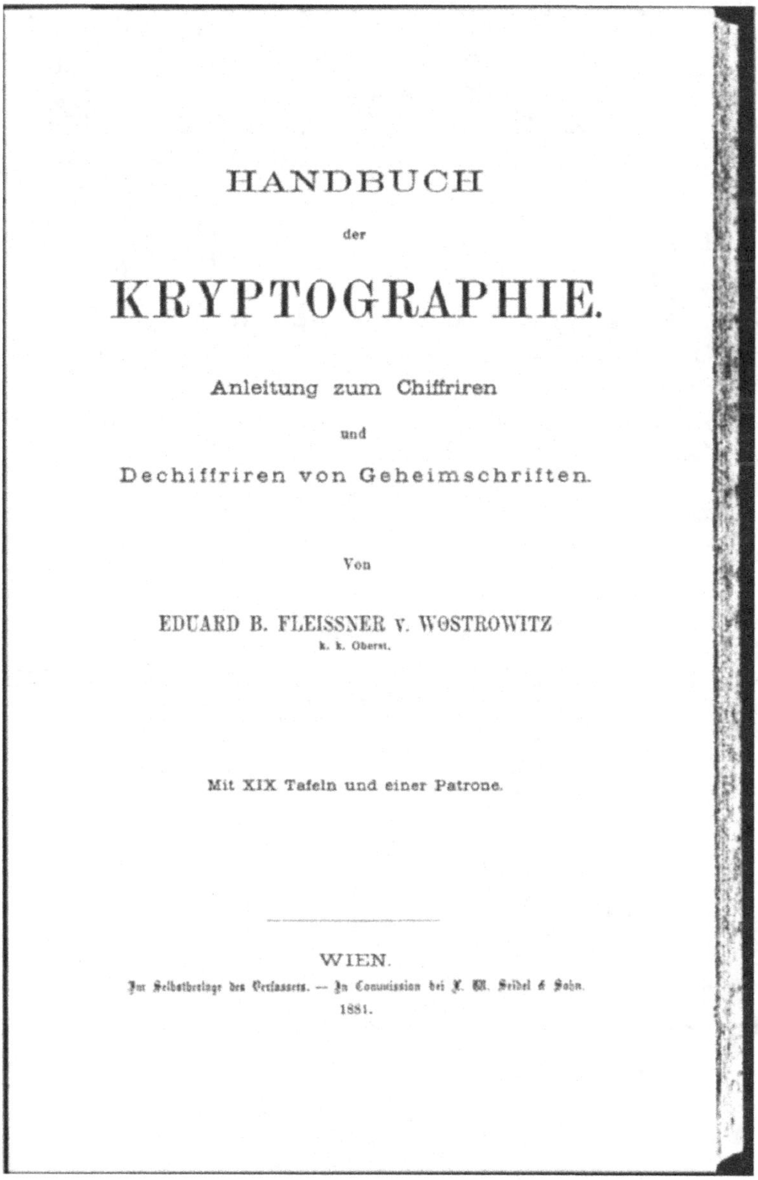

HANDBUCH

der

KRYPTOGRAPHIE.

Anleitung zum Chiffriren

und

Dechiffriren von Geheimschriften.

Von

EDUARD B. FLEISSNER v. WOSTROWITZ

k. k. Oberst.

Mit XIX Tafeln und einer Patrone.

WIEN.

Im Selbstverlage des Verfassers. — In Commission bei L. W. Seidel & Sohn.

1881.

FIGURE 1

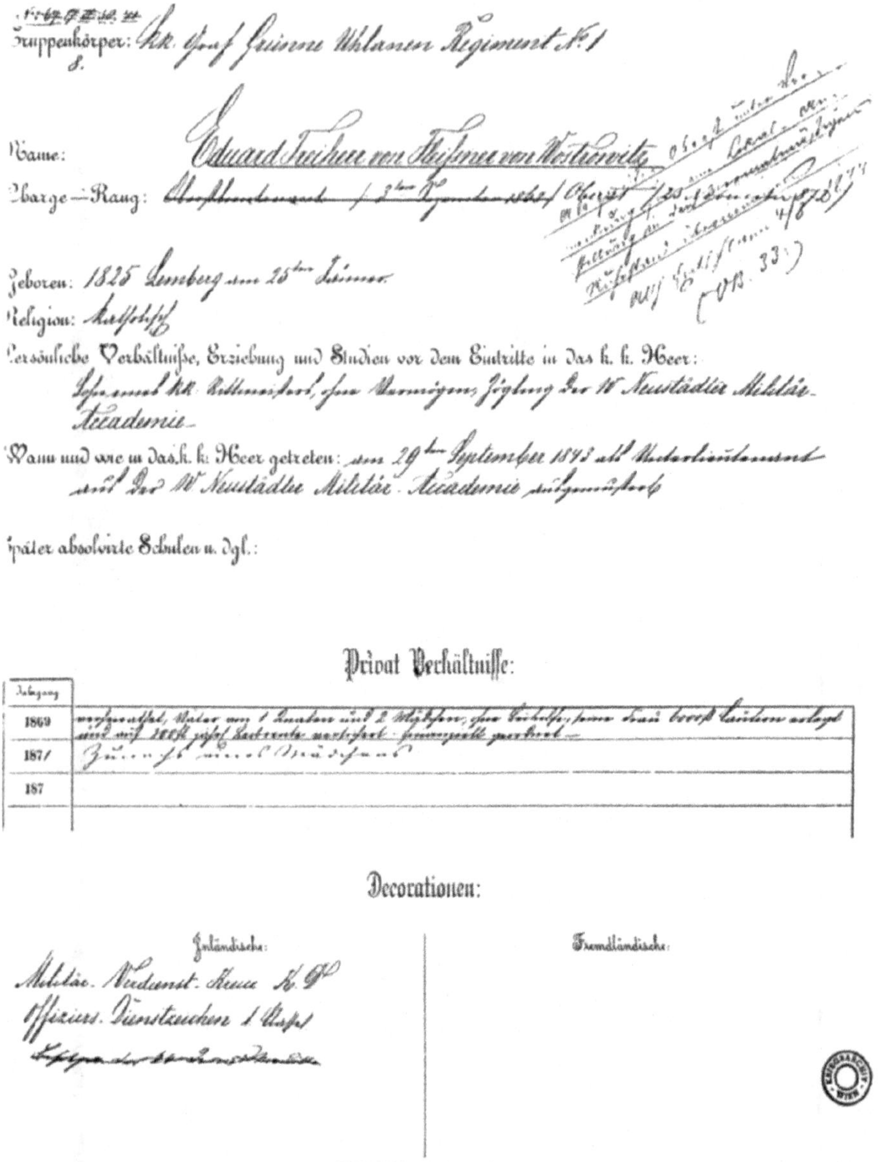

Truppenkörper: k.k. Graf Grünne Uhlanen Regiment No 1

Name: Eduard Freiherr von Fleissner von Wostrowitz

Charge—Rang: ~~Oberstlieutenant~~ / Oberst

Geboren: 1825 Lemberg am 25ten Jänner

Religion: katholisch

Persönliche Verhältnisse, Erziehung und Studien vor dem Eintritte in das k. k. Heer: Sohn eines k.k. Rittmeisters, ohne Vermögen, Zögling der W. Neustädter Militär-Academie

Wann und wie in das k. k. Heer getreten: am 29ten September 1843 als Unterlieutenant aus der W. Neustädter Militär-Academie ausgemustert

Später absolvirte Schulen u. dgl.:

Privat Verhältnisse:

| Jahrgang | |
|---|---|
| 1869 | ~~verheiratet, Vater von 1 Knaben und 2 Mädchen~~ [illegible] |
| 1871 | [illegible] |
| 187 | |
| | |

Decorationen:

Inländische:

Militär-Verdienst-Kreuz K.D.

Offiziers-Dienstzeichen 1. Classe

~~[illegible]~~

Fremdländische:

FIGURE 2

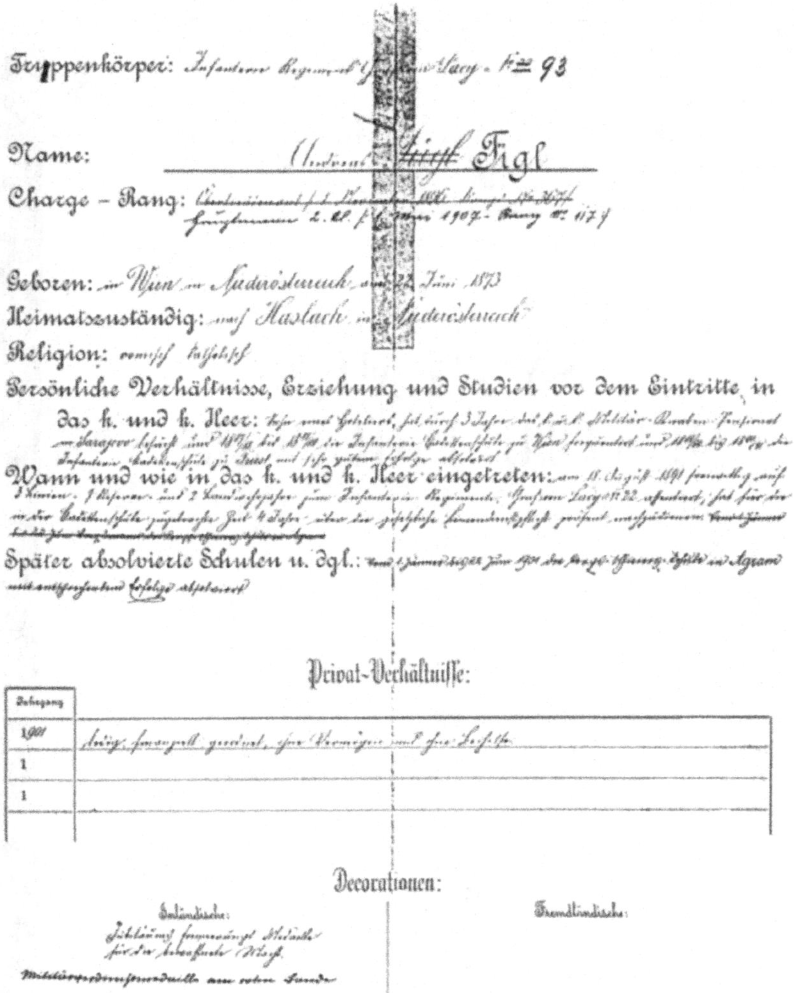

Truppenkörper: Infanterie Regiment [illegible] Nr. 93

Name: Andreas [illegible] Figl

Charge – Rang: ~~Oberleutnant [illegible]~~ Hauptmann 2. Cl. [illegible] Mai 1907 – Rang Nr. 117

Geboren: in Wien in Niederösterreich am [illegible] Juni 1873

Heimatszuständig: nach Haslach in Niederösterreich

Religion: römisch katholisch

Persönliche Verhältnisse, Erziehung und Studien vor dem Eintritte in das k. und k. Heer: [illegible] Infanterie Cadettenschule [illegible] Wien [illegible]

Wann und wie in das k. und k. Heer eingetreten: am [illegible] August 1891 [illegible] Infanterie Regiment [illegible] Nr. 22 [illegible]

Später absolvierte Schulen u. dgl.: [illegible] 1901 [illegible] Agram [illegible]

Privat-Verhältnisse:

| Jahrgang | |
|---|---|
| 1901 | ledig [illegible] |
| 1 | |
| 1 | |
| | |

Decorationen:

Inländische:

Jubiläums Erinnerungs Medaille für die bewaffnete Macht.

~~Militärverdienstmedaille am roten Bande~~

Fremdländische:

Lag. Nr. 87 a. — Aus der k. k. Hof- und Staatsdruckerei — IV/1900.

FIGURE 3

Wissenschaftliche Veröffentlichungen des Kriminalistischen Laboratoriums der Polizeidirektion Wien
(Wissenschaftl. Vorstand: Dozent Dr. Siegfried Türkel).

# SYSTEME DES CHIFFRIERENS

von

A. FIGL
Oberst und Regierungsrat

GRAZ 1926

Verlag von Ulr. Mosers Buchhandlung (J. Meyerhoff)

FIGURE 4

# VORWORT.

Durch Einführung der Post-Correspondenz-Karten und durch den Umstand, dass in Geheimschrift abgefasste Telegramme im Privatverkehre gestattet sind, hat die Kryptographie oder die Kunst des Chiffrirens und Dechiffrirens, die bisher die Wissenschaft weniger Stände war, an Bedeutung und Interesse auch für das grössere Publicum gewonnen.

Wenn bisher nur ausschliesslich die Diplomatie und die Generalstäbe der Armeen diese Kunst cultivirten, manchmal auch die grossen Bankhäuser, Kaufherren und Rheder in Verfolgung ihrer Interessen, endlich der Untersuchungsrichter und der Polizeibeamte bei Erfüllung ihres Berufes öfters in die Lage kamen, sich mit der Kryptographie beschäftigen zu müssen, so ist sie jetzt für Jeden, der seine kleinen Geheimnisse nicht einer offenen Post-Correspondenz-Karte anvertrauen will, gewiss von einigem Nutzen.

Da aber die Kenntniss der Kryptographie trotz ihrer vielfältigen Anwendung im Allgemeinen eine sehr ungenügende ist, indem man selbst von staatlichen Behörden und Personen, von denen man schon wegen ihres Berufes eine grössere Vertrautheit mit der Kryptographie voraussetzen sollte, Chiffre-Methoden in Anwendung bringen sieht, die das Geheimniss, also die Hauptsache, nicht sicher zu wahren vermögen, so dürfte ein Werkchen über Kryptographie vielleicht willkommen sein.

VIII Vorwort.

Die günstige Beurtheilung, welche das Manuscript zu diesem Buche von Autoritäten erfuhr, bestimmt mich, dasselbe der Oeffentlichkeit zu übergeben.

Von einem Nichtfachmanne geschrieben, ist es nicht für Fachmänner bestimmt, wenn ich auch hoffe, dass selbst diese in meinem Buche manches Neue finden werden. Die Bestimmung desselben ist vielmehr die, dem Laien als treuer Rathgeber bei der Wahl eines verlässlichen Chiffre-Schlüssels zu dienen und dem angehenden Diplomaten, Officier, insbesondere Generalstabs-Officier und überhaupt Allen, deren Beruf sie öfters in die Lage versetzt, von Geheimschriften Gebrauch machen zu müssen, in das weite Gebiet der Kryptographie einzuführen.

Sollte dieses Handbuch den gewünschten Leserkreis finden, so würde ich demselben als zweiten Theil folgen lassen:

Die Patronen-Geheimschrift als Wort-Chiffre und

Ueber das Dechiffriren in fremden Sprachen, erläutert durch Aufstellung von Regeln, Wörter-Sammlungen und Beispiele für die französische, englische, italienische, russische und ungarische Sprache, damit auch Nichtkenner dieser Sprachen selbe dechiffriren lernen.

Wien, im März 1881.

*Der Verfasser.*

FIGURE 5

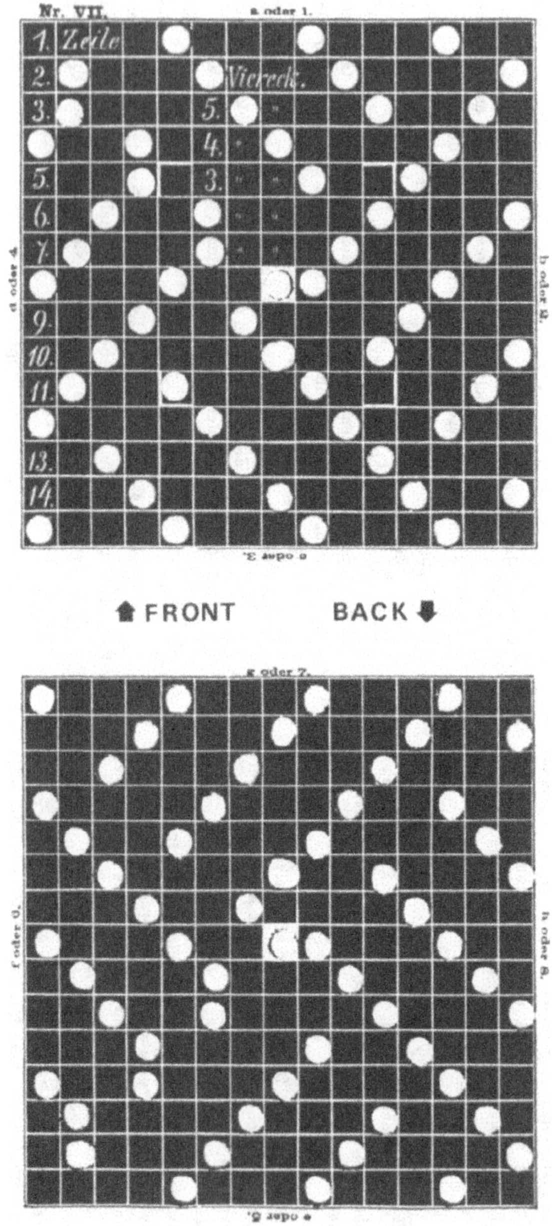
Nr. VII.
a oder 1.
1. Zeile
2.
3.
4.
5.
6.
7.
9.
10.
11.
13.
14.
Viereck.
5.
4.
3.
d oder 4.
b oder 2.
c oder 3.
↑ FRONT
BACK ↓
g oder 7.
f oder 6.
h oder 8.
e oder 5.

FIGURE 6

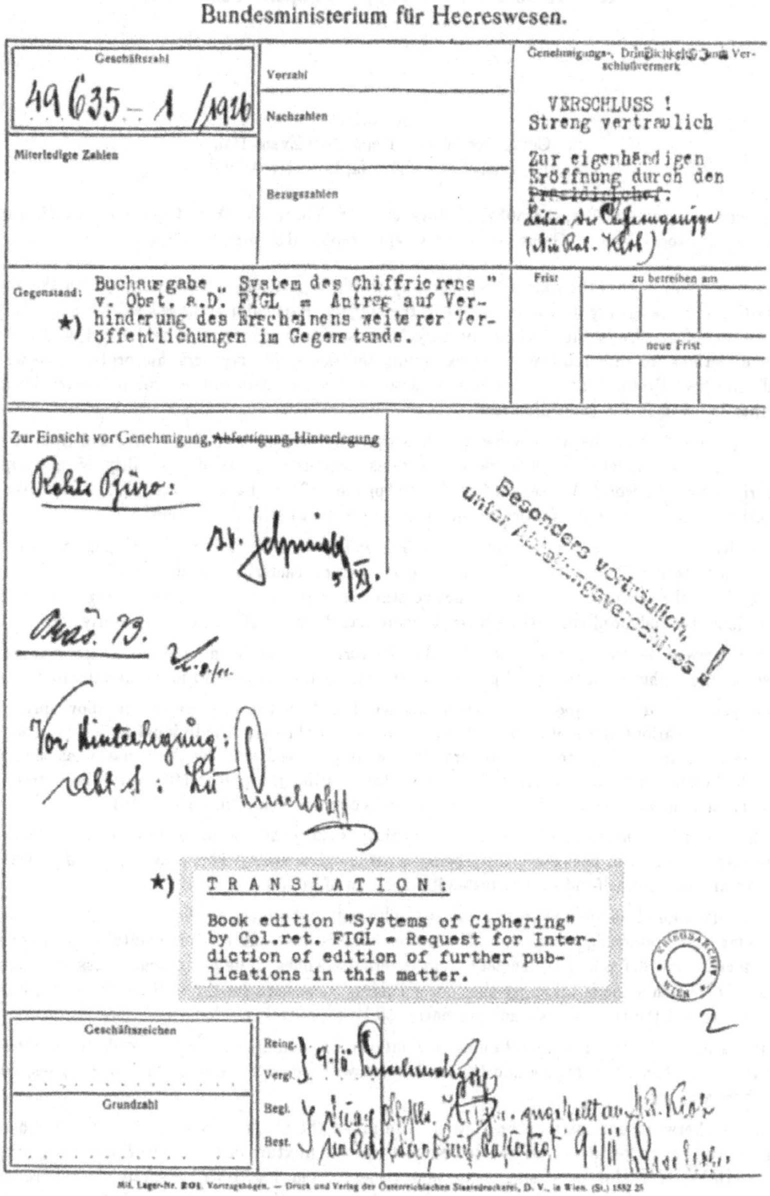

Bundesministerium für Heereswesen.

| Geschäftszahl | Vorzahl / Nachzahlen / Bezugszahlen | Genehmigungs-, Dringlichkeits- und Verschlußvermerk |
|---|---|---|
| 49635 – 1 /1926 | | VERSCHLUSS ! Streng vertraulich Zur eigenhändigen Eröffnung durch den ~~Präsidialchef:~~ Leiter der Chiffriergruppe (Min.Rat. Kloß) |
| Miterledigte Zahlen | | |

Gegenstand: Buchausgabe „ System des Chiffrierens " v. Obst. a.D. FIGL = Antrag auf Verhinderung des Erscheinens weiterer Veröffentlichungen im Gegenstande. *)

Frist — zu betreiben am — neue Frist

Zur Einsicht vor Genehmigung, ~~Abfertigung, Hinterlegung~~

Rechts Büro:

Besonders vertraulich, unter Abteilungsverschluss !

Vor Hinterlegung:
Abt. 1:

*) TRANSLATION:

Book edition "Systems of Ciphering" by Col.ret. FIGL = Request for Interdiction of edition of further publications in this matter.

KRIEGSARCHIV WIEN

Geschäftszeichen — Grundzahl

Reing. Vergl. Begl. Best.

Mil. Lager-Nr. 201 Vortragsbogen. — Druck und Verlag der Österreichischen Staatsdruckerei, D. V., in Wien. (St.) 1552 25

FIGURE 7

# On the history of cryptography during WW2, and possible new directions for cryptographic research.

Tom Tedrick
Computer Science Dept., 570 Evans Hall
University of California, Berkeley 94720

Keywords: History of Cryptography, History of War, Theory of War, Cryptographic Protocols, Abstract Protocol Theory, Game Theoretic Cryptography, Rommel, ULTRA.

This paper will discuss the role of cryptography within a particular "world view", with the aim of investigating the history and foundations of the subject. Particular emphasis will be placed of the role of cryptography in the German military failures of WW2, lessons to be derived, and possible new directions for research (including extending the theory of cryptographic protocols to what I call "Abstract Protocol Theory".) I hope that some of the readers will become interested in doing further research in the areas discussed.

To begin we describe the world view, which is partially derived from the Vedas, and from Aristotle. Of course, Godel's incompleteness theorems demonstrate the impossibility of a complete description of the world. We seek a few simple "primitive", or "basic", notions (somewhat like the practice in axiomatic mathematics) from which to create a useful description.

3 primitive notions are seen as fundamental principles operative in the lives of men, described as "inactive","active","balanced". The inactive state is characterized as slow, dull, lazy, dormant, weak, sluggish, confused, chaotic; the active state as passionate, aggressive, strong, competitive, ambitious; the balanced state as intelligent, coordinated, cooperative, skillful, orderly, careful.

Man is viewed as having a soul which takes on form repeatedly in order to progress from the lower to the higher condition (and perhaps to something further beyond my understanding).

Society is viewed as composed of various classes, based on the mixture of the above principles operative in various types of men, and the interests and abilities of individual men. It is sufficient for the purposes of this paper to deliberately oversimplify and describe these classes as the workers, the commercial class (motivated by desire for wealth), the political/military class (desire for power), and the class consisting of the intellectual community (desire for knowledge).

Each class has a necessary function in a healthy society and is dependent on the others for existence, antagonism between classes being a pathological state. This may happen if power and wealth are used for self-indulgence instead of social welfare, for example.

The intellectual class has the role of guiding, advising, and educating the other classes, as well as pursuing and preserving knowledge. The power holders have the role of maintaining an orderly, just society and defending the society from external enemies. The commercial class accumulates wealth, of which some is taken by the power holders to be used for the welfare of society, leaving enough so that the commercials have incentive to keep producing.

A fundamental problem is maintaining the intellectual community and an orderly, progressive society in the face of ignorance and the tendency towards disorder among the lower classes, whose numbers are larger.

Relations between nations may be viewed in terms of the above primitive notions as indifferent, competitive, or cooperative. Of course always there is a mixture of these 3 in various proportions. Competition is useful in raising man and society from inactivity to activity, for reducing inefficiency, etc. Excessive competition may lead to the pathological state called war (as well as to other unpleasantness). A fundamental problem is to reach a state of cooperation between nations, for mutual benefit, avoiding unneccessary war (this includes the problem of de-escalation of tensions).

(Cryptography is intimately linked to war. In war, the forces of the nation must cooperate in order to function effectively, which requires exchange of information. At the same time this information needs to be kept hidden from the enemy.)

One means for avoiding war has been exchange of information between states, so as to avoid fatal misunderstandings. This includes dialogue (including meetings between political leaders), travel and cultural exchange, and such proposals as a joint USA-USSR crisis communications center. History shows that there is a great danger of war due to accidents, misunderstandings, or miscalculation (witness WW1 and WW2), hence such proposals are extremely important.

Historically, cryptography has sometimes played a role in information exchange. Compromised ciphers have knowingly been used in order to give away certain information. (This practice goes back at least as far as Bismarck.) The use of compromised encoding schemes will likely continue to be important for this purpose, and for purposes of giving away false or misleading information in intelligence operations. (So in some cases a perfectly secure encryption scheme might be undesirable.) One possibly new idea is for adversaries to agree to use jointly constructed codes for certain purposes so that both may be aware of certain information, while outsiders remain in the dark. This idea involves many difficulties, including the problem of ciphertext which appears to be plaintext. If they could be overcome this scheme might be useful in certain situations, so that military exercises, test firings of missiles, etc., would not be mistaken for hostile activity.

It is interesting that encryption schemes can be constructed so that with very high probability the scheme can be broken after a prechosen amount of computation (plus or minus epsilon). So information can be released now and read at a quite precisely predetermined time in the future.

We now leave the subject of peaceful cooperation between nations and examine the situation where competition has degenerated to war. The theory of war in certain of its aspects was brought to a high level in Germany earlier in the century (especially the theory of land warfare). We mention some of the principles of war: Concentration of force, mobility, divide and conquer, breakthrough and pursuit, mass exploitation of new weapons and tactics, surprise, extensive training of troops, proper organizational structure of military groups, propaganda (these principles can be interpreted in terms of the 3 primitive notions mentioned earlier, as seeking to maximize cooperation and effective activity of one's forces in order to disrupt and destroy the activity of enemy forces, and cooperation between enemy forces, creating chaos, weakness, confusion, uncertainty and demoralization in the enemy camp, so as to impose one's will on the enemy.). Ideally the aim of war is to destroy the power of the enemy to resist in a single blow, thus achieving victory at minimum cost. Failing this a war of attrition may result, extremely costly to both sides. In that case it is essential to preserve one's strength as much as possible while weakening the enemy. (It might be mentioned that this ideal of achieving victory in a single blow does not seem to be fully understood. Witness the gradual escalation in Vietnam, the war against Nicaragua, etc. Such gradualism allows the enemy time to develop countermeasures. Then the victor is the one who endures the longest, and it should be no surprise when a weaker power on its own territory is victorious. In terms of the present world view, small scale attacks may have the effect of raising the enemy from a state of inactivity to a state of greater activity, thus being of limited value. One should quietly accumulate strength, then suddenly deal an overwhelming suprise blow. Even after war has broken out this principle remains valid: when preparing for battle giving the enemy a temporary respite from harassment may induce some degree of inertia in him.)

It might be mentioned here that long term intelligence operations which may not bear fruit for many years are a fundamental part of the modern political struggle. Also the scientific, technological, economic, and educational levels of the country are critical. These are lessons clearly demonstrated in WW2.

Let us examine briefly the role of cryptography in WW1. Development of wireless technology, mechanized transport, and very large scale armies led to the practice of controlling troop movements from remote headquarters via wireless communications. Cryptography was needed to hide the transmitted information from the enemy, but was in a pre-scientific stage leaving much room for code breaking and exploitation of information gained.

On the eastern front, the Russians employed primitive ciphers which were easily broken by the Germans. Knowing Russian intentions, the numerically inferior (of course qualitatively superior) German forces were, in the early stages of the war, able to remove troops from certain defensive sectors and concentrate forces to attack and defeat separated parts of the Russian forces in turn (witness Tannenburg, the Maurian Lakes). This is an early example of using cryptographic information in order to make optimal use of scarce resources in battle. Later it was possible to exploit the tendency of the Russians to employ human wave attacks and inflict heavy casualties, knowing in advance the time and location of these attacks. This slaughter led to the breakdown of the Czarist regime and the resulting so called communist state. The information gained through compromised Russian codes was almost the only source of intelligence information about the Russians available to Germany.

On the western front German codes were broken frequently and information given away was of much value to their enemies. Broken codes played a large part in bringing the United States into the war against Germany (witness the Zimmerman affair). Another, fundamental reason for the German defeat lay in the bad judgement of her military and political leaders. (Bismarck's successors did not have his level of judgement.) It was not in Germany's interest to become involved in a war in the first place (Marshall Foch said that given 20 more years of peace Germany would have become the dominant world power). The removal of troops from France before achieving victory in the initial invasion was an unnecessary violation of principle. Antagonizing the USA through U-boat warfare violated the divide and conquer principle. Finally the attempt to decide the issue late in the war by taking the offensive without sufficient superiority was very risky. Given the superiority of defense at that time an alternative plan could have been temporary withdrawal followed by massive counterattack before the enemy had time to establish strong defensive positions, hopefully leading to breakthrough and pursuit, etc. (this method also has the virtue that it forces the enemy to be more cautious in pursuit and is consistent with a game theoretical attempt to optimize strategy). It was particularly important for Germany not to waste troop strength in the attack unless a decisive victory was likely, given the numerical inferiority of the German armies.

Another failure that should be mentioned is the German loss of the propaganda war. Her enemies succeeded in portraying the Germans as brutal and inhuman aggressors, while not so much was heard of the German point of view. The importance of intelligence operations, such as long term propaganda efforts in foreign countries should again be emphasized. Cryptography has a role here, as in the case of the Zimmerman affair. Information gained through broken codes can be useful in propaganda campaigns. Use of this information has to be weighed against the cost of revealing to the enemy that his codes are compromised. Here we see a dilemna for the intellectual community, who are presumably responsible for cryptographic efforts. The political leadership may not have sufficient understanding of the difficulty and importance of breaking enemy codes, and too readily allow the secret out. It is the responsibility of those in charge of cryptographic efforts to impress upon the political leadership the vital importance of secrecy. This problem is still with us (witness the revelation that Soviet encryption methods had been compromised after the shooting down of the Korean airlines flight 007, the revelation that Cuban codes had been compromised after Grenada, etc.)

All in all, we see that cryptography played a vital role in WW1, with fateful consequences for human history that are not widely understood. I view cryptography as a "weak link in the chain", or vital point on which events turned, rendering the immense efforts of millions of people all for nought. The efforts to unify Germany and make her a leading world power led to disaster. The importance of subtle ideas and the intellectual community as opposed to the more direct, forceful, active type of person has at times been neglected. Perhaps more subtle judgement would have preserved the pre-WW1 European empires.

Between wars, cryptography has played a role during negotiations, among other uses.

Let us turn to WW2. For many years I was baffled by the failures of German military operations in WW2. It was only when I became aware of ULTRA that I began to believe that I understood the reasons for Germany's defeat. It is my thesis that without ULTRA the Allies would have had a very difficult time defeating Germany. The possible result might have been the use of atomic weapons in Europe. It is also possible that ULTRA prevented the German atomic effort from succeeding, although the information I have seen has been incomplete and sometimes inconsistent. I believe the full story of the German atomic effort has not been made public.

To clarify more exactly what role ULTRA played, it is important to mention some mistakes which were more or less independent of ULTRA. Principally these were a consequence of Hitler's overeliance on intuition as opposed to logic, perhaps as a consequence of his lack of formal education at the higher levels (his limited experience in foreign countries also contributed to mistakes in judgement, as did excessive use of drugs). (Information gained from ULTRA was useful in the campaign of psychological warfare aimed at unbalancing Hitler, creating dissension in his camp, etc.) It was again not in Germany's interest to fight a war at the time. Most of the principles of war which were so well understand by the German military theorists were violated. For example, the pursuit was halted and the British forces allowed to escape at Dunkirk. After the fall of France, full mobilization of the German war effort did not occur for some time, in the belief that the war was essentially over. While still at war with Britain, the Soviet Union was invaded, in violation of the divide and conquer principle. If anything, the invasion of Britain should have been attempted instead (ULTRA played a role here, as the Luftwaffe's failure to drive the RAF from the skies made the invasion seem too dangerous to Hitler). Then war was declared on the United States without anything to gain except perhaps the goodwill of Japan. German military forces were separated and sent off on uncoordinated missions instead of being concentrated. Despite the success and German superiority in mobile warfare, Hitler reverted to a strategy of static warfare on the Eastern front. (Of course this strategy would have been more successful were it not for ULTRA.) Overemphasis on appearances led him to refuse to allow construction of defensive positions in rear areas, and to reject the strategy of temporary withdrawal followed by counterattack so necessary for the numerically inferior side. (That this also might have failed due to ULTRA is beside the point.) Local commanders were not given the proper amount of discretion in tactical and operational matters, nor was there unified tactical command of all the branches of the armed services on the battlefield. The commander on the battlefield has direct perception of the particular local conditions, and should be free to react accordingly, in order to make optimal use of temporary opportunities which may arise, etc. Also lack of freedom to take the initiative is demoralizing. Hitler was often too remote from the battlefield to be in a position to make correct judgements. (This is an example of the problem of abstract vs. particular knowledge.) New weapons were not developed as rapidly as possible, nor on the largest possible scale, due to Hitler's interference, vacillation, amateurishness, and irrationality, instead being employed piecemeal (again this gives the enemy time to develop countermeasures). (ULTRA also played a role in hindering weapons development, reducing their surprise value, etc.) Before the war, scientific and technological development was hindered by Hitler's persecution of the Jewish and the intellectual community (this also strengthened his enemies). Mistreatment of subject peoples made them less useful in the war effort, when many would willingly have become allies. His choice of Japan as an ally was disastrous. ( Japan refused to relieve pressure on the Eastern front by attacking the Soviet Union, instead bringing the United States into the war.)

In spite of all these mistakes, Germany had very good chances for military success up to the point where atomic weapons could come into play (at that point war takes on a new aspect and the theory of war has to be reconsidered). Let us examine some examples.

ULTRA was indispensible during the battle of Britain, allowing the British to make optimal use of limited resources in fighting the Luftwaffe. Knowledge of enemy numbers, locations, and plans was of extreme importance. Without ULTRA the expected outcome should have been German control of the skies and much more severe damage, along with a possible invasion of Britain. It should be mentioned that production of German aircraft should have been increased at an earlier date and that the diversion of planes to the Eastern front weakened the German effort.

The U-boat war failed primarily for 2 reasons. First they were not employed on a massive scale. Production should have been underway on a large scale well in advance of any war. This is in accordance with the principal that new weapons and tactics should be employed on a massive scale in order to overwhelm the enemy at the very beginning of the conflict. Incidentally this principle is still being violated in the West. For example the United States has only on the order of a hundred submarines in service, to my knowledge. No matter how high the quality, weapons have to be employed on a large scale for full effectiveness. Production has to begin early, as it may be too late after the conflict begins. Production of military equipment should be a long term continuing effort, and can be tied to economic cycles in order to counter cyclical downturns (i.e. vary production so that it increases when unemployment rises, etc.). A surplus of equipment should be the goal (this is perhaps more useful than Keynes' idea of putting the unemployed to work digging holes and filling them again).

The other fundamental reason for the failure of the U-boat campaign was ULTRA. The new tactical methods developed in Germany relied on coordination from a central location, hence wireless encrypted messages. Included in these messages were locations of U-boats, places and times to rendezvous, etc. Over and over again this information was used to attack and sink German submarines. This was carried to such an extreme that the U-boat commanders had no doubt that the Admiralty codes had been broken, despite official denials that this was even possible. (Here we see an example of the need for the empirical method in cryptography: if things aren't going well consider changing your cryptosystem, even if the experts "prove" it to be secure. Any proof of security is necessarily based on certain assumptions within a model and can be invalidated if the enemy can escape the restrictions in the model.) As early as 1955 unequivocal statements to the effect that the German codes had been compromised appeared in print, although it was much later that more complete information was published. We see another principle at work here, namely that in exploiting information gained through code breaking the enemy may be given a hint that his cryptosystem has been broken. It is a difficult problem for intelligence agencies to disguise activities in such a way that broken codes remain in use by the enemy. This leads naturally to a game theoretic approach to cryptography: One can predict the probable outcome of a military operation and if it fails to achieve the expected outcome change the cryptosystem in use. Thus either one achieves one's military goal, or the enemy loses access to the information from a compromised code, if such a code has been in use. In military games (both in the field and in computer simulations) various assumptions about the security of cryptosystems can be incorporated, to gain more experience about how broken cryptosystems are likely to affect combat, and to enable commanders to recognize situations where codes have been compromised. Another subtle point that has crept in is the notion of independence of cryptosystems. It is no use changing to a new cryptosystem which can be broken in the same way as the old one. We saw this in WW2, continuing modifications of enigma being broken one after the other. And in some cases the modifications actually made it easier to break. We would like to be able to switch to a cryptosystem independent of the old one. Finally, it should be stated that cryptography needs to be seen as a part of a larger subject that includes the problem of how to make proper use of information gained.

To conclude the discussion of the U-boat war, without ULTRA the U-boats would have been an extremely difficult problem for the allies, despite their not being employed on a sufficiently large scale. The invasions of North Africa, Italy, and France, and the supply of British forces in North Africa, as well as the shipment of supplies to the Soviet Union, would have been much more problematic.

Let us examine the North African campaign. Here ULTRA was used to discover Rommel's plans, and to sink ships carrying supplies to him. He suffered severely due to a supply shortage during most of the campaign.

The thing that impresses me most about Rommel's operations is how finely calculated they were, and how they reflect nearly perfectly the optimal practical application of the theory of mobile warfare, and the principles of war in general. Rommel has not been given full credit for his superior understanding and application of military principles. Almost invariably, his failures in North Africa were due to information leaked to ULTRA. The one mistaken assumption which upset all his plans was that enigma was secure. He became convinced that enigma must have been broken, but was assured by experts that this was not possible (here we see the principle that one relies on the judgement of so-called experts at one's peril: again any deduction must be based on assumptions which cannot be proven, hence one must sometimes allow empiricism some sway, not accepting advice which contradicts one's experience). This led to suspicion of his Italian allies (reinforced by Allied intelligence operations designed to confirm that suspicion), loss of confidence in his leaders, and perhaps to his decision to join the opposition to Hitler. Were it not for the accident of July 17, it is likely that Rommel within a few days would have openly broken with Hitler, with the most unpredictable consequences. (Information about the events around this time related to the plot against Hitler seems still to be incomplete.) In any case history has yet to do justice to Rommel and his work. It is perhaps interesting that one of his ambitions was to redesign the waterways of Europe during the postwar reconstruction (which he did not live to see, having lost his life to the Nazis for having accepted the role as the leader of Germany in case the plot against Hitler had succeeded. Had Rommel become Germany's leader he would likely have sought peace with the West, withdrawn from occupied countries, removed the Nazis from power, and kept the Soviets out of Eastern Europe.)

One particular characteristic of Rommel's methods was the attempt to exploit confusion and uncertainty on the battlefield (where the superior mobility and training of his troops, their ability to function independently of command supervision, and Rommel's personal style of leadership and initiative could have its maximum effect), to lead the opposing commanders to become confused, disoriented, and make fatal misjudgements. This happened, and it was only ULTRA and Churchill's consequent intervention that saved the British forces from being completely routed.

One other point worth mentioning is that much of Rommel's early success was due to his own cryptographic section. Unfortunately a typically ignorant officer ordered these "do-nothings" into combat at El Alamein, resulting in their destruction. This is an example of the danger of the lack of respect for the more intellectual types by more primitive men.

Finally Montgomery found the correct method of fighting against Rommel (with ULTRA). Use ULTRA to discover Rommel's plans, prepare accordingly, take no risks of being drawn into mobile warfare, acquire an overwhelming material superiority and grind down the numerically inferior opponent. Montgomery has been criticized for not engaging in mobile warfare or more vigorous pursuit when fighting Rommel, but given that his source of information about Rommel's activities tended to vanish in this type of battle, that Montgomery had an almost mathematical certainty of success following the methods he actually used, and that the Germans could little afford material losses while the British could, Montgomery deserves historical credit for following exactly the correct plan, against all opposition.

Turning to the Eastern Front, we see ULTRA being used by the Soviets in the Stalingrad campaign, their plan of encirclement being based on information from ULTRA. Without ULTRA Stalingrad must have taken a different course.

Again at Kursk, we see the Russian defensive system (extremely extensive and thoroughly prepared, on the order of a hundred miles deep!) being based on knowledge of the plans for the German attack gained months in advance via ULTRA. The attack must have had much greater success had it not been for ULTRA. The failure of the attack was of course a military disaster of the highest order for the Germans. (Note that the enormous and costly efforts to create such a defensive system could only be justified by foreknowledge of enemy plans.)

Information from ULTRA was available to the Soviets from the beginning of the campaign in the east (and even earlier), until the end. Much more could be said, but the above 2 examples should demonstrate that ULTRA had the most serious consequences in the east.

Information gained from ULTRA was invaluable in planning and executing the Normandy invasion, etc., etc.

One point worthy of note is that the Allies came to rely too heavily on ULTRA, so that when the Ardennes offensive came without warning (for reasons other than fear for the security of the enigma, plans for this offensive were not broadcast), the Allied forces were immediately in serious trouble, being caught unprepared and unawares. This brings up 2 points: (1): One should develop as many alternative sources of intelligence as possible in case some sources fail, and (2): It may be possible to deliberately compromise a source of information to the enemy, lead him to rely on it too heavily, then strike a sudden blow, without warning being given through the compromised channel.

Summing up, in all theatres of war ULTRA had the most serious consequences for the German war effort. Without ULTRA Rommel should have overrun the British in North Africa and been able to carry out his plan for moving into southern Russia, the Allies should not have been able to invade North Africa or Europe, and the war on the Eastern front should have been at least a stalemate. When Atomic weapons came into play the most uncertain consequences could be expected.

Let us examine the theory of war in the Atomic age. It is no longer likely that one side will be able to accumulate a decisive superiority and deliver an overwhelming blow which destroys the enemy, without risk of being destroyed in turn. (Let us hope that the so-called superpowers will realize that their mutual self-interest is in maintaining peaceful relations and the status quo, preventing the spread of atomic weapons, etc.) However, there is always the chance that a flaw in one side's military scheme will be uncovered. One weak point currently may be communication systems. Being able to disable or interfere with the enemy's communication system could make a succesful first strike possible. Another danger is simulating a compomised cryptographic scheme, delivering false information to an enemy while an attack is underway. Hence the need for the utmost care in such matters. Multiple, fault tolerant communication and cryptographic systems would make such a first strike strategy more difficult.

With regards to conventional weapons systems, some of the interesting developments are in bad weather and night fighting equipment, satellite vision systems able to penetrate cloud cover, etc. Many varied types of surveilance systems are needed to guard against a Soviet surprise invasion of Western Europe. Cryptography of course has an important role here. Particularly interesting are cryptosystems related to error-correcting codes (B. Chor has done some interesting work in this area).

We now turn to some possible new directions for cryptographic research. Let us examine some speculative cryptographic ideas. We have seen in Brassard's Quantum Cryptography how ideas on the frontiers of science can be used to develop unusual cryptographic schemes, both for practical and theoretical purposes. Let us look at "Psychic Attacks" on cryptosystems. It might seem that not much can be done about such attacks. However, suppose we model the situation as follows: A "psychic" can look at say N bits of information hidden by an enemy. Then a cryptosystem with a short key is at risk, while the one time pad is optimally secure, since seeing N bits of the key is no better than seeing N bits of the real message. In any case, some interesting theoretical and perhaps practical consequences are derivable in this and other models of psychic attack. One practical question might be what storage medium to use in order to hide a key to a cryptosystem. It may be safer on a hard disk, say, than written on paper. An interesting theoretical problem is whether there are "Quantum" methods for storing information so that it is invulnerable to psychic attack.

Let us examine research and education in relation to cryptography. One lesson from WW2 is that genius (i.e. Alan Turing) can be of vital importance. How to tap such genius? No bureaucratic set of rules can hope to produce such genius, rather red tape tends to inhibit researchers. I propose to look at the problem of getting research done as follows: research by its very nature defies preconceived explanations. We cannot dictate how to go about solving unsolved problems, at least not in all cases. Still, the effort in case of war or political struggle needs to be organized in some way. Using the 3 primitive principles stated earlier, I look at it as follows. Research should be subsidized to a certain funding level. (The function representing yearly funding should normally be "smooth" as radical changes from year to year are wasteful. Rates of change may be more important than particular yearly amounts, with the long run in view.) Whether a particular researcher continues to be subsidized depends on competitive principles, i.e. after a certain number of years the output of various researchers is investigated and a certain percentage receive continued funding, others lose their funding. A certain number of new researchers are given funding each year. A certain number of researchers who have done good work are given lifetime support. (So they can pursue their work with the long term in view, without having to compromise by seeking quick results in order to justify continued support, etc.) While sometimes the "critical mass" needed to solve a problem needs to form in the mind of a single individual, at other times it helps to bring together a number of individuals working in related areas, who then form another type of critical mass. Additionally, more researchers than are currently needed should be subsidized, so as to be available with no lag time in case of emergency. The above applies to cryptographic research in particular, as well as research in general. It might be noted that as weapons development is a part of war, the theory of weapons development needs to be studied. As in the case of research in general, preconceived specifications for weapon systems are likely to lead to problems. Many researchers should be given funding to develop systems on their own, and the best creations put into production. Overall guidelines may be helpful, but overprecise specifications are likely to be counterproductive. Instead competition between researchers for funding should be used to get the best possible systems created. Also developments in other countries should be monitored and the best creations copied.

Of course there are times when scarcity of resources (or other factors) requires a single cooperative effort to solve a particular problem. Cooperative efforts have some theoretical advantages. Applying the principle of competition to good effect requires intelligence. No appeals to an "Invisible Hand" allowed. So called "competitive markets" really exist within a larger framework of cooperation. Competition carried to the extreme is destructive (i.e. spillover costs, war, etc.)

I now discuss the role of cryptography in education. The problem of teaching students to think independently in addition to giving them a technical education is a difficult one. Logic and cryptography can be useful here.

As logic can be used for discerning truth and falsity in certain circumstances, its study is useful in helping students develop the ability to think independently and develop the faculty of critical analysis. One danger in this study is that the student when first introduced to logic may become too concerned with truth and not understand the need for falsehood and deception (including social pleasantries) under certain circumstances, instead having to learn this through painful experience. Cryptography is in some sense a dual science to logic, concerned with hiding the truth. Its study sheds some light on the ages old problem in philosophy of knowing the truth, speaking the truth, etc. (Recall Diogenes). Why is it that it is so hard to find an honest man? In terms of the present world view, the answer is simple. In competition, as in war, information is valuable to the opponent, helpful to ones allies. So information should be truthfully shared with those working in cooperation towards a common goal, and hidden from those working towards antagonistic ends, with a view to the consequences in mind. Teaching cryptography as well as logic in colleges and universities could be a valuable part of student education, in understanding the proper role of truth and deception in life, further developing the power of discrimination in judgement and independent thought. A one semester course in cryptography could easily be given, containing perhaps history, computer programming assignments related to cryptography, the problems of data security in computer systems, theory (illustrating such things as computational complexity theory when dealing with public key cryptography, beautiful mathematical topics like information theory ...), etc. If such courses were implemented on a wide scale, increasing the number of students aware of cryptographic issues, there is a greater likelihood of outstanding researchers appearing from this larger population. Also cryptographers would have greater employment opportunities given the need for instructors for such courses, thus increasing the size of the cryptographic community. The history of cryptography provides an excellent example of the importance of the intellectual in society, and the tragic consequences of the weakening of the intellectual community in a particular society.

A curious question is the relation between cryptography and chess. A number of outstanding cryptographers have also had a serious interest in chess in one way or another. The question of whether there is some causual relation, or whether chess develops some faculty useful in cryptography, is open, to my knowledge. Perhaps including courses in chess in schools would have some unexpected benefits. This has been done on a very large scale in the Soviet Union. At the very least this has resulted in a great many strong chess players. Besides being a pleasant form of mental exercise which can strengthen memory, etc., chess (as well as other competitive games) can be useful in developing a more objective view of oneself and respect for the opposition (if only Hitler had been a chess player, perhaps his megalomania would not have been so pronounced. Usually only world champions can maintain illusions of grandeur for long. Poor Fischer ...).

## ABSTRACT PROTOCOL THEORY

We now turn to the subject of Cryptographic Protocols, and "Abstract Protocol Theory". Recent research has investigated cryptographic protocols such as "Exchange of Secret Keys", "Contract Signing", "Digital Money", "Certified Mail", "Oblivious Transfer", etc. When dealing with these protocols certain principles appear repeatedly. I would like to propose considering "Abstract Protocol Theory", abstracting certain underlying principles from the theory of Cryptographic Protocols. We will take the view that we have a number of parties who interact under some rules (the rules of the protocol). We assume certain functions exist, say functions representing the wealth of each individual, the probability of being caught cheating (violating the rules of the protocol), the penalty for cheating, the probability that an individual will attempt to cheat, the amount of information each individual has, etc. These functions may vary with time, wealth, information, etc. We do not specify these functions more precisely as we want to remain somewhat abstract for now.

Suppose that the protocol is insecure in the sense that the penalty for cheating is less than the benefits. Suppose some individuals are more likely to cheat than others. Then immediately we see that over time wealth will tend to accrue to the cheaters. Suppose that willingness to cheat is increased by lack of wealth and/or information that cheating is profitable. Then as time passes and cheaters accumulate wealth, presumably this will become more and more evident and formerly honest participants will become more inclined to cheat. In the extreme we may imagine all participants forced to cheat in order to survive.

So we immediately see a relation between the mathematical model and such issues as honesty, morality, law, social and economic policy. By studying abstract protocol theory, my hope is that the certainty of deductive methods can be applied to certain problems which are presently treated in a haphazard and unscientific way.

Some interesting questions arise. Is it possible to design fair protocols where the chance of successfully cheating is low and the benefits from cheating do not outweigh the penalties? In some cases (such as with Income Tax Protocols), we may ask, is it even possible to have a well defined protocol? Godel's incompleteness theorems might lead us to suspect that in some cases no well defined protocol can exist. (After all, arithmetic is used in income tax protocols.) What are the consequences? We might conclude that the efforts to establish such protocols have the unintended effect of creating a haven for clever and unscrupulous individuals. Also that the moral elements of society may be either reduced to poverty or forced to compromise their morality.

Let us look at some examples, to indicate a few of the many directions research might take.

In the USA, the income tax system is notoriously badly designed, and easily cheated, either through outright fraud or through exploiting poorly designed rules (i.e. "loopholes"). In consequence a greater segment of the population seems to be violating at least the spirit of the law, an underground economy has developed, honest citizens pay a disproportionate share of taxes, etc.

Some interesting points come out when considering traffic laws. Certain laws (i.e. speeding) are widely broken. Logically, when an individual breaks one such law, where is he to stop? The result may be a breakdown in the social order, as individuals no longer respect the laws in general, having broken some particular law. Having no protocol may be better than a badly designed or unenforced one.

Sometimes traffic laws make conflict between drivers inevitable, whereupon the drivers get angry with each other while the real culprits (the protocol designers) escape blame.

Drug laws against such substances as marijuana, etc., have had the effect of restricting supplies, with the obvious result that price increases, giving more incentive for individuals to become growers, etc. Hence a great deal of effort on both sides is wasted to the detriment of the overall economy and society. An alternative approach would be for the government to license producers and tax it, thereby eliminating a segment of the underground economy, returning individuals to more productive occupations, eliminating the violent drug wars which are ruining some parts of the country and the lives of many people, saving costs of anti-drug enforcement, and increasing tax revenues, not to mention removing a source of social conflict, eliminating a source of funding for revolutionary groups, etc. (It has also been suggested that a great deal of crime is due to drug users seeking money to support drug habits.) In this way closer supervision could be maintained over drug users and drug purity, casualties of drug use could be given medical treatment, etc. After some years, when the underground supply system had disappeared, it might then be possible to eliminate the drug from society, if desired.

One problem that can arise is that a badly designed protocol can be difficult to get rid of. In practice human beings seem to have a habit of constructing ill-conceived protocols ("red-tape", "catch-22", etc. Individuals who have been graduate students at Berkeley may be able to discuss other surprising examples.) A possible solution is a "meta-protocol" which requires all protocols to have an expiration date set when they are created, thus killing off bad protocols eventually instead of giving them eternal life. Protocols which turned out to be useful could be renewed. One of the main tasks I envision for researchers in Abstract Protocol Theory is getting rid of existing undesirable protocols.

We might note that given the likelihood that certain protocols cannot be designed in a provably secure way, we need to consider an empirical approach where protocols are tried for a certain period of time, later being modified or terminated based on experience. Of course this is often what happens in practice. When new protocols are implemented, criminals get to work seeking flaws. After the flaws become evident, the protocol is altered, new flaws are sought, etc.

Also to be considered is the problem of propaganda/disinformation campaigns designed to mislead the population into obeying the rules of certain insecure protocols. This practice may start during childhood ...

Integrating some of the principles mentioned earlier, let us look at education from the viewpoint of Abstract Protocol Theory. We saw that competition is a force that can reduce inefficiency. In the USA the public school system is subsidized with only moderate competition. The result is frequently mediocre public education for the students (it must be clear that education is for the benefit not only of the student but also of the society he lives in). A simple method of introducing competition is the so called "school voucher" proposal, where individuals are given vouchers which they can take to any school of their choice. This would force schools to compete for students, hopefully resulting in better quality education.

In general the possibility of applying the competition principle in protocol design might be investigated.

Turning to another example, suppose that when receiving "transfer payments" or services subsidized by the government, the total is recorded by the IRS. Then when paying taxes, a surcharge, say 10%, is levied on those with a positive balance. This would provide incentive not to use such services needlessly while minimizing economic hardship for those in need.

Political systems can also be looked upon as protocols.

From an anthropological point of view, protocols might be linked to the notion of ritual as fufilling some innate need. It might be noted that the chance of cheating without being caught increases in societies with larger populations, where interaction between strangers is frequent, while in smaller tribal groups one cannot so easily hide, as everyone has more information about the other participants. Perhaps it can be proven that attempts to organize large groups inevitably create opportunities for criminal activity. Perhaps dissimilar genetic or cultural backgrounds within a population make certain types of protocols (social organization) impossible, due to lack of certain common implicit assumptions.

In conclusion, I believe integrating abstract protocol theory with theories from other fields such as economics, etc., can yield a useful tool for improving social conditions, and an interesting model for understanding events.

# SECTION II

# PUBLIC KEY CRYPTOGRAPHY

# EFFICIENT FACTORING BASED ON PARTIAL INFORMATION

Ronald L. Rivest* and Adi Shamir**

*MIT Laboratory for Computer Science
Cambridge, Mass. 02139, U.S.A.

**Applied Math. Dept., The Weizmann Institute of Science
Rehovot 76100, Israel

Many recently proposed cryptosystems are based on the assumption that factoring large composite integers is computationally difficult. In this paper we examine this assumption when the cryptanalyst has "side information" available.

Let N be the product of two large primes P and Q, where N is n bits in length, and P, P are each n/2 bits in length. Given N, it is possible to compute P and Q in time approximately

$$L(N) = \exp(\mathrm{sgrt}(\ln(N)\ln\ln(N))) \quad [1]$$

using, for example, the recent algorithm of Lenstra.

In cryptographic applications, however, the cryptanalyst may have available additional "side information" above and beyond the number N itself. In practice, one of the parties typically knows P and Q already, and uses these factors explicitly during his cryptographic computations. The results of these computations may become known to the cryptanalyst, who thereby may find himself at an advantage compared to a pure factoring situation.

For example, the cryptanalyst might become privy to:

(1) the procedure that generated P and Q (but not the random inputs to that procedure).

(2) the lengths of P and Q.

(3) a square root of 2, modulo N.

(4) the RSA signature of a message M using modulus N corresponding to a public RSA exponent of 3.

(5) the least-significant n/4 bits of P.

The point to be understood is that in practice additional side information may become available to the cryptanalyst, for one of the following reasons:

- loss of the equipment that generated P and Q.
- explicit release of partial side information as part of a protocol (e.g., "exchange of secrets" [Bl83]).
- routine usage of P , Q to decrypt mail, sign messages, etc.
- poor physical or electrical security by crypto equipment that uses and guards P and Q.

We formalize this notion, in a worst-case manner, as follows. Suppose that the cryptanalyst is allowed to ask a certain number k of arbitrary "Yes/No" questions at the beginning. He is given the answers to these questions before he attempts to factor N. (We do not care about the difficulty of answering these questions -- the answers are supplied free of charge to the cryptanalyst.) To be precise, we assume he is given the answer to question i before he poses question i + 1.

As we increase k , the cryptanalyst's task becomes easier and easier. For example, with $k = n/2$ his task is trivial: he asks for the binary representation of P. We ask our fundamental question: for what values of k (as a function of N) can the cryptanalyst factor N in polynomial time? Our main result is the following:

Theorem. The cryptanalyst can factor $N = P \cdot Q$ (where P and Q are n/2-bit numbers, and N is an n-bit number in time polynomial in n , if he is first given the answers to $n/3 + O(1)$ "Yes/No" questions about N for free.

This is not a dramatic improvement over the obvious n/2 result mentioned above. However, the proof is not trivial, and we do not know how to improve on this result. We conjecture that $O(n^{\varepsilon})$ questions suffice, for some $\varepsilon < 1$.

Proof (sketch): Suppose the cryptanalyst asks for the top $k = n/3$ bits of the factor P . He can then represent P in the form

$$P = P_1 \cdot 2^m + P_o \qquad [2]$$

where $m = (n/2) - k = n/6$,

$$0 \leq P_1 \leq 2^k \qquad [3]$$

$$0 \leq P_o \leq 2^m \qquad [4]$$

$P_1$ is known, and $P_o$ is unknown. The factor Q can be represented similarly:

$$Q = Q_1 \cdot 2^m + Q_o \qquad [5]$$

where

$$0 \leq Q_1 \leq 2^k \text{ , and} \qquad [6]$$

$$0 \leq Q_o \leq 2^m. \qquad [7]$$

Since N and $P_1$ are known, $Q_1$ can be easily computed. (We know N and P to at least k bits of precision, so we know their quotient to k bits of precision.) The unknowns to be solved for are $P_o$ and $Q_o$.

Compute

$$X = N - P_1Q_1 2^{2m}, \qquad [8]$$

$$A = P_1 \cdot 2^m, \text{ and} \qquad [9]$$

$$B = Q_1 \cdot 2^m . \qquad [10]$$

Then we have the equation

$$X = A \cdot P_o + B \cdot Q_o + P_oQ_o \qquad [11]$$

to solve for $P_o$ and $Q_o$. When k is large, m is small, and the product $P_oQ_o$ (of length 2m) is also small. We can thus attempt to solve [11] by trying to find a linear combination of A and B that closely approximates X. (We treat the term $P_oQ_o$ as similar to the "approximation error".) We set this up as a two-dimensional integer programming problem:

<u>Minimize</u>: $Z = X - A \cdot P_o - BQ_o$ [12]

<u>Subject to</u>: $0 \leq P_o \leq 2^m$ [13]

$0 \leq Q_o \leq 2^m$ [14]

We note that X is approximately n - k bits in length. We use a heuristic argument here that for each degree of freedom (bit) we can set in $P_o$ or $Q_o$, we can reduce the length of Z by one bit. Since we have

$$|P_o| + |Q_o| = 2m \qquad [15]$$

we expect that Z will be $|X| - 2m = n - 2k = n/3$ bits in length; our "approximation error" is about n/3 bits in length. We note that $P_oQ_o$ also has length $2m = n/3$, so that the "modelling error" we introduced by moving from the nonlinear equation [11] to the linear approximation [12] will also be about n/3 bits in length. We can thus expect the solution to [12]-[14] to be a solution for [11] as well. We note that [12]-[14] can be solved in polynomial time using Lenstra's algorithm for integer programming in a fixed number of dimensions. [Le81]

The preceding proof sketch is not a rigorous argument, but can be made so (although the number of questions may need to be increased by O(1) to handle some details about the precision).

A similar argument can be made to show that the cryptanalyst can factor N using the <u>low</u>-order k bits of N rather than the high-order k bits. ■

## Open Problems

Prove or disprove that $\Omega(n)$ questions are necessary in the theorem, if the cryptanalyst may only ask for bits in the binary representation of $P$.

Prove or disprove that $\Omega(n)$ questions are necessary in general.

## Acknowledgment

This research was supported in part by NSF grant MCS 8006938.

## References

[B183] Blum, Manuel. "How to exchange secrets," Proc. 15th Annual ACM STOC Conference (1983), 440-447.

[Le81] Lenstra, H. W., Jr. "Integer programming in a fixed number of variables," Report 81-03, Mathematisch Institut, Universitat ban Amsterdam (1981).

# A PUBLIC-KEY CRYPTOSYSTEM BASED ON SHIFT REGISTER SEQUENCES

Harald Niederreiter
Mathematical Institute
Austrian Academy of Sciences
A-1010 Vienna/Austria

Various cryptosystems using finite field arithmetic have been introduced recently, e.g. cryptosystems based on permutations of finite fields (Lidl and Müller [8], Nöbauer [12]), cryptosystems of the knapsack type (Chor and Rivest [4], Niederreiter [11]), and cryptosystems based on discrete exponentiation in finite fields (Odlyzko [13], Wah and Wang [14]). Finite fields also play a role in the construction of stream ciphers (Beker and Piper [1], Beth et al. [2], Lidl and Niederreiter [10]). The security of cryptosystems based on discrete exponentiation has recently been diminished by significant progress on the discrete logarithm problem (Blake et al. [3], Coppersmith [5], Coppersmith et al. [6]). In this paper we propose a public-key cryptosystem that has a more complex structure than the corresponding discrete-exponentiation cryptosystem and is therefore potentially harder to break. This cryptosystem uses feedback shift register (FSR) sequences in finite fields and is thus easy to implement.

To set up the cryptosystem, let $q$ be a prime power, let $F_q$ be the finite field with $q$ elements, and let

$$g(x) = x^n - b_{n-1}x^{n-1} - \dots - b_1x - b_0$$

be a publicly known polynomial over $F_q$ with $n \geq 1$ and $b_0 \neq 0$. Let $(s_i)$ be an FSR sequence in $F_q$ with

$$s_{i+n} = b_{n-1}s_{i+n-1} + \dots + b_1s_{i+1} + b_0s_i \quad \text{for} \quad i = 0,1,\dots .$$

This sequence can be generated by an n-stage FSR and has characteristic polynomial $g(x)$. The basic idea of our cryptosystem is to replace discrete exponentiation by the operation of decimation for FSR sequences. By definition, the <u>decimation</u> of $(s_i)$ by the factor $k$ yields the sequence $(s_{ik})$, i.e. we take every kth term of $(s_i)$ starting from $s_0$. Let $M$ be the least positive integer such that $g(x)$ divides $x^M - 1$. If $g(x)$ is also the minimal polynomial of $(s_i)$, then the least period of $(s_i)$ is equal to $M$. We refer to [9, Ch. 8] for the necessary background on FSR sequences.

FSR Public-Key Cryptosystem. Let $A$ and $B$ be two correspondents in a communication system. The private key of $A$ is a random integer $h$ with $1 < h < M$ and $\gcd(h,M) = 1$. Let $(s_i)$ be the FSR sequence with characteristic polynomial $g(x)$ and initial values $s_0 = \dots = s_{n-2} = 0, s_{n-1} = 1 (s_0 = 1$ if $n = 1)$. Then the public key of $A$ is the string $s_h s_{2h} \dots s_{(2n-1)h}$ of $2n - 1$ elements of $F_q$.
Encryption: If $B$ wants to send a message to $A$ that consists of a string $a_0 a_1 \dots a_{n-1}$ of $n$ elements of $F_q$ which are not all 0, then $B$ picks a random integer $k$ with $1 < k < M$ and $\gcd(k,M) = 1$. From A's public key, B determines the minimal polynomial of the decimated sequence $(t_i) = (s_{ih})$. Thus $B$ can calculate any $u_i = t_{ik}$. Now $B$ forms the Hankel matrix

$$U = \begin{pmatrix} u_0 & u_1 & \dots & u_{n-1} \\ u_1 & u_2 & \dots & u_n \\ \vdots & \vdots & & \vdots \\ u_{n-1} & u_n & \dots & u_{2n-2} \end{pmatrix}$$

and transmits to $A$ the following two strings as ciphertexts: $s_k s_{2k} \dots s_{(2n-1)k}$ and $(a_0 a_1 \dots a_{n-1})U$.
Decryption: From the ciphertext $s_k s_{2k} \dots s_{(2n-1)k}$, $A$ determines the minimal polynomial of the decimated sequence $(v_i) = (s_{ik})$. Thus $A$ can calculate any $u_i = s_{ihk} = v_{ih}$ and so finds the matrix $U$. Then $A$ recovers the plaintext $a_0 a_1 \dots a_{n-1}$ by postmultiplying the ciphertext $(a_0 a_1 \dots a_{n-1})U$ by $U^{-1}$.

Some comments on this cryptosystem are in order. A task we face several times is the calculation of remote terms in an FSR sequence. This task can be solved by very efficient algorithms. For instance, a recent algorithm of Fiduccia [7] allows the calculation of the ith term of an n-stage FSR sequence in $F_q$ by $O(n(\log n)(\log i))$ arithmetic operations in $F_q$; for earlier algorithms see the references in [9, p. 458]. We note further that the given initial values of the FSR sequence $(s_i)$ guarantee that $g(x)$ is the minimal polynomial of $(s_i)$. The following general results on FSR sequences are also needed.

Lemma 1. If the characteristic polynomial $g(x)$ of an arbitrary FSR sequence $(s_i)$ in $F_q$ has the factorization $g(x) = \prod_{j=1}^{n} (x - \beta_j)$ in its splitting field over $F_q$, then the decimated sequence $(s_{ik})$ has the characteristic polynomial $g_k(x) = \prod_{j=1}^{n} (x - \beta_j^k)$, which is again a polynomial over $F_q$.

Lemma 2. If $(s_i)$ is an arbitrary FSR sequence in $F_q$ with minimal polynomial $g(x)$, if $\gcd(k,M) = 1$ and $x^2$ does not divide $g(x)$, then $(s_{ik})$ has the minimal polynomial $g_k(x)$.

These two lemmas show that all the decimated sequences appearing in our cryptosystem are again n-stage FSR sequences in $F_q$ with minimal polynomials of degree n. It is known that the minimal polynomial of an n-stage FSR sequence can be calculated quickly from the first 2n terms of the sequence, e.g. by the Berlekamp-Massey algorithm (see [9, Ch. 8]). In our case, the first 2n terms of the relevant sequences are always available since the first term $s_0$ is known anyway and the next 2n - 1 terms are either published or transmitted over the channel. In the deciphering procedure we have to make use of the nonsingularity of the matrix U, which follows from the fact that the sequence $(u_i)$ has a minimal polynomial of degree n and from [9, Theorem 8.75].

In the special case n = 1 our cryptosystem reduces to one based on discrete exponentiation. The presence of the free parameter n allows for a greater flexibility and for a more complex structure as compared to a discrete-exponentiation cryptosystem. An additional advantage is the possibility of error-correcting cryptography. This means that if the channel $B \rightarrow A$ is noisy, then we can add some check symbols to the ciphertexts in a natural way to reduce the probability of transmission errors. In detail, we take the ciphertext $v_1 v_2 \ldots v_{2n-1}$ and add to it a string $v_{2n} v_{2n+1} \ldots v_{2n+m}$ of subsequent terms of the FSR sequence $(v_i)$ as check symbols. The receiver A still determines the minimal polynomial of $(v_i)$ from the string $v_1 v_2 \ldots v_{2n-1}$, and if the check symbols do not fit, he can ask for a retransmission. We note also that there is a second version of the FSR public-key cryptosystem in which the sequence $(s_i)$ is replaced by the power-sum sequence associated with g(x), i.e. the sequence which in the notation of Lemma 1 is given by $s_i = \sum_{j=1}^{n} \beta_j^i$ for $i = 0,1,\ldots$ . In this case the strings of length 2n - 1 can be replaced by strings of length n, but on the other hand we can only work with fields $F_q$ of characteristic $p > n$.

A cryptanalyst can basically pursue two lines of attack against the FSR public-key cryptosystem. The first type of attack is directed against the keys h and k. This amounts to inferring the value of k from knowledge of the polynomials g(x) and $g_k(x)$ in Lemma 1. The following three steps are required:

(i) calculating the roots of g(x) and $g_k(x)$;

(ii) pairing off the roots of g(x) with those of $g_k(x)$ in a correct manner (which may require up to n! trials);

(iii) solving discrete logarithm problems in various extensions of $F_q$.

The least favorable case is the one where g(x) is irreducible over $F_q$, for then step (ii) is not needed and the problem of inferring k is equivalent to a discrete logarithm problem. The polynomial g(x) should be chosen in such a way that a large value of M is obtained and the factorization of g(x) into irreducibles over $F_q$ is fairly complicated. A good choice for g(x) appears to be the following: let q be a large prime and let g(x) be a product of many irreducibles over $F_q$ of small degree such that a large value of M is obtained. Alternatively, we could use q = 2 and let $g(x)$ be a product of many irreducibles over $F_2$ of moderately large degree such that a large value of $M$ is obtained.

The second line of attack is aimed at a direct determination of the matrix U. This succeeds immediately if there are two message strings $a_0a_1 \dots a_{n-1}$ that are scalar multiples of 10 ... 0 and 0 ... 01, respectively, for then a knowledge of the corresponding ciphertexts $(a_0a_1 \dots a_{n-1})U$ determines U completely (because of the special structure of a Hankel matrix). In general, the system is vulnerable to this type of attack if there are several messages of low weight. We can defend against this attack by using a different enciphering scheme for low-weight messages, such as those in [4] and [11] designed especially for low-weight messages. Another defense is based on first encoding all messages via a linear code C over $F_q$ of length n, dimension $d < n$, and large minimum distance (in the sense of algebraic coding theory). The resulting system works as follows. The acceptable messages consist of nonzero strings of d elements of $F_q$. Each message is transformed via the coding scheme of C into a code word $a_0a_1 \dots a_{n-1}$, which is then postmultiplied by U to get the second ciphertext in the FSR public-key cryptosystem. Decryption proceeds by determining U as before from the first ciphertext, postmultiplying the second ciphertext by $U^{-1}$ to recover $a_0a_1 \dots a_{n-1}$, and then applying the inverse coding scheme to recover the original message. By using the code C we make sure that each string $a_0a_1 \dots a_{n-1}$ entering the encryption phase has a relatively large weight. In all cases it should be noted that U is determined once we have used n linearly independent message strings, and so the value of the key k should be changed before that.

The principle employed in the design of our cryptosystem, namely to replace discrete exponentiation by the more complex operation of decimation of FSR sequences, can be used to construct other cryptosystems. We have obtained in this way new conventional cryptosystems, key-exchange schemes, and variants of Shamir's no-key algorithm. The most intricate of these cryptosystems work with message-dependent FSR sequences.

## References


1. H. Beker and F. Piper: Cipher Systems. The Protection of Communications, Northwood Books, London, 1982.
2. T. Beth, P. Heß, and K. Wirl: Kryptographie, Teubner, Stuttgart, 1983.
3. I. F. Blake, R. Fuji-Hara, R. C. Mullin, and S. A. Vanstone: Computing logarithms in finite fields of characteristic two, SIAM J. Alg. Discr. Methods 5, 276-285 (1984).
4. B. Chor and R. L. Rivest: A knapsack type public key cryptosystem based on arithmetic in finite fields, Proc. CRYPTO '84, to appear.
5. D. Coppersmith: Fast evaluation of logarithms in fields of characteristic two, IEEE Trans. Inform. Theory 30, 587-594 (1984).
6. D. Coppersmith, A. M. Odlyzko, and R. Schroeppel: Discrete logarithms in GF(p), preprint.
7. C. M. Fiduccia: An efficient formula for linear recurrences, SIAM J. Comput. 14, 106-112 (1985).

8. R. Lidl and W. B. Müller: A note on polynomials and functions in algebraic cryptography, Ars Combin. 17A, 223-229 (1984).
9. R. Lidl and H. Niederreiter: Finite Fields, Addison-Wesley, Reading, Mass., 1983.
10. R. Lidl and H. Niederreiter: Introduction to Finite Fields and Their Applications, Cambridge Univ. Press, in press.
11. H. Niederreiter: Knapsack-type cryptosystems and algebraic coding theory, Problems of Control and Information Theory, to appear.
12. R. Nöbauer: Rédei-Funktionen und ihre Anwendung in der Kryptographie, Acta Sci. Math. Szeged, to appear.
13. A. M. Odlyzko: Discrete logarithms in finite fields and their cryptographic significance, Proc. EUROCRYPT '84, to appear.
14. P. K. S. Wah and M. Z. Wang: Realization and application of the Massey-Omura lock, Proc. Intern. Sem. on Digital Communications (Zürich, 1984), pp. 175-182.

# A COMMENT ON NIEDERREITER'S PUBLIC KEY CRYPTOSYSTEM

Bernard Smeets
Department of Computer Engineering
University of Lund
P.O. Box 118, S-221 00 Lund, SWEDEN

**Summary** - In this comment we show that a recently proposed public key cryptosystem is not safe for most of the practical cases. Furthermore, it is shown that the security of this system is closely connected with the problem of computing logarithms over a finite field.

## 1 Introduction

At the EUROCRYPT 85 workshop H. Niederreiter proposed a public key distribution system based on shift register sequences. In this comment we show that the proposed system that works with sequences over a finite field of characteristic 2 will be unsecure for most of the practical cases.

Let us briefly summarize what is known publicly in one of the proposed systems. For a full description we refer to [1]. First a polynomial $g(x)$ of degree n over some finite prime field $K=GF(p)$, p prime, is chosen, i.e.

$$g(x)=x^n-b_{n-1}x^{n-1}-\dots-b_1x^1-b_0 \in K[x].$$

We demand that

$$n\geq 2 \quad \text{and} \quad (b_0,b_1)\neq(0,0).$$

For the moment let p=2 and $g(x)$ a prime polynomial over $K(=GF(2))$. Furthermore, let s be the sequence obtained from a linear feedback shift register with $g(x)$ as its feedback polynomial and initial conditions $s_0=\dots=s_{n-2}=0, s_{n-1}=1$. Besides $g(x)$ two sequences are public; $s^{(h)}:=s_h,s_{2h},\dots,s_{(2n-1)h}$ and $s^{(k)}:=s_k,s_{2k},\dots,s_{(2n-1)k}$, where h and k are two integers such that $1\leq h,k<\mathrm{ord}(g(x))=e$ and $\gcd(h,e)=\gcd(k,e)=1$. The task of the cryptanalyst is to determine h and k.

## 2 A possible attack

Since $s^{(k)}$ is known the cryptanalyst can compute the minimal polynomial $g^{(k)}(x)$ of this decimated sequence. From gcd(k,e)=1, it follows that $g^{(k)}(x)$ is prime over K and deg $g^{(k)}(x)=n$, [2]. Hence the roots of g(x) and $g^{(k)}(x)$ lie in an extension field F of K of degree n. The cryptanalyst proceeds by writing

$$g(x) = \prod_{i=1}^{n} (x-r_i),\ r_i \in F(=GF(2^n)),$$

and

$$g^{(k)}(x)= \prod_{j=1}^{n} (x-t_j),\ t_i \in F.$$

Both polynomials are prime, hence the roots of each of them are distinct. In general, obtaining all the roots of g(x) (or $g^{(k)}(x)$) in F requires $O((n\ln n)^2 \ln\ln n \ln p)$ operations in F by one of the root finding algorithms, [3], see also [4]. The field F is realized as K[x]/p(x)K[x], where p(x) is a maximum length polynomial of degree n over K. The polynomial p(x) is chosen such that the choice has a profitable effect on the algorithm for computing discrete logarithms in F, [5]. Now there exist a j such that $t_1=r_j^k$. Let us assume that j=1. If $j\neq1$ then the cryptanalyst has to try an other value of j. The latter implies that when our cryptanalyst is very unlucky he has to repeat n times the computations that remain at this point. Having expressed both $r_1$ and $t_1$ as elements in the field K[x]/p(x)K[x], the cryptanalyst can compute the logarithms of these two elements. Let l denote log $r_1$ and let l′ denote log $t_1$. From the relation $t_1=r_1^k$ follows the equation $l'=kl \bmod 2^n-1$. This equation has to be solved for k under the condition $1\leq k<e$. Using the fact that $e=(2^n-1)/d$, where $d=\gcd(l,2^n-1)$, and recalling that gcd(k,e)=1 and thus $\gcd(k,2^n-1)=1$, the cryptanalyst obtains

$$k=l'l^{-1} \bmod (2^n-1)/d.$$

Now it is clear that the values of h and k can be computed. When ignoring the computations of the roots the amount of work is roughly O(nf(n)), where O(f(n)) is the required work to compute a logarithm in F when the necessary precomputations have been done. In [6] it is indicated that for n=460 these precomputations require about a year on a modern supercomputer. In the same paper it is shown that O(f(n)) can be done in much less time.

## 3 Conclusions

When g(x) is not a prime polynomial then mutatis mutandis the same approach can be used to obtain h and k. And since the logarithm algorithm also works when one would have taken $GF(2^m)$ instead of GF(2), the PKC is vulnerable even in those cases. Summerizing, for the most interesting practical situations, i.e. p=2 and n<500, the proposed PKC system is not secure. In general the system is at most n times as complex as the discrete logarithm problem after precomputations.

## REFERENCES


[1] H. Niederreiter, "A public-key cryptosystem based on shift register sequences", Proceedings of EUROCRYPT 85 , (F. Pichler,T. Beth, ed), Springer Lecture Notes, to appear.

[2] N. Zierler, "Linear recurring sequences", SIAM Journ., vol. 7, (1959), pp. 31-48, Reprinted in Linear sequential switching circuits , (W.H. Kautz, ed), Holden-Day, San Fransisco, 1965.

[3] M. Ben-Or, "Probabilistic algorithms in finite fields", Proceedings of Foundations of Computer Science , 1981, pp.394-398.

[4] E.R. Berlekamp, "Factoring polynomials over large finite fields", Math. Comp., vol. 24, (1970), pp. 713-735.

[5] D. Coppersmith, "Fast evaluation of logarithms in finite fields of characteristic two, "IEEE Trans. on Inform. Theory, IT-30, (1984), pp. 587-594.

[6] A.M. Odlyzko, "Discrete logarithms in finite fields and their cryptographic significance", preliminary report, Bell Labs.

# IMPLEMENTATION STUDY OF PUBLIC KEY CRYPTOGRAPHIC PROTECTION IN AN EXISTING ELECTRONIC MAIL AND DOCUMENT HANDLING SYSTEM*

J. Vandewalle, R. Govaerts, W. De Becker, M. Decroos+
ESAT Laboratory, K.U. Leuven
Kardinaal Mercierlaan 94, 3030 Leuven, Belgium
and G. Speybrouck
Telindus, Geldenaakse Baan 335, 3030 Leuven, Belgium.

## 1. Introduction.

The problem which is addressed in this paper is to study the public key data protection (privacy, integrity and signatures) of an existing electronic mail and document handling system. This is not a trivial and straightforward problem since the protocols have to be tailored to the user's needs and since many trade-offs are involved between speed, security and ease of use. Moreover the final security of the overall system not only depends on the choice of the cryptographic algorithm, but also on the communication protocol, the key management and their implementation (physical security and computer security). In other words the security is a property of the whole system [3]. Although many of the arguments described in the paper are rather system dependent, it is expected that the approaches taken here are valuable for other applications too. The readers are however cautioned not to transfer the conclusions blindly.

In the paper we first describe in Section 2 the protection needs in and threats to the existing system. Section 3 presents a protection scheme which is tailored to these needs and to the system. A choice of the cryptographic system is made (RSA public key). In Section 4 the key management is described, while in Section 5 the communication protocol is presented. Section 6 presents the conclusions.

## 2. Protection needs in the existing system.

The Belgian Information System by Telephone (BISTEL) is the information network of the Belgian Goverment. It comprises more than 120 videoterminals, word processors, laserprinters and telexterminals spread over the remote ministerial departments. In the department of the Prime Minister an interconnection through a Local Area Network (LAN) is provided. All these remote sites are connected with a central computerroom

*Supported by the Services of the Prime Minister of Belgium under the BISTEL projekt.
+Part of this text has been elaborated within the framework of the Belgian Programme for the reinforcement of the scientific potential in the new technologies - PREST (Prime Minister's Office for Science Policy). The scientific responsibility for the text is assumed by its authors.

through the Public Switching Telephone Network (PSTN), the telexnetwork, or the X.25 packet switching network (DCS) of the Belgian R.T.T. The central computerroom is equipped with computers, databases and disk storage and a communication processor controlling the local network. This computerroom is physically protected against unauthorized access. The system is highly automated and can be operated day and night in a very user-friendly way (menu driven) by politicians as well as administrators. The system first of all performs the function of electronic mail between the terminals (editing and mailing of texts, chats). The electronic mail system operates in much the same way as ordinary mail. A sender A makes the central computer store a letter in the mailbox of the receiver B. B can read this message at his leisure. With the document handling facility one can store electronic mail, documents and telexes temporarily (3000 Mbyte disc) or archive (4000 Mbyte disc) them in a central database (document handling). The system also distributes telexes of international press agencies (UPI,AFP, Reuter, Belga) (media). The system also allows to consult databases. The general experience with the system is positive.
It is well known that passwords do not provide data protection and can only provide some barrier against unauthorized access. Even this barrier is not very resistant against computer hackers. The goal of this project is to study and evaluate protection alternatives for the system with a net speed which is not too much lower than the actual speed of 1200 bps, while maintaining the user-friendliness. One should achieve high standards of privacy protection, message as well as sender authentication and signature protection during the transmission through the network as well as during temporary or permanent storage. Here one should bear in mind that the protection of the system should not be based on a simultaneous presence of both the sender and the receiver (handshaking or mutual protocols) since it is more intended for electronic mail than for chats. In order to be able to compare the effectiveness of alternative protection schemes it is important to understand the major security threats of the system. By wiretapping the telephone, telex or packet switching network or by unauthorized access to the computer, one can obtain sensitive data (threat to privacy). The authenticity of messages is threatened by the injection of false or old messages or modification of blocks (replacing, inserting, deleting, modifying, ...) of existing messages either through the network or inside the computer. Moreover the classical subjective recognition of a sender by his handwriting in a letter or by his voice in the phone is no longer possible in the electronic mail. Hence it is important that the transmission as well as the storage of data in the system is protected against masquerade i.e. an intruder pretending to be an authorized user of the system (sender authentication). Finally it should not be possible for a sender to deny his sending a message nor for the receiver to deny the receipt (certified mail and electronically signed documents [1;4,p.14]). This implies that an independent third party can confirm the identity of the sender and the receiver of a message.

## 3. Selection of the protection scheme.

In the next three sections we compare and motivate the engineering choices related to the kind of encryption (symmetric versus asymmetric), the encryption algorithm and scheme, the key management and the communication protocol. Then we explain how the proposed protection scheme counters the major threats described in the previous Section. The choice between three kinds of encryption [4] classical or symmetric system, public key distribution system, and public key system is made in favor of the last one because of several reasons. First of all classical cryptography requires much processing of keys. Either it needs a different key for any pair of users which implies already 7140 keys for 120 users or in case session keys are used a vast key management is necessary. For practical algorithms (like DES) the key may have to change often in time. Hence this requires much bookkeeping of the encrypted documents and the corresponding keys. Of course these keys have to be stored in a protected way. Moreover the symmetric nature does not provide a signature protection. The second alternative (the combination of a public key distribution scheme for key transmission and a classical algorithm for data transmission) is not so appealing because it requires the implementation of two algorithms (more hardware or software). Moreover the inconvenience of updating and securely storing the keys of the classical scheme remains. A public key encryption is preferred because it requires less keys which last longer and because only one algorithm can provide many different protections (privacy, authentication, signature and even special needs [5]).

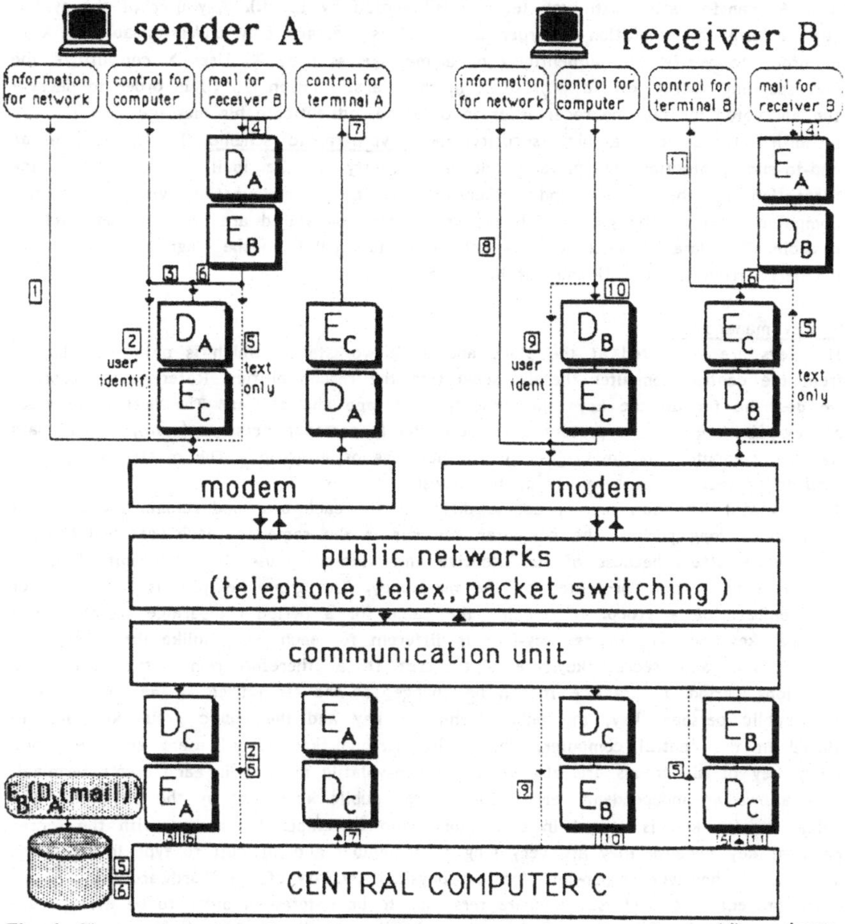


Fig. 1. The cryptographic scheme for mailing a message from A to B, providing privacy protection and authentication.

Although classical schemes and public key distribution schemes generally provide higher speed of data transmission, the required speed of 1200 bps does not exclude public key schemes.

The selection of RSA [6] as the public key cryptographic algorithm is motivated by the following arguments. The alternative algorithms are either broken (Merkle Hellman knapsack [7]) or not yet fully investigated (the most general knapsack [8]). The RSA algorithm with 200 decimal digits however is generally considered to be secure for several years to come [9]. Indeed intensive and diverse efforts over more than 5 years have shown only weaknesses which can be easily overcome. The scheme allows all types of protection and is most likely to become an ISO standard in a couple of years [1]. Moreover encryption and decryption speed of 1200 bps required for this system is certainly feasible.

In the sequel we denote by $(e_X,n_X)$ the public key of user X (exponent $e_X$, modulus $n_X$). A transformation with key $(e_X,n_X)$ is denoted by $E_X$ (.). Any user of the system can perform this operation in order to make his message only understandable by X or in order to verify the authenticity of a message sent by X. User X can utilize the corresponding secret key $(d_X,n_X)$ of X in the transformation $D_X$ (.) in order to decrypt the encrypted message he receives or in order to authenticate his message.

In order to achieve a high security the cryptographic scheme (Fig.1) provides an end-to-end protection of privacy and authenticity of the mail as well as a link protection of the privacy and authenticity of the communication with the central computer. Thereby the data which are transmitted or stored are protected as much as possible. The data (i) which are available at certain points in the diagram of fig. 1 are numbered from (1) to (11) and put in a box in Fig. 1.

## 4. Key management.

The keys are generated at the place and on a workstation which is physically disjoint from the central computer thereby separating the responsibilities. Referring to Table 1 we describe for all the keys their function, storage and back-up. The first three types of key-pairs are used to protect data, respectively personal messages (mail), control data for the computer and messages to all members of a group. The master key-pair is used to protect the authenticity of the transmitted keys.

The personal key-pairs are of course different for each user and remain the same at least for a long period. The computer key-pair is the same for each user and changes much more often, because of its intensive and widespread use. It is transmitted to the user at each session, protected by the masterkey. The group key-pair is the same for all members of a group. It remains the same for a period comparable to that of a personal key-pair. The master key-pair is different for each user. Unlike the other keys, both "public" and "secret" key are kept secret. It can therefore remain the same for a very long period. In practice it can be changed at the same time as the personal key. The public personal key, the public computer key and the public group key are all stored in the central computer. The public personal key of all users and the public group key of all groups are also stored in non-volatile memory in each user's terminal. This allows an independent verification of the public keys sent by the computer. The public master key is stored in a memory chip or chipcard together with the secret personal key because they are very long to remember and difficult to type in correctly. The user is however responsible for the physical security of the "hardware" key. As an extra protection a part (say 6 characters) has to be entered in order to be able to use the keys in the memory. This is an extra barrier for the finder or thief to overcome

| KEYS | FUNCTION(S) | STORAGE | BACK-UP |
|---|---|---|---|
| 1.a)public personal key of A $(e_A,n_A)$ | encrypt and verify authenticity of mail | locally on diskette verified with a copy authenticated by computer | no problem |
| b)secret personal key of A $(d_A,n_A)$ | decrypt and authenticate mail | memory chip or chipcard a part is entered on the keyboard | in safe (sharing) |
| 2.a)public computer key $(e_C,n_C)$ | encrypt and verify authenticity of communication with computer | sent by computer with secret masterkey authentication and public personal key protection then stored on cryptocard in terminal | no problem |
| b)secret computer key $(d_C,n_C)$ | decrypt and authenticate communication with computer (same for all users but varies often) | control computer | no problem |
| 3.a)public group key of group A $(e_G,n_G)$ | encrypt messages to group G | same as 1 | no problem |
| b)secret group key of group G $(d_G,n_G)$ | decrypt messages to the group | same as 1b) or 2a) | same as 1 |
| 4.a)public master key of A $(e_{MA},n_{MA})$ | verify authenticity of computer key | memorychip or chipcard | no problem |
| b)secret master key of A $(d_{MA},n_{MA})$ | transmit computer key (different for each user A) | central computer in protected memory | no problem |

Table 1. Key management.

before (s)he can use the key. The secret computer key remains in protected area in the computer. The secret group keys are stored in the same protected area. The keys are authenticated with the secret personal key of the groupleader and for each groupmember they are protected by his (her) public personal key. The secret master keys are stored in protected area in the computer as it is used for authentication of the keys transmitted by the computer.
The back-up of keys requires special attention only for the secret personal key and the secret group key since no messages are stored with encryption under either master key or computer key. In order to have a secure back-up when the secret personal key and the secret group key are lost or destroyed, the keys are partitioned over different safes so that only a sufficiently large subset of parts can reconstruct a key (sharing). Of course if a lost key is compromised a new key should be generated and the stored data which were protected with the compromised key should be recuperated quickly. If certificates are used in the protocol, a backup of the public masterkey of each user is necessary.

## 5. Basic steps of communication protocol for securely sending mail from A to B.

Part I Transmission of a protected message from A to the central computer.

1. The network information like the phone number (1) is sent to the network in clear

2. After connection to the host computer the electronic mail function is activated.
3. Then the identification (name) of the sender (2) is transferred in clear to the computer. After receiving the necessary keys (see Section 6) the encrypted password is sent to the computer. Though the security of the system does not depend critically on the password protection, its barrier along with a possible call-back system can detract many computer hackers.
4. The control for the computer mail program (3) is then sent authenticated by A with $D_A$ and encrypted with $E_C$. Of course in order to be able to verify the authenticity each block has to contain a sufficient number of redundant bits.
5. The control to the terminal in response (7) is authenticated by the computer with $D_C$ and encrypted with $E_A$.
6. The mail (4) from A to B is authenticated by A with $D_A$ and encrypted with $E_B$. When it is combined in a block with control (6) an additional authentication with $D_A$ and encryption with $E_C$ of the complete block happens as in step 4. The authenticated and privacy protected mail is stored on disk.
7. At the end of the session A sends a disconnection message to the computer authenticated by $D_A$ and encrypted with $E_C$.
8. The terminal switches to off-line condition.

Part II Reading of the protected message by B from the central computer.
As shown in Fig. 1 B proceeds analogously as A in part A. Of course in 6 the computer sends the protected message to B.

6. Basic steps of the key transfer protocol.
Communication beween user A and computer (Part I,3)
1. The computer sends $(e_C,n_C)$ authenticated with $(d_{MA},n_{MA})$ to A. Remember from Table 1 that $(d_{MA},n_{MA})$ is stored in protected memory in the central computer.
2 A sends the initialization of the message (author, destinee, subject) to the computer authenticated with $(d_A,n_A)$ and privacy protected with $(e_C,n_C)$.
3. a. The computer sends $(e_B,n_B)$ authenticated with $(d_{MA},n_{MA})$.
b. If a signature is desired the computer sends a certificate of $(e_A,n_A)$ and $(e_B, n_B)$ containing among others (A, B, $(e_A,n_A)$ $(e_B,n_B)$, time T, subject) authenticated with $(d_{MA},n_{MA})$. Each user has the obligation to report to the central computer a loss of his secret key immediately. Hence this certificate states that $(d_A,n_A)$ and $(d_B,n_B)$ were not compromised at time T.
4. A obtains $(e_B,n_B)$ from $D_{MA}$ $((e_B,n_B))$ or from the certificate.
At this moment user A disposes of all the keys $(e_C,n_C)$, $(e_B,n_B)$ (s)he needs for sending securely his mail to B and communicating securely with the computer C.

Communication between user B and computer. (Part II, 3.)
1. The computer sends $(e_C,n_C)$ authenticated with $(d_{MB},n_{MB})$ to B.
2. B sends the number of the message (s)he wants to read to the computer authenticated with $(d_B,n_B)$ and privacy protected with $(e_C,n_C)$.
3. a. Computer sends $(e_A,n_A)$ authenticated with $(d_{MB},n_{MB})$.
b. If a signature is desired the computer sends a certificate of $(e_A,n_A)$ and $(e_B, n_B)$ containing among others (A,B,$(e_B,n_B)$, time T', subject). $(e_A,n_A)$ and $(e_B,n_B)$ are the keys that were used to generate $E_B(D_A(\text{Mail}))$ at instant T.

4. B obtains $(e_A,n_A)$ from $D_{MB}((e_A,n_A))$ or from the certificate.
At this moment user B disposes of all the keys $(e_C,n_C)$, $(e_A,n_A)$ (s)he needs for reading the protected mail from A and for the secure communication with the computer C.

Let us now verify that this protocol meets the requirements of privacy, authenticity and if desired signature of Section 2. First of all the storage as well as the transmission of the mail can only be deciphered by B (end-to-end encryption). The transmission of the control data between computer and terminal is privacy protected (link encryption). The same reasoning can be given for the authenticity of the sender and the message. Observe that a message is always first authenticated and then encrypted (privacy protection). If the order was reversed, anybody could easily take off the authentication and abuse the resulting encrypted data. The signature with the mail is guaranteed by a certificate by the computer with $(d_{MA}, n_{MA})$ of the authenticity of the sender, the receiver and the keys used at time instant T. Users A and B are unable to alter the certificate, nor can they claim that their keys were lost, because they have the responsibility to report any loss of their keys. A can prove to a third party that B and only B has read the message, while B can prove to the same third party that A and only A has sent the message.

## 7. Conclusions.

The cryptographic protection of the BISTEL system is both necessary and feasible. The use of RSA and a hardware implementation is advocated. A proposal for the cryptographic scheme and the communication protocol is presented. It provides privacy protection, authentication and signature protection. Additional physical and computer security measures have to be taken. It appears that an acceptable trade-off between security, speed and ease of the use can be realised for this system.

## REFERENCES

[1] ISO, "Public key cryptosystem and mode of use, Annual report 1984", Report ISO/TC 97/SC 20/WG 2 N, Dec. 1984.

[2] S. Weinstein, "Smart credit cards; the answer to cashless shopping", IEEE Spectrum, Vol. 21, n°2, pp.43-49, Febr. 1984.

[3] D. Davies and W. Price, "Engineering secure information systems," Proc. Eurocr.1985.

[4] D.E. Denning, "Cryptography and data security," Addison-Wesley, Reading, 1982

[5] D. Chaum, "Untracable electronic mail, return addresses, and digital pseudonyms", Comm. ACM, Vol. 24, pp. 84-88, Febr. 1981.

[6] R.L. Rivest, A. Shamir, and L. Adleman, "A method for obtaining digital signatures and public key cryptosystems," Comm. ACM, Vol. 21, pp. 294-299, April 1978.

[7] R. Merkle and M. Hellman, "Hiding information and signatures in trapdoor knapsacks", IEEE Trans. Inform. Theory, Vol. 24, pp. 525-530, Sept. 1978.

[8] Y. Desmedt, J. Vandewalle, and R. Govaerts, "A general public key cryptographic knapsack algorithm based on linear algebra", IEEE Proc ISIT, pp. 129-130, 1980.

[9] Davis J.A., Holdridge D.B., Simmons G.J., "Status Report on factoring", Sandia National Laboratories 1-33, 1984.

[10] S. Serpell, C. Brookson, B. Clark, "A prototype encryption system using public key", Proc. Crypto 84.

# CRYPTANALYSIS OF THE DICKSON-SCHEME *

Winfried B. Müller and Rupert Nöbauer
Institut für Mathematik
Universität Klagenfurt
A - 9010 Klagenfurt, Austria

## 1. Introduction

In Müller and W. Nöbauer (1981) a new public-key cryptosystem was introduced. Similar to the well-known RSA-scheme, the plaintext alphabet and the code alphabet of this cryptosystem are given by Z/(n), the ring of residue classes of the integers Z modulo a natural number n. In contrast to the RSA-scheme, however, n need not be squarefree, but can be an arbitrary positive integer. The encryption polynomials $x^k$ of the RSA-scheme are replaced by another class of polynomials, namely by the so-called Dickson-polynomials. We call this cryptosystem the Dickson-scheme.
So far, there is not known very much about the security of the Dickson-scheme. The goal of this paper is to perform a cryptanalysis of the Dickson-scheme. We start with some basic facts on Dickson-polynomials, outline a fast algorithm for the computation of function values for the Dickson-polynomials and then give a short description of the Dickson-scheme. Afterwards, several possible cryptanalytic attacks on the system are discussed and as a consequence requirements to the key parameters are formulated, which guarantee the system to be secure from the described attacks.

---

*) The work presented in this paper was supported by the Österreichischen Fonds zur Förderung der Wissenschaftlichen Forschung under FWF-Project No. P 5452.
The final version of this paper was prepared during a visiting appointment of the author W.B. Müller in the Department of Mathematics at Monash University, Clayton, Vic. 3168, Australia.

## 2. Some basic facts

Let R be a commutative ring with identity, and let $a \in R$. The Dickson-polynomial $g_k(a,x) \in R[x]$ of degree k is given by

$$g_k(a,x) = \sum_{i=0}^{[k/2]} \frac{k}{k-i} \binom{k-i}{i} (-a)^i \, x^{k-2i},$$

where [k/2] denotes the greatest integer $i \le k/2$.
If $R_1$ is an extension ring of R and if $u \in R_1$ is a unit, then the equation

$$g_k(a, u + \tfrac{a}{u}) = u^k + (\tfrac{a}{u})^k \tag{1}$$

holds, as can be proved by using Waring's inversion formula (cf. Lidl and Niederreiter (1983)).
In this paper we restrict ourselves to the case $a = 1$ and write $g_k(1,x) =: g_k(x)$. Since for $a = 1$ from (1) the functional equation $g_k(x) \circ g_t(x) = g_{kt}(x)$ follows, the Dickson-polynomials $g_k(x)$ are closed under composition.

In order to use Dickson-polynomials in public-key cryptography, we put $R = Z/(n)$. The plaintext messages $m \in Z/(n)$ are encrypted by $m \to g_k(m) \bmod n$.
If the factorization of n is given by $n = \prod_{i=1}^{r} p_i^{e_i}$, then in the Dickson-scheme the number [1]

$$v(n) = [p_1^{e_1-1}(p_1^2-1),\ p_2^{e_2-1}(p_2^2-1), \ldots,\ p_r^{e_r-1}(p_r^2-1)]$$

plays the same role as the number $w(n) = [p_1-1, p_2-1, \ldots, p_r-1]$ for a squarefree n in the RSA-scheme. For example, whereas the power polynomial $x^k$ induces a permutation of Z/(n) for a squarefree n, iff[2] $(k,w(n)) = 1$, the Dickson-polynomial $g_k(x)$ induces a permutation of Z/(n), n arbitrary, iff $(k,v(n)) = 1$ (cf. W. Nöbauer (1965)). Another obvious analogy to the RSA-scheme is given by the following fact:
If the permutation $\pi$ of Z/(n) is induced by a Dickson-polynomial $g_k(x)$, then $\pi^{-1}$ is also induced by a Dickson-polynomial, namely by $g_t(x)$, where $kt \equiv 1 \bmod v(n)$ (cf. Lausch, Müller and W. Nöbauer (1973)).

---

1) By $[a_1,\ldots,a_r]$ we denote the least common multiple of the integers $a_1,\ldots,a_r$.
2) By $(a_1,\ldots,a_r)$ we denote the greatest common divisor of the integers $a_1,\ldots,a_r$.

Thus, exactly like in the RSA-scheme, the trapdoor information of the Dickson-scheme consists in the factorization of n: All known methods for computing the inverse of an encryption function $x \to g_k(x) \bmod n$ need the prime factor decomposition of n.

## 3. A fast evaluation algorithm for Dickson-polynomials

We now give an evaluation algorithm of complexity O(ld(k)), which permits to calculate function values of $g_k(x)$ (cf. also R. Nöbauer (1985/86)). Given $b \in Z/(n)$, we want to compute $g_k(b) \bmod n$. For doing this, we have to solve

$$u + \frac{1}{u} = b, \tag{2}$$

or equivalently

$$u^2 - bu + 1 = 0 \tag{3}$$

in some extension ring of Z/(n).

As can be seen easily, the factor ring $R_b = Z/(n)[u]/(u^2-bu+1)$ is an extension ring of Z/(n), and every element $s \in R_b$ can be represented uniquely in the form

$$s = a_1u + a_0, \quad a_0, a_1 \in Z/(n).$$

Multiplication in $R_b$ can be implemented by using the formula

$$(a_1u+a_0)(b_1u+b_0) = (a_1b_0+a_0b_1+a_1b_1b)u + a_0b_0 - a_1b_1. \tag{4}$$

Obviously, the element $u \in R_b$ is a solution of (3). Since $u(b-u) = 1$, u is always invertible.

Now, for the evaluation of $g_k(b)$ just calculate the power $u^k$ in the ring $R_b$ by using the "square- and multiply-technique": That is, first compute

$$u,\ u^2,\ (u^2)^2,\ \ldots$$

and then multiply together the appropriate factors, thus finding elements $a_0, a_1 \in Z/(n)$ with

$$u^k = a_1u + a_0.$$

Since $u^{-1}$ also satisfies (3), the equation

$$\frac{1}{u^k} = a_1\frac{1}{u} + a_0$$

holds, and therefore

$$g_k(b) = g_k(u + \frac{1}{u}) = u^k + \frac{1}{u^k} = a_1(u + \frac{1}{u}) + 2a_0 = a_1b + 2a_0.$$

The number of required steps is O(ld(k)).

We summarize our procedure in the following

Algorithm 1:

  Input  $n,k,b$

  Compute $a_0, a_1 \in Z/(n)$ with $u^k \equiv a_1 u + a_0 \bmod u^2 - bu + 1$.

  Comment [use the square-and multiply-technique].

  Compute $g_k(b) \equiv a_1 b + 2a_0 \bmod n$.

  End.

## 4. The Dickson-scheme

Every participant C of the communication network chooses a positive integer $r_C := r$, $r$ odd prime powers $p_i^{e_i}$ (if also a power $2^e$ is chosen, the following formulas have to be modified slightly), and an encryption key $k_C := k$ with $(k, p_i^{e_i - 1}(p_i^2 - 1)) = 1$ for $i = 1,2,\ldots,r$.

Then C calculates the numbers

$n_C := n = \prod_{i=1}^{r} p_i^{e_i}$, $v(n) = [p_1^{e_1-1}(p_1^2-1),\ldots, p_r^{e_r-1}(p_1^2-1)]$, and computes

a decryption key $t_C := t$, that is a natural number satisfying the linear congruence

$$kt \equiv 1 \bmod v(n). \tag{5}$$

The public key of C consists in the parameters $n$ and $k$, and the secret key is given by the prime factorization of $n$ and by $t$.

If A intends to send the secret message $m \in Z/(n_B)$ to B, he has to encrypt $m$ by calculating $c \equiv g_{k_B}(m) \bmod n_B$ and then he sends $c$ to B. The receiver B decrypts $c$ by calculating $g_{t_B}(c) \equiv g_{t_B}(g_{k_B}(m)) \equiv m \bmod n_B$.

## 5. Cryptanalysis

Since unlike to B a spy does not know the factorization of $n_B$, he cannot compute a decryption key $t_B$ in the same way as B does. However, he might try to use other methods of decryption, especially to do partial decryption, that is to decrypt certain ciphertexts without knowing a decryption key $t_B$.

In the following we discuss several procedures of partial decryption. We show, that in some cases these attacks can be used also for factoring n. All discussed attacks are analogues to well-known attacks

on the RSA-scheme (cf. Schnorr (1981), Simmons and Norris (1977), Berkowitz (1982), Herlestam (1978), Rivest (1978)). For a more algebraic discussion of superenciphering attacks on variants of the RSA-scheme see also W. Nöbauer (1985).
In the following we restrict ourselves to the cryptographically most important case where n is the product of two distinct odd prime numbers, that is $n = p_1 p_2$. We show that the Dickson-scheme is secure from the described attacks, if $p_i - 1$ $(i = 1,2)$ contains a large prime factor $p_i'$, if $p_i + 1$ $(i = 1,2)$ contains a large prime factor $p_i^*$, and if as well the order of $k \bmod p_i'$ as the order of $k \bmod p_i^*$ $(i = 1,2)$ is large. These requirements are fulfilled, if e.g. for $i = 1,2$

$$(6) \qquad \begin{cases} p_i - 1 = a_i p_i', \ a_i < 10^5, \ p_i' > 10^{80} \\ p_i + 1 = b_i p_i^*, \ b_i < 10^5, \ p_i^* > 10^{80}, \end{cases}$$

$$(7) \qquad \begin{cases} \operatorname{ord} p_i' \ (k) > 10^{11} \\ \operatorname{ord} p_i^* \ (k) > 10^{11}. \end{cases}$$

## 5.1. Attacks by finding an s with $g_s(c) \equiv 2 \bmod n$

### 5.1.1. Partial decryption

Let $c \in Z/(n)$ be a given ciphertext. Suppose, the cryptanalyst succeeds in finding a natural number s with $g_s(c) \equiv 2 \bmod n$. Let $s = s_1 s_2$, where $s_1$ contains all those prime factors of s which divide k, and $s_2$ contains the remaining prime factors. The numbers $s_1$ and $s_2$ can be computed without the knowledge of the prime factorization of s, by using the following

Algorithm 2:

- Input $k, s$.
- Initialize $s_1 = 1$; $s_2 = s$.
- While $(s_2, k) > 1$ do $s_1 = s_1 (s_2, k)$; $s_2 = \frac{s_2}{(s_2, k)}$.
- End.

Let $u_i \in GF(p_i^2)$, $i = 1,2$, be solutions of $u + \frac{1}{u} = c$. (Such solutions always exist.) From $g_s(c) \equiv 2 \bmod n$ we obtain $g_s(c) \equiv 2 \bmod p_i$ for $i = 1,2$, and using (1) it follows, that in $GF(p_i^2)$ the equation $g_s(c) = g_s(u_i + \frac{1}{u_i}) = u_i^s + \frac{1}{u_i^s} = 2$ holds. This is equivalent with $u_i^s = 1$, hence with $u_i^{s_1 s_2} = 1$. Since $(k, p_i^2 - 1) = 1$, we have also $(s_1, p_i^2 - 1) = 1$.

Let $o_i$ be the order of $u_i$ in $GF(p_i^2)^*$, the multiplicative group of

$GF(p_i^2)$. As $o_i | p_i^2-1$, there holds

(8) $$(s_1, o_i) = 1.$$

From $u_i^{s_1 s_2} = 1$ we get $o_i | s_1 s_2$, hence $o_i | s_2$ by (8), that is $u_i^{s_2} = 1$.
By definition of $s_2$ we have $(k, s_2) = 1$. Thus there exists a natural number $\bar{k}$ such that $k\bar{k} \equiv 1 \bmod s_2$. Suppose that $k\bar{k} = s_2 r + 1$.
If $m \equiv g_k^{-1}(c) \equiv g_t(c) \bmod n$ is the plaintext corresponding to c, then the equation $m = g_t(c) = g_t(u_i + \frac{1}{u_i}) = u_i^t + \frac{1}{u_i^t}$ holds in $GF(p_i^2)$ for $i = 1,2$.
Therefore we have

$$g_{\bar{k}}(c) = g_{\bar{k}}(g_k(m)) = g_{\bar{k}k}(m) = g_{\bar{k}k}(u_i^t + \frac{1}{u_i^t}) = u_i^{t\bar{k}k} + \frac{1}{u_i^{t\bar{k}k}} =$$

$$= u_i^{ts_2 r+t} + \frac{1}{u_i^{ts_2 r+t}} = u_i^t + \frac{1}{u_i^t} = m$$

in $GF(p_i^2)$. By the Chinese remainder theorem we obtain $g_{\bar{k}}(c) = m \bmod n$.

If we assume that the search for an s such that $g_s(c) \equiv 2 \bmod n$ is done by trial and error, and more concretely by testing all s between 1 and $10^5$, we can summarize our attack in the following

<u>Algorithm 3</u> (Deciphering the cryptogram $c \in Z/(n)$):

<u>Input</u> n,k,c.
<u>Initialize</u> s = 1.
<u>While</u> $s < 10^5$ <u>and</u> $g_s(c) \not\equiv 2 \bmod n$ <u>do</u> s = s+1.
<u>If</u> $g_s(c) \not\equiv 2 \bmod n$ <u>then</u> stop; <u>comment</u> [algorithm unsuccessful].
<u>Else</u>
<u>Compute</u> $s = s_1 s_2$, where $s_1$ contains all those prime factors of s which divide k, and $s_2$ consists of the remaining prime factors of s; <u>comment</u> [use algorithm 2].
<u>Compute</u> a natural number $\bar{k}$ such that $k\bar{k} \equiv 1 \bmod s_2$.
<u>Decipher</u> c by calculating $g_{\bar{k}}(c) \equiv m \bmod n$.
<u>End.</u>

Now we will show that the Dickson-scheme is secure from attack 5.1.1., if the key parameters satisfy (6). For $i = 1,2$, we consider the $p_i$ equations

(9) $$z + \frac{1}{z} = q, \quad q \in GF(p_i),$$

or equivalently, the $p_i$ quadratic equations $z^2-qz+1 = 0$. Let $M_i$ be the set of elements of $GF(p_i^2)$, which are solutions of anyone of the equations (9). In W. Nöbauer (1968) it is shown that $M_i = K_i \cup L_i$, where $K_i = \{u \in GF(p_i^2) : u^{p_i-1} = 1\}$ and $L_i = \{u \in GF(p_i^2) : u^{p_i+1} = 1\}$. Obviously, $K_i$ and $L_i$ are subgroups of $GF(p_i^2)^*$. If $w$ is a generator of $GF(p_i^2)^*$, then $K_i = \{w^{(p_i+1)r_1} : r_1 = 0,1,\dots,p_i-2\}$ and $L_i = \{w^{(p_i-1)r_2} : r_2 = 0,1,\dots,p_i\}$.

For $q \neq \pm 2$, the equations (9) have exactly two solutions $u,v \in GF(p_i^2)$, which are either both elements of $K_i$ or of $L_i$ (cf. W. Nöbauer (1968)). For $q = \pm 2$, these equations have exactly one solution $u \in GF(p_i^2)$, namely $u = 1$ or $u = -1$ respectively.

The groups $K_i$ and $L_i$ are cyclic, and by (6) the orders of $K_i$ and $L_i$ are given by $|K_i| = p_i-1 = a_i p_i'$ and by $|L_i| = p_i+1 = b_i p_i^*$. If $u \in K_i$, then $\mathrm{ord}(u) \leq 10^5$ holds if and only if $\mathrm{ord}(u) | a_i$. If $d | a_i$, then the number of elements $u \in K_i$ with $\mathrm{ord}_{K_i}(u) = d$ is given by $\varphi(d)$, and therefore the number of elements $u \in K_i$ with $\mathrm{ord}_{K_i}(u) \leq 10^5$ is given by $\sum_{d|a_i} \varphi(d) = a_i$. Thus we have proved

$$(10) \qquad |\{u \in K_i : \mathrm{ord}_{K_i}(u) \leq 10^5\}| = a_i,$$

and similarly, we obtain

$$(11) \qquad |\{u \in L_i : \mathrm{ord}_{L_i}(u) \leq 10^5\}| = b_i.$$

For a given ciphertext $c \in Z/(n)$, algorithm 3 is successful, if and only if there exists an $s$ with $1 \leq s \leq 10^5$, such that $g_s(c) \equiv 2 \bmod n$, or equivalently, such that $g_s(c) \equiv 2 \bmod p_i$, $i = 1,2$. If $u \in K_i \cup L_i$ is a solution of $u + \frac{1}{u} = c$, then $g_s(c) \equiv 2 \bmod p_i$ holds if and only if $u^s + \frac{1}{u^s} = 2$, that is, if and only if $u^s = 1$. Using the Chinese remainder theorem and the equations (10) and (11), we obtain

$$\begin{aligned}
&|\{c \in Z/(n) : \exists\ s \text{ with } 1 \leq s \leq 10^5 \text{ such that } g_s(c) \equiv 2 \bmod n\}| \leq \\
&\leq \prod_{i=1}^{2} |\{c \in Z/(p_i) : \exists\, s \text{ with } 1 \leq s \leq 10^5 \text{ such that } g_s(c) \equiv 2 \bmod p_i\}| = \\
&= \prod_{i=1}^{2} [\tfrac{1}{2}|\{u \in K_i \backslash \{\pm 1\} : \mathrm{ord}_{K_i}(u) \leq 10^5\}| + \tfrac{1}{2}|\{u \in L_i \backslash \{\pm 1\} : \mathrm{ord}_{L_i}(u) \leq 10^5\}| + 2] = \\
&= \prod_{i=1}^{2} [\tfrac{1}{2}(a_i-2) + \tfrac{1}{2}(b_i-2) + 2] = \tfrac{1}{4} \prod_{i=1}^{2} (a_i+b_i) < 10^{10}.
\end{aligned}$$

Therefore, if (6) holds and if $c$ is uniformly distributed on $Z/(n)$, then the probability that $c$ can be decrypted by algorithm 3 is bounded by $10^{10}/10^{160} = 10^{-150}$.

## 5.1.2. Factoring of n

In certain cases, knowing an s such that $g_s(c) \equiv 2 \bmod n$ not only allows to decipher c, but also to factorize n.
For the following considerations we put $v_2(s) := \max\{e \in \mathbb{N} : 2^e | s\}$.
Suppose that a cryptanalyst succeeds in finding an even s such that $g_s(c) \equiv 2 \bmod n$. Let $u_i \in GF(p_i^2)$, $i = 1,2$, be a solution of $u_i + \frac{1}{u_i} = c$.

Then we have $u_i^s = 1$ for $i = 1,2$.
Let $j := \max \{r \in \{0,1,\dots,v_2(s)\} : u_i^{s/2^r} = 1,\ i = 1,2\} =$

$= \max \{r \in \{0,1,\dots,v_2(s)\} : g_{s/2^r}(c) \equiv 2 \bmod n\}$.

Since the equation $x^2 = 1$ has just the two solutions 1 and -1 in the cyclic group $GF(p_i^2)^*$, $i = 1,2$, one of the following four cases holds:

(i) $j = v_2(s)$

(ii) $j < v_2(s)$, $u_1^{s/2^{j+1}} = 1$, $u_2^{s/2^{j+1}} = -1$

(iii) $j < v_2(s)$, $u_1^{s/2^{j+1}} = -1$, $u_2^{s/2^{j+1}} = 1$

(iv) $j < v_2(s)$, $u_1^{s/2^{j+1}} = -1$, $u_2^{s/2^{j+1}} = -1$.

Case (i) is equivalent to $g_{s/2^{v_2(s)}}(c) \equiv 2 \bmod n$, case (iv) is equivalent to $g_{s/2^{j+1}}(c) \equiv -2 \bmod n$, and in these cases our procedure does not provide the factorization of n.
If case (ii) holds, then $g_{s/2^{j+1}}(c) \equiv 2 \bmod p_1$ and $g_{s/2^{j+1}}(c) \not\equiv 2 \bmod p_2$, and therefore $(g_{s/2^{j+1}}(c)-2,n) = p_1$. Similarly, in case (iii) there holds $(g_{s/2^{j+1}}(c)-2,n) = p_2$.
If we assume that searching for an s such that $g_s(c) \equiv 2 \bmod n$ is done by testing all even s between 1 and $10^5$, we can summarize the attack in the following

Algorithm 4:

Input n,c.
Initialize $s = 2$.
While $s < 10^5$ and $g_s(c) \not\equiv 2 \bmod n$ do $s = s+2$.
If $g_s(c) \not\equiv 2 \bmod n$ then goto 10.
Compute $v_2(s)$.
Compute $j = \max \{r \in \{0,1,\dots,v_2(s)\} : g_{s/2^r}(c) \equiv 2 \bmod n\}$.

<u>If</u> $j = v_2(s)$ <u>goto</u> 10; <u>comment</u> [case (i)].

<u>Else if</u> $g_{s/2^{j+1}}(c) \equiv -2 \bmod n$ <u>goto</u> 10; <u>comment</u> [case (iv)].

<u>Else compute</u> $d = (g_{s/2^{j+1}}(c) - 2, n)$; <u>comment</u> [d is a non-trivial factor of n].

10 <u>Comment</u> [algorithm unsuccessful].

Since algorithm 4 is successful only with ciphertexts c which can be decrypted by algorithm 3, this algorithm does not represent a real threat to the Dickson-scheme: If condition (6) holds and if c is uniformly distributed on $Z/(n)$, then the probability that algorithm 4 provides a nontrivial factor of n is bounded by $10^{-150}$.

## 5.2 Factoring by means of fixed points

Let s be an odd natural number, and let $c \not\equiv \pm 2 \bmod n$ be a fixed point of $g_s(x) \bmod n$. Clearly c is also a fixed point of $g_s(x) \bmod p_i$ for $i = 1,2$. Let $u_i \in GF(p_i^2)$ be a solution of $u_i + \frac{1}{u_i} = c$, $i = 1,2$. Then we have

$g_s(u_i + \frac{1}{u_i}) = u_i^s + \frac{1}{u_i^s} = u_i + \frac{1}{u_i}$, hence $(u_i^{s+1}-1)(u_i^{s-1}-1) = 0$, and therefore one of the equations $u_i^{s+1} = 1$ or $u_i^{s-1} = 1$ holds. Clearly, $u_i^{s+1} = 1$ is equivalent to $g_{s+1}(c) \equiv 2 \bmod p_i$, and $u_i^{s-1} = 1$ is equivalent to $g_{s-1}(c) \equiv 2 \bmod p_i$.

If $u_1^{s+1} = 1$ and $u_2^{s-1} = 1$, but not $u_2^{s+1} = 1$,
or $u_1^{s-1} = 1$ and $u_2^{s+1} = 1$, but not $u_2^{s-1} = 1$,
then $(g_{s+1}(c)-2,n) \in \{p_1,p_2\}$, and a factor of n is found. However, if $u_1^{s+1} = 1$ and $u_2^{s+1} = 1$ or $u_1^{s-1} = 1$ and $u_2^{s-1} = 1$, then we have found an even number $\bar{s}$ with $g_{\bar{s}}(c) \equiv 2 \bmod n$, and therefore attack 5.1.2. can be applied.

A special case of this attack is given, when $s = k$. Then c is a fixed point of the enciphering polynomial $g_k(x) \bmod n$.

As there is not known any systematic algorithm for the search for fixed points of $g_s(x) \bmod n$, only trial and error methods can be used. Therefore, the Dickson-scheme is secure from attack 5.2., if the number fix(n,s) of fixed points of $g_s(x) \bmod n$ is small. By the Chinese remainder theorem $\mathrm{fix}(n,s) = \prod_{i=1}^{2} \mathrm{fix}(p_i,s)$, and according to R. Nöbauer (1985) $\mathrm{fix}(p_i,s) = \frac{1}{2}[(s-1,p_i-1) + (s+1,p_i-1) + (s-1,p_i+1) + (s+1,p_i+1)] - 2$.

If the key parameters satisfy (6), then

$$\text{fix}(p_i,s) = \frac{1}{2}\,[(s-1,a_i)(s-1,p_i') + (s+1,a_i)(s+1,p_i') + (s-1,b_i)(s-1,p_i^*) + (s+1,b_i)(s+1,p_i^*)] - 2.$$

If for $i = 1,2$

(12)[1] $\quad p_i' \nmid s-1,\ p_i' \nmid s+1,\ p_i^* \nmid s-1,\ p_i^* \nmid s+1,$

we have $\text{fix}(p_i,s) < 10^6$, and consequently $\text{fix}(n,s) < 10^{12}$. In this case, the probability that a uniformly distributed $c \in Z(n)$ is a fixed point of $g_s(x) \bmod n$ is bounded by $10^{12}/10^{160} = 10^{-148}$, and the task of finding any fixed point is computationally infeasible.

Let us assume that the number s itself is chosen according to a uniform distribution on $M = \{1,2,\ldots,r\}$, where r is a large positive integer, e.g. $r = 10^{100}$. In the following we write $[x]$ for the greatest integer which is less or equal than the real number x. There are exactly $[\frac{r-1}{p_i'}]+1$ numbers $s \in M$ such that $p_i' | s-1$, namely the numbers $1,\ 1+p_i',\ 1+2p_i',\ \ldots,\ 1+[\frac{r-1}{p_i'}]p_i'$. Similarly, there are exactly $[\frac{r-1}{p_i^*}]+1$ numbers $s \in M$ such that $p_i^* | s-1$, there are exactly $[\frac{r+1}{p_i'}]$ numbers $s \in M$ sucht that $p_i' | s+1$, and there are exactly $[\frac{r+1}{p_i^*}]$ numbers $s \in M$ such that $p_i^* | s+1$. Since $p_i' > 10^{80}$, we obtain

$$[\frac{r-1}{p_i'}]+1 \le [\frac{r}{p_i'}]+1 \le [\frac{r}{10^{80}}]+1,$$

$$[\frac{r+1}{p_i'}] \le [\frac{r}{p_i'}]+1 \le [\frac{r}{10^{80}}]+1,$$

and the same inequalities hold also with $p_i^*$ instead of $p_i'$. Therefore, an upper bound for the number of elements $s \in M$ with

$$p_i' | s-1 \quad\text{or}\quad p_i' | s+1 \quad\text{or}\quad p_i^* | s-1 \quad\text{or}\quad p_i^* | s+1$$

is given by $4([\frac{r}{10^{80}}]+1)$. Consequently, a lower bound for the probability that a uniformly distributed $s \in M$ satisfies (12), is given by

$$(r - \frac{4r}{10^{80}} - 4)/r = 1 - \frac{4}{10^{80}} - \frac{4}{r}\ .$$

Therefore, a uniformly distributed $s \in \{1,2,\ldots r\}$ satisfies (12) almost certainly.

---

[1] We write $a \nmid b$ for "a does not divide b".

Altogether we obtain: If the key parameters satisfy (6), then the task of finding an $s \in \mathbb{N}$ and a $c \in Z/(n)$ such that c is a fixed point of $g_s(x) \bmod n$ is computationally infeasible.

## 5.3 Superenciphering

Let $c \in Z/(n)$ be a given ciphertext. We consider $g_k(c), g_k^2(c), g_k^3(c), \ldots,$ where $g_k^r(x)$ denotes the function $g_k(x)$ iterated r times. Since $Z/(n)$ is finite, there are two exponents r and s such that $g_k^r(c) \equiv g_k^s(c) \bmod n$. This implies the existence of a positive integer t such that $g_k^t(c) \equiv c \bmod n$, or equivalently, $g_{k^t}(c) \equiv c \bmod n$. If m denotes the plaintext corresponding to c, it follows from $c \equiv g_k(m) \bmod n$ that $g_k^{t+1}(m) \equiv g_k(m) \bmod n$. Hence $g_k^t(m) \equiv m \bmod n$, and therefore $g_k^{t-1}(c) \equiv m \bmod n$, and the plaintext is obtained.

Sometimes superciphering also yields the factorization of n. Namely, from $g_k^t(c) \equiv c \bmod n$ follows $g_{k^t}(c) \equiv c \bmod n$. That means, c is a fixed point of $g_{k^t}(x) \bmod n$. Since $k^t$ is odd, attack 5.2. can be applied. Superenciphering is only successful if there exists a small t - say $t \leq 10^{10}$ - such that c is a fixed point of $g_{k^t}(x) \bmod n$. Thus the Dickson-scheme is secure from superenciphering, if for all $t \leq 10^{10}$ the mapping $x \to g_{k^t}(x) \bmod n$ has only a small number of fixed points. Let us assume that the conditions (6) and (7) are satisfied. Then all t between 1 and $10^{10}$ fulfil $k^t \not\equiv \pm 1 \bmod p_i'$ and $k^t \not\equiv \pm 1 \bmod p_i^*$. Hence

$$\begin{aligned} \mathrm{fix}(p_i, k^t) &= \tfrac{1}{2}\,[(k^t-1, a_i p_i') + (k^t+1, a_i p_i') + (k^t-1, b_i p_i^*) + \\ &\quad + (k^t+1, b_i p_i^*)] - 2 \leq \\ &\leq a_i + b_i - 2 < 10^6, \end{aligned}$$

and therefore $\mathrm{fix}(n, k^t) < 10^{12}$.

This yields

$$|\{c \in Z/(n) : \exists\, t \quad \text{with} \quad 1 \leq t \leq 10^{10} \quad \text{and}$$

$$g_{k^t}(c) \equiv c \bmod n\}| < \sum_{t=1}^{10^{10}} \mathrm{fix}(n, k^t) < 10^{10} \cdot 10^{12} = 10^{22}.$$

Therefore, if the conditions (6) and (7) hold, then the fraction of ciphertexts $c \in Z/(n)$ which can be decrypted by superenciphering is bounded by $10^{22}/10^{160} = 10^{-138}$.

References

Berkowitz, S. (1982): Factoring via superencryption. Cryptologia 6, 229-237.

Herlestam, T. (1978): Critical remarks on some public-key cryptosystems. BIT 18, 493-496.

Lausch, H., Müller, W.B. and Nöbauer, W. (1973): Über die Struktur einer durch Dicksonpolynome dargestellten Permutationsgruppe des Restklassenringes modulo n. J. reine angew. Math. 261, 88-99.

Lidl, R. and Niederreiter, H. (1983): Finite Fields. Vol. 20 of the Encyclopedia of Mathematics and Its Applications. Addison-Wesley, Reading, Massachusetts.

Müller, W.B. and Nöbauer, W. (1981): Some remarks on public-key cryptosystems. Studia Sci. Math. Hungar. 16, 71-76.

Nöbauer, R. (1985): Über die Fixpunkte von durch Dicksonpolynome dargestellten Permutationen. Acta Arithmetica 45, 91-99.

Nöbauer, R. (1985/86): Key distribution systems based on polynomial functions and on Rédei-functions. To appear in Problems of Control and Information Theory.

Nöbauer, W. (1965): Über Permutationspolynome und Permutationsfunktionen für Primzahlpotenzen. Monatsh. Math. 69, 230-238.

Nöbauer, W. (1968): Über eine Klasse von Permutationspolynomen und die dadurch dargestellten Gruppen. J. reine angew. Math. 231, 215-219.

Nöbauer, W. (1985): On the length of cycles of polynomial permutations. To appear in Contributions to General Algebra 3, Verlag B.G. Teubner, Stuttgart.

Rivest, R. L. (1978): Remarks on a proposed cryptanalytic attack on the M.I.T. public-key cryptosystem. Cryptologia 2, 62-65.

Schnorr, C.P. (1981): Zur Analyse des RSA-Schemas. Preprint. Fachbereich Mathematik, Universität Frankfurt.

Simmons, G.J. and Norris, N.J. (1977): Preliminary comments on the M.I.T. public-key cryptosystem. Cryptologia 1, 406-414.

# Simultaneous Security of Bits in the Discrete Log.

*René Peralta (*)*

Computer Science Division

University of California

Berkeley, California.

*ABSTRACT*

We show that $c \log\log P$ simultaneously secure bits can be extracted from the discrete log function. These bits satisfy the next-bit unpredictability condition of Blum and Micali. Therefore we can construct a cryptographically secure pseudo random number generator which produces $c \log\log P$ bits per modular exponentiation under the assumption that the discrete log is hard.

## 1. Introduction.

Let $P = 2^S q + 1$ (q odd) be an odd prime and $\alpha$ a generator for the multiplicative group of integers modulo P. The problem of solving $\alpha^X = \beta \ (mod\ P\ )$ for X is called the **discrete log problem.** The fastest known algorithm for solving the discrete log runs in time $e^{\sqrt{\ln P \ln\ln P} + o(1)}$. (Coppersmith, ) However, certain bits of X (for example the least significant bit) can be retrieved in polynomial time in $\log P$ . It is of theoretical and practical interest to identify the hard bits of X, as well as groups of bits which are hard simultaneously.

(*) Research sponsored in part by NSF grant MCS-82-04506

We start by defining the concept of a secure single bit with respect to an underlying function f.

**Definition 1** . A boolean predicate B(X) of X is **hard** with respect to a function f if an oracle which outputs B(X) on input f(X) can be used to invert f in polynomial time.

We now extend this notion to consider the simultaneous security of several bits. Call a boolean predicate trivial if it is identically 0 or identically 1.

**Definition 2** . A k-bit predicate $B_k(X)$ is **hard** with respect to a function f if for every non-trivial boolean predicate B on k bits, an oracle which outputs $B\ (B_k(X))$ on input f(X) can be used to invert f in polynomial time. If $B_k$ is a hard predicate then we say that bits $B_k(X)$ of X are **weak simultaneously secure.**

Blum and Micali (Blum, 1982) showed a hard boolean predicate for the discrete log. Long and Widgerson (Long, 1983) show that $c \log \log P$ high order bits of X are weak simultaneously secure. Long (Long, 1984) shows that $c \log \log P$ low order bits are also weak simultaneously secure.

Weak simultaneous security, however, is not the strongest possible notion of security. In particular, weak simultaneous security of k bits is **not enough** to use all k bits in a cryptographically secure pseudo random number generator.

The notion of next-bit unpredictability came up in the study of pseudo random number generators. Blum and Micali (Blum, 1982) showed the first pseudo random number generator which had this property. Yao (Yao, 1982) later showed that pseudo random number generators with this property pass all polynomial statistical tests for randomness. Below we define this notion outside the context of pseudo random number generators. In section 5 we show that next-bit unpredictability is stronger than weak simultaneous security in the sense that if k bits of X are next-bit unpredictable then they are also weak simultaneously secure.

**Definition 3** . Let f be a function from $Z_N$ to $Z_N$. k bits $x_1, \cdots, x_k$ of X are **next-bit**

**unpredictable** if for every $l$ $(1 \le l < k)$ an oracle which on input $f(X), x_1, \ldots, x_l$ outputs $x_{l+1}$ on $\frac{1}{2} + \epsilon$ fraction of all inputs X, can be used to invert f in probabilistic polynomial time. (Here, $\epsilon > (log\ N)^{-c}$ for some constant c)

The main result in this paper is that if $P = 2^S q + 1$, with q an odd integer, then the $k = c \log\log P$ bits immediately following the s-th. least significant bit of X are next-bit unpredictable in the discrete log. Thus we can extract $c \log\log P$ bits per modular exponentiation in a pseudo random number generator based on the discrete log:

Let $x_0$ be a random number in $Z_P$. Let $\alpha$ be a generator for $Z_P$. Let $x_i = \alpha^{x_{i-1}} (mod\ P)$. Extracting the $c \log\log P$ bits immediately following the s-th. lsb. of $x_L, x_{L-1}, \ldots, x_0$, we obtain the **discrete log pseudo random sequence.**

Vazirani and Vazirani (Vazirani, 1984) have recently shown that $c \log\log P$ secure bits can also be extracted from the $x^2\ mod\ N$ generator of Blum, Blum, and Shub, (Blum, 1982) as well as from other encryption schemes based on factoring.

## 2. The S least significant bits of X are easy

In this section we show that the discrete log problem reduces to the problem of computing $\alpha^{2^{S-1}T} (mod\ P)$ from $\alpha^{2^S T} (mod\ P)$.

Pohlig Hellman (Pohlig, 1978) first gave an algorithm to compute the discrete log in the special case that $P = 2^S + 1$. In fact, their techniques show that the S least significant bits of X can be efficiently computed from $\alpha^X (mod\ P)$ where $P = 2^S q + 1$.

We use a slightly different method, introducing the technique of shifting X to the right by computing the square root of $\alpha^X$. This technique will be used throughout this paper.

Square roots modulo a prime number are computable in probabilistic polynomial time. (Rabin, 1980) A quadratic residue modulo P is of the form $\alpha^{2t} (mod\ P)$. Therefore, if $\alpha^X = \beta (mod\ P)$, the least significant bit of X is 0 if and only if $\beta$ is a quadratic residue. In this case the roots of $\beta$ are $\alpha^{\frac{X}{2}} (mod\ P)$ and $\alpha^{\frac{X}{2} + \frac{P-1}{2}} = \alpha^{\frac{X}{2} + 2^{S-1}q} (mod\ P)$. The first of these is called the **principal square root** of $\beta$ (with respect to the generator $\alpha$).

Blum and Micali (Blum, 1982) have shown that if we could compute the principal square root of $\beta$ then we would be able to solve the discrete log in polynomial time: If $\beta$ is a nonresidue we know that the lsb. of X is 1. We can set this bit to 0 by dividing $\beta$ by $\alpha$. Then we divide X by 2 by computing the principal square root. Thus we have shifted X to the right, moving X's 2nd. lsb. to the lsb. position, where it can be determined by testing quadratic residuosity. We can keep shifting until we obtain all bits of X. Thus we have shown the following:

**(Blum-Micali) the discrete log reduces to**
**the principal square root problem.**

We cannot in general compute the principal square root of X. Notice, however, that if $\beta$ is a quadratic residue, then both roots $\alpha^{\frac{X}{2}}$ and $\alpha^{\frac{X}{2}+2^{S-1}q}$ of $\beta$ have the same quadratic character provided $S > 1$ i.e. the lsb. of the roots are equal. Choose an arbitrary root, set its lsb. to 0, and again compute a root of the result. This time there are four possible results , but provided $S > 2$ they all have the same quadratic character. We can in this manner compute the S least significant bits of X. The computation tree is shown below. Any path down this tree yields the correct bits. If we can compute these bits then we can set them to 0. Thus we have shown the following:

**the discrete log reduces to solving the**
**equation $\alpha^{2^S T} = \beta \,(mod\ P\,)$ for T.**

Combining the two results we have:

**the discrete log reduces to finding the principal**
**square root $\alpha^{2^{S-1}T}$ of $\beta = \alpha^{2^S T}\,(mod\ P\,)$**

Computation tree for $S \geq 4$.

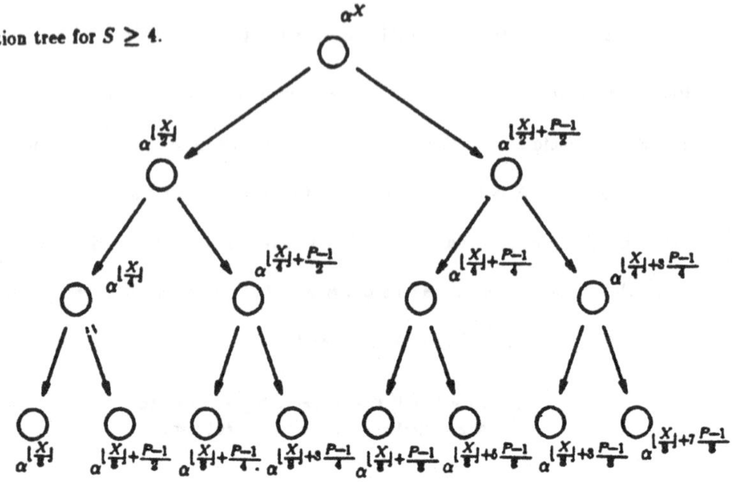


Nodes at the same level have the same quadratic character.

**3. The $s+1$ st. lsb. of X is a hard bit in the discrete log.**

Suppose we have an oracle which on input P,$\alpha$,$\beta$ , outputs the $s+1$ st. lsb. of X. Then we can set this bit to 0 by dividing by $\alpha^{S+1}$ if necessary. Using the results of the previous section (and the oracle), the discrete log problem then reduces to finding the principal square root of $\beta = \alpha^{2^S T} \ (mod\ P)$ where T is even. But this is easy since the principal square root $\gamma = \alpha^{2^{S-1} T} \ (mod\ P)$ of $\beta$ is the unique root which satisfies $\gamma^q = 1 \ (mod\ P)$ . To see this recall that $\alpha^{P-1} = \alpha^{2^S q} = 1 \ (mod\ P)$. Then $\gamma^q = \alpha^{2^S q \frac{T}{2}} = 1 \ (mod\ P)$, whereas $(-\gamma)^q = -1 \ (mod\ P)$ since q is odd.

It will follow from Theorem 1 of the next section that this result holds even in the case where the oracle is correct in $\frac{1}{2} + \epsilon$ fraction of inputs. This result is included in (Long, 1984) along with a proof that almost all bits of X are hard with respect to oracles which are always correct.

## 4. $c \log\log P$ next-bit unpredictable bits

Let $x_i$ be the ith. least significant bit of X.

**Theorem 1**. Let $k = c \log\log P$ for some constant c. Then $x_{s+1}, \cdots, x_{s+k}$ are next-bit unpredictable in the discrete log if we require the oracle to predict correctly on every input.

**Proof:** Suppose there exists $l$, $1 \leq l < k$, and an oracle $O$ which on input $(P, \alpha, \beta, x_{s+1}, \cdots, x_{s+l})$ outputs $x_{s+l+1}$. As before, we may assume $X = 2^s T$. Algorithm I computes X in probabilistic polynomial time. Several operations are performed on the value of X. These can be done in polynomial time even when the value of X is not known but $\alpha^X \pmod{P}$ is. The operations are:

- test whether X equals a particular value.
- assignment (Y := X).
- division by 2 when the $S + 1$ least significant bits of X are known.
- setting a particular bit of X to 0 when the value of the bit is known.

**Algorithm I - Solve $\alpha^X = \alpha^{2^S T} = \beta$ for X.**

```
begin

Y := X ;
for every possible value of x_{s+1} ··· x_{s+l} do
begin
 i := 0;
 repeat until Y = 0 or i > log P

  begin
   i := i + 1;
   obtain bit s+l+1 of Y from the oracle;
   { assume this is also the s+l+i th. bit of X}
   set the s+1 st. bit of Y to 0
   Y := Y/2 { compute the principal square root of α^Y }
  end

 test the value constructed for X in the equation α^X = β (mod P );
 if the equation holds then stop - X has been found
end

end.
```

Consider the iteration of the for-loop in which the correct value of $x_{s+1} \cdots x_{s+l}$ is assumed. Recall that to compute the principal square root of $\alpha^Y$, where $Y = 2^S T$, all we need to know is $y_{s+1}$. This bit is known correctly in the first iteration of the repeat loop. At each iteration of the repeat loop, the $s+1$ st. bit of Y is discarded and the higher order bits are shifted to the right by one position. The oracle allows the algorithm to see the bit which is shifted into th $s+l$ th. position. Thus , at each iteration , the algorithm knows bits $s+1$ through $s+l$ of Y, and in particular bit $s+1$ of Y .$_\nabla$

**Theorem 2** . Let $k = c \log\log P$ for some constant c. Then $x_{s+1}, \cdots, x_{s+k}$ are next-bit unpredictable in the discrete log.

**Proof:** Algorithm-I computes the discrete log using an oracle which is always correct. Now suppose the oracle is correct on $\frac{1}{2} + \epsilon$ fraction of inputs, with $\epsilon = \frac{1}{2^u}$ ( $u = O(\log\log P)$ ). We will construct an oracle which is correct with probability exponentially close to 1 for all $X < \frac{P}{2^{u+1}}$. Note that, in the iteration of the for loop in which the correct value of $x_{s+1} \cdots x_{s+l}$ is assumed, the oracle is queried for monotonically decreasing values of Y. Therefore, for the algorithm to work, we need only **start** with an initial value of X which is less than $\frac{P}{2^{u+1}}$.

Note that Algorithm-I always knows the $s+l$ least significant bits of X. Therefore, if $X < \frac{P}{2^{u+1}}$ then $x_{s+l+1}$ can be determined from the $s+l+1$ st. bit of $X + r$ provided $0 \le r < P\frac{2^{u+1}-1}{2^{u+1}}$ , since then $X + r < P$. This gives us a way of randomizing queries to the oracle. To determine the $s+l+1$ st. bit of X we query the oracle on the $s+l+1$ st. bit of X+ r for random values of r in the specified range. We now show that the probability of obtaining a correct answer on each such random query is $\ge \frac{1}{2} + \frac{3\epsilon}{4}$.

Let $S = \{X + r \;/\; 0 \le r < P\frac{2^{u+1}-1}{2^{u+1}}\}$. Notice $|S| = P\frac{2^{u+1}-1}{2^{u+1}}$, and every element of S is less than P provided $X < \frac{P}{2^{u+1}}$.

Let $\frac{1}{2} + \hat{\epsilon}$ be the fraction of elements in S for which the oracle is correct. Then the total number of correct answers of O is less than or equal to the number of correct answers in S plus the cardinality of the complement of S. Thus

$$P(\frac{1}{2}+\epsilon) \leq (\frac{1}{2}+\hat{\epsilon})|S| + P - |S| \quad ==>$$

$$P(\epsilon - \frac{1}{2}) \leq |S|(\hat{\epsilon} - \frac{1}{2}) \quad ==>$$

$$\hat{\epsilon} \geq \frac{P}{|S|}(\epsilon - \frac{1}{2}) + \frac{1}{2} = \frac{2-2^u}{2^{u+1}-1} + \frac{1}{2} = \frac{3}{2}(\frac{1}{2^{u+1}-1}) \geq \frac{3}{2}(\frac{1}{2^{u+1}}) = \frac{3\epsilon}{4}.$$

Thus the oracle is correct on $\frac{1}{2} + \frac{3\epsilon}{4}$ fraction of all elements in the set S. Therefore, by querying the oracle on a polynomial number (in log P) of points we obtain the $s+l+1$ st. least significant bit of X with negligible probability of error.

A problem remains in that we have assumed that $X < \frac{P}{2^{u+1}}$. This is solved by randomizing X i.e. we try to solve the equation $\alpha^{(X+R) \bmod (P-1)} = \hat{\beta} = \beta\alpha^R \pmod P$ for random values of R ( $0 \leq R < P-1$). With probability $\frac{1}{2^{u+1}}$ , $(X+R) \bmod (P-1) < \frac{P}{2^{u+1}}$. Alternatively, we could simply try all possible values of the $u+1st.$ most significant bits of X, setting these bits to 0 by dividing by the appropiate power of $\alpha$. Thus our algorithm computes X in probabilistic polynomial time .$\nabla$

## 5. Next bit unpredictability implies weak simultaneous security

The next theorem shows that next bit unpredictability is a stronger notion than weak simultaneous security. Although this result is implied by a fundamental theorem of Yao, (Yao, 1982) it is included here because it has a straightforward proof.

**Theorem 3**. Let f be a function from $Z_N$ to $Z_N$. If $k = c \log\log N$ bits are next-bit unpredictable with respect to f then they are also weak simultaneously secure with respect to f.

**Proof:** Suppose bits $(x_1, \cdots, x_k)$ are next-bit unpredictable. Let B be a non-trivial predicate on

$(x_1, \cdots, x_k)$. Let $O$ be an oracle for B given f(X). Let T be the set of values of $(x_1, \cdots, x_k)$ for which $B(x_1, \cdots, x_k) = 1$. Since B is non trivial , there exists a prefix $\vec{u} = u_1 \cdots u_l$ (possibly the empty string $\lambda$) for which the number of elements in T with prefix $\vec{u}1$ is distinct from the number of elements in T with prefix $\vec{u}0$. Assume, without loss of generality, that T contains more elements with prefix $\vec{u}1$ than with prefix $\vec{u}0$.

Let $\vec{x} = (x_1, \cdots, x_l)$. We make the simplifying assumption that all values of $(x_1, \cdots, x_k)$ are equally probable when X is random. Then, if $\vec{x} = \vec{u}$, the probability that $O$ outputs $x_{l+1}$ on input f(X) is $> \frac{1}{2}$. We construct an oracle $\hat{O}$ for $x_{l+1}$ given ( $f(X), x_1, \cdots, x_l$) as follows:

$\hat{O}$ : *If* $\vec{x} = \vec{u}$ *then output* $O(f(X))$ *else output the flip of a fair coin.*

Now we show $\hat{O}$ is correct on at least $\frac{1}{2} + (log\ N)^{-c}$ fraction of all inputs. Thus, by the next-bit unpredictability assumption we can use $\hat{O}$ ( hence $O$ ) to invert f in polynomial time.

Let $\rho$ be the probability that $\hat{O}$ is correct when X is chosen at random. Then

$$\begin{aligned}\rho &= Prob.(\vec{x} \neq \vec{u})*\frac{1}{2} + Prob.(\vec{x} = \vec{u})*Prob.(\hat{O}(f(X),\vec{x}) = x_{l+1} \mid \vec{x} = \vec{u}) \\ &= (1 - 2^{-l})*\frac{1}{2} + 2^{-l}*Prob.(\hat{O}(f(X),\vec{x}) = x_{l+1} \mid \vec{x} = \vec{u}) \\ &= (1 - 2^{-l})*\frac{1}{2} + 2^{-l}*Prob.(O(f(X)) = x_{l+1} \mid \vec{x} = \vec{u}) \qquad (*)\end{aligned}$$

There are $2^{k-l}$ elements $x_1, \cdots, x_k$ with prefix $\vec{u}$, and we know the fraction of these elements for which O outputs $x_{l+1}$ is $> \frac{1}{2}$. Therefore $Prob.(O(f(X)) = x_{l+1} \mid \vec{x} = \vec{u}) \geq \frac{2^{k-l-1} + 1}{2^{k-l}}$.

Substituting in (*) we get

$$\begin{aligned}\rho &\geq (1 - 2^{-l})*\frac{1}{2} + 2^{-l}*\frac{2^{k-l-1} + 1}{2^{k-l}} \\ &= \frac{1}{2} + \frac{1}{2^k} = \frac{1}{2} + (logN)^{-c}. \nabla\end{aligned}$$

**Acknowledgements:**

Much of the inspiration for this work comes from a wonderful course in cryptography taught by Clauss Schnorr at Berkeley in the Fall of 84.

I also wish to thank Manuel Blum and Umesh Vazirani for their constructive criticism and support.

**References**

Blum,.L. Blum, M. Blum, and M. Shub, "A Simple Secure Pseudo-Random Number Generator," *CRYPTO 82*, 1982.

Blum,.M. Blum and S. Micali, "How to Generate Cryptographically Strong Sequences of Pseudo Random Bits," *23rd. FOCS*, pp. 112-117, 1982.

Coppersmith,.

Coppersmith, "Unpublished Result," *Private Communication through C.P. Schnorr.*

Long,.D. Long and A. Widgerson, "How Discreet is the Discrete Log," *15th. STOC*, 1983.

Long,.D. Long, "The Security of Bits in the Discrete Logarithm," *PhD Dissertation*, Princeton University, January, 1984.

Pohlig,.

S. Pohlig and M. Hellman, "An Improved Algorithm for Computing Logarithms over GF(p) and Its Cryptographic Significance.," *IEEE Transactions on Information Theory*, vol. 1, no. 1, January 1978.

Rabin,.

M. Rabin, "Probabilistic Algorithms in Finite Fields," *Siam J. Comp.* , vol. 9, pp. 273-280, 1980.

Vazirani,.

U. Vazirani and V. Vazirani, "Efficient and Secure Pseudo Random Number Generation," *Proceedings of the 25th. FOCS* , 1984.

Yao,. A. Yao, "Theory and Applications of Trapdoor Functions," *1982 FOCS*, 1982.

# ON PUBLIC-KEY CRYPTOSYSTEMS BUILT USING POLYNOMIAL RINGS

Józef P. Pieprzyk
Institute of Telecommunication
Technical Academy of Bydgoszcz
85-763 Bydgoszcz, Poland

**Abstract**

In the paper, a public-key cryptosystem that is, as a matter of fact, a modification of the Merkle-Hellman system has been described. However, unlike the Merkle-Hellman system, it has been built using a polynomial ring. Finally, its quality has been given.

## 1. Introduction

Although several solutions of public-key cryptosystems (PKC) have already been published, intensive studies are still pursued to gain new cryptosystems which couple advantages of existing ones while some of their drawbacks are removed. In the work, a variation of the public-key cryptosystem based on idempotent elements [5] is presented.

The variation relies on inserting idempotent elements into a polynomial ring. Clearly, operations defined in a polynomial ring over a finite field are more tractable than in an integer ring.

## 2. Description of the PKC

Presented in [5], the cryptosystem like the Merkle-Hellman cryptosystem (MH system) is based on the NP-complete knapsack problem. The best known algorithm [2] for solving the knapsack problem of size n requires $O(2^{\frac{n}{2}})$ time. So, n=100 what was originally suggested by Merkle and Hellman [4] seems to be too small. However for n=200, $2^{100} \approx 10^{30}$ and the algorithm is computationally infeasible.

On the other hand, the design of the PKC with idempotent elements over an integer ring proves to be somewhat burdensome. Difficulties will be removed applying polynomial algebraic structures. Moreover, the quality of the PKC based on a polynomial ring will be given taking into account steps needed to carry out cryptographic processes.

First of all, necessary notations are now introduced. A cryptosystem is known to be described by five components [2]:

$\mathcal{M}$ - a message space,

$\mathcal{C}$ - a ciphertext space,

$\mathcal{K}$ - a key space,

$E_K: \mathcal{M} \rightarrow \mathcal{C}$ - a family of enciphering transformations, where $K \in \mathcal{K}$ ,

$D_K: \mathcal{C} \rightarrow \mathcal{M}$ - a family of deciphering transformations, where $K \in \mathcal{K}$ .

Let us assume that the PKC is used to encipher a message $M=(m_1(x), \ldots, m_n(x))$, where $M \in \mathcal{M}$ and $m_i(x)$ is a binary polynomial for i=1,...,n. Furthermore at the receiver's side, the polynomial ring $R=R[x]/\varphi_1(x)\cdots\varphi_n(x)$ over GF(2) is created, where $\varphi_i(x)$ is irreducible and $\deg \varphi_i(x) = \deg m_i(x)+1$ for i=1,...,n. Also, idempotent polynomials $p_i(x)$ (i=1,..., n) of R are calculated. Therefore

$$\underset{i=1,\ldots,n}{\forall} \quad p_i^2(x) = p_i(x) \pmod{\varphi(x)} \tag{1}$$

whereas $\varphi(x) = \varphi_1(x) \ldots \varphi_n(x)$.

Notice that, for the message $M=(m_1(x),\ldots,m_n(x))$, the polynomial

$$\sum_i p_i(x)\, m_i(x) \tag{2}$$

can be computed. In order to get back $m_j(x)$ from (2), the following congruence is applied:

$$m_j(x) = \sum_i m_i(x)\, p_i(x) \pmod{\varphi_j(x)}\, ; \quad j=1,\ldots,n \, . \tag{3}$$

The public key $K=(k_1(x),\ldots,k_n(x))$ is created as follows:

$$\underset{i=1,\ldots,n}{\forall} \quad k_i(x) = p_i(x)\, a(x) \pmod{\psi(x)} \, , \tag{4}$$

while $\psi(x)$ is randomly selected and it generates a Galois field $GF(2^u)$ $\left(u=\deg \psi(x) = \sum_i \deg \varphi_i(x) + \max_i \deg m_i(x)\right)$, whereas a(x) is an arbitrarily chosen element of $GF(2^u)$.

At the sender's side, for the message $M=(m_1(x),\ldots,m_n(x))$, the ciphertext $C\in\mathcal{C}$ is created according to the equation

$$C = \sum_i m_i(x)\, k_i(x) \tag{5}$$

and it is sent to the receiver. On receipt, the ciphertext is transformed in $GF(2^u)$ so that

$$C' = C\, a^{-1}(x)\ (\mathrm{mod}\ \psi(x)) \ . \tag{6}$$

By (4) and (5), (6) may be converted into the form

$$C' = \sum_i m_i(x)\, p_i(x)\ (\mathrm{mod}\ \psi(x)) \ . \tag{7}$$

Next by applying (3), the message M can be recreated.

Example: Let us consider a cryptosystem defined by the ring $R= R[x]/\varphi_1(x)\,\varphi_2(x)$ over $GF(2)$ where $\varphi_1(x)=x+1$, $\varphi_2(x)=x^3+x+1$ and $\varphi(x)=\varphi_1(x)\,\varphi_2(x)=x^4+x^3+x^2+1$. For the message $M=(m_1(x),m_2(x))$, the following equalities have to be fulfilled:

$\deg m_1(x)=\deg \varphi_1(x)-1 =0,$

$\deg m_2(x)=\deg \varphi_2(x)-1 =2.$

At the receiver's side, idempotent polynomials are also calculated and they are:

$p_1(x)= x^3+x+1$ ,

$p_2(x)= x^3+x$ .

As $\deg \sum_i p_i(x)\, m_i(x)=5$, $\deg \psi(x)=6$. We are now looking for $\psi(x)$. Although it should be chosen randomly, we take into account the cyclotomic polynomial $Q^{(9)}(x)$ and accept $\psi(x)=Q^{(9)}(x)=x^6+x^3+1$ (see [1]). Now, we select the polynomial $a(x)=x^3+1$ and calculate its inverse $a^{-1}(x)=x^3$ in the field $GF(2^6)$. Then, the public key consists of two polynomials, namely:

$k_1(x)= p_1(x)\,a(x)= x^4+x^3+x\ (\mathrm{mod}\ x^6+x^3+1)$ ,

$k_2(x)= p_2(x)\,a(x)= x^4+x+1\ (\mathrm{mod}\ x^6+x^3+1)$ .

At the sender's side, $K=(k_1(x),k_2(x))$ is used to create a ciphertext. For instance, for the message $M=(1,1,0,1)=(1,\ x^2+1)$, the ciphertext takes on the form

$$C = (x^4+x^3+x)+(x^2+1)\,(x^4+x+1)= x^6+x^2+1 \ .$$

At the receiver's side, the ciphertext is transformed and

$$C' = C\,a^{-1}(x)=(x^6+x^2+1)\,x^3 = x^5+x^3+1\ (\mathrm{mod}\ x^6+x^3+1) \ .$$

The message M can be easily recreated as

$m_1(x)= C' \bmod \varphi_1(x) = x^5+x^3+1 = 1\ (\mathrm{mod}\ x+1)$ and

$m_2(x)= C' \bmod \varphi_2(x) = x^5+x^3+1 = x^2+1\ (\mathrm{mod}\ x^3+x+1)$ .

## 3. Determination of the polynomial ring

As is known, the algebraic ring ought to be defined by the polynomial $\varphi(x)$ whose factorization gives n different irreducible polynomials ($n > 200$). In Table 1, numbers of irreducible polynomials over GF(2) for successive degrees are shown. Suppose that a designer of the cryptosystem chooses randomly a hundred irreducible polynomials from among all ones of degree 11 and a hundred irreducible polynomials of degree 12 as well. These polynomials are multiplied to get the polynomial $\varphi(x)$. Obtaining $\varphi(x)$ $\left(\deg \varphi(x) = \sum_{i=1}^{n} d_i\right.$, where $\left.d_i = \deg \varphi_i(x)\right)$ needs $O(dn^2)$ elementary operations while d is the average degree of $\varphi_i(x)$ $(i=1,\ldots,n)$. Clearly, the probability of $\varphi(x)$ disclosure by an enemy observer is less than $2^{-200}$. As the knowledge of all irreducible polynomials of degrees 11 and 12 is needed at the receiver s side, their list has to be given and stored all the time.

Table 1

| polynomial degree | number of irreducible polynomials over GF(2) |
|---|---|
| 1 | 2 |
| 2 | 1 |
| 3 | 2 |
| 4 | 3 |
| 5 | 6 |
| 6 | 9 |
| 7 | 18 |
| 8 | 30 |
| 9 | 56 |
| 10 | 99 |
| 11 | 186 |
| 12 | 335 |
| 13 | 630 |

Knowing $\varphi(x)$, we can determine idempotent polynomials $p_i(x)$, $i=1,\ldots,n$. Any polynomial $p_i(x)$ fulfills the two following congruences:

$$\forall_{i=1,\ldots,n} \quad p_i(x) \equiv 1 \bmod \varphi_i(x) \quad , \tag{8}$$

$$\forall_{i=1,\ldots,n} \quad \forall_{j \neq i} \quad p_i(x) \equiv 0 \bmod \varphi_j(x) \quad . \tag{9}$$

The congruence (9) implies that

$$p_i(x) = \alpha_i(x)\, \varphi_1(x) \ldots \varphi_{i-1}(x)\, \varphi_{i+1}(x) \ldots \varphi_n(x) \quad . \tag{10}$$

Of course, $\alpha_i(x)$ is unknown. Let us denote

$$\beta_i(x) = \varphi_1(x) \dots \varphi_{i-1}(x)\, \varphi_{i+1}(x) \dots \varphi_n(x) \; (\mathrm{mod}\; \varphi_i(x)) \quad . \tag{11}$$

Applying (11) to (8), we get

$$\alpha_i(x)\, \beta_i(x) = 1 \bmod \varphi_i(x) \quad . \tag{12}$$

Otherwise

$$\alpha_i(x) = \beta_i^{-1}(x) \bmod \varphi_i(x) \quad . \tag{13}$$

So, finding $\alpha_i(x)$ relies on the calculation of the inverse element in $GF(2^{d_i})$. As is known [1], reckoning the inverse element requires $O(4d_i)$ units of time. Thus, in order to calculate all elements $\{\alpha_i(x)\,;\, i=1, \dots, n\}$, we need $O(4nd)$ steps. Háving the set $\{\alpha_i(x)\,;\, i=1,\dots,n\}$, we can compute $\{p_i(x)\,;\, i=1,\dots,n\}$ in time $O(n^2)$.

We now assume that $d_i=d$ for $i=1,\dots,n$. Next, we pay our attention to determine an irreducible polynomial that defines $GF(2^{(n+1)d})$. The most obvious solution of the problem would be a random choice of a polynomial of a required degree and verification of its irreducibility. Probability of choosing an irreducible polynomial from among all polynomials of degree $(n+1)d$ is known to be $\frac{1}{(n+1)d}$ [1].

On the other hand, to test if a polynomial is reducible or not, we may adapt Berlekamp s factoring algorithm [1] that requires $O((n+1)^3 d^3)$ units of time. Clearly, it can be considerable simplified for it sometimes ends at the beginning when, for example, a polynomial is not squarefree.

Irreducible polynomials may be pointed out by applying well-known properties of Galois fields. For instance, cyclotomic polynomials may be used as their forms can be easily computed even for high degrees [1]. Now assume that an irreducible polynomial $g(x)$ has been found ($\deg g(x) = (n+1)d$). If w is a root of $g(x)$ $(w \in GF(2^{(n+1)d}))$, any element $v \in GF(2^{(n+1)d})$ may be presented as a polynomial for w of degree at most $(n+1)d$ and, moreover, it is a root of some minimal polynomial whose degree divides $(n+1)d$.

Therefore, we propose to fix the irreducible polynomial $\psi(x)$ by random choice of a binary polynomial $\xi(x)$ which defines the relation between elements w and v in the form

$$v = \xi(W)$$

whereas the irreducible polynomial $g(x)$ assigns $GF(2^{(n+1)d})$ $(w, v \in GF(2^{(n+1)d}))$ and w is a primitive element. Hence, $\psi(x)$ is the minimal polynomial of v. Described in [1], the algorithm gives minimal polynomials in $O(\frac{1}{3}(n+1)^3 d^3)$ steps.

The rest operations needed to get both a public key and a message from a ciphertext requires $O((n+1)d)$ units of time.

## 4. Conclusions

The breaking of the cryptosystem may rely upon either the message disclosure by solving the suitable knapsack problem or determination of the algebraic ring R by searching the public key. Of course, the knapsack problem is NP-complete and, in general, it is shown [2] to be solvable in time $O(2^{n/2})$, where n is the size of the problem.

On the other hand, Brickell [3] has shown in his presentation at this conference that determination of the ring R is possible in polynomial time. It is due to modular multiplications which are used to disguise the shape of idempotent elements.

## 5. Bibiography


[1] Berlekamp E.R., Algebraic Coding Theory, McGraw-Hill Book Company, New York, 1968

[2] Denning D.E., Cryptography and Data Security, Addison-Wesley Publishing Company, Reading, Massachusetts, 1982

[3] Brickell E.F., Attacks on Generalized Knapsack Schemes, EUROCRYPT 85, Linz, Austria, 1985

[4] Merkle R.C., Hellman M.E., Hiding Information and Signatures in Trapdoor Knapsack, IEEE Trans. on Inf. Theory, Vol. IT-24, September 1978, pp.525-530

[5] Pieprzyk J.P., Rutkowski D.A., Design of Public-Key Cryptosystems Using Idempotent Elements, Proc. of EUROCON, Brighton, UK, 26-28 September, 1984, pp.64-8

# SECTION III

# SECRET KEY CRYPTOGRAPHY

# Is the Data Encryption Standard a Group?[1] (Preliminary Abstract)[2]

*Burton S. Kaliski, Jr., Ronald L. Rivest, and Alan T. Sherman*

*MIT Laboratory for Computer Science*
*545 Technology Square*
*Cambridge, MA 02139*

**Abstract**

The Data Encryption Standard (DES) defines an indexed set of permutations acting on the message space $\mathcal{M} = \{0,1\}^{64}$. If this set of permutations were closed under functional composition, then DES would be vulnerable to a known-plaintext attack that runs in $2^{28}$ steps, on the average. It is unknown in the open literature whether or not DES has this weakness.

We describe two statistical tests for determining if an indexed set of permutations acting on a finite message space forms a group under functional composition. The first test is a "meet-in-the-middle" algorithm which uses $O(\sqrt{K})$ time and space, where $K$ is the size of the key space. The second test, a novel cycling algorithm, uses the same amount of time but only a small constant amount of space. Each test yields a known-plaintext attack against any finite, deterministic cryptosystem that generates a small group.

The cycling test takes a pseudo-random walk in the message space until a cycle is detected. For each step of the pseudo-random walk, the previous ciphertext is encrypted under a key chosen by a pseudo-random function of the previous ciphertext. Results of the test are asymmetrical: long cycles are overwhelming evidence that the set of permutations is not a group; short cycles are strong evidence that the set of permutations has a structure different from that expected from a set of randomly chosen permutations.

Using a combination of software and special-purpose hardware, we applied the cycling test to DES. Our experiments show, with a high degree of confidence, that DES is not a group.

**Key Words and Phrases**
Birthday Paradox, closed cipher, cryptanalysis, cycle-detection algorithm, Data Encryption Standard (DES), finite permutation group, idempotent cryptosystem, multiple encryption, pure cipher.

---

[1]This research was supported by NSF grant MCS-8006938 and IBM.

[2]A revised and more detailed version of this paper will be available from the authors sometime in the future. In August 1985, the authors reported results of additional cycling experiments on DES at the Crypto 85 conference at the University of California, Santa Barbara [41].

# 1 Introduction

On November 23, 1976, the United States National Bureau of Standards (NBS) adopted the Data Encryption Standard (DES) as a federal standard for the cryptographic protection of computer data [2] [28].[3] Although a few studies on DES have been openly published [4] [30] [35] [38],[4] to date, numerous fundamental questions about the standard remain unanswered in the open literature. In this paper, we address one such important question: "Is the set of DES transformations closed under functional composition?"

It is important to know whether or not DES is closed since, if DES were closed, it would have the following two weaknesses. First, both sequential multiple encryption and Tuchman's multiple encryption scheme—the two most popular proposals for strengthening DES through using multiple encryption—would be equivalent to single encryption.[5] Even worse, DES would be vulnerable to a known-plaintext attack that runs in $2^{28}$ steps, on the average. Each weakness follows from the fact that the set of cryptographic transformations of any closed cipher forms a group under functional composition. Although most researchers believe DES is not closed, no one has proven this conjecture in the open literature.

In this paper we present two statistical tests for determining if a finite, deterministic cryptosystem is a closed under functional composition. The first test is based on a "meet-in-the-middle" strategy and takes $O(\sqrt{K})$ time and space, where $K$ is the size of the key space. The second test follows a pseudo-random walk in the message space until a cycle is detected, using $O(\sqrt{K})$ time and constant space. Although we focus on DES, the methods presented here are general in nature.

Using a combination of software and special-purpose hardware, we applied the cycling test to DES. Our initial experiments revealed no algebraic weaknesses with DES.

The body of this paper is organized in six sections. Section 2 discusses the contrasting properties of closed and random ciphers. Section 3 presents two statistical closure tests. Section 4 describes how each test can be modified into a known-plaintext attack against closed ciphers. Section 5 lists our initial experimental results and explains how to interpret them. Section 6 poses several open problems, and section 7 summarizes our conclusions. An appendix, which briefly describes our implementation of the cycling test, is also included.

## 1.1 Definitions and Notations

A ***(finite, deterministic) cryptosystem*** is an ordered 4-tuple $(\mathcal{K}, \mathcal{M}, \mathcal{C}, T)$, where $\mathcal{K}, \mathcal{M}$, and $\mathcal{C}$ are finite sets called the ***key space***, ***message space***, and ***ciphertext space***, and $T : \mathcal{K} \times \mathcal{M} \to \mathcal{C}$ is a transformation such that, for each $k \in \mathcal{K}$, the mapping $T_k = T(k, \cdot)$ is invertible. The ***order*** of a cryptosystem is the number of distinct transformations; the ***degree*** of a cryptosystem is the size of the message space. A cryptosystem is ***endomorphic*** iff the message space and ciphertext space are the same set.

Thus, for any cryptosystem $(\mathcal{K}, \mathcal{M}, \mathcal{C}, T)$, each key $k \in \mathcal{K}$ represents a transformation $T_k : \mathcal{M} \to \mathcal{C}$. In an endomorphic cryptosystem, each key represents a permutation on $\mathcal{M}$. A cryptosystem is ***faithful*** iff every key represents a distinct transformation.

We shall use the following notations throughout the paper. For any cryptosystem $\Pi = (\mathcal{K}, \mathcal{M}, \mathcal{C}, T)$, let $\mathcal{T}_\Pi = \bigcup\{T_k : k \in \mathcal{K}\}$ be the set of all encryption transformations, and let $G_\Pi = \langle \mathcal{T}_\Pi \rangle$ be the group generated by $\Pi$. For any transformation $T_k \in \mathcal{T}_\Pi$, let $T_k^{-1}$ denote the inverse of $T_k$. In addition, let $K = |\mathcal{K}|$ be the size of the key space; let $M = |\mathcal{M}|$ be the degree of $\Pi$; and let $m = |\mathcal{T}_\Pi|$ be the order of $\Pi$. Whenever the meaning is clear, we will omit the subscript $\Pi$.

Let $I$ be the identity permutation on $\mathcal{M}$, and let $\mathcal{A}_\mathcal{M}$ and $\mathcal{S}_\mathcal{M}$ be, respectively, the ***alternating group*** and ***symmetric group*** on $\mathcal{M}$ [13]. For any permutations $g, h$ we will denote the composition of $g$ and $h$ by

[3] We expect the reader to be familiar with the fundamentals of cryptology (as presented in [3] or [1], for example), as well as with the basics of DES (as described in [2] or [4], for example).

[4] See bibliography for a list of additional technical works on DES.

[5] To encrypt a message $x$ using *sequential multiple encryption* is to compute $T_i T_j(x)$, where the keys $i$ and $j$ are chosen independently. Similarly, to encrypt a message $x$ under *Tuchman's scheme* is to compute $T_i T_j^{-1} T_k(x)$, where the keys $i, j$, and $k$ are independently chosen [44] [4] [42].

$gh = g \circ h = g[h(\cdot)]$.

An endomorphic cryptosystem is *closed* iff its set of encryption transformations is closed under functional composition.[6] Shannon's notion of a pure cipher generalizes the idea of closure to non-endomorphic cryptosystems [57]. A cryptosystem $\Pi = (\mathcal{K}, \mathcal{M}, \mathcal{C}, \mathcal{T})$ is *pure* iff, for every $T_0 \in \mathcal{T}_\Pi$, the set $T_0^{-1}\mathcal{T}_\Pi$ is closed.[7] Every closed cryptosystem is pure, but not every endomorphic pure cryptosystem is closed (see section 2.2).

To analyze the cycling test, it is useful to introduce the following standard terminology from permutation group theory [13] [15] [16]. For any subgroup $G \subseteq S_\mathcal{M}$, for any $x \in \mathcal{M}$, the *G-orbit of x* is the set $G\text{-orbit}(x) = \{g(x) : g \in G\}$ and the *G-stabilizer of x* is the set $G\text{-stabilizer}(x) = \{g \in G : g(x) = x\}$. If $f$ is any function (not necessarily a permutation) and if $x \in \text{Domain}(f)$, the *f-closure of x* is the set $f\text{-closure}(x) = \{f^i(x) : i \geq 0\}$. For any permutation $g \in S_\mathcal{M}$, we will sometimes write $g$-orbit$(x)$ to denote the $\langle g \rangle$-orbit of $x$. For any subgroup $G \subseteq S_\mathcal{M}$, the *order of G* is the number of elements in $G$; for any $g \in S_\mathcal{M}$, the *order of g* is the order of $\langle g \rangle$.

Whenever $\mathcal{T} \subseteq S_\mathcal{M}$, we say $\mathcal{T}$ *acts transitively on* $\mathcal{M}$ iff, for every pair of messages $x, y \in \mathcal{M}$, there exists some transformation $T_k \in \mathcal{T}$ such that $T_k(x) = y$.

For any any string $s \in \{0,1\}^*$, let $\bar{s}$ denote the bitwise complement of $s$.

The Data Encryption Standard defines a particular endomorphic cryptosystem with $\mathcal{M} = \mathcal{C} = \{0,1\}^{64}$ and $\mathcal{K} = \{0,1\}^{56}$. Because DES has degree $2^{64}$, but order at most $2^{56}$, DES is intransitive. It is unknown if DES is faithful, closed, or pure. It is also unknown whether or not any DES transformation is the identity permutation. See NBS FIPS publication 46 [28] or most any cryptography survey work (*e.g.* [2] or [4]) for a detailed definition of the DES encryption function.

## 1.2 A Priori Beliefs

The question of whether or not DES is closed is a question about the order of the group generated by DES. Grossman and Coppersmith observed that $G_{DES} \subseteq \mathcal{A}_\mathcal{M}$ [48], but no one has disproved the possibility that $G_{DES} = \mathcal{T}_{DES}$.[8]

There are several reasons to suspect DES is not closed. First, Coppersmith and Grossman proved "DES-like" permutations generate the alternating group [48].[9] Second, if even just two permutations are chosen at random from $S_\mathcal{M}$, then there is an overwhelming chance (greater than $1 - e^{-\sqrt{M}}$) that these permutations generate either $\mathcal{A}_\mathcal{M}$ or $S_\mathcal{M}$ [12] [14]. Third, no one has announced finding any three keys $i, j, k \in \mathcal{K}$ such that $T_k = T_i T_j$. Finally, according to a 1977 unclassified summary of a report of the Senate Select Committee on Intelligence, the National Security Agency certified that "the final DES algorithm was, to the best of their knowledge, free of any statistical or mathematical weaknesses" [58].

On the other hand, DES is not a set of randomly chosen permutations, and Coppersmith and Grossman did not prove that DES generates $\mathcal{A}_\mathcal{M}$. Furthermore, DES is known to have the following three regularities [2] [4] [30] [38].

1. *Complementation Property.* For every key $k$ and every message $x$, $T_{\bar{k}}(\bar{x}) = \overline{T_k(x)}$.

2. *Existence of Weak Keys.* There exist at least four distinct keys $k$ such that $T_k^2 = I$.

3. *Existence of Semi-Weak Keys.* There exist at least six distinct pairs of keys $k_1 \neq k_2$ such that $T_{k_2}T_{k_1} = I$.

[6] Note that we are using the term *closed cipher* to refer to what Shannon calls an *idempotent cipher* [57]. Shannon defines a closed cipher to be any cryptosystem with the property that each cryptographic transformation is surjective.

[7] Shannon defines purity in a different but essentially equivalent way. Shannon also requires each transformation of a pure cipher to be equally likely.

[8] To see that $G_{DES} \subseteq \mathcal{A}_\mathcal{M}$, note that each round of DES is an even permutation.

[9] See Goldreich's paper [37] for a minor extension of this result.

The last two properties, however, apparently involve only a small fraction of the total number of DES transformations. While many people may have a strong belief that DES is not closed, there is a need for convincing objective evidence to answer this question.

## 1.3 Previous Cycling Studies on DES

To the best of our knowledge, only three other cycling experiments on DES have been reported in the open literature. These experiments were performed by Gait; Davies and Parkin; and Hellman and Reyneri. Each of these experiments differs from our cycling closure test, and none of these previous experiments answered the question, "Does DES generate a small group?"

The analysis of each of these previous experiments depends heavily on the following two facts [8] [10] ([20], exercise 3.1.12]). Let $x_0 \in \mathcal{M}$ be any message. For a randomly selected *function* $f$ on $\mathcal{M}$, the expected size of $f$-closure($x_0$) is about $\sqrt{M}$. (This follows from the Birthday Paradox.) But for a randomly selected *permutation* $g$ on $\mathcal{M}$, the expected size of $g$-orbit($x_0$) is about $M/2$. (This is true because, for any $1 \leq l \leq M$, the probability that the cycle containing $x_0$ has length exactly $l$ is $1/M$.)

Gait [36] investigated the statistical properties of pseudo-random key streams produced by DES in output-feedback mode [29]. Provided the feedback width is exactly 64 bits, each such key stream describes the orbit of a DES transformation on some initial message. In a series of software experiments, Gait computed the key stream produced by DES in output-feedback mode to at most $10^6 \cong 2^{20}$ places. Gait found no cycles for nonweak keys.[10] Unfortunately, Gait did not state what feedback width he used. Gait also proposed a new power-spectrum test for nonrandomness and applied it to each of the pseudo-sequences he computed from non-weak keys. Gait observed that each of these sequences was considered random by his test.

Provided a feedback width of 64 bits is used, the cycling study considered by Gait can be viewed as a closure test. If DES were closed, then each of the orbits considered by Gait would have at most $K = 2^{56}$ messages (see lemma 2.2). Hence, observing an orbit of length greater than $2^{56}$ would be direct proof that DES is not closed. Although we will not do so in this preliminary abstract, it is also possible to interpret Gait's orbit test as a statistical closure test. Viewed as a statistical closure test, the orbit test can be strengthened by combining the test with tests for other algebraic properties.

Davies and Parkin [31] [32] and Jueneman [40] studied mathematically the cycle structure of the key stream produced in output-feedback mode. Each of these studies concluded that, if DES is used in output-feedback mode with a feedback-width of less than 64 bits, then the resulting key stream will cycle in about $2^{32}$ steps, on the average (the exact expected cycle length depends slightly on the feedback width). If all 64 bits are fed back, then the expected cycle length is about $2^{63}$. The point is that the state transition function in output-feedback mode is a permutation if and only if all 64 bits are fed back. Although Davies and Parkin did not report performing any experiments on the full DES algorithm, Davies and Parkin did run a series of experiments on DES substitutes consisting of random permutations on $\{0,1\}^8$. Their experimental results agreed with their theoretical predictions.

In an attempt to better understand how effectively the Hellman time-space tradeoff [53] could be applied to DES, Hellman and Reyneri [39] examined the cycle structure of mappings induced by DES on the keyspace. Specifically, they considered mappings $F_x : \mathcal{K} \to \mathcal{K}$ defined by $F_x(k) = \rho(T_k(x))$, where $\rho : \mathcal{M} \to \mathcal{K}$ is a projection[11] and $x \in \mathcal{M}$ is some fixed message. Their studies detected no significant statistical irregularities. Whether or not DES is closed, the expected cycle length of the Hellman/Reyneri experiment is about $\sqrt{K} = 2^{28}$.

Each of these previous cycling projects studied the behavior of the powers of some indexed function (*i.e.* $T_k^i(x_0)$ or $F_x^i(k_0)$ for $i = 1, 2, \ldots$) where the index of the function was held fixed throughout the experiment: Gait and Davies and Parkin held the key fixed; Hellman and Reyneri held the message fixed. By contrast, our cycling test computes the sequence $x_i = T_{k_i} T_{k_{i-1}} \cdots T_{k_1}(x_0)$ for $i = 1, 2, \ldots$ where at each

[10] Since $T_k^2 = I$ for any weak key $k$, the key stream produced in output-feedback mode with feedback width 64 bits cycles after 128 bits whenever a weak key is used.

[11] Hellman and Reyneri used the projection that removes each of the 8 parity bits.

step $i$ the key $k_i$ is chosen as a pseudo-random function of the previous ciphertext $x_{i-1}$.

## 2 Closed Ciphers versus Random Ciphers

In this section, we review several important differences between closed cryptosystems and cryptosystems that consist of randomly chosen permutations. These differences will form the basis of the statistical closure tests.[12]

### 2.1 Algebraic Properties of Closed and Random Ciphers

Since every finite cancellation semigroup is a group [15], any endomorphic cryptosystem is closed iff its set of encryption transformations forms a group under functional composition. Thus, closed ciphers have a great deal of algebraic structure. By contrast, one expects a set of randomly chosen permutations to have virtually no algebraic structure, as the following lemmas makes precise.

Properties of cryptosystems can be studied both by examining abstractly the set of encryption transformations and by examining how the transformations act on the message space. Lemma 2.1 captures one important difference between closed and random ciphers by focusing on a property of the set of encryption transformations. This lemma says that if a cryptosystem is closed, then for every transformation $T_k$ there are many pairs $T_i, T_j$ such that $T_k = T_iT_j$; but, if a cryptosystem consists of randomly chosen permutations, then for every transformation $T_k$ it is unlikely to find any pair $T_i, T_j$ such that $T_k = T_iT_j$. This lemma provides the basis of the meet-in-the-middle closure test.

**Lemma 2.1** Let $\Pi = (\mathcal{K}, \mathcal{M}, \mathcal{M}, \mathcal{T})$ be any endomorphic cryptosystem of order $m$, and let $k \in \mathcal{K}$ be any key. If $\Pi$ is closed, then there are exactly $m$ pairs of keys $T_i, T_j \in \mathcal{T}$ such that $T_iT_j = T_k$. If $\mathcal{T}$ is selected at random from $S_{\mathcal{M}}$, then the expected number of pairs of transformations $T_i, T_j \in \mathcal{T}$ such that $T_iT_j = T_k$ is $m^2/M!$.

**Proof.** Part 1: Assume $\Pi$ is closed. For every transformation $T_i \in \mathcal{T}$, there is exactly one transformation $T_j \in \mathcal{T}_\Pi$ such that $T_iT_j = T_k$. Part 2: Assume $\mathcal{T}_\Pi$ is chosen at random. There are $m^2$ pairs $T_i, T_j \in \mathcal{T}_\Pi$ and each pair has a $1/|S_{\mathcal{M}}|$ chance of corresponding to $T_k$. Moreover, these probabilities are independent. ∎

For unfaithful cryptosystems, it is important to distinguish between drawing a transformation from the set of transformations and picking a representation of a transformation from the keyspace. Mathematically, it is usually more convenient to think about selecting a transformation from a set of transformations, but in practice, one must often select a transformation by choosing a key. Let $\mathcal{T}$ be the set of cryptographic transformations in any cryptosystem with keyspace $\mathcal{K}$. If $T_k$ is selected from $\mathcal{T}$ at random, then the probability of picking any particular transformation in $\mathcal{T}$ is exactly $1/m$, where $m = |\mathcal{T}|$. However, if a key $k$ is selected at random from $\mathcal{K}$, then the probability that $k$ represents any particular transformation in $\mathcal{T}$ is between $1/m$ and $1/K$, where $K = |\mathcal{K}|$. If the underlying cryptosystem is unfaithful, then $m < K$.

The next lemma describes the structure imposed on the message space by any closed cipher; specifically, lemma 2.2 says that the orbits of any closed cipher partition the message space into transitive sets. This lemma provides the basis of the cycling closure test. (See section 1.1 for a review of some basic definitions from permutation group theory.)

**Lemma 2.2** Let $\Pi = (\mathcal{K}, \mathcal{M}, \mathcal{M}, \mathcal{T})$ be any endomorphic cryptosystem of order $m$. If $\Pi$ is closed, then, for some $1 \leq r \leq m$, the $\mathcal{T}$-orbits of $\mathcal{M}$ partition $\mathcal{M}$ into $r$ mutually disjoint sets $\mathcal{M} = B_1 \cup \cdots \cup B_r$ such that, for each $1 \leq i \leq r$, the following two statements hold:

1. $\mathcal{T}$ acts transitively on $B_i$.
2. $|B_i|$ divides $m$; in fact, for any $x \in B_i$, $|B_i| = m/|H_x|$, where $H_x$ is the $\mathcal{T}$-stabilizer of $x$.

**Proof.** (Sketch) For each $x \in \mathcal{M}$, consider the left cosets of $H_x$ in $\mathcal{T}$ [15]. ∎

[12] This section draws heavily from basic results in permutation group theory and from Shannon's classic paper [57] [55].

**Corollary 2.3** If DES is closed, then DES partitions its message space into at least $2^8$ mutually disjoint transitive sets, each of size at most $2^{56}$.
**Proof.** DES has degree $2^{64}$, but order at most $2^{56}$. ∎

To implement the cycling test, it is especially convenient that order(DES) < degree(DES). Note, however, that for any cryptosystem one can create a similar situation by considering the action of the set of transformations on the Cartesian product $\mathcal{M}^l$, for a sufficiently large integer $l \geq 1$.

The next lemma calculates the expected number of spurious decipherments of closed and random ciphers; this lemma is useful in the analysis of the tests.

**Lemma 2.4** Let $\Pi = (\mathcal{K}, \mathcal{M}, \mathcal{M}, \mathcal{T})$ be any endomorphic cryptosystem of order $m$, let $p \in \mathcal{M}$ be any message, let $k \in \mathcal{K}$ be any key, and let $c = T_k(p)$. If $\Pi$ is closed, then the number of transformations that map $p$ to $c$ is $m/|B_p| = |H_p|$, where $B_p$ is the $\mathcal{T}$-orbit of $p$, and $H_p$ is the $\mathcal{T}$-stabilizer of $p$. If $\mathcal{T}_\Pi$ is chosen at random, then the expected number of transformations that map $p$ to $c$ is $m/M$.
**Proof.** Part 1: (Sketch) By lemma 2.2 and the fact that, for any $x, y \in B_p$, $|\{T_i \in \mathcal{T}_\Pi : T_i(x) = y\}| = |\{T_i \in \mathcal{T}_\Pi : T_i(p) = c\}|$. Note that $|H_p| = |H_c|$. Part 2: Each transformation in $\mathcal{T}$ other than $T_k$ maps $p$ to $c$ with probability $1/M$. ∎

## 2.2 Closed Ciphers: Two Examples

One interesting example of a closed cipher is a single-key variation of the RSA cryptosystem [56] in which the same modulus is used for every key. Only the encryption exponent varies. In this cryptosystem, the modulus $n$ is chosen to be the product of two large primes $p, q$. The message space is the multiplicative group modulo $n$, and the key space is the set of all integers $1 < e < \phi(n)$ such that $e$ has a multiplicative inverse modulo $\phi(n)$, where $\phi(n) = (p-1)(q-1)$ is the *totient* function. The encryption function is defined by $T_{e,n}(x) = x^e \bmod n$. It is easy to verify that this cryptosystem is closed.

Although this variation of RSA is vulnerable to the known-plaintext attacks described in this paper, these attacks are less efficient at breaking the cryptosystem than are known factoring techniques [23]. We view this example as evidence that, provided the key space is large enough to withstand an $O(\sqrt{K})$ time and space attack, closed ciphers are not necessarily insecure. Of course, the security of this variation of RSA remains to be further evaluated [49].

Simple substitution [50] is also a closed cipher. Note that the restriction of simple substitution where the letter 'A' is always mapped to 'B' is an endomorphic system that is pure but not closed.

# 3 Statistical Closure Tests

In this section we describe two statistical tests for determining if an indexed set of permutations $\mathcal{T}$ generates a small group. Each test tries to distinguish between the two competing hypotheses: "$\mathcal{T}$ is closed" and "$\mathcal{T}$ was selected at random." Both tests are based heavily on the Birthday Paradox.

## 3.1 The Birthday Paradox

The Birthday Paradox [6] involves the question, "If $r$ people are selected at random, what is the chance that no two people will have the same birthday?" If birthdays are independently and uniformly distributed between 1 and $m$, then the answer to this question is about $p_r = 1 - \frac{1}{m}\binom{r}{2}$, since there are $\binom{r}{2}$ pairs of people and each pair has a $1/m$ chance of having the same birthday. This approximate analysis, however, ignores the possibility that more than two people might have the same birthday. The "paradox" is that many students are surprised to learn that the probability $p_r$ is so low: with only $r = \sqrt{m}$ people, the chance is about .5 that at least two people will have the same birthday.

More exactly,

$$p_r = \frac{(m)_r}{m^r} = \frac{m!}{m^r(m-r)!} \tag{1}$$

where $(m)_r = m(m-1)\cdots(m-r+1)$. Using Stirling's formula [6] [24], it can be shown that, for any constant $c > 0$, if $r = c\sqrt{m}$ then for sufficiently large $m$

$$p_r \approx e^{-c^2/2}. \tag{2}$$

Thus, by choosing $r = c\sqrt{m}$ with $c$ sufficiently large, $p_r$ can be made as small as desired.

The meet-in-the-middle test uses a variation of the Birthday Paradox in which two samples $X$ and $Y$, each of size $r$, are drawn at random from a universe of $m$ elements. If $X$ and $Y$ each are drawn without replacement, and if each element is drawn independently with probability $1/m$ then, the chance that $X$ and $Y$ do not intersect is exactly $(m)_{2r}/((m)_r)^2$. If $r = c\sqrt{m}$, then this chance is about $e^{-3c^2}$.

### 3.2 Meet-in-the-Middle Closure Test

The meet-in-the-middle closure test is based on lemma 2.1 and the Birthday Paradox: given any endomorphic cryptosystem $\Pi = (\mathcal{K}, \mathcal{M}, \mathcal{M}, \mathcal{T})$, pick any key $k \in \mathcal{K}$ and search for keys $a, b \in \mathcal{K}$ such that $T_k = T_b T_a$. If $\Pi$ is closed, then such a pair of keys $a, b$ can be efficiently found, on the average. If $\mathcal{T}$ were selected at random, then it is unlikely to find any such pair.

To search for a pair of keys $a, b \in \mathcal{K}$ such that $T_k = T_b T_a$, we use a standard "meet-in-the-middle" attack similar to that described in [42], for example. To wit, choose $2r$ keys $a_1, a_2, \ldots, a_r$ and $b_1, b_2, \ldots, b_r$ at random[13] and look for a pair of keys $a_i, b_j$ for some $1 \le i, j \le r$ such that $T_k = T_{b_j} T_{a_i}$. To find such a match, represent the cryptographic transformations by their images or preimages of some particular message. Specifically, pick any message $p \in \mathcal{M}$, calculate $c = T_k^{-1}(p)$, and compute $x_i = T_{a_i}(p)$ and $y_i = T_{b_i}^{-1}(c)$, for $1 \le i \le r$. Then, look for matches $x_i = y_j$ by sorting the triples $(x_i, a_i, \text{"A"})$ and $(y_j, b_j, \text{"B"})$ for $1 \le i, j \le r$ on their first components. Screen out false matches by testing if $T_k(p_i) = T_{b_j} T_{a_i}(p_i)$, for all $1 \le i \le l$, for a small number of additional messages $p_1, p_2, \ldots, p_l \in \mathcal{M}$. (A false match is a pair of keys $a', b' \in \mathcal{K}$ such that $T_k(p) = T_{b'} T_{a'}(p)$ even though $T_k \neq T_{b'} T_{a'}$.)

If $\Pi$ is closed, this procedure will find a match $T_k = T_b T_a$ with probability $q_r \ge 1 - e^{3r^2/K}$. The situation is a variation of the Birthday Paradox in which we are drawing two samples $X$ and $Y$, each of size $r$, from an urn containing $m$ elements. We are interested in the probability that the samples overlap. If $\Pi$ is faithful, each element is drawn with probability exactly $1/K$; otherwise, each element is drawn with probability at least $1/K$. If $\mathcal{T}$ was chosen at random, then, for any $T_k \in \mathcal{T}$, we would expect $\mathcal{T}$ to contain a pair $T_a, T_b \in \mathcal{T}$ such that $T_k = T_b T_a$ with probability at most $K^2/M! \cong 0$. By choosing $r = c\sqrt{m}$ with $c$ sufficiently large, we can make the probability $q_r \cong 1 - e^{-3c^2}$ of finding a match as large as desired.

The expected number of false matches is very small, as shown by lemma 2.4. If $\Pi$ is closed, then at most $(K-1)/|B_p|$ keys other than $k$ map $p$ to $c$, where $B_p$ is the $\mathcal{T}$-orbit of $p$. Conversely, if $\mathcal{T}$ was chosen at random, then we would expect at most $(m-1)/M \le 2^{-8}$ keys other than $k$ to map $p$ to $c$.

This statistical test requires $O(r)$ steps and $O(r)$ words of memory. The two most time consuming operations are generating and sorting the lists $x_1, x_2, \ldots, x_r$ and $y_1, y_2, \ldots, y_r$. The required number of encryptions is $2r$ plus the number of additional evaluations used to screen out false matches. If sorting is performed in main memory using radix sort, then sorting will take $O(r)$ machine operations; otherwise, $O(r \log r)$ external memory operations would be needed. The main problem with carrying out this test on DES is the high space requirement, but even today using $2^{28}$ words of external tape storage is not totally unreasonable. Most steps of this test can be performed in parallel.

### 3.3 Cycling Closure Test

Given any endomorphic cryptosystem $\Pi = (\mathcal{K}, \mathcal{M}, \mathcal{M}, \mathcal{T})$, the cycling test takes a pseudo-random walk in $G_\Pi$, the group generated by $\Pi$. By the Birthday Paradox, the expected cycle length of such a walk is about $\sqrt{\hat{m}}$, where $\hat{m} = |G_\Pi|$. If $\Pi$ is closed, then $\hat{m} = m$, where $m = order(\Pi)$. But if $\mathcal{T}_\Pi$ is chosen at random, then with extremely high probability $\mathcal{T}_\Pi = \mathcal{A}_\mathcal{M}$ or $\mathcal{T}_\Pi = \mathcal{S}_\mathcal{M}$ and hence $\hat{m} \ge (M!)/2$.

[13] Actually, it suffices to choose $b_i = a_i$, for $1 \le i \le r$.

The walk $\hat{g}_1, \hat{g}_2, \ldots$ in $G_\Pi$ is computed from a pseudo-random sequence of transformations $g_0, g_1, \ldots \in \mathcal{T}_\Pi$ by letting $\hat{g}_0 = I$ and $\hat{g}_i = g_i \hat{g}_{i-1}$, for $i \geq 1$. Each $g_i$ is chosen by selecting a key $k_i$ and letting $g_i = T_{k_i}$.

To implement this cycling test efficiently, represent the walk $\hat{g}_1, \hat{g}_2, \ldots$ in $G_\Pi$ by an induced walk $\hat{x}_1, \hat{x}_2, \ldots$ in $\mathcal{M}^l$, for some $l$. Specifically, select some message sequence $\hat{x}_0 \in \mathcal{M}^l$ at random and represent each $\hat{g}_i$ by its image $\hat{x}_i = \hat{g}_i(\hat{x}_0)$. To prevent the induced walk in $\mathcal{M}^l$ from cycling before the main walk in $G_\Pi$ cycles, the integer $l$ must be chosen sufficiently large. For DES, $l = 1$ suffices, since DES has many more messages than keys.

To enable the cycle length of the walk to be computed efficiently and exactly, take a deterministic pseudo-random walk rather than a truly random walk. In particular, for $i = 1, 2, \ldots$, choose the key $k_i$ as a pseudo-random function of $\hat{x}_{i-1}$. For $i = 1, 2, \ldots$, let $\hat{x}_i = T_{k_i}(\hat{x}_0)$, where $k_i = \rho(\hat{x}_{i-1})$ for some deterministic pseudo-random function $\rho : \mathcal{M}^l \rightarrow \mathcal{K}$. Finally, to detect cycles and to compute the lengths of cycles and their leaders, use the efficient algorithms described by Sedgewick and Szymanski [27] that generalize the well-known "two-finger" algorithm due to Floyd [20].

The validity of the cycling test depends in part on the extent to which the pseudo-random walk behaves like a truly random walk. To increase one's confidence that the pseudo-random function does not interact with the cryptosystem in a way that would invalidate the statistical analysis, we recommend that each trial of the experiment be repeated with several different types of pseudo-random functions.[14] (See section 5.2 and Appendix A for a description of the particular pseudo-random functions used in our experiments.)

In other words, the cycling closure test picks an initial message $x_0$ at random and computes the $\psi_\rho$-closure of $x_0$, where the function $\psi_\rho : \mathcal{M} \rightarrow \mathcal{M}$ is defined by $\psi_\rho(x) = T_{\rho(x)}(x)$ whenever $x \in \mathcal{M}$, and $\rho : \mathcal{M} \rightarrow \mathcal{K}$ is a deterministic pseudo-random function. If $\rho$ is "random," then $\psi_\rho$ acts like a random function on the $\langle \mathcal{T} \rangle$-orbit of $x_0$. The expected length of the $\psi_\rho$-closure computed by the test is about the square root of the length of the $\langle \mathcal{T} \rangle$-orbit of $x_0$. If DES acts like a set of randomly chosen permutations, then we would expect $\langle \mathcal{T} \rangle\text{-orbit}(x_0) = \mathcal{M}$, in which case we would expect $|\psi_\rho\text{-closure}(x_0)| \cong \sqrt{M} = 2^{32}$. However, if DES were closed, then $|\langle \mathcal{T} \rangle\text{-orbit}(x_0)| \leq K$, in which case we would expect $|\psi_\rho\text{-closure}(x_0)| \leq \sqrt{K} = 2^{28}$.

The second test is similar in spirit to Pollard's $\rho$-factoring method [22] [18]. It is also similar to but different from the algorithm discovered by Sattler and Schnorr for determining the order of any element in any finite group that has an efficient multiplication procedure [25]. The cycling test differs from the cycling experiments performed by Gait [36] and Hellman and Reyneri [39], who held either the key or message fixed (see section 1.3).

If $\mathcal{T}_\Pi$ is chosen at random, then the walk in $G_\Pi$ induces a pseudo-random walk in $\mathcal{M}^l$. If $r = cM^{l/2}$ for some constant $c > 0$, then the chance that the induced walk in $\mathcal{M}^l$ cycles within $r$ steps is only about $e^{-c^2/2}$.

For the case that $\Pi$ is closed, it helpful to model the pseudo-random walk $\hat{g}_1, \hat{g}_2, \ldots$ in $G_\Pi$ as a discrete finite Markov Process with a $K \times K$ transition matrix $A$. For each $1 \leq i, j \leq K$, the $(i, j)$th entry $a_{ij}$ of $A$ denotes the probability of selecting $\hat{g}_i$ next, given that $\hat{g}_j$ was the last selected transformation. Each pseudo-random selection depends only on the immediately preceding state. If $\Pi$ is faithful, then each entry of $A$ is exactly $1/K$; otherwise, each entry of $A$ is at least $1/K$. In either case, the probability of a pseudo-random walk not cycling within $r$ steps is at most $(K)_r / K^r$.

The second test computes a statistic $w = \lambda + \mu$, where $\lambda$ and $\mu$ are respectively the leader length and cycle length of a particular pseudo-random walk in $\mathcal{M}^l$, starting at some randomly selected point $\hat{x}_0$. The value of this statistic depends on the size of the $G_\Pi$-orbit of $x_0$. If $\Pi$ is closed, then by lemma 2.2 this orbit contains at most $K$ messages. However, if $\mathcal{T}_\Pi$ is chosen at random, then with very high confidence the $G_\Pi$-orbit of $x_0$ is $\mathcal{M}^l$. Therefore, if $\Pi$ is closed, the expected value of $w$ is at most approximately $\sqrt{K}$; but, if $\mathcal{T}_\Pi$ is chosen at random, then the expected value of $w$ is approximately $M^{l/2}$. For DES with $l = 1$, the expected value of $w$ is about $2^{28}$ if DES is closed and about $2^{32}$ if $\mathcal{T}_{DES}$ is chosen at random.

It is possible for the random walk to cycle prematurely if certain special keys are chosen during the walk. For example, the cycle will close if a pair of semi-weak keys are chosen one after the other, or, if

[14]For example, the pseudo-random function might be table look-up into a table of randomly generated values, modification of table look-up in which each input into the table is first XOR'd with the previous output from the table, or DES under a randomly chosen fixed key.

the identity permutation is selected. Such events would be interesting, but are unlikely to happen. In any case, such events would not contradict any of our analysis, since short cycles are evidence that $\mathcal{T}$ is not a random set of permutations.

This test requires $O(w)$ time and a constant amount of space, where $w$ is the statistic computed by the test. The cycle detection and cycle length computations use a small constant amount of space and require about $w$ encryptions [27].

By picking any $T_0 \in \mathcal{T}$, and by applying the test to $T_0^{-1}\mathcal{T}$, the cycling test can be used to test for purity as well.

# 4 Known-Plaintext Attacks against Closed Ciphers

Each of the closure tests can be used with only slight modifications as a known-plaintext attack against any closed cipher. The input to each attack is a short sequence $(p_1, c_1), (p_2, c_2), \ldots, (p_l, c_l)$ of matched plaintext/ciphertext pairs derived from the same secret key $k$. With high probability each attack finds a representation of $T_k$ as a product of two or more transformations. The cryptanalyst can use this representation of $T_k$ to decrypt additional ciphertexts also encrypted under the same key $k$. This attack does not find $k$.

## 4.1 Meet-in-the-Middle Known-Plaintext Attack

The meet-in-the-middle test first picks any message $p$ and any key $k$ at random and then computes the ciphertext $c = T_k(p)$. Next, the test searches for a pair of keys $a, b$ such that $T_k = T_b T_a$. Alternately, a cryptanalyst could begin with any matched plaintext/ciphertext pair $(p, c)$ that was encrypted using some unknown key $k$, and then search for a representation of the secret transformation $T_k$ as a product $T_b T_a$. This attack requires $O(\sqrt{K})$ time and space on the average.

## 4.2 Cycling Known-Plaintext Attack

The cycling test also yields a known-plaintext attack. Given a matched plaintext/ciphertext pair $(p, c)$ that was encrypted under some secret key $k$, the cryptanalyst computes two pseudo-random walks of the type used in the cycling test, starting from messages $p$ and $c$. The same pseudo-random function is used for each of the walks. If the attacked cryptosystem is closed, then, since $p$ and $c$ lie in the same orbit, with very high probability the two pseudo-random walks will intersect within about $\sqrt{K}$ steps. Since the same deterministic pseudo-random function is used for each of the walks, once the two walks intersect, they will forever follow exactly the same path and will therefore drain into the same cycle. By running the Sedgewick/Szymanski [27] cycle-detection algorithm for each of the pseudo-random walks, and by sharing the same memory for both algorithms, it is easy to find a specific point at which the walks intersect, provided the walks intersect. The two walks can be computed sequentially or simultaneously.

Thus, the cycling test gives a way to generate two sequences of keys $a_1, a_2, \ldots, a_i$ and $b_1, b_2, \ldots, b_j$ such that $g(p) = h(c) = hT_k(p)$, where $g = T_{a_i} T_{a_{i-1}} \cdots T_{a_1}$ and $h = T_{b_j} T_{b_{j-1}} \cdots T_{b_1}$. With high probability, $T_k = h^{-1}g$, which can be statistically verified by applying $h^{-1}g$ to additional matched plaintext/ciphertext pairs. If $T_k \neq h^{-1}g$, then the entire procedure can be repeated on the next plaintext/ciphertext pair.

To decrypt each additional ciphertext $c_0$, the cryptanalyst computes $T_k^{-1}(c_0) = g^{-1}h(c_0)$. To compute $h$ in constant space is easy—simply generate the sequence of keys $b_1, b_2, \ldots, b_j$ by retracing the pseudo-random walk starting from $c$. The difficulty is to compute $g^{-1}$ in a time- and space-efficient manner. The problem is that each pseudo-random walk is a "one-way walk" in the sense that reversing any step of the walk requires inverting the encryption function.

One could save each of the keys $a_1, a_2, \ldots, a_i$, but that would require $O(i)$ space, where $i$ is the length of the walk starting at $p$. If the attacked cryptosystem is closed, then $i$ will be about $\sqrt{K}$, on the average. On the other hand, one could reverse any step of the walk in constant space by retracing the the walk from the beginning, but this procedure would yield an $O(i^2)$ time algorithm for computing $g^{-1}$. Chandra shows that a range of time-space tradeoffs can be used to solve this type of problem. In particular, for any $\epsilon > 0$, it is possible to compute $g^{-1}$ in constant space and time $i^{1+\epsilon}$ [19]. Therefore, if the attacked cryptosystem is closed, then, for any $\epsilon > 0$, the cycling known-plaintext attack can be carried out in constant space and time $O\left(K^{(1+\epsilon)/2}\right)$, on the average.

### 4.3 Application of Attacks to DES

Each of the known-plaintext attacks can be applied to any finite, deterministic cryptosystem by launching the attack against the group generated by the cryptosystem. For this reason, it is very important to know the order of the group generated by DES.

Since DES's relatively small key space of $2^{56}$ keys allows no margin of safety even for 1977 technology [35], these attacks would be a devastating weakness for DES, if DES generated a small group. In particular, if DES were closed, a personal computer equipped with special-purpose hardware could decrypt DES ciphertexts under a known-plaintext attack in less than two hours, on the average (See appendix A).

## 5 Experimental Results

This section explains how to interpret the results of the statistical closure tests and summarizes the initial results we obtained by applying the cycling test to DES.

### 5.1 Interpreting the Experimental Results

Each statistical test gives a method for collecting evidence that can be used to compute a measure of our relative degree of belief in the following two competing hypotheses:

- $H_G$ = "DES is a group."
- $H_R$ = "Each DES transformation was chosen independently with uniform probability from the symmetric group on $\mathcal{M}$."

To compute this measure, we will apply the *theory of the weight of evidence*, as explained by Good [9] [7].

Each test is asymmetrical in the sense that it allows us to compute the conditional probabilities $P(E \mid H_G)$ and $P(E \mid H_R)$, but not $P(E \mid \overline{H_G})$ nor $P(E \mid \overline{H_R})$, where $E$ is experimental evidence and $\overline{H_G}$ and $\overline{H_R}$ are the complements of $H_G$ and $H_R$ respectively. This means that, on the basis of experimental evidence, we would be able to conclude only that DES is *not* closed or that DES has a structure different from that expected from a set of randomly chosen permutations; we would not be able to conclude that DES is closed. In the worst case, DES could be closed, except for some isolated pair of keys $a, b$ such that $T_bT_a$ is not in $\mathcal{T}$, even though there exists some key $k$ and some message $x_0$ such that $T_bT_a(x) = T_k(x)$ for all messages $x \in \mathcal{M}$, $x \neq x_0$.

Initially, each person may have some (subjective) degrees of belief $P(H_G)$ and $P(H_R)$ in hypotheses $H_G$ and $H_R$ respectively. From these initial degrees of belief, each person can compute $O(H_G/H_R) = P(H_G)/P(H_R)$ as his or her initial *odds in favor of $H_G$ over $H_R$*. After seeing any experimental evidence $E$, however, each rational person should update his or her own odds in favor of $H_G$ over $H_R$.

Given any evidence $E$, each believer in the theory of the weight of evidence should update his or her odds in favor of $H_G$ over $H_R$ as follows:

$$O(H_G/H_R \mid E) \longleftarrow \frac{P(E \mid H_G)}{P(E \mid H_R)} O(H_G/H_R). \tag{3}$$

where $O(H_G/H_R \mid E)$ is the *odds in favor of $H_G$ as opposed to $H_R$ given $E$*.

In light of the our experimental evidence, we encourage each reader to update his or her own odds in favor of $H_G$ over $H_R$.

### 5.2 Summary of Experimental Results

On April 4, 1985, we completed the first trial of the cycling test, detecting a cycle of length nearly $2^{33}$. For this test, we chose the pseudo-random function to be the "identity" projection.[15] Starting with the initial message $x_0 = $ 0123 4567 89AB CDEF (in hexadecimal notation), we found a cycle of length exactly $\mu = 7,985,051,916$ with a leader of length $\lambda = 34,293,589$. As one test of the correctness of our computations, we ran a software implementation of the cycling test for 30,000 steps. The software and hardware implementations of the cycling test agreed on all values. As a second test of correctness, we repeated the initial experiment and obtained identical results.

This single experiment gives strong evidence that DES is not closed. Let $E$ denote the evidence from our experiment. Since $\mu + \lambda \approx 2^{33} = 2\sqrt{M} = 32\sqrt{K}$, it follows that $P(E \mid H_G)/P(E \mid H_R) \approx e^{-32^2/2}/e^{-2^2/2} = e^{-510}$. Therefore, each reader should decrease his or her odds in favor of $H_G$ over $H_R$ by a factor of about $e^{-510}$.

During May through August 1985, we performed additional trials of the cycling closure test as well as other cycling experiments on DES. Results of these experiments were described at the Crypto 85 conference [41]. All additional trials of the cycling closure test supported our initial findings.

## 6 Open Problems

Although our experiments give strong statistical evidence that DES is not closed, numerous interesting questions remain unanswered. We begin with several questions about the algebraic structure of DES.

- Does DES generate $\mathcal{A}_\mathcal{M}$? What is the order of the group generated by DES? What is the group generated by DES? For how many keys $i, j, k$ is it true that $T_k = T_i T_j$?
- Is DES faithful? What is the order of DES?
- What subsets of DES transformations generate small groups? (Note that each weak key represents a transformation that generates the cyclic group of order 2.)
- Is DES *homogeneous* in the sense that for every $k \in \mathcal{K}$ it is true that $T_k^{-1} \in \mathcal{T}$? For how many $k \in \mathcal{K}$ is it true that $T_k^{-1} \in \mathcal{T}$?
- Is $I \in \mathcal{T}$?

Knowing whether or not $I \in \mathcal{T}_{DES}$ is interesting—not because this property would necessarily be a weakness in DES—but because this question would answer several other questions about DES. By the complementation property, for any key $k$, $T_k = I$ implies $T_{\bar{k}}$=I. Hence, if $I \in \mathcal{T}_{DES}$, then DES is not faithful. In particular, if DES is closed, then DES is not faithful. Conversely, if $I \notin \mathcal{T}_{DES}$, then DES is not closed.

Each of the known-plaintext attacks finds a representation of the secret transformation $T_k$ as a product of two or more transformations. In practice, it would suffice to find an approximate representation of $T_k$. To this end, we could say that two permutations $T_1, T_2 \in \mathcal{T}$ are *q-approximately equal on* $X \subseteq \mathcal{M}$ iff, for all $x \in X$, $T_1(x)$ and $T_2(x)$ always agree on at least $q$ bits.

- For each $1 \le q \le 64$, for how many keys $i, j, k$ is it true that $T_k$ is *q-approximately equal* to $T_i T_j$ on $\mathcal{M}$ ?
- What other notions of "approximately equal" transformations would be useful in finding approximate representations?

Since the closure tests do not depend on the detailed definition of DES, it is natural to ask:

[15]More specifically, we used the projection that removes each of the eight parity bits.

- What can be proven from the detailed definition of DES about the order of the group generated by DES?
- Are there more powerful statistical closure tests than the two tests presented in this paper that are based on the detailed definition of DES?

Our research also raises questions involving the design of cryptosystems.

- Is it possible to build a secure, practical cryptosystem for which it can be proven that the cryptosystem generates either $\mathcal{A}_{\mathcal{M}}$ or $\mathcal{S}_{\mathcal{M}}$? (See [48] for one suggestion.)
- Is it possible to hide a trapdoor in a cryptosystem by concealing a secret set of generators for a small group? (Note that it does not work simply to have a large subset of the transformations generate a small group, since the enemy could guess a small number of transformations in the subset and apply the cycling closure test to the guessed transformations.)

We presented two known-plaintext attacks against closed ciphers, but other attacks may also exist.

- What attacks are possible against closed ciphers? How can knowledge of the specific group help?

Finally, it would be interesting to apply the closure tests to variations of DES that exaggerate certain types of possible weaknesses in the standard.

- What is the order of "crippled" DES transformations formed by reducing the number of rounds or by replacing one or more of the S-boxes with linear mappings?

## 7 Summary

We have presented two statistical tests for determining whether or not any finite, deterministic cryptosystem generates a small group. Each test yields a known-plaintext attack against closed cryptosystems.

Using a combination of software and special-purpose hardware, we applied the cycling test to DES. Our experiments show, with a high degree of confidence, that DES does not generate a small group. These results should increase our confidence in the security of using DES with multiple encryption. However, since cryptosystems that generate large groups are not necessarily secure, our experiments say only that DES does not fail in one extreme way.

This work leaves open the possibility of proving that DES is not closed directly from the detailed definition of DES.

## 8 Acknowledgments

We would like to thank four people who contributed to this paper. Leon Roisenberg helped out with the design and construction of our special-purpose hardware. John Hinsdale wrote the C software used by our host IBM personal computer to control our special-purpose hardware and to carry out the cycle-detection algorithm. Gary Miller answered several of our questions about permutation group theory, and Oded Goldreich participated in a conversation that led to the meet-in-the-middle closure test. Finally, we would like to thank the Functional Languages and Architectures (FLA) research group of the MIT Laboratory for Computer Science (LCS) for use of their new state-of-the-art hardware laboratory during the construction and testing of our special-purpose hardware.

# A A Fast Implementation of the Cycling Closure Test

To test the DES for closure, we designed and built special-purpose hardware for an IBM PC. Our experiment required special-purpose hardware for two reasons: we needed to compute about $2^{32}$ encryptions[16] and we needed to change the key at each step.[17]

The special-purpose hardware is a custom wire-wrap board for an IBM personal computer,[18] containing a microprogrammed finite-state controller and an AMD AmZ8068 DES chip [52]. Data paths connect the DES chip, a 16-byte ciphertext buffer, a PROM computing the next-key function, and the host computer (see figure 1). The next-key function is computed byte-by-byte. A read-write counter indicates the number of consecutive messages to compute. To increase the board's flexibility, the microprogram is stored in RAM accessible to the host computer. The PROM can be easily replaced to implement different next-key functions.

We perform cycle detection in two passes: data acquisition and analysis. During data acquisition, the host computer stores every $2^{20}$th message on a floppy disk. During analysis, these messages are loaded into main memory, and up to $2^{20}$ consecutive messages are computed and compared to those already present. In effect, we perform the Sedgewick-Szymanski [26] algorithm with a fixed estimate of the cycle length. We use an open-addressing, double-hashing scheme for stores and lookups [21]. We wrote all data acquisition and analysis routines in C.

Including all overhead for computing and loading a new key for each encryption, our board performs about 45K encryptions/second, or almost $2^{32}$ per day. This enables us to carry out each trial of the experiment within a few days. Our board also supports all approved modes of operation for DES.

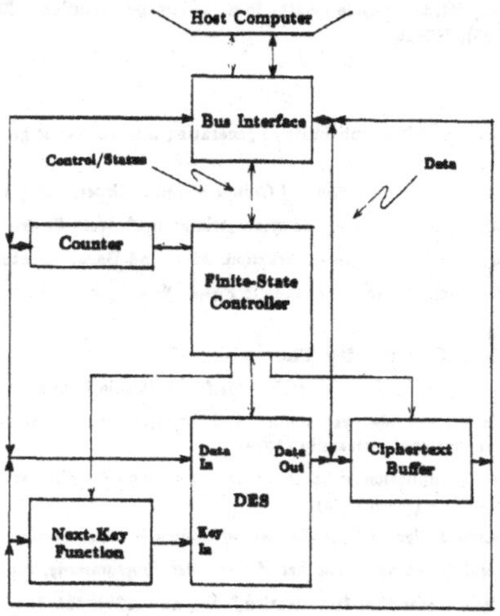


Figure 1: Block diagram of special-purpose hardware

[16] Software implementations of the DES for the IBM PC run at about 200-300 encryptions/second. According to Davio, by using an efficient space-intensive implementation of the DES, it is possible to perform about 2.5K encryptions/second on the VAX 11/780 [33]. Thus, it would take the IBM PC about 10 to 16 days to compute $2^{28}$ DES encryptions; a VAX 11/780 would require about a day and a half. Running the test for $2^{32}$ steps would take at least 16 times longer.

[17] Commercially available DES boards are not suited for our purposes. To compute and load a new key for each encryption would require interaction by the host computer, introducing tremendous overhead.

[18] We chose to use an IBM PC because an IBM PC was available to us, and because it is easy to attach special-purpose hardware to an IBM PC [54].

# References


[] **Survey Works on Cryptology**

[1] Beker, Henry; and Fred Piper, *Cipher Systems: The Protection of Communications*, John Wiley (New York, 1982).

[2] Davies, Donald W.; and W. L. Price, *Security for Computer Networks: An Introduction to Data Security in Teleprocessing and Electronic Funds Transfer*, John Wiley (Chichester, England, 1984).

[3] Diffie, Whitfield; and Martin E. Hellman, "Privacy and authentication: An introduction to cryptography," *Proceedings of the IEEE*, **67** (March 1979), 397–427.

[4] Meyer, Carl H.; and Stephen M. Matyas, *Cryptology: A New Dimension in Computer Data Security*, John Wiley (New York, 1982).

See also [50] [55].

**Works on Probability and Statistics**

[5] Bovey, J. D., "An approximate probability distribution for the order of elements of the symmetric group," *Bull. London Math Society*, **12** (1980), 41–46.

[6] Feller, W., *An Introduction to Probability Theory and its Applications*, vol. I, John Wiley (New York, 1971).

[7] Good, Irving John, *The Estimation of Probabilities: An Essay on Modern Bayesian Methods*, MIT Press (1965).

[8] Harris, Bernard, "Probability distributions related to random mappings," *Annals of Math. Statistics*, **31** (1959), 1045–1062.

[9] Osteyee, David Bridston; and Irving John Good, *Information, Weight of Evidence, the Singularity between Probability Measures and Signal Detection*, Springer (Berlin, 1974).

[10] Purdom, Paul W.; and J. H. Williams, "Cycle length in a random function," *Transactions of the American Mathematics Society*, **133** (1968), 547–551.

[11] Shepp, L. A.; and S. P. Lloyd, "Ordered cycle lengths in a random permutation," *Transactions of the American Mathematics Society*, (February 1966), 340–357.

See also [12] [14] [25].

**Works on Algebra**

[12] Bovey, John; and Alan Williamson, "The probability of generating the symmetric group," *Bull. London Math Society*, **10** (1978), 91–96.

[13] Carmichael, Robert D., *Introduction to the Theory of Groups of Finite Order*, Dover (New York, 1956).

[14] Dixon, John D., "The probability of generating the symmetric group," *Math Zentrum*, **110** (1969), 199–205.

[15] Rotman, Joseph J., *The Theory of Groups: An Introduction*, Allyn and Bacon (Boston, 1978).

[16] Wielandt, Helmut, *Finite Permutation Groups*, Academic Press (New York, 1964).

See also [5] [8] [10] [25] [11].

**Works on Algorithms and Complexity Theory**

[17] Allender, Eric; and Maria Klawa, "Improved Lower Bounds for the Cycle Detection Problem," working paper.

[18] Brent, Richard P., "Analysis of some new cycle-finding and factorisation algorithms," technical report, Department of Computer Science, Australian National University (1979).

[19] Chandra, Ashok K., "Efficient compilation of linear recursive programs," technical report no. ŞTAN-CS-72-282, Computer Science Dept., Stanford Univ (April 1972).

[20] Knuth, Donald E., *Seminumerical Algorithms* in *The Art of Computer Programming*, vol. 2, Addison-Wesley (1969).

[21] Knuth, Donald E., *Sorting and Searching* in *The Art of Computer Programming*, vol. 3, Addison-Wesley (1973).

[22] Pollard, J. M., "A Monte Carlo method for factorization," *Bit*, **15** (1975), 331–334.

[23] Pomerance, Carl, "Analysis and comparison of some integer factoring algorithms," technical report, Math Dept., Univ. of Georgia.

[24] Purdom, Paul W. Jr.; and Cynthia A. Brown, *The Analysis of Algorithms*, Holt, Rinehart, and Winston (New York, 1985).

[25] Sattler, J.; and C. P. Schnorr, "Generating random walks in groups," unpublished manuscript (October 1983).

[26] Sedgewick, Robert; and Thomas G. Szymanski, "The complexity of finding periods," *Proceedings of the 11th Annual STOC Conference* (1979), 74–80.

[27] Sedgewick, Robert; Thomas G. Szymanski; and Andrew C. Yao, "The complexity of finding cycles in periodic functions," *Siam Journal on Computing*, **11** (1982), 376–390.

### Selected Federal Standards Involving DES

[28] "Data Encryption Standard," National Bureau of Standards, Federal Information Processing Standards Publications No. 46 (January 15, 1977).

[29] "DES modes of operations," Federal Information Standards Publication No. 81 (December 1980).

### Selected Technical Works on DES

[30] Davies, Donald W., "Some regular properties of the DES," in [46], 89–96.

[31] Davies, Donald W.; and G. I. P. Parkin, "The average size of the key stream in output feedback mode," in [46], 97–98.

[32] Davies, Donald W.; and G. I. P. Parkin, "The average size of the key stream in output feedback encipherment," in [45], 263–279.

[33] Davio, Mark; Yvo Desmedt; Josef Goubert; Frank Hoornaert; and Jean-Jacques Quisquater, "Efficient hardware and software implementations for the DES," *Proceedings of Crypto 84*, Springer (1985).

[34] Desmedt, Yvo, "Analysis of the security and new algorithms for modern industrial cryptography," dissertation, Department Elektrotechniek, Katholieke Universiteit Leuven (October 1984).

[35] Diffie, Whitfield; and Martin E. Hellman, "Exhaustive cryptanalysis of the NBS Data Encryption Standard," *Computer*, **10** (March 6, 1980), 74–84.

[36] Gait, Jason, "A new nonlinear pseudorandom number generator," *IEEE Transactions on Software Engineering*, **SE-3** (September 1977), 359–363.

[37] Goldreich, Oded, "DES-like functions can generate the alternating group," *IEEE Transactions on Information Theory*, **IT–29** (1983), 863–865.

[38] Hellman, Martin E., *et al.*, "Results of an initial attempt to cryptanalyze the NBS Data Encryption Standard," technical report SEL 76–042, Information Systems Laboratory, Stanford Univ. (November 1976).

[39] Hellman, Martin E.; and Justin M. Reyneri, "Distribution of Drainage in the DES," in [46] (1982), 129–131.

[40] Jueneman, Robert R., "Analysis of certain aspects of output-feedback mode," in [46] (1982), 99–127.

[41] Kaliski, Burton S., Jr.; Ronald L. Rivest; and Alan T. Sherman, "Is DES a pure cipher? (Results of more cycling experiments on DES)," *Proceedings of Crypto 85*, to appear.

[42] Merkle, Ralph C.; and Martin E. Hellman, "On the security of multiple encryption," *CACM*, **24** (July 1981), 465–467.

[43] Reeds, J. A.; and J. L. Manferdell, "DES has no per round linear factors," *Proceedings of Crypto 84*, Springer (1985).

[44] Tuchman, W. L., talk presented at the National Computer Conference, (June 1978).

See also [2] [4] [48] [51] [53].

### Other Works

[45] Beth, Thomas, *ed.*, *Cryptography, Proceedings of the Workshop on Cryptography, Burg Feuerstein, Germany, March 29–April 2, 1982*, Springer (Berlin, 1983).

[46] Chaum, David; Ronald L. Rivest; and Alan T. Sherman, *eds.*, *Advances in Cryptology: Proceedings of Crypto 82*, Plenum Press (New York, 1983).

[47] Chaum, David, *ed.*, *Advances in Cryptology: Proceedings of Crypto 83*, Plenum Press (New York, 1984).

[48] Coppersmith, Don; and Edna Grossman, "Generators for certain alternating groups with applications to cryptology," *Siam Journal on Applied Mathematics*, **29** (December 1975), 624–627.

[49] DeLaurentis, John M., "A further weakness in the common modulus protocol for the RSA cryptosystem," *Cryptologia*, **8** (July 1984), 253–259.

[50] Gaines, Helen Fouché, *Cryptanalysis: A Study of Ciphers and Their Solution*, Dover (1956).

[51] Grossman, Edna; and Bryant Tuckerman, "Analysis of a Feistel-like cipher weakened by having no rotating key," IBM research report RC 6375 (#27489), (January 31, 1977).

[52] *Data Ciphering Processors Am9518, Am9568, AmZ8068 Technical Manual*, Advanced Micro Devices, Inc. (1984).

[53] Hellman, Martin E., "A cryptanalytic time-memory tradeoff," technical report, Stanford Univ. (1978).

[54] *IBM Personal Computer Technical Reference* (July 1982).

[55] Longo, G., *ed.*, *Secure Digital Communications*, Springer (Vienna 1983).

[56] Rivest, Ronald; Adi Shamir; and Leonard Adleman, "On digital signatures and public-key cryptosystems," *CACM*, **21** (February 1978), 120–126.

[57] Shannon, Claude E., "Communication theory of secrecy systems," *Bell System Technical Journal*, **28** (October 1949), 656–715.

[58] "Unclassified summary: Involvement of NSA in the development of the Data Encryption Standard," staff report of the Senate Select Committee on Intelligence, United States Senate (April 1978).

# TWO NEW SECRET KEY CRYPTOSYSTEMS

Eurocrypt 1985, Linz, Austria

Henk Meijer & Selim Akl
Department of Computing & Information Science
Queen's University
Kingston, Ontario

## 1. Introduction

Since the Data Encryption Algorithm DES was accepted as a standard in 1977 [4], few new conventional cryptosystems have been proposed in the open literature [5]. However DES is not necessarily the most suitable encryption procedure for all applications. For example two people desiring to set up a private secure communication channel may not want to use a standardized encryption algorithm; or communicating parties may want to choose from a set of encryption algorithms, trading off speed against security. In this paper we propose two new conventional cryptosystems that are

- adaptable (parameters can be chosen to increase or decrease execution time and level of security),
- efficient (the algorithms are fast, even when implemented in a high level computer language),
- easy to program (both algorithm can be written in less than 100 lines) and
- conceptually simple.

The above properties make the systems attractive to users that do not have the time, expertise and/or money to install special hardware chips or to write long and complicated programs. It is hoped that the last property will increase the trust we can have in the security of the systems. Since no practical cryptosystem can be proven to be secure, we have to use encryption algorithms that we believe to be secure. By using only conceptually simple operations and transformations, we hope that weaknesses are easier to detect. And even if such weaknesses should exist, we claim that in some applications a system with known deficiencies is preferable to an apparently secure, but difficult to analyze cryptosystem.

## 2. Convential cryptosystem, based on permutations and multiplications.

This cryptosystem consists of three multiplication and two permutation stages. We will first describe the system and then examine its security properties.

### 2.1 The system

Let m be a message consisting of 2n bits. We write

$$m = \langle m_0, m_1 \rangle$$

where $m_0$ and $m_1$ are the n most significant and n least-significant bits of m, respectively. The encryption key k is a block of 3n bits; we can write $k = \langle k_0,k_1,k_2 \rangle$, where each $k_i$ is a block of n bits. P is a permutation of size 2n. The encryption algorithm $E_k(m)$ can be stated as follows:

$$\begin{aligned} E_k(m) : \quad & \langle a_0,a_1 \rangle = \langle m_0*k_0, m_1*k_2 \rangle \\ & \langle b_0,b_1 \rangle = P(\langle a_0,a_1 \rangle) \\ & \langle c_0,c_1 \rangle = \langle b_0*k_1, b_1*k_1 \rangle \\ & \langle d_0,d_1 \rangle = P(\langle c_0,c_1 \rangle) \\ & \langle e_0,e_1 \rangle = \langle d_0*k_2, d_1*k_0 \rangle \\ & \text{return } (\langle e_0,e_1 \rangle). \end{aligned}$$

In the above algorithm, the operation * is defined by

$$\begin{aligned} a * b &= 2^n-1 \text{ if } a = 2^n-1 \text{ and } b > 0 \\ &= ab \bmod 2^n-1 \text{ otherwise.} \end{aligned}$$

If the permutation P is chosen such that $P = P^{-1}$ and if $k_0$, $k_1$ and $k_2$ are such that

$$\gcd(k_i, 2^n-1) = 1 \text{ for } i = 0,1,2,$$

then we have

$$E_{\langle k_0,k_1,k_2 \rangle}(m) = c \text{ iff } E_{\langle k_2^{-1},k_1^{-1},k_0^{-1} \rangle}(c) = m,$$

where $k_i^{-1}$ is the multiplicative inverse of $k_i$ modulo $2^n-1$.

### 2.2. Efficiency and implementation

The above algorithm can be implemented efficiently by using n-bit integers rather than arrays of length n. Since $2^n \equiv 1 \bmod 2^n-1$, an algorithm for multiplication modulo $2^n-1$ can be written as a sequence of regular additions, while adding overflow bits to the least significant bits. For example, in the language C, using 32-bit unsigned integers, we can add modulo $2^n-1$ with n=32 by

```
add (a,b) :  if (a+b) <  a return (a+b+1)
                         else return (a+b)
```

since overflow bits are automatically truncated. Or, in Pascal, with 32-bit signed integers and the largest positive integer max = $2^{31}-1$, we can add modulo $2^{31}-1$ by

```
add (a,b) :  if max-a < b then return (a-max+b)
                           else return (a+b).
```

Given an addition function, an algorithm for multiplication modulo $2^n-1$ can be written as

```
multiply (a,b) :
     product = 0
     while b > 0 do
          if b is odd then product = add (product,a)
          right-shift (b)
          cyclic-left-shift (a)

     endwhile
     return (product).
```

Notice that the above algorithm returns $2^n-1$ if a = $2^n-1$ and b>0, as required for the encryption algorithm. The permutation step can be executed by a sequence of modulo reductions, integer divisions and additions, all with powers of 2. In C, this can be done with the standard shift operation. For example the following algorithm swaps bit i of integer a with bit j of integer b:

```
if ((a>>i)&01) != ((b>>j&01)
{        a xor= 01 << i; /* change bit i */
         b xor= 01 << j; /* change bit j */  }
```

In languages in which shift operations do not exist, integers can be mapped into arrays before being permuted, or bits can be swapped directly by code looking like:

$a_i$ = (a div $2^i$) mod 2
$b_j$ = (b div $2^j$) mod 2

$$\text{if } a_i = b_j \text{ then } a = a + (1 - 2a_i)\, 2^i$$
$$b = b + (1 - 2b_j)\, 2^j .$$

## 2.3. Analysis

We first note that 2 * x, where * is the operation introduction in section 2.1, is equal to a cyclic left shift of the n-bit integer x. So if cs(x) denotes the cyclic left shift of x, we have

$$2^i * x = cs^i(x).$$

From this we can see that the multiplication step of the encryption algorithm has the property

$$cs^i(a) * k = cs^i(a * k).$$

Therefore, in order to ensure that cyclic shifts will not be preserved under the encryption function, the permutation P has to be chosen such that for all (i,j) ≠ (0,0), there exist x,y, such that

$$P(< cs^i(x),\ cs^j(y) > ) \neq$$
$$< cs^i(P(<x,y>)_0,\ cs^j(P(<x,y>)_1) >$$

where $P(<x,y>)_0$ and $P(<x,y>)_1$ denote the n most-significant and n least-significant bits of P(<x,y>) respectively.

For all permutations P and keys $k = <k_0, k_1, k_2>$ we have

$$E_k(\bar{m}) = E_{\bar{k}}(m) = \overline{E_k(m)} ,$$

where $\bar{x}$ denotes the bitwise complement of x. This can easily be seen from the fact that for all x with $0 <= x <= 2^n-1$,

$$\bar{x} = 2^n-1 - x.$$

This property enables a cryptanalyst to

(i) reduce a search of the keyspace by 50% in case of a known plaintext attack,

(ii) obtain a message-cyphertext pair $(\bar{m},\bar{c})$ for each known pair (m,c).

However, disadvantage (i) is not serious if the key space is sufficiently large and (ii) can be prevented by, for example, requiring that all messages end with a zero.

The encryption algorithm has good statistical properties, even if it is reduced to two multiplications and one permutation. In fact it can be proven that the multiplication step is complete, i.e. the function $f_k(.)$ defined by

$f_k(x) = k * x$

is complete [3] for all k with gcd (k, $2^n-1$) = 1.

## 3. Secret-key cryptosystem and random-bit generator

The sender and receiver choose and agree on two n-bit (n = 64, say) vectors V and W. The pair (V,W) represents the secret key.

The sender and receiver also choose and agree on two n-integer vectors X and Y such that

$$X = x_1\ x_2\ \dots\ x_n \qquad \text{where } 1 \le x_i \le i, \text{ and}$$
$$Y = y_1\ y_2\ \dots\ y_n \qquad \text{where } 1 \le y_i \le i.$$

Each of X and Y is thus a permutation [2]. The pair (X,Y) is a parameter of the system which may - but needs not to - be kept secret.

Each plaintext message consists of n-bit vectors $M_i$, i = 1,2, ...,r.

### 3.1. Encryption

With every message to be transmitted a n-bit vector U which is a function of the date and time is created.

This vector is used by the sender to compute two n-bit vectors $M_0$ and $C_0$ as follows:

$$M_0 = \text{middle-n bits of } UxV \quad (\text{i.e. } M_0 = \lfloor (UxV \bmod 2^{3n/2})/2^{n/2} \rfloor),$$

$$C_0 = \text{middle-n bits of } UxW \quad (\text{i.e. } C_0 = \lfloor (UxW \bmod 2^{3n/2})/2^{n/2} \rfloor).$$

Let $N_0$ equal the reverse of the bit pattern for $M_0$, i.e. if $M_0 = m_1\ m_2 \dots m_n$, then $N_0 = m_n\ m_{n-1} \dots m_2\ m_1$.

The message is now encrypted using the procedure below.

$$\begin{array}{l} \text{for } i=1 \text{ to } n \text{ do} \\ \qquad (M'_{i-1}, N_i) = S(M_{i-1}, N_{i-1}) \\ \qquad C'_{i-1} = C_{i-1} \oplus M'_{i-1} \\ \qquad C_i = P(M_{i-1} \oplus C'_{i-1}, M_i \oplus C'_{i-1}) \\ \text{endfor.} \end{array}$$

The functions S and P are defined as follows. Let $K = k_1\ k_2 \dots k_n$ and $H = h_1\ h_2 \dots h_n$.

1) function S(K,H) :

$Q = K \times H$ $\{Q = q_1 q_2 \dots q_{2n}$, i.e. Q is a 2n-bit vector$\}$

$K = q_{n/2+1}\, q_{n/2+2} \dots q_{3n/2}$ $\{K = \lfloor (K\mathrm{x}H \bmod 2^{3n/2})/2^{n/2} \rfloor\}$

$H = q_{3n/2}\, q_{3n/2-1} \dots q_{n/2+2}\, q_{n/2+1}$ $\{$H is the reverse of K$\}$

return (K,H).

2) function P(K,H) :

```
        for i=n  to  2  do
              if  k_i = 0  then  h_i <--> h_{x_i}
                               else  h_i <--> h_{y_i}
              endif
        endfor
return H.
```

The sender now transmits $U, C_1, C_2, \dots, C_r$ to the receiver.

### 3.2. Decryption

The receiver goes through the same steps to compute $M_0, C_0, N_0$. Then he recovers $M_1, M_2, \dots, M_r$ using the following procedure.

for i=1 to r do

$(M'_{i-1}, N_i) = S(M_{i-1}, N_{i-1})$

$C'_{i-1} = C_{i-1} \oplus M'_{i-1}$

$M_i = C'_{i-1} \oplus P^{-1}(M_{i-1} \oplus C'_{i-1}, C_i)$ endfor.

The function $P^{-1}$ (K,H) is the same as P(K,H) except that the for loop goes from i=2 to n.

## 4. Conclusions

Both systems introduced in this paper can easily be implemented. They withstand initial attempts to break them and possess no obvious statistical weaknesses [1,3]. More statistical and analytical validation will be done in the future. Notice that the second system is an example of a randomized encryption system, so if a message is encrypted twice under the same key, it will result in two different cyphertexts.

## References

[1] H. Beker and F. Piper, Cipher Systems, John Wiley, 1982.

[2] D.E. Knuth, The Art of Computer Programming, Vol.2, Addison Wes-

ley, 1981.

[3] A.G. Konheim, Cryptography: a Primer, John Wiley, 1981.

[4] National Bureau of Standards, Data Encryption Standard, FIPS publication 46, U.S. Department of Commerce, January 1979.

[5] J.A. Thomas and J. Thersites, An infinite encryption system, Dr. Dobb's Journal, August 1984.

## CRYPTANALYSTS REPRESENTATION OF NONLINEARLY FILTERED ML-SEQUENCES

T.Siegenthaler
Institute for Communication Technology
Federal Institute of Technology
8092 Zurich,Switzerland

Abstract

A running key generator consisting of a maximum-length (ML) linear feedback shift register (LFSR) and some nonlinear feedforward state filter function is investigated. It is shown how a cryptanalyst can find an equivalent system in a ciphertext-only attack. The analysis uses a Walsh orthogonal expansion of the state filter function and its relation to the crosscorrelation function (CCF) between the ML-sequence and the produced running key sequence.

### I Introduction

Nonlinearly filtered ML-sequences are frequently used as the running key sequence in stream ciphers. It will be shown how, under some assumptions, a cryptanalyst can find a system which generates the same running key sequence. The following system will be investigated:

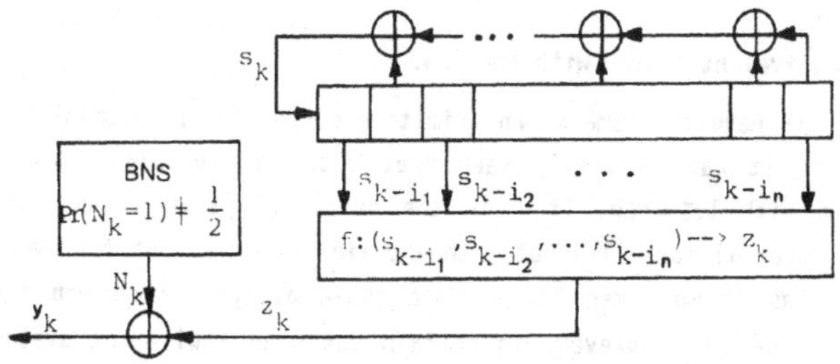


Fig. 1. A nonlinearly state filtered ML-sequence

In Fig. 1 it is assumed that the stages $i_j$ with $1 \leq i_1 \leq i_2 \ldots i_n \leq L$ of the LFSR of length L are tapped as inputs to the nonlinear function f. The described method, however, applies to any choice $1 \leq i_1 \leq i_2 \ldots i_n \leq 2^L-1$ and is useful if $n<L$. The binary noise source (BNS) models the generation of the plaintext to be enciphered. We shall require that $Pr(N_k=1) \neq 1/2$ and the analysis will make use of the resulting redundancy in the plaintext. It is assumed that the task for the

cryptanalyst is to find an equivalent system which generates the full period of the sequence $(z_k)$, given only the primitive connection polynomial of the LFSR and some portion of $(z_k)$ or of $(y_k)$. The number n, and thus the positions $i_1$, $i_2$, ..., $i_n$ of the taps, as well as the function f and the initial state of the LFSR are not known to the cryptanalyst. The described system could of course be simulated by a binary counter, counting through $2^L-1$ states and an appropriate function of L variables. In a worst case situation, the cryptanalyst could do nothing better than this. A necessary but not sufficient condition for this worst case is n=L. Alternatively the above system could be simulated by the shortest LFSR generating the sequence $(z_k)$, but this seems not be possible if only a portion of $(y_k)$ instead of $(z_k)$ is known. However, if the cryptanalyst knows the connection polynomial used in the original system given in Fig. 1 (if not he could try all possible primitive polynomials of degree L), he can try to determine an equivalent system as given in Fig. 2.

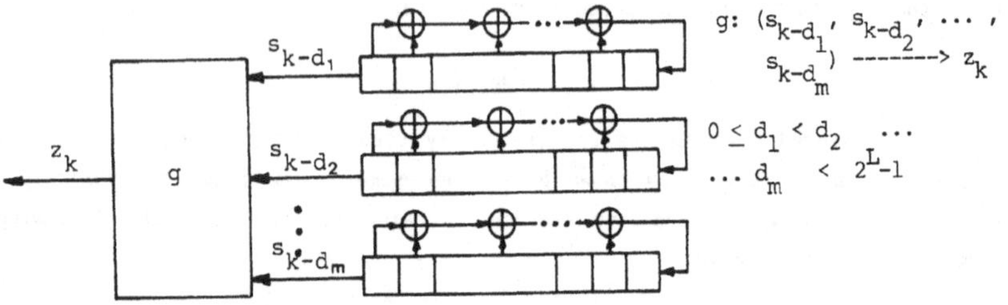


Fig. 2. Cryptanalyst's equivalent system with $1 \le m \le n$.

The m LFSR's in Fig. 2 all have the same known primitive connection polynomial but different initial states. It can be easily seen that such an equivalent system always exists for an m with $1 \le m \le n$. If f in the original system is not the constant function $z_k = 0$ (or 1) for all inputs, then obviously $m \ge 1$. But for every f the above equivalent has at most m=n because one could always choose m=n and $d_1=i_1$, $d_2=i_2$, ..., $d_n=i_n$ and g=f. However, in certain cases an equivalent system with m<n exists. The cryptanalyst generally finds the equivalent in two steps. He determines first m initial states $S^1, S^2, \dots, S^m$ for the LFSR's which then generate the sequences$(s_{k-d_1})$, $(s_{k-d_2})$, ...,$(s_{k-d_m})$, $1 \le m \le n$, and afterwards he determines the function g from the known inputs $s_{k-d_i}$, i=1,2, ...,m, and the observed $y_k$. The sequences generated by the given primitive polynomial form a vectorspace $V^L$ of dimension L over GF(2). The sequences $(s_{k-i_1})$,$(s_{k-i_2})$, ...,$(s_{k-i_n})$ and its linear combinations form a subspace $V^n$ of $V^L$. It will be shown that the sequences $(s_{k-d_1})$,$(s_{k-d_2})$, ...,$(s_{k-d_m})$ are elements of $V^n$ and can be found by inspection of the CCF between $(s_k)$ and $(y_k)$.

## II Walsh orthogonal expansion of the state filter function

To show that the sequences used in the equivalent system are in fact elements of the subspace $V^n$ mentioned in chapter I and can be found by inspection of a crosscorrelation function, a Walsh orthogonal expansion of the state filter function will be applied. In this section, the Walsh-Transform is reviewed. Let f be any real-valued function of binary (0,1) variables $x_1,x_2, \ldots, x_n$. The domain of f is then the set of $2^n$ binary vectors $\underline{x}=[x_1,x_2, \ldots, x_n]$ in the vectorspace $Z^n$. Since f is completely specified by its value at each of these $2^n$ points in $Z^n$, we may consider f as a member of a $2^n$-dimensional vectorspace Q. For any fixed $\underline{w}=[w_1,w_2,\ldots,w_n]$ in $Z^n$, we can write the corresponding Walsh function $W_{\underline{w}}(\underline{x}) \in Q$ as

$$W_{\underline{w}}(\underline{x}) = (-1)^{\underline{x}\cdot\underline{w}} = (-1)^{x_1w_1 \oplus x_2w_2 \oplus \ldots \oplus x_nw_n} \quad . \tag{1}$$

There are exactly $2^n$ different Walsh-Functions $W_{\underline{w}}(\underline{x})$ corresponding to the $2^n$ vectors $\underline{w}$ in $Z^n$. These functions form a complete orthogonal basis for Q [2].

We now write $f(\underline{x})$ to denote $f(x_1,x_2,\ldots,x_n)$. The function f can be expanded in a Walsh function expansion as

$$f(\underline{x}) = \sum_{\underline{w}} F(\underline{w})W_{\underline{w}}(\underline{x}) \tag{2}$$

where

$$F(\underline{w}) = 2^{-n}\sum_{\underline{x}} f(\underline{x})W_{\underline{w}}(\underline{x}) \tag{3}$$

is the Walsh-Spectrum [2] of f. The following properties will be used later on.

Property 1: (initial value)

$$\sum_{\underline{w}} F(\underline{w}) = f(\underline{0}) \tag{4}$$

Proof: $F(\underline{w}) = 2^{-n}\sum_{\underline{x}} f(\underline{x})W_{\underline{w}}(\underline{x})$. Note, however, that $W_{\underline{w}}(\underline{0}) = 1$ for all $\underline{w}$. Hence, summing on $\underline{w}$, $\sum_{\underline{w}} F(\underline{w}) = 2^{-n}\sum_{\underline{x}} f(\underline{x}) \sum_{\underline{w}} W_{\underline{w}}(\underline{x})W_{\underline{w}}(\underline{0}) = f(\underline{0})$ from the orthogonality of Walsh-Functions.

Property 2: (idle variables)

If the variable $x_j$ in $f(x_1,x_2,\ldots,x_n)$ is idle, then

$$F(\underline{w}) = 0 \quad \text{for } \underline{w} \in (\underline{w}\colon w_j=1). \tag{5}$$

Proof (Titsworth [1]):

$$F(\underline{w}) = 2^{-n}\sum_{\underline{x}} f(\underline{x})(-1)^{\underline{x}\cdot\underline{w}}$$

$$= 2^{-n}\sum_{\underline{x}:x_j=0} f(\underline{x})\prod_{k\neq j}(-1)^{x_k\cdot w_k}\left[\sum_{x_j=0}^{1}(-1)^{x_j}\right]$$

but the last bracket vanishes for every choice of $x_k$, all $k \neq j$.

Property 3: (degenerate functions)

It has been shown by Lechner [3] that if the smallest subspace of $Z^n$ which contains the set $S=(\underline{w}:F(\underline{w}) \neq 0)$ has dimension $m \leq n$ then it is guaranteed that a function $g(\underline{y})$ with $g(\underline{y}) = g(\underline{x}H^t) = f(\underline{x})$ exists, where $H^t$ is the transpose of

$$H = \begin{bmatrix} \underline{w}_1 \\ \underline{w}_2 \\ \cdot \\ \cdot \\ \underline{w}_m \end{bmatrix}$$

and where any m linear independent elements of S can be chosen as the row vectors $\underline{w}_i$, $i=1,2,\ldots,m$. For $m < n$, $f(\underline{x})$ is called a degenerate function and $y_1,y_2,\ldots,y_m$ are called essential variables.

## III Crosscorrelation function

In this section, the CCF C(d) of the sequences $(s_k)$ and $(z_k)$ will be computed. By definition,

$$C(d) = (1/p)\sum_{k=0}^{p-1}(-1)^{z_k}(-1)^{s_{k-d}}, \quad \text{for } d=0,1,\ldots,p-1 \;, \tag{6}$$

where $p=2^L-1$ denotes the period of the ML-sequence $(s_k)$. First, we consider the general case, where n=L and $i_1=1$, $i_2=2$, ..., $i_L=L$ (see Fig.1). The L sequences $(s_{k-1})$, $(s_{k-2})$, $\ldots(s_{k-L})$ are linearly independent and form a basis for the vector space $V^L$. This follows from the assumption that a primitive and hence irreducible connection polynomial is used. The sequence $(s_{k-d})$ can be expressed as a linear combination of the above basis for every $d \in (0,1,\ldots,p-1)$. Therefore, we can express $s_{k-d}$ using the binary vectors $\underline{v}(d) = [v_1(d),v_2(d),\ldots,v_L(d)]$ and $\underline{x}_k = [s_{k-1},s_{k-2},\ldots,s_{k-L}]$ as $s_{k-d} = \underline{v}(d)\underline{x}_k$ :

$$s_{k-d} = v_1(d)s_{k-1} \oplus v_2(d)s_{k-2} \oplus \ldots \oplus v_L(d)s_{k-L} \quad . \tag{7}$$

To simplify the notation, we will sometimes write

$$f^*(\underline{x}) = (-1)^{f(\underline{x})}$$

to denote the (1,-1) function corresponding to $f(\underline{x})$. $F^*(\underline{w})$ denotes the Walsh-Transform of $f^*(\underline{x})$. From (2),(6) and (7) we get

$$C(d) = (1/p)\sum_{k=0}^{p-1} \sum_{\underline{w}} F^*(\underline{w})(-1)^{\underline{w}\cdot\underline{x}_k}(-1)^{\underline{v}(d)\cdot\underline{x}_k} =$$

$$= (1/p)\sum_{\underline{w}} F^*(\underline{w}) \sum_{k=0}^{p-1} (-1)^{\underline{x}_k\,(\underline{w}\oplus\underline{v}(d))} \quad . \tag{8}$$

The exponent $\underline{x}_k\cdot(\underline{w} \oplus \underline{v}(d))$ for $k = 0,1,\ldots,p-1$ corresponds, for some fixed binary vector $\underline{w} \oplus \underline{v}(d) \neq 0$, to a linear combination of ML-sequences and therefore is itself a ML-sequence. Hence, the last sum in (8) is equal to -1 unless $\underline{w} \oplus \underline{v}(d) = 0$ and we obtain

$$C(d) = (1/p)\,[p\,F^*(\underline{v}(d)) - \sum_{\underline{w}:\underline{w}\neq\underline{v}(d)} F^*(\underline{w})] \quad . \tag{9}$$

Using property 1 from sec. II, we get

$$C(d) = (1 + 1/p)\,F^*(\underline{v}(d)) - (1/p)\,f^*(\underline{0}) \quad , \tag{10}$$

where $F^*$ and $f^*$ are functions of L variables. Expression (10) gives, for an arbitrary state filter function f, the value of the CCF between the ML-sequence $(s_k)$ and the running key sequence $(z_k)$. In the sequel, the case $n < L$ is of interest. We consider C(d) as given in (6) at some position d. Assume that some variable $s_{k-i}$, for a fixed i in (7), belongs to the L-n idle variables. Then we have from property 2 of sec. II:

$$F^*(\underline{v}(d)) = 0 \;, \qquad \text{for} \quad \underline{v}(d) \in (\, \underline{v}((d)\colon v_i(d) = 1 \,). \tag{11}$$

Therefore, we have from (10) for all d such that $\underline{v}(d)$ contains at least one component $v_i(d) = 1$, for which the corresponding variable $x_i$ is idle,

$$C(d) = -(1/p)\,f^*(\underline{0}) = \text{constant}. \tag{12}$$

Hence, the only d's where C(d) may be different from the constant given in (12) are those where all components $v_i(d)$, $i \in (1,2,,\ldots,L)$, in $\underline{v}(d)$ are zero for all $i \notin (i_1,i_2,\ldots,i_n)$. Note that the only non-idle variables are $s_{k-i_1}$, $s_{k-i_2}$, ..., $s_{k-i_n}$. Therefore, we have finally our desired result:

$$C(d) = \begin{cases} -(1/p)\,f^*(\underline{0}) & , \; d \notin M \\ (1 + 1/p)\,F^*(\underline{v}(d)) - (1/p)\,f^*(\underline{0}) & , \; d \in M \text{ and } \underline{v}(d) \neq 0, \end{cases} \tag{13}$$

where M denotes the set of all d such that the sequence $(s_{k-d})$ can be obtained as a linear combination of the sequences $(s_{k-i_1})$, $(s_{k-i_2})$, ... $(s_{k-i_n})$. Note that $f^*$ and $F^*$ in (13) are functions of the n non-idle variables only and that $\underline{v}(d)$ can be considered as the corresponding vector of n components only.

The following facts follow from (13):

1) A peak in the CCF (value different from $-(1/p)f^*(\underline{0})$ ) occurs at d if and only if d is such that $(s_{k-d})$ can be obtained as some linear combination of tap-sequences $(s_{k-i_1}),(s_{k-i_2})$ ..., $(s_{k-i_n})$ and $F^*(\underline{v}(d)) \neq 0$.
2) The magnitude of a peak depends only on $F^*$ (or equivalently on $f^*$), not on the tap positions or the chosen primitive connection polynomial.
3) The positions of peaks in the CCF depend only on the chosen connection polynomial and the tap positions $i_1,i_2,\ldots,i_n$.
4) The number of peaks in the CCF is the number of $\underline{w} \neq \underline{0}$ such that $F^*(\underline{w}) \neq 0$, and thus is at most $2^n-1$.

Example 1: (L=7, n=3)
Consider the state filter function $f(\underline{x}) = x_1x_2 \oplus x_1x_3 \oplus x_2x_3$, where addition and multiplication is in GF(2).

| $w_1$ $x_1$ | $w_2$ $x_2$ | $w_3$ $x_3$ | $f(\underline{x})$ | $F(\underline{w})$ | $f^*(\underline{x})$ | $F^*(\underline{w})$ |
|---|---|---|---|---|---|---|
| 0 | 0 | 0 | 0 | 1/2 | 1 | 0 |
| 0 | 0 | 1 | 0 | -1/4 | 1 | 1/2 |
| 0 | 1 | 0 | 0 | -1/4 | 1 | 1/2 |
| 0 | 1 | 1 | 1 | 0 | -1 | 0 |
| 1 | 0 | 0 | 0 | -1/4 | 1 | 1/2 |
| 1 | 0 | 1 | 1 | 0 | -1 | 0 |
| 1 | 1 | 0 | 1 | 0 | -1 | 0 |
| 1 | 1 | 1 | 1 | 1/4 | -1 | -1/2 |

$C(d_1)=C(d_2)=C(d_3)= (1 + 1/127)(1/2) - 1/127 = 63/127 \approx 1/2$

$C(d_4)=(1 + 1/127)(-1/2) - 1/127 = -65/127 \approx -1/2$

$C(d_i)=-1/127$, for $i=5,6,\ldots,127$ $\approx 0$

$\underline{v}(d_1) = [001]$ ; $\underline{v}(d_2) = [010]$ ; $\underline{v}(d_3) = [100]$ ; $\underline{v}(d_4) = [111]$

and $(s_{k-d_j}) = (s_{k-i_j})$ for $j=1,2,3$ and $(s_{k-d_4}) = (s_{k-i_1} \oplus s_{k-i_2} \oplus s_{k-i_3})$.

## IV Cryptanalyst´s equivalent

From the inverse Walsh-Transform (3), it follows that the function $f(\underline{x})$ is uniquely determined by its nonzero Walsh coefficients $F(\underline{w})$. These coefficients can be recognized as peaks in the CCF at positions $d_1,d_2,\ldots$as pointed out in chapter III. Up to now we have assumed that the CCF is computed as given in expression (6), where the sum is over the full period p. Moreover, the influence of the plaintext has not been considered. In practice, the CCF will be corrupted by the plaintext source as shown in Fig. 1; moreover, the cryptanalyst may usually use only a small portion of ciphertext instead of a full period. In this case, the values of the peaks are only estimates of the nonzero coefficients in $F(\underline{w})$. Therefore, the cryptanalyst proceeds in two steps. For the sequences $(s_{k-d_1})$, $(s_{k-d_2})$, $\ldots \in V^n$ corresponding to the positions $d_1,d_2, \ldots$ of the observed peaks, an arbitrary basis $(s_{k-d_1})$, $(s_{k-d_2})$ ,..., $(s_{k-d_m})$ of dimension $m \leq n$ is chosen, where $s_{k-d_1}$, $s_{k-d_2}$, ... $s_{k-d_m}$ correspond to the essential variables mentioned in sec. II, property 3. The above sequences are generated by m LFSR´s with appropriate initial loadings $S^1,S^2,\ldots,S^m$. It then remains to determine the function g: $(s_{k-d_1},s_{k-d_2},\ldots, s_{k-d_m}) \dashrightarrow z_k$. This is an easy task because the inputs $s_{k-d_1},s_{k-d_2},\ldots,s_{k-d_m}$ are known and the corresponding noisy output $y_k$ can also be observed for $k = 1,2,\ldots$ as ciphertext from the original system. If the same input vector $(s_{k-d_1}, s_{k-d_2},\ldots,s_{k-d_m})$ occurred a sufficient number of times, the corresponding mapping for this input-output pair could be estimated by a simple majority decision.

<u>Example 2:</u> The following system is cryptanalyzed: L=13

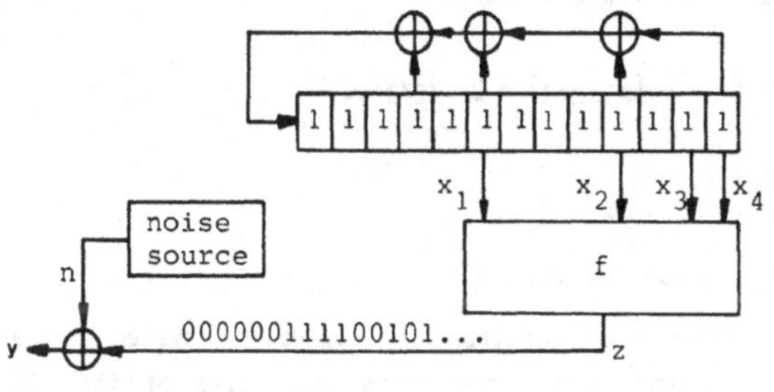


<u>unknown to cryptanalyst:</u>

$n=4$ ,
$i_1 = 6,\ i_2 = 10$ ,
$i_3 = 12,\ i_4 = 13$ ,
$Pr\ (n=1) = 0.1$ ,
$z = x_1 \oplus x_4 \oplus x_1x_3 \oplus$
$\oplus\ x_2x_3 \oplus x_1x_4 \oplus x_2x_4$

Fig. 3. The original system

The cryptanalyst knows only the connection polynomial and observes only 800 digits of ciphertext. However, from the shift-register states corresponding to the four observed peaks in the CCF (see Fig. 4), three linearly independent initial states $S^1, S^2, S^3$ can be determined, corresponding to the positions of (any) three of these peaks.

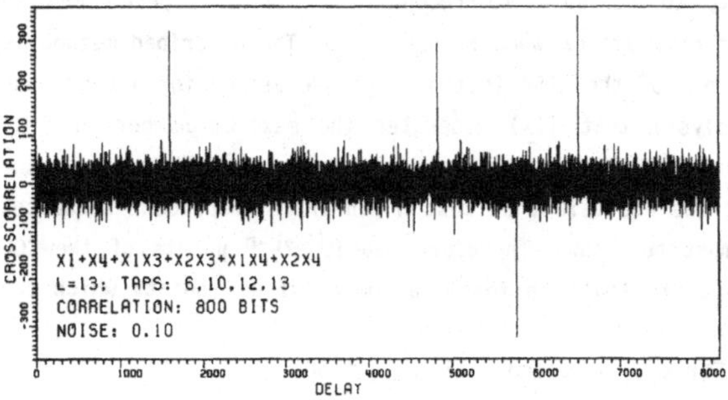


| delay | peak | sr-state |
|---|---|---|
| 325 | -90 | 0001010101110 |
| •1603 | 320 | 0000001111001 |
| 3200 | -98 | 0011011100110 |
| 4488 | -92 | 1011110001110 |
| 4552 | -100 | 1001111101101 |
| •4835 | 294 | 0000001111000 |
| 5031 | -108 | 1001110110110 |
| •5775 | -326 | 0000000000110 |
| •6513 | 352 | 0000000000111 |
| 7987 | -98 | 0101101010100 |

Fig.4. CCF for the system of Fig. 3 with protocol of 10 strongest values together with the corresponding states of cryptanalyst's LFSR.

It turns out that, for this example, the equivalent function g determined by the procedure described above is $z = y_1 \oplus y_2 \oplus y_1y_3 \oplus y_1y_2 \oplus y_2y_3$; hence, m=3 and the representation is:

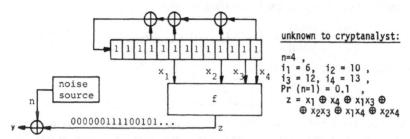

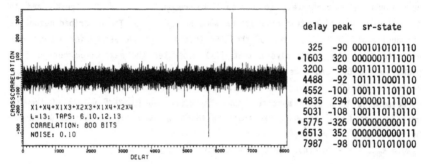

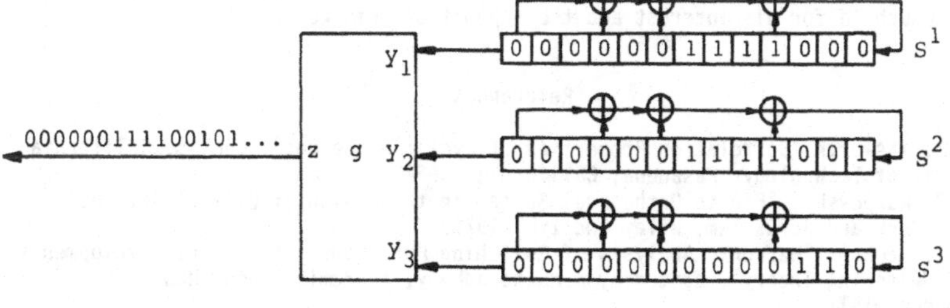


Fig. 5. Cryptanalyst's equivalent system

In fact, it can be seen from the Walsh-Transform of $f(\underline{x})$ that the cryptanalyst implicitly used the linear transformation

$$H = \begin{bmatrix} \underline{w}_1 \\ \underline{w}_2 \\ \underline{w}_3 \end{bmatrix} = \begin{bmatrix} 1010 \\ 1001 \\ 0110 \end{bmatrix} \text{ where } \underline{y} = [y_1 y_2 y_3] = [x_1 x_2 x_3 x_4]\, H^t ,$$

even if he did not do this explicitly.

## V Conclusions

It has been shown how a cryptanalyst can construct an equivalent system for a certain type of running key generator. The method uses properties of the CCF between the driving ML-sequence and the produced running key sequence. The Walsh-Transform of the state filter function played a crucial role in the computation and interpretation of this CCF. The advantage of the described method is that an equivalent system can be found in a ciphertext-only attack. To determine the equivalent function g even in a known plaintext attack (where $Pr(N_k=1) = 0$), at least $2^m$ ciphertext digits are required. However, generally one needs much more ciphertext to be able to recognize enough CCF peaks and to determine g in a ciphertext-only attack when $Pr(N_k=1) \neq 0$. The described method is not applicable if the length L of the LFSR is too large. We assume for a best case estimate (for the cryptanalyst) that $f(\underline{x})$ generates the maximum number of $\approx 2^n$ peaks in the CCF and moreover that these peaks are equally distributed over the period of the CCF. To find the equivalent at most n linearly independent sequences corresponding to n peaks must be found. Therefore, about $n2^{L-n}$ points of the CCF must be considered. If we assume that the feasible number of CCF points which can be tested is $2^{k_{max}}$ we obtain:

$L_{max} \approx k_{max} + n - \log_2(n)$. For $k_{max} = 40$ and n=15, $L_{max} \approx 50$.

## Acknowledgement

The author is greatful to Prof. Dr. J. Massey and Dr. P. Schöbi of the Institute for Signal and Information Processing, ETH, Zurich, for valuable discussions and suggestions concerning this work and to A. Clivio from the Mathematics Department, ETH, Zurich, for helpful discussions concerning Ref. [3]. Also thanks go to Prof. Dr. P. Leuthold for his interest and the support of this work.

## References

[1] R.C.Titsworth,"Correlation Properties of Cyclic Sequences", Thesis, California Inst. of Technology, Pasadena, California, 1962.

[2] M.G. Karpovsky, "Finite Orthogonal Series in the Design of Digital Devices", New York and Jerusalem, Wiley and IVP, 1976.

[3] R.J. Lechner,"Harmonic Analysis of Switching Functions",in "Recent Developments in Switching Theory", edited by A.Mukhopadhyay, Academic Press, New York and London, 1971.

# AUTHORIZED WRITING FOR "WRITE-ONCE" MEMORIES

Philippe Godlewski and Gérard D. Cohen
ENST, Département SYC,
46 rue Barrault, 75013 PARIS, France.

**Abstract**

We describe a method for storing information on a "write-once" memory with the following feature : reading is easy, whereas writing is difficult, except for the designer.

## 1. Introduction

We start from the following problem, (see [1] for details and terminology) : how to reuse a "Write-Once" memory. That is, we have a storage medium, called **wom** , consisting of n binary positions or **wits** , initially containing a "0". At some step, a wit can be irreversibly overwriten with a "1" (e.g. by some laser beam in digital optical disks or burning microscopic fuses in PROMS).

We consider a coding technique, which we call **coset coding** ([2], [3]), based on error-correcting codes, enabling many rewritings on a wom. We denote by C[n,k] a binary linear code with length n and dimension k. It is used to encode r=n-k bits on a wom as follows : every message $s \in F_2^{n-k}$ is one-to-one associated with a coset of C, say x+C, having for syndrome s. That is $s = x.H^t = s(x)$ where H is a generator matrix for $C^*[n,n-k]$, the dual of C. To encode s (or "write" or "update") envolves finding a vector y in x+C (i.e. with syndrome s), and writing it in the wom. Then writing thriftly (using a minimum number of wits) needs a complete decoding algorithm in the sense of error-correcting codes. Reading on the wom (or decoding the womcode) is simply a syndrome computation retrieving s from y. Notice that, whereas the writing procedure is NP-hard for general codes, see [4], reading only takes $O(n^2)$ mod 2-additions. This is a desirable feature for many applications, where the most frequent operation is reading, but updating is exceptionnal. Our method also has a cryptographic flavour, inspired by McEliece ([5]) which we describe now.

**2. An easy reading - reserved writing procedure**

A disk designer D proposes a data storing system which enables him to keep "economic" control on updatings. This "authorized writer" chooses a code possessing a simple complete decoding scheme which allows him easy updating. He keeps secret $H'$, the parity matrix of the code, and publishes $H$, a random permutation of the columns of an equivalent matrix $MH'$. Then

$H = M H' P$,

where $M$ is a $(n-k)x(n-k)$ invertible matrix, and $P$ a $nxn$ permutation matrix. A guaranteed number of possible updatings is also made public. Everybody can use $H$ to read in the wom by syndrome computation. However, anyone, apart from D, willing to write syndrome s is faced with the following alternative :

- find y, with minimum or upperbounded weight, representing s, by use of H : reputed untractable ([4]).
- find any y representing s, hereby losing updating possibilities ; in that case the weight of y is likely to be large ( $\sim (n-k)/2$, see section 4).

**3. The updating problem**

The designer needs a complete decoding algorithm or a maximum likelihood decoding algorithm (a difference with McEliece scheme). He must solve the following :

Problem :

Given a message $s \in F_2^{n-k}$

and a set I of written wits $I \subset \{1,2,\ldots,n\}$

Find a word y with minimum weight satisfying

(i) $yH^t = s$

(ii) $I \subset supp(y)$.

The updating procedure is depicted in figure 1.

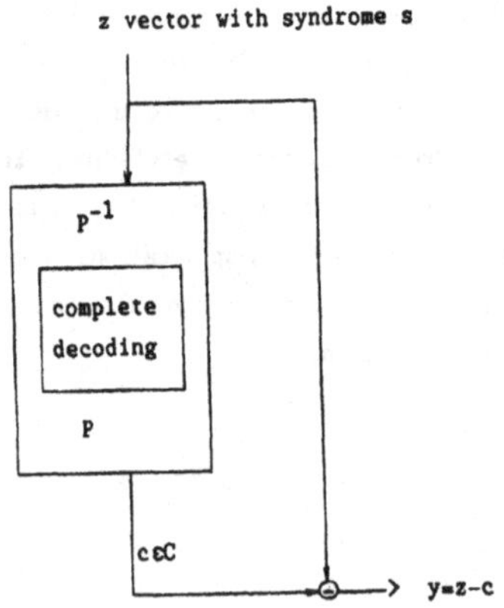


**Figure 1**

In fact, because of point (ii), D needs a little bit more than a complete decoding, that is, a kind of weigthed decoding. This does not bring additional complexity for Viterbi type or treilis decoding ; just consider for instance some metric modification in the treillis when $i \in I$ :

$$d(z_i, c_i) = 0 \text{ if } z_i \neq c_i$$
$$= \infty \text{ if } z_i = c_i.$$

We now give a list of block codes with "practical" complete decoding algorithms.

- block codes with k or n-k not too large,
- some high rate BCH codes.

Such codes may not be used isolated in the scheme but can be part of the following constructions :

- product and concatenated codes ([6]),
- block codes constructed from time-varying convolutional codes ([7]).

## 4. Strategy for the unauthorized writer

Hereafter could be a strategy of the unauthorized writer (UW) :

- Pick any set S of $r=n-k$ columns in the parity-check matrix H.
- Check whether S has full rank r : this is easy, and the answer is "yes" with probability $\sim 1-2^r$ ("no" means S is the support of a codeword in C, an event of probability $\sim 2^r$).
- Write syndrome s as a linear combination of elements in S.

The average number of wits used in this operation is r/2. More precisely, the probability that this number would be essentially smaller, that is, $\lambda r$, for some fixed $\lambda$, $0 \leq \lambda \leq 1/2$ is

$$2^{-r} \sum_{i=0}^{\lambda r} \binom{r}{i} \sim 2^{r(h_2(\lambda)-1)},$$

where $h_2(.)$ is the binary entropy function. In other words, when r becomes large, the unauthorized writer almost surely uses effectively r/2 wits to write s.

Let us now compare this with the situation of the designer (D).
We call t(C) the **covering radius** of C, i.e. the maximal weight of a coset leader, or equivalently, the greatest possible distance between vectors in $F_2^n$ and C. Then it is clear that the coset coding procedure uses at most t(C) wits. For most codes, it is known (cf. e.g. [8]) that, for $r/n = \mu$,

$$t(C) < nh_2^{-1}(\mu).$$

where $h_2^{-1}$ is the inverse of $h_2$ on [0,1/2]. Let us summarize these facts

| F : fraction of the wom used by coset coding with $C[n,n(1-\mu)]$ | UW | D |
|---|---|---|
| | $\frac{1}{2}\mu$ | $h_2^{-1}(\mu)$ |

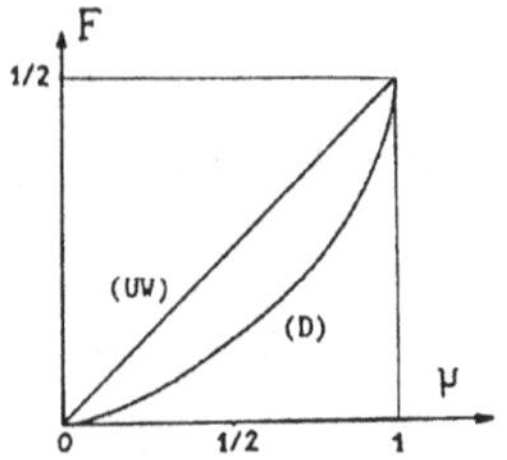


Finally, we give a cleverer strategy for UW which gives slightly (but not essentially) better results :

- Transform H into a equivalent matrix $H''=M''.H$ containing as a submatrix a rxr identity matrix ; M" is an invertible rxr matrix. Let V be the set of the n-r other columns of H".
- For given parameters $\lambda$ and j, compute the Hamming distances between the transformed syndrome $s''=sM''^t$ to be written and the sums of at most j columns of V. Call the algorithm successful if one of these distances is at most $\lambda r$.
- In case of success, take the associated set of columns in V, and add the appropriate columns from the identity submatrix (at most $\lambda r$ of them), getting s as a linear combination of at most $\lambda r+j$ columns in H" and then in H.

The number of basic operations to perform is

$$\sum_{i=0}^{j} \binom{n-r}{i} < (n-r)^j .$$

For $\lambda$ fixed, the probability of success is upperbounded by

$$1 - \left[1-2^{-r(1-h_2(\lambda))}\right]^{(n-r)^j} \sim (n-r)^j\, 2^{-r(1-h_2(\lambda))},$$

i.e. goes to zero for $\lambda < 1/2$ and fixed r/n when r goes to infinity.

For $\lambda=(1/2)-\theta.r^{-1/2}$, $\theta$ constant, the probability of success is non vanishing, but the average number of wits written is $\lambda r \sim r/2$, like with the previous strategy.

**References**


[1] R.L.Rivest and A.Shamir, "How to Reuse a "Write-Once" Memory", Inform. and Control 55, 1-19 (1982).

[2] Heegard, "An efficient Encoder for Algebraic Optical Disk Codes", Preprint.

[3] G.D. Cohen, P. Godlewski, F. Merkx, "Linear Binary Codes for Write-Once Memories", submitted to IEEE-IT.

[4] E.R. Berlekamp, R.J. McEliece and H.C.A. Van Tilborg, "On the Inherent intractability of certain Coding Problems", IEEE Trans. Inform. Theory, vol. IT-24, pp.384-386, May 1978.

[5] R.J. McEliece, "A Public-Key Cryptosystem based on Algebraic Coding Theory", DSN Progress Report, Jan 1978.

[6] J.K. Wolf, "Efficient Maximum Likelihood Decoding of Linear Block Codes Using a Trellis", IEEE Trans. Inform. Theory, vol. IT-24, No. 1, pp. 76-80, Jan. 1978.

[7] J.L. Massey, "Error Bounds for Tree codes, Treillis Codes and Convolutional Codes with Encoding and Decoding Procedures", in Coding and Complexity, G. Longo Ed., C.I.S.M. Courses and Lectures No. 216, New York, Springer-Verlag, 1974, pp. 1-57.

[8] G.D. Cohen, "A Nonconstructive Upper Bound on Covering Radius", IEEE Trans. Inform. Theory, vol. IT-29, pp. 352-353, May 1983.

# SECTION IV

# SHIFTREGISTER SEQUENCES AND RELATED TOPICS

# ON FUNCTIONS OF LINEAR SHIFT REGISTER SEQUENCES*

Tore Herlestam

Dept. of Computer Engineering
University of Lund
P.O. Box 118
S-221 00 LUND, Sweden

and

Dept. of Signal Security
General Staff of Defense
Bankogårdsgatan 74
S-252 60 HELSINGBORG, Sweden

**Abstract**

This paper is intended as an overview, presenting several results on the linear complexity of sequences obtained from functions applied to linear shift register sequences. Especially for cryptologic applications it is of course highly desirable that the linear complexity be as large as possible, and not only to get a huge period. The theory reviewed in this paper contains several criteria on how to achieve such goals.

## 1. INTRODUCTION

In what follows we shall consider shift register sequences $(x_k)_{k\geq 0}$, over a finite field GF(q), q a prime power. Two well-known models for shift registers are in use. The Fibonacci model consists of cascaded memory boxes. The contents of each box is multiplied by a feedback coefficient before being taken to a common summing device to produce the feedback element. The feedback coefficients are numbered $c_1, c_2, ..., c_n$ from the feedback terminal.

In the Galois model adders are inserted between the memory boxes, the system output is multiplied by the feedback coefficients, numbered $c_1, c_2, ..., c_n$ from the output terminal, and the products are taken to the adders.

In both cases the same shift register recurrence is obtained:

$$x_k = c_1 x_{k-1} + c_2 x_{k-2} + \ldots + c_n x_{k-n}, \quad k \geq n.$$

Three different methods for handling this recurrence are in use. The linear algebraic (matrix) method is the most commonly used (e.g. Golomb (1967)), in particular in coding theory. Here the

*This research was supported in part by the National Swedish Board for Technical Development under grants 81-3323, 83-4364, and 85-3759 at the University of Lund.

state $(x_{k-1}, x_{k-2}, \ldots, x_{k-n})$ of the Fibonacci model is transformed by the next-state-function

$$\begin{pmatrix} x_k \\ x_{k-1} \\ \vdots \\ x_{k-n+1} \end{pmatrix} = \begin{pmatrix} c_1 & \ldots & c_{n-1} & c_n \\ 1 & \ldots & 0 & 0 \\ \vdots & \ddots & \vdots & \vdots \\ 0 & \ldots & 1 & 0 \end{pmatrix} \begin{pmatrix} x_{k-1} \\ x_{k-2} \\ \vdots \\ x_{k-n} \end{pmatrix}$$

most often written in the transposed form

$$(x_k, x_{k-1}, \ldots, x_{k-n+1}) = (x_{k-1}, x_{k-2}, \ldots, x_{k-n}) \begin{pmatrix} c_1 & 1 & \ldots & 0 \\ \vdots & \vdots & \ddots & \vdots \\ c_{n-1} & 0 & \ldots & 1 \\ c_n & 0 & \ldots & 0 \end{pmatrix}$$

by means of the so-called companion matrix. By iteration

$$\begin{pmatrix} x_{k-1} \\ x_{k-2} \\ \vdots \\ x_{k-n} \end{pmatrix} = \begin{pmatrix} c_1 & \ldots & c_{n-1} & c_n \\ 1 & \ldots & 0 & 0 \\ \vdots & \ddots & \vdots & \vdots \\ 0 & \ldots & 1 & 0 \end{pmatrix}^{k-n} \begin{pmatrix} x_{n-1} \\ x_{n-2} \\ \vdots \\ x_0 \end{pmatrix}$$

where $(x_{n-1}, x_{n-2}, ..., x_0)$ is the starting state of the Fibonacci model of the register.

A closely related finite automaton model is used by Nyffeler (1975).

Rewriting the shift register recurrence as a homogeneous linear difference equation

$$x_k - c_1 x_{k-1} - c_2 x_{k-2} - \ldots - c_n x_{k-n}, k \geq n,$$

we can apply the classical technique as used by Selmer (1966) and Key (1976) among others. Here the characteristic polynomial

$$c(t) = t^n - c_1 t^{n-1} - \ldots - c_n$$

plays a dominant role.

If the characteristic polynomial is factorized over its splitting field $\mathrm{GF}(q^s)$,

$$c(t) = \prod_j (t - z_j)^{m_j}, \; z_j \in \mathrm{GF}(q^s) \text{ with multiplicity } m_j ,$$

then the general solution of the difference equation can be written

$$x_k = \sum_{j,r} A_{jr} \binom{k+r-1}{r} z_j^k, \; A_{jr} \in \mathrm{GF}(q^s).$$

Note that, compared with difference or differential equations over the field of reals or the complex numbers, $\binom{k+r-1}{r}$ is used instead of $k^r$ in order to achieve linear independence over $\mathrm{GF}(q)$.

Finally, the generating function method, used by Zierler (1959), can be applied to the shift register recurrence. Here the feedback polynomial

$$f(t) = 1 - c_1 t - c_2 t^2 - \ldots - c_n t^n,$$

reciprocal to the characteristic polynomial, plays a major role. The shift register sequence $(x_k)_{k\geq 0}$, is identified with the formal power series

$$x(t) = \sum_{k=0}^{\infty} x_k t^k$$

and then the shift register equation is equivalent to

$$\mathrm{f}(t)x(t) = \mathrm{x}^*(t)$$

a polynomial of degree < deg f, so that

$$x(t) = \frac{\mathrm{x}^*(t)}{\mathrm{f}(t)},$$

a rational form over GF(q).

Note that $(x_0, x_1, \ldots, x_{n-1})$ is the starting state of the Fibonacci model, while $(x_0^*, x_1^*, \ldots, x_{n-1}^*)$ is the starting state of the Galois model.

Zierler also introduced the linear spaces over GF(q)

$$G(\mathrm{f}) = \{\, \mathrm{x}^*/\mathrm{f};\ \deg \mathrm{x}^* < \deg \mathrm{f}\},$$

consisting of all shift register sequences with f as feedback polynomial.

The rational forms $x=\mathrm{x}^*/\mathrm{f}$ are ideally suited to handle linear shift register sequences, e.g.

- f equals the minimum polynomial $\mathrm{f}_x$ of the sequence $x$ if and only if $\mathrm{x}^*$ and f are coprime, $\gcd(\mathrm{x}^*,\mathrm{f}) = 1$
- $x + y = \frac{\mathrm{x}^*}{\mathrm{f}} + \frac{\mathrm{y}^*}{\mathrm{g}} = \frac{\mathrm{z}^*}{\mathrm{lcm(f,g)}}$ implies that $\mathrm{f}_{x+y}$ divides lcm(f,g).

## 2. THE LINEAR COMPLEXITY CONCEPT

Given a periodic sequence $x$ over a finite field GF(q) we can always write it as

$$x(t) = \frac{\mathrm{g}(t)}{1 - t^{\mathrm{per}\,x}},$$

i.e. a linear shift register sequence. The length of the shortest possible linear shift register being able to produce the sequence, i.e. the degree of the minimum polynomial $\mathrm{f}_x$

$$\mathrm{L}(x) = \deg \mathrm{f}_x$$

is called the *linear complexity* of the sequence.

It is readily generalized by

$$\mathrm{L}(S) = \deg \mathrm{f}_S$$

to any finite set $S$ of periodic sequences.

The problem of determining the linear complexity of a given sequence is completely solved in practice by the well-known Berlekamp-Massey algorithm (Berlekamp (1968), Massey (1969)). However, when the linear complexity becomes very large or when we want to derive some nice criteria on how to obtain maximal complexity, another technique is needed.

Any memoryless function of a number of linear shift register sequences over GF(q) can be implemented by means of a function $F$ from $GF(q)^n$ to GF(q). Since GF(q) is finite, $F$ has to be a polynomial function

$$F(x) = \sum_{\underline{a}} A_{\underline{a}} x^{\underline{a}}, \quad A_{\underline{a}} = A_{a_1 a_2 \ldots a_n}, \quad x^{\underline{a}} = x_1^{a_1} x_2^{a_2} \ldots x_n^{a_n}$$

This is the algebraic normal form used by Müller (1954), Reed (1954) for q=2, and by Benjauthrit and Reed (1976) for general q.

Thus we have to study

1. $L(x+y)$ and $L(ax)$, $(x+y)_k = x_k + y_k$, $(ax)_k = ax_k$
2. $L(xy)$, $(xy)_k = x_k y_k$ (Hadamard product)
3. $L(x^a)$, $(x^a)_k = x_k^a$ (Hadamard power)

The simplest case is $L(ax)$. Defining the content

$$c(a)=0 \text{ when } a=0, =1 \text{ when } a \neq 0,$$

we find immediately

$$L(ax) = c(a)L(x).$$

For $x+y$ we have

**Theorem 2.1:** $L(x+y) \leq L(x)+L(y)$ with equality if and only if the minimum polynomials $f_x$ and $f_y$ are coprime i.e. $\gcd(f_x,f_y)=1$.

**Corollary 2.2:** $L(G(f)+G(g)) \leq L(G(f)) + L(G(g))$ with equality if and only if f and g are coprime i.e. gcd(f,g)=1.

## 3. THE COMPLEXITY OF THE HADAMARD PRODUCT

The Hadamard product was first considered by Selmer (1966). When $f(t) = \prod_u (1-\frac{t}{u})$, $g(t) = \prod_v (1-\frac{t}{v})$ with mere simple zeroes, Selmer defined $f§g = \prod_{u,v}(1-\frac{t}{uv})$ and showed

**Theorem 3.1:** Assuming $x$ belongs to $G(f)$, $y$ to $G(g)$ then $xy$ belongs to $G(f§g)$. Further, if f and g are prime (irreducible) then f§g is prime too.

**Corollary 3.2:** If f and g are prime then $f_{xy} = f§g$.

Note the analogy with Hadamard's well-known theorem for analytic functions:

If $\sum_{n=0}^{\infty} a_n z^n$, $\sum_{n=0}^{\infty} a_n z^n$ are analytic around the origin with singularities in the points $z_j(a)$, $1 \le j \le r$ , $z_k(b)$, $1 \le k \le s$, then the Hadamard product $\sum_{n=0}^{\infty} a_n b_n z^n$ has all its singularities at the points $z_j(a)z_k(b)$, $1 \le j \le r$, $1 \le k \le s$.

Zierler and Mills (1973) defined f$\vee$g = f§g when f and g have mere simple zeroes and transferred it to the general case by means of an algebraic algorithm, utilizing the prime factorizations of f and g. No bounds on deg f$\vee$g or conditions for maximality were given.

*Remark.* Zierler and Mills used $\vee$ although it has nothing in common with the logical OR.

Herlestam (1977, 1982) defined f$\wedge$g as the minimum polynomial of

$$G(\mathrm{f})G(\mathrm{g}) = \{\ xy;\ x \text{ in } G(\mathrm{f}),\ y \text{ in } G(\mathrm{g})\ \}$$

and showed

**Theorem 3.3:** deg f$\wedge$g $\le$ deg f $\cdot$ deg g with equality if and only if at least one of f and g has mere simple zeroes and all the zero products $z(\mathrm{f})z(\mathrm{g})$ are different.

**Corollary 3.4:** If f and g are prime and of coprime degrees then deg f$\wedge$g = deg f $\cdot$ deg g.

(Selmer (1966): in this case f$\wedge$g is prime.)

**Corollary 3.5:** $\mathrm{L}(xy) \le \mathrm{L}(x)\mathrm{L}(y)$ with equality if and only if at least one of $\mathrm{f}_x$ and $\mathrm{f}_y$ has mere simple zeroes and all the zero products $z(\mathrm{f}_x)z(\mathrm{f}_y)$ are different.

**Corollary 3.6:** If $\mathrm{f}_x$ and $\mathrm{f}_y$ are prime and of coprime degrees then $\mathrm{L}(xy) = \mathrm{L}(x)\mathrm{L}(y)$.

(Selmer (1966): in this case $\mathrm{f}_{xy}$ is prime.)

*Remark.* Using the classical approach when q=2 and $\mathrm{f}_x$ and $\mathrm{f}_y$ prime and of coprime degrees, Key (1976) proved Corollary 3.6.

The period of a sequence $x \ne 0$ in $G(\mathrm{f})$ is trivially upperbounded

$$\text{per } x \le \mathrm{q}^{\deg \mathrm{f}} - 1.$$

When equality is attained $x$ is called a maximum length sequence (ML for short). The period of a feedback polynomial is defined by

$$\text{per f} = \min r \text{ for which } \mathrm{f}(t) \text{ divides } 1 - t^r.$$

Apparently per $x$ = per $\mathrm{f}_x$ so if $x$ is ML then all $x \ne 0$ in $G(\mathrm{f})$ are ML and

$$\text{per f} = \mathrm{q}^{\deg \mathrm{f}} - 1.$$

In this case f is called a maximum length polynomial (ML for short). Many authors use 'primitive polynomial' instead of ML-polynomial (but not 'primitive sequence' instead of ML-sequence !).

## 4. THE POWER FUNCTION

The power function $x^a$ is of interest only when q>2 since $u^2=u$ holds in GF(2). If $a \geq$q it can be reduced by means of $u^q=u$ in GF(q). Thus we may assume $0 \leq a <$q.

Since q is a prime power, q=$p^e$, we can proceed by writing $a$ in the p-ary number system

$$a = a_0 + a_1 p + a_2 p^2 + \ldots + a_{e-1} p^{e-1},$$

where the digits $a_i$ are $\geq 0$ and <p.

In order to handle a power of a shift register sequence we may use the well-known multinomial formula (see e.g. Tucker (1980))

$$(\sum_{j=1}^{n} X_j)^s = \sum_{\underline{u}} \frac{s!}{u_1! \ldots u_n!} X_1^{u_1} \ldots X_n^{u_n}$$

summed over all nonnegative solutions $\underline{u}$ of $\sum_i u_i = s$.

Note that $\frac{s!}{u_1! \ldots u_n!}$ should be interpreted by first considering it over the integers, then reducing it modulo the characteristic of the field.

Utilizing this multinomial formula Herlestam (1982 and later) derived the following results.

**Theorem 4.1:** If $0 \leq a <$q, $a = \sum_{i=0}^{e-1} a_i p^i$, $0 \leq a_i < p$, q=$p^e$, then

$$L(x^a) \leq \prod_i \binom{L(x) + a_i - 1}{a_i}$$

with equality if $x$ is a ML-sequence. In particular, when p=2,

$$L(x^a) \leq L(x)^{H(a)},$$

where $H(a)$ is the Hamming weight of $a$ and where equality holds if $x$ is a ML-sequence.

(Brynielsson (1985): equality in the ML-case).

Now we have at our disposal all the components for handling any function of any finite number of shift register sequences. In the general case it may of course be quite hard to guarantee that maximal complexity be attained, but in many instances this can be achieved.

The following case is closely connected with the power function. Let $x_1, x_2, \ldots, x_s$ be a number of different shift register sequences with the same feedback polynominal f. The power function technique yields

$$L(x_1, x_2, \ldots, x_s) \leq \binom{\deg f + s - 1}{s},$$

a not particularly good estimate however. Instead, Herlestam (1983) derived the following

**Theorem 4.2:** Assume $f$ prime over GF(q) and that $x_1, x_2, \ldots, x_s$, all $\neq 0$, be shift register sequences with f as feedback polynomial so that $L(x_i)$=L=deg f. Further, let $x_1, x_2, \ldots, x_s = y$. Then

1. $L(y) \leq A_q(L,s) = \sum_{k=1}^{s} c_q(s,k)\binom{L}{k}$, where

$$c_q(s,k) = \sum_{r=0}^{k-1}(-1)^r\binom{k-1}{r}\binom{s-r(q-1)-1}{k-1}$$

so that $A_q(L,s) = \sum_{j=0}^{s-1}(-1)^j\binom{s-j(q-1)-1}{j}\binom{L+s-jq-1}{L-j-1}$

2. if g is a prime factor of $f_y$ then deg g divides deg $f_y$.

In particular, when $s < q$, $A_q(L,s) = \binom{L+s-1}{s}$

and when q=2, $A_2(L,s) = \sum_{k=1}^{s}\binom{L}{k}$.

*Remark.* In the case of nonlinear feedforward, where q=2 and f a ML-polynomial, this result was stated without proof by Ristenbatt et al. (1973) and obtained later by Key (1976).

## 5. NONLINEAR FEEDFORWARD

The GF(2) case has been investigated by Groth (1971), Key (1976), Jennings (1980), Beker and Piper (1982), Rueppel (1984).

In the GF(q) case Herlestam (1983) derived

**Theorem 5.1:** Assume that f is prime over GF(q) and that $x_i$, $1 \leq i \leq s \leq$ deg f, are sequences taken from different taps in a linear shift register with f as feedback polynomial. Let $y = x_1, x_2, \ldots, x_s$. Then

1. L($y$) is independent of the starting state
2. if g is a prime factor of $f_y$ then deg g divides deg $f_y$ so if deg $f_y$ is prime then $f_y$ must be prime unless it has a first-degree factor
3. all zeroes of $f_y$ are simple and belong to the set

$$S = \{\prod_i z_i^{w_i};\quad \sum_i w_i = s;\quad w_i \geq 0;\quad f(z_i) = 0\}.$$

Lower bounds on the linear complexity have been obtained by Rueppel (1984) in the GF(2) case for some special classes of feedforward functions.

## 6. SOME SKETCHES OF PROOFS

**Th. 2.1:** From $f_{x+y} | \mathrm{lcm}(f_x,f_y) \mid f_x f_y$ it follows that $L(x+y) \leq L(x)+L(y)$. If $\gcd(f_x,f_y)=1$ and g | $f_x f_y$, g prime, then g | $f_x$ or g | $f_y$ but not both so assume g | $f_x$. Should $L(x+y) < L(x)+L(y)$ then g | $(x^* f_y + y^* f_x)$ i.e. g | $x^* f_y$. Since $\gcd(g,f_y)=1$ this implies g | $x^*$, against the minimality of $f_x$.

Conversely, if gcd($f_x$,$f_y$)=h, deg h > 0, then h | ($x^*f_x+y^*f_y$), implying $L(x+y) < L(x)+L(y)$.

**Th. 3.3:** If f and g are feedback polynomials over GF(q) so that

$$f(t) = \prod (1 - \frac{t}{z_i(f)})^{m_i(f)}, \quad g(t) = \prod (1 - \frac{t}{z_j(g)})^{m_j(g)}$$

over a common splitting field GF($q^e$), and if $x=x^*/f$, $y=y^*/g$, then the partial fractions expansions are

$$x = \sum_{i=0}^{n(f)-1} \sum_{r=0}^{m_i(f)-1} A_{ir}(1 - \frac{t}{z_i(f)})^{-r-1}, y = \sum_{j=0}^{n(g)-1} \sum_{s=0}^{m_j(g)-1} B_{js}(1 - \frac{t}{z_j(g)})^{-s-1}$$

By means of the binomial formal power series

$$(1-t)^{-a-1} = \sum_{k=0}^{\infty} \binom{a+k}{k} t^k$$

it follows that

$$x_k y_k = \sum_{i,r,j,s} A_{ir} B_{js} \binom{r+k}{k} \binom{s+k}{k} (z_i(f) z_j(g))^{-k},$$

As is easily shown

$$\binom{r+k}{k} \binom{s+k}{k} = \sum_m d_m(r,s) \binom{m+k}{k},$$

where $\max(r,s) \le m \le r+s$, and the integers $d_m(r,s)$ are independent of k. This shows that, over GF($q^e$), $xy$ is a partial fractions expansion of a rational form, the denominator of which has the zeroes $z_i(f)z_j(g)$ of multiplicity $\le m_i(f)+m_j(g)-1$.

Using the power sums of the roots to show that some polynomials over GF($q^e$) are in fact polynomials over GF(q), it follows that deg $f_{xy} \le$ deg f$\cdot$ deg g, and, after some further manipulations, the theorem follows.

**Th. 4.1:** When the characteristic coincides with the exponent the multinomial formula is particularly simple

$$(\sum X_j)^p = \sum X_j^p$$

since all multinomial coefficients $\neq 1$ are divisible by p.

By iteration

$$(\sum X_j)^{p^i} = \sum X_j^{p^i}$$

When $0 \le a < p$,

$$(\sum X_j)^a = \sum_{\underline{u}} \frac{a!}{u_1! \ldots u_n!} X_1^{u_1} X_2^{u_2} \ldots X_n^{u_n}$$

where all the coefficients are $\neq 0$ since $a!$ cannot be divisible by p. Applied to an arbitrary element

$$x_k = \sum_{i,r} A_{ir} \binom{r+k}{k} z_i^{-k}$$

of a shift register sequence, one obtains for each term in the p-ary representation $a = \sum_i a_i p^i$ the inequality

$$\deg f_{x^{a_i p^i}} \leq \binom{L(x) + a_i - 1}{a_i}$$

and finally, by Th. 3.3,

$$\deg f_{x^a} \leq \prod \binom{L(x) + a_i - 1}{a_i}$$

The clause on equality follows from the facts that if $x$ is a maximum length sequence, the zeroes of $f_x$ can be written as

$$z^{q^i}, 0 \leq i < L(x),$$

where $z$ is a primitive ($q^n$-1)-st root of unity, and that the q-ary representation of a number is unique.

**Th. 4.2:** Assume first that $x_1, x_2, \ldots, x_s$ are ML-sequences so that

$$x_i = x_i^*/f = \sum_{j=1}^{n} \frac{A_{ij}}{1 - t/z_j}$$

where all $A_{ij}$'s are nonzero. Thus

$$x_{ik} = \sum_{\underline{u}} A(\underline{u})(\underline{z}^{\underline{u}})^{-k}$$

where the summing interval is the set of all nonnegative solutions $\underline{u}$ of $\sum_j u_j = s$, and

$$A(\underline{u}) = \sum_{\underline{j}} \prod_{i=1}^{s} A_{ij_i}$$

summed over all permutations $\underline{j}$ of $u_1$ 1's, $u_2$ 2's,..., $u_s$ s's. The minimum polynomial $f_y$ cannot have any multiple zeroes, since the coefficients $A(\underline{u})$ are independent of $k$.

The zeroes of f can be written $z_j = z^{q^j}$ where $z$ is a primitive ($q^n$-1)-st root of unity and

$$\underline{z}^{\underline{u}} = z^a, \quad 0 \leq a < q^n - 1,$$

where $\sum_j u_j q^j = a \pmod{q^n - 1}$, $\underline{u}$ being a partition of $s = \sum_j u_j$, $u_j \geq 0$.

Let $A_q(n, s)$ denote the number of $a$'s obtainable this way. It can also be described as the number of q-ary $n$-strings

$$a = \sum_{j=0}^{n-1} a_j q^j, \text{ not all } a_j = 0$$

such that $\sum_{j=0}^{n-1} a_j = s - k(q-1)$, $0 \leq k < s/(q-1)$. This leads rather quickly to the form

$$A_q(n,s) = \sum_{k=1}^{s} c_q(s,k)\binom{n}{k}$$

where the integers $c_q(s,k)$ are independent of $n$ and

$$c_q(s,k) = \sum_{j=1}^{q-1} c_q(s-j,k-1)\,, \quad c_q(s,1) = c_q(s,s) = 1.$$

When f is prime only, per f divides $q^n$-1 and $z$ is a primitive root of unity of order per f. Hence the number of different $(\underline{z}^{\underline{u}})$'s must still be $\leq A_q(n,s)$.

The clause on a prime factor of $f_y$ follows quite easily from the fact that per $f_y$ divides per f.

**Th. 5.1:** Follows from

$$x_i^*(t) = t^{e_i} x^*(t) \qquad (\text{mod } f(t)),$$

where $x^*$ is associated solely with the starting state and the exponent $e_i \geq 0$ with the position of the tap from which $x_i$ is taken.

### Acknowledgement

The author wants to express his deep gratitude to Prof J. L. Massey and Prof R. Johannesson for many fruitful discussions on the subject.

### SOME SELECTED REFERENCES (in chronological order)

L. Fibonacci, *Liber Abaci*, 1202

E. Galois, "Sur la theorie des nombres", Bull. Sci. Math. de M. Ferussac, 1830; J. Math. Pures Appl., 1846

L. Kronecker, *Werke Bd. 2*, pp. 146-149, 1881

D. E. Müller, "Application of Boolean Algebra to Switching Circuit Design and to Error Detection", IRE Trans. on Electron, Comp., 1954

I. S, Reed, "A Class of Error Correcting Codes and the Decoding Scheme", IRE Trans. on Electron. Comp., 1954

N. Zierler, "Linear Recurring Sequences", J. SIAM, 1959; also in W. H. Kautz, *Linear Sequential Switching Circuits*, Holden-Day, San Francisco, 1965

E. S. Selmer, *Linear Recurrence Relations over Finite Fields*, Univ. of Bergen, Norway, 1966

B. L. van der Waerden, *Algebra I*, Springer, Berlin, 1966

S. W. Golomb, *Shift Register Sequences*, Holden-Day, San Francisco, 1967

E. R. Berlekamp, *Algebraic Coding Theory*, McGraw-Hill, New York, 1968

J. L. Massey, "Shift-Register Synthesis and BCH Decoding", IEEE Trans on Inform. Th., 1969

E. J. Groth, "Generation of Binary Sequences with Controllable Complexity", IEEE Trans. on Inform. Th., 1971

N. Zierler and W. H. Mills, "Products of Linear Recurring Sequences", J. Algebra, 1973

M. P. Ristenbatt et al., "Crack-Resistant Sequences for Data Security", IEEE Nat. Telecomm. Conf., 1973

P. R. Geffe, "How to Protect Data with Ciphers That Are Really Hard to Break", Electronics, 1973

P. Nyffeler, *Binäre Automaten und ihren linearen Rekursionen*, Ph.D. Thesis, Bern, 1975

B. Benjauthrit and I. S. Reed, "Galois Switching Functions and Their Applications", IEEE Trans. on Comp., 1976

E. L. Key, "An Analysis of the Structure and Complexity of Nonlinear Binary Sequences Generators", IEEE Trans. on Inform. Th., 1976

K. P. Yiu and R. B. Ward, "A Method for Deciphering a Maximal-Length Sequence", Proc. IEEE, 1977

T. Herlestam, "On Linearization of Nonlinear Combinations of Linear Shift Register Sequences", IEEE ISIT, Ithaca, New York, 1977

H. Lüneburg, *Galoisfelder, Kreisteilungskörper und Schieberegisterfolgen*, Bibliogr. Inst., Zürich, 1979

A. Tucker, *Applied Combinatorics*, Wiley, New York, 1980

S. M. Jennings, *A Special Class of Binary Sequences*, Ph.D. Thesis, London, 1980

T. Herlestam, "On Using Prime Polynomials in Crypto Generators", in *Cryptography, Proc. Burg Feuerstein, 1982*, ed. by T. Beth, Springer, Berlin, 1983

T. Herlestam, "On the Complexity of Functions of Linear Shift Register Sequences", IEEE ISIT, Les Arcs, France, 1982

H. Beker and F. Piper, *Cipher Systems*, Northwood Publ., London, 1982

R. Lidl and H. Niederreiter, *Finite Fields*, Encycl. Math. and Its Appl. Vol. 20, Addison-Wesley, 1983

T. Herlestam, "On the Complexity of Certain Crypto Generators", in *security, IFIP/sec'83*, ed. by V. Fåk, North-Holland, 1983

R. Rueppel, *New Approaches to Stream Ciphers*, Ph.D. Thesis, Zürich, 1984

L. Brynielsson, "On the Linear Complexity of Combined Shift Register Sequences", Eurocrypt 85, Linz, Austria, 1985

# ON FEEDFORWARD TRANSFORMS AND p-FOLD PERIODIC p-ARRAYS

Dong-sheng Chen
Graduate School
Academia Sinica
Beijing China

Zong-duo Dai
Institute of Math.
Academia Sinica
Beijing, China

Abstract

In this paper we discuss non-linear feedforward transforms of arbitrary non-singular linear shift register sequences. The approach is to give an algebraic representation of p-array modules together with description of the structure of such modules. On the basis of this, an algebraic description of the non-linear transformas is given.

## I. Introduction

Let

$$u_i=(u_i(0),\ u_i(1),\ldots\ldots,u_i(j),\ldots\ldots)\qquad 1\leqslant i\leqslant p \tag{1}$$

be binary periodic sequences with periods $T_i$, and $n_i$ be the degrees of the minimal generating polynomials $f_i(x)$ of $u_i$. Consider an arbitrary Boolean function

$$\phi(x_{11},\ldots,x_{1n_1},\ldots,x_{p1},\ldots,x_{pn_p})=\sum_{0\leqslant s<n} a_{s_1,\ldots,s_p}\, x_{1s_1}\ldots x_{ps_p} \tag{2}$$

put

$$u(j)=\sum_{0\leqslant s_i<n_i} a_{s_1\ldots s_p}\, u_1(j-s_1)\ldots u_p(j-s_p)$$

$$u=(u(0),u(1),\ldots,u(j),\ldots) \tag{3}$$

then u is called feedforward sequence of $u_i$ $(1\leqslant i\leqslant p)$ defined by the feedforward transform $\phi$ .

The problem we enface is of a twofold character, namely, to analyse the structure of the sequence u given the transform $\phi$ and to determine the transform $\phi$ given the sequence u.

A p-array u is defined to be a mapping from $I^p$ to the binary field $F_2$ where I is the set of nonnegative integers, $I^p=\{(i_1,\ldots,i_p)\,|\,i_j\in I\}$.

A p-fold p-array (i.e. p.p-array) is defined to be a p-array u with $T_i \in I$ $(1 \leq i \leq p)$, such that $u(T_i e_i + \bar{j}) = u(\bar{j})$, $\forall \bar{j} \in I^p$, where $e_i = (0\ldots0\underset{i}{1}0\ldots0) \in I^p$.

Set

$$\mathcal{M}_p = \{v \mid v \text{ is a p.p-array}\}, \quad R = F_2[x_1, \ldots, x_p]$$

For any $v$, $v_i \in \mathcal{M}_p$, $f \in R$, $f = \sum a_{\bar{s}} \bar{x}^{\bar{s}}$, the operations

$$(v_1 + v_2)(\bar{j}) = v_1(\bar{j}) + v_2(\bar{j}), \quad (fv)(\bar{j}) = \sum a_{\bar{s}} v(\bar{j} - \bar{s})$$

introduce in $\mathcal{M}_p$ a structure of an R-module.

A product p-array $w = u_1 \times \ldots \times u_p$ $(u_i \in \mathcal{M}_1)$ is defined to be a p-array such that $w(j_1, \ldots, j_p) = \prod_{i=1}^{p} u_i(j_i)$, $\forall (j_1, \ldots, j_p) \in I^p$. It is obvious that $w \in \mathcal{M}_p$.

Operator $\pi$ is defined to be a mapping from $\mathcal{M}_p$ to $\mathcal{M}_1$ such that $(\pi v)(j) = v(\bar{j})$, $\forall v \in \mathcal{M}_p$, $\bar{j} = (j, \ldots, j) \in I^p$.

Let $u_i$ be as in (1), $w = u_1 \times \ldots \times u_p$, $a_{s_1 \ldots s_p}$ be as in (2), $f = \sum a_{s_1 \ldots s_p} x_1^{s_1} \ldots x_p^{s_p}$ and u be as in (3). It is easy to see $\pi f w = u$. So the problem of determing $\phi$ and u from each other is thus reduced to the problem of solving the equation $\pi f w = u$ for u or f.

The approach is to analyse the structure of the module $\langle w \rangle$ (the R-module generated by w). In [1], using languages of algebraic geometry, A.A.Grigoriev discussed the equation $\pi f w = u$ for the case where the minimal generating polynomial of $u_i$ have no multiple factors. In this paper, relying on an algebraic representation of R-module $\mathcal{M}_p$, we'll discuss the equation $\pi f w = u$ without any restriction on $u_i$.

For the limitation of space, in this paper we omit proofs of Theorems.

## II. Algebraic representations of the modules

If $u = (u(0), u(1), \ldots, u(j), \ldots) \in \mathcal{M}_p$ with period T, then its generating function is

$$A(u) = \sum_{i=0}^{\infty} u(i) x^i = \frac{A_0(x)}{1 - x^T} = \frac{h(x)}{f(x)}, \tag{4}$$

where $A_0(x) = \sum_{0 \leq i < T} u(i) x^i$, $(h, f) = 1$, $\deg[h] < \deg[f]$, $f(0) = 1$. f(x) is called the minimal generating polynomial of u . Similarly, if $u \in \mathcal{M}_p$, Its generating function is

$$A(x) = \sum_{0 \leq j_i < \infty} u(j_1 \ldots j_p) x_1^{j_1} \ldots x_p^{j_p} = \frac{A_0(x)}{(1 - x_1^{T_1}) \ldots (1 - x_p^{T_p})}$$

where $A_0(x) = \sum_{0 \leq j_i < T_i} u(j_1 \ldots j_p) x_1^{j_1} \ldots x_p^{j_p}$. In particular, for product p.p-array $w = u_1 \times \ldots \times u_p$. its generating function is

$$A(w) = \prod_{i=1}^{p} \frac{h_i(x_i)}{f_i(x_i)} \tag{5}$$

where $A(u_i)=\frac{h_i(x)}{f_i(x)}$ as in (4).

Set

$$\mathcal{A}_p=\{\frac{G}{F}|\, G,F\in R, F=\prod_{i=1}^{p} f_i(x_i),\ f_i(0)=1,\ \deg_i[G]<\deg_i[F]\} \tag{6}$$

Let $\frac{G}{F}$ be as in (6), write

$$I_F=(f_1(x_1),\dots,f_p(x_p)) \tag{7}$$

(the ideal generated by $f(x)$). $\mathcal{A}_p$ is an additive subgroup of $F_2(x_1,\dots,x_p)$. For any $f\in R$, $\frac{G}{F}\in\mathcal{A}_p$, the operation

$$f\,\frac{G}{F}=\frac{G_1}{F} \tag{8}$$

where $G_1\equiv fG \pmod{I_F}$, $\deg_i[G_1]<\deg_i[F]$, $\forall i$, introduce in additive group $\mathcal{A}_p$ a structure of an R-module.

Theorem 1 The mapping $u\mapsto A(u)$ is a module isomorphism from $\mathcal{M}_p$ onto $\mathcal{A}_p$.

By Thm.1, we can identify u with A(u).

## III. Structure of p.p-array modules.

For $v\in\mathcal{M}_p$, let $\mathrm{Ann}_R\langle v\rangle=\{f|\,fv=0,\ f\in R\}$. Let $\frac{G}{F}$ as in (6), $I_F$ as in (7). It is easy to see that 1) $\mathrm{Ann}_R\langle\frac{G}{F}\rangle=(I_F:G)$, 2) if $(G,I_F)=R$, then $\langle\frac{G}{F}\rangle=\langle\frac{1}{F}\rangle$, 3) $\dim_{F_2}\langle\frac{1}{F}\rangle=\prod_{i=1}^{p}\deg[f_i(x_i)]$.

If $w=u_1\times\dots\times u_p$, and $u_i$ have powers of irreducible polynomials as their minimal generating polynomials, we call w as a standard product p.p-array. Let w be an arbitrary product p.p-array, it is easy to see that $w=\sum_{j=1}^{m} w_j$, $w=\oplus\langle w_j\rangle$, where $w_j$ are standard product p.p-arrays, and can calculate $\mu_j(x)\in R$, such that $w_j=\mu_j(\bar{x})w$.

By the above, w.l.g., we only consider standard product p.p-arrays w as in (5), and

$$f_i(x)=p_i(x)^{1+t_i},\qquad \frac{h_i(x)}{p_i(x)}=\sum_{j=1}^{p}\frac{\lambda_i^{2^j}}{(1-\theta_i^{2^j}x)^{1+t_i}} \tag{9}$$

where $p_i(x)$ are irreducible, $p_i(0)=1$, $t_i\geq 0$, $\theta_i$ is one of the roots of $p_i(x)$, $n_i=\deg[p_i]$, $\lambda_i\in F_2(\theta_i)$.

Before stating Theorem 2, we make some preparations. Let $N=[n_1,\dots,n_p]$, then $F_{2^N}=F_2(\theta_1,\dots,\theta_p)$. Let $V=\{(\theta_1^{2^{j_1}}\dots\theta_p^{2^{j_p}})\,|\,0\leq j_i<n_i\}$. For any $\bar\theta$, $\bar\theta'\in V$, we say $\bar\theta=(\theta_1^{2^{j_1}},\dots,\theta_p^{2^{j_p}})$ is conjugate to $\bar\theta'$, if $\exists$ $\sigma\in \mathrm{Gal}\,F_{2^N}/F_2$, such that $(\sigma\theta_1^{j_1},\dots,\sigma\theta_p^{j_p})=\bar\theta'$. Let $r_1=1$,

$r_i=([n_1,\dots,n_{i-1}],\ n_i)$, $2\le i\le p$. For any $\bar{j}=(j_1,\dots,j_p)$, $\{\bar{\theta}_{\bar{j}+k\bar{1}}\ |\ 0\le k<N$, $\bar{\theta}_{\bar{j}+k\bar{1}}=(\theta_1^{2^{j_1+k}},\dots,\theta_p^{2^{j_p+k}})\}$ is a complete conjugate class in V. Write $Z_{r_1,\dots,r_p}=\{\bar{j}\,|\,\bar{j}=(j_1,\dots,j_p),\ 0\le j_i<r_i\}$. It is known that V is the union of $\{\bar{\theta}_{\bar{j}+k\bar{1}}\ |\ 0\le K<N\}$, $\bar{j}\in Z_{r_1,\dots,r_p}$. Let $f(\bar{x})=\Sigma\, a_{\bar{s}}\bar{x}^{\bar{s}}\in R$, define $f^{\bar{k}}(\bar{x})=$ $=\Sigma\, a_{\bar{s}}\binom{\bar{s}}{\bar{k}}\bar{x}^{\bar{s}}$, where $\bar{s}=(s_1,\dots,s_p)$, $\bar{x}^{\bar{s}}=x_1^{s_1}\dots x_p^{s_p}$, $\bar{k}=(k_1,\dots,k_p)$, $\binom{\bar{s}}{\bar{k}}=$ $=\prod_{i=1}^{p}\binom{s_i}{k_i}$. For any i, let $\{e_j(i)\,|\,0\le j<n_i\}$ be the duel base of $\{\theta_i^j\ |\ 0\le j<n_i\}$.

Theorem 2 Let w be as in (5) and (9), $I_F$ as in (7). Then

1.
$$w=\sum_{\bar{j}\in Z_{r_1,\dots,r_p}} u(\bar{\theta}_{\bar{j}},\bar{t},\lambda_{\bar{j}}),\ \text{where } u(\bar{\theta}_{\bar{j}},\bar{t},\lambda_{\bar{j}})=\sum_{0\le K<N}\frac{\lambda_{\bar{j}}^{2^k}}{\prod_{i=1}^{p}(1-\theta_i^{2^{j_i+k}}x_i)^{1+t_i}},$$

$$\bar{j}=(j_1,\dots,j_p),\ \lambda_{\bar{j}}=\prod_{i=1}^{p}\lambda_i^{2^{j_i}},\ \bar{t}=(t_1,\dots,t_p).$$

2. **Let n be any integer with** $2^n\ge 1+\Sigma\, t_i$. Take

$$e_{\bar{j}}(\bar{x})=\sum_{0\le i_k<n_i}\mathrm{Tr}_{F_{2^N}/F_2}(e_{i_1}(1)e_{i_2}(2)^{2^{j_2}}\dots e_{i_p}(p)^{2^{j_p}})x^{i_1}x^{i_2}\dots x^{i_p}$$

$$\varepsilon_{\bar{j}}(\bar{x})=e_{\bar{j}}(\bar{x})^{2^n}\qquad (\mathrm{mod}\ I_F).$$

Then $u(\bar{\theta}_{\bar{j}},\bar{t},\lambda_{\bar{j}})=\varepsilon_{\bar{j}}(\bar{x})w$.

3. $$\langle w\rangle=\bigoplus_{j\in Z_{r_1,\dots,r_p}}\langle u(\bar{\theta}_{\bar{j}},\bar{t},\lambda_{\bar{j}})\rangle.$$

4. $f.u(\bar{\theta}_{\bar{j}},\bar{t},\lambda)=\sum_{\bar{0}\le \bar{k}\le\bar{t}} u(\bar{\theta}_{\bar{j}},\bar{t}-\bar{k},\lambda f^{\bar{k}}(\bar{\theta}_{\bar{j}}^{-1}))$, where $\bar{\theta}_{\bar{j}}^{-1}=(\theta_1^{-2^{j_1}},\dots,\theta_p^{-2^{j_p}})$.

5. $\langle u(\bar{\theta},\bar{t},\lambda)\rangle=\langle u(\bar{\theta},\bar{t},1)\rangle=\{\sum_{\bar{0}\le\bar{k}\le\bar{t}} u(\bar{\theta},\bar{k},\alpha_{\bar{k}})\,|\,\alpha_{\bar{k}}\in F_{2^N}\}$

where $\lambda\ne 0\in F_{2^N}$ and $\sum_{\bar{0}\le\bar{k}\le\bar{t}} u(\bar{\theta},\bar{k},\alpha_{\bar{k}})=0$ iff. $\alpha=0$, $\forall\bar{k}$.

6. $\mathrm{Ann}_R\langle u(\bar{\theta}_{\bar{j}},\bar{t},1)\rangle=(I_F,1-\varepsilon_{\bar{j}}(\bar{x}))$.

## IV The operator $\pi$

First we make some conventions. Let $S=\{\rho_{\bar{j}}\,|\,\rho_{\bar{j}}=\prod_{i=1}^{p}\theta_i^{2^{j_i}},\ \bar{j}\in Z_{r_1,\dots,r_p}\}$ Let $Z'_{r_1,\dots,r_p}\subset Z_{r_1,\dots,r_p}$, and $\{\rho_{\bar{j}}\,|\,\bar{j}\in Z'_{r_1,\dots,r_p}\}$ be a complete set of representatives of the conjugate classes over $F_2$ in S. Let $q_{\bar{j}}(x)$ be an irreducible polynomial with $\rho_{\bar{j}}$ being a root. If $k=\Sigma k_i 2^i$, $j=\Sigma\, j_i 2^i$, $k_i$, $j_i=0$ or 1, define $k\vee j=\Sigma(k_i\vee j_i)2^i$, $k\vee j\vee m=(k\vee j)\vee m$ and so on.

Let $V_{\bar{t}} = t_1 \vee t_2 \vee \ldots \vee t_p$, $L_{\bar{t}} = \max\limits_{\bar{0} \leq \bar{k} \leq \bar{t}} V_{\bar{k}}$. It is known that $L_{\bar{t}} = -1 + 2^{\bar{j}_0} + \sum\limits_{j \geq j_0} (\sum\limits_{i=1}^{p} t_{ij}) 2^{j}$,
where $t_i = \sum t_{ij} 2^j$, $t = 0$ or $1$, $j_0$ is the smallest integer such that
$\sum\limits_{i=1}^{p} t_{ij} < 2$, $\forall j \geq j_0$.

Theorem 4. (The notations being as above)

1. $\pi u(\bar{\theta}_{\bar{J}}, \bar{t}, \lambda) = u(\rho_{\bar{J}}, V\bar{t}, Tr_{F_{2^N}/F_2(\rho_{\bar{J}})}(\lambda))$
2. $\pi\langle u(\bar{\theta}_{\bar{J}}, \bar{t}, \lambda)\rangle = \langle u(\rho_{\bar{J}}, L_{\bar{t}}, 1)\rangle$
3. $\pi\langle w\rangle = \pi(\bigoplus\limits_{\bar{j} \in Z'_{r_1, \ldots, r_p}} \langle u(\bar{\theta}_{\bar{j}}, \bar{t}, \lambda_{\bar{j}})\rangle) = \bigoplus\limits_{\bar{j} \in Z'_{r_1, \ldots, r_p}} \langle u(\rho_{\bar{j}}, L_{\bar{t}}, 1)\rangle =$

$$= \langle \frac{1}{H(x)^{1+L_{\bar{t}}}} \rangle, \text{ where } H(x) = \prod_{\bar{j} \in Z'_{r_1, \ldots, r_p}} q_{\bar{j}}(x)$$

V. The equation $\pi fw = u$.

From the above, it is not difficult to see that the equation $\pi fw = u$ could be reduced to the two kinds of algebraic equations:

1. For any $\alpha \in F(\rho)$, $\rho \in F_{2^N}$, to find y such that

$$Tr_{F_{2^N}/F_2(\rho)}(y) = \alpha$$

2. For $\beta_{\bar{k}} \in F_{2^N}$, $\bar{0} \leq \bar{k} \leq \bar{t}$, to find $f(\bar{x}) \in R$, such that

$$f^{\bar{k}}(\theta_1^{-1}, \ldots, \theta_p^{-1}) = \beta_{\bar{k}} \qquad \bar{0} \leq \bar{k} \leq \bar{t}, \forall \bar{k} \tag{10}$$

By the Theorem 2, there exists unique $f(x) \bmod (Ann_R \langle u(\theta, t, 1)\rangle)$, satisfying (10).

References

1. A.A.Grigoriev, Problems of Control and Information Theory Vol. 9(4) (1980).
2. Neal Zievler and W.H.Mills, J.Algebra, 27.(1973).
3. 陶仁骥, 有限自动机的可逆性, 科学出版社.

# GENERALIZED MULTIPLEXED SEQUENCES

Mu-lan Liu and Zhe-xian Wan
Institute of Systems Science, Academia Sinica
Beijing, 100080 China

## 1. Introduction

Let $LSR_1, LSR_2, \ldots, LSR_k$ and LSR be k+1 linear feedback shift registers with characteristic polynomials $f_1(x), f_2(x), \ldots, f_k(x)$ and $g(x)$ over $\mathbb{F}_2$ and output sequences $\underline{a}_1, \underline{a}_2, \ldots, \underline{a}_k$ and $\underline{b}$ respectively, where $\underline{a}_i=(a_{io}, a_{i1}, \ldots)$, $i=1,2,\ldots,k$, $\underline{b}=(b_o, b_1, \ldots)$. Let $\mathbb{F}_2^k = \{(c_1, c_2, \ldots, c_k) \mid c_i \in \mathbb{F}_2\}_k$ be the k-dimensional space over $\mathbb{F}_2$ and $\gamma$ be an injective map from $\mathbb{F}_2^k$ into the set $\{0,1,2,\ldots,n-1\}$, $2^k \leqslant n$, of course. Constructing k-dimensional vector sequence $A=(A_o, A_1, \ldots)$ where $A_t=(a_{1t}, a_{2t}, \ldots, a_{kt})$, $t=0,1,2,3,\ldots$ and applying $\gamma$ to each term of the sequence A, we get the sequence $\gamma(A)= (\gamma(A_o), \gamma(A_1), \ldots)$ where $\gamma(A_t) \in \{0,1,\ldots,n-1\}$, for all t. Using $\gamma(A)$ to scramble the output sequence $\underline{b}$ of LSR, we get the sequence $\underline{u}=(u_o, u_1, \ldots)$ where $u_t=b_{t+\gamma(A_t)}$, for all t. we call $\gamma$ a scrambling function and $\underline{u}$ the Generalized Multiplexed Sequence (generalizing Jenning's Multiplexed Sequence, see ref.[1]), in brief, GMS. In the present paper, the period, characteristic polynomial, minimum polynomial and translation equivalence properties of the GMS are studied under certain assumptions. Let $\Omega$ be the algebraic closure of $\mathbb{F}_2$. Throughout this paper, any algebraic extension of $\mathbb{F}_2$ are assumed to be contained in $\Omega$. Let f(x) and g(x) be polynomials over $\mathbb{F}_2$ without multiple roots. Let f*g be the monic polynomial whose roots are all the distinct elements of the set $S= \{\alpha \cdot \beta \mid \alpha, \beta \in \Omega,\ f(\alpha)=0,\ g(\beta)=0\}$. It is well known that f*g is a polynomial over $\mathbb{F}_2$. Let G(f) denote the vector space consisting of all output sequences of LSR with characteristic polynomial f(x).

2. <u>The minimum polynomial and characteristic polynomial of GMS u</u>

For proof of the following, we list some familiar results.

Lemma 1. 1) Suppose $f(x)=p_1(x)^{e_1}\dots p_m(x)^{e_m}$ is the characteristic polynomial of LSR, where $e_1,e_2,\dots,e_m$ are integers, $p_1(x),\dots,p_m(x)$ are irreducible polynomials of degrees $n_1,n_2,\dots,n_m$ over $\mathbb{F}_2$ respectively. For $i=1,2,\dots,m$, let $\alpha_i$ be one of the roots of $p_i(x)$. Let $\underline{a}\in G(f)$, then there exist uniquely determined elements $\xi_{ri}\in\mathbb{F}_{2^{n_r}}$, $r=1,2,\dots,m$, $i=1,2,\dots,e_r$, such that

$$a_t=\sum_{r=1}^{m}\sum_{i=1}^{e}\binom{i+t-1}{i-1}Tr_{2^{n_r}}(\xi_{ri}\alpha_r^t),\ t=0,1,\dots. \tag{1}$$

where $Tr_{2^{n_r}}$ is the trace function from $\mathbb{F}_{2^{n_r}}$ to $\mathbb{F}_2$.

2) $f(x)$ is the minimum polynomial of the sequence $\underline{a}$ iff $\xi_{re_r}\neq 0$, $r=1,2,\dots,m$.

3) If there exist elements $\xi_{ri}\in\mathbb{F}_2[\alpha_1,\dots,\alpha_m]$, $r=1,2,\dots,m$, $i=1,2,\dots,e_r$, such that (1) holds and $a_t\in\mathbb{F}_2$, $t=0,1,2,\dots$. Then $f(x)$ is the characteristic polynomial of the sequence $\underline{a}$.

Corollary 1. 1)Under the conditions of Lemma 1, if $e_1=e_2=\dots=e_m=1$, i.e. $f(x)=p_1(x)p_2(x)\dots p_m(x)$, then there exist uniquely determined elements $\xi_r$, $r=1,2,\dots,m$, such that

$$a_t=\sum_{r=1}^{m}Tr_{2^{n_r}}(\xi_r\alpha_r^t),\qquad t=0,1,2,\dots \tag{2}$$

2) $f(x)$ is the minimum polynomial of $\underline{a}$ iff $\xi_r\neq 0$, $r=1,2,\dots,m$.

3) If there exist elements $\xi_r$ such that (2) holds and $a_t\in\mathbb{F}_2$, $t=0,1,2,\dots$. Then $f(x)$ is a characteristic polynomial of $\underline{a}$.

Lemma2. Let m,n be two integers, l be the least common multiple of m and n, i.e. $l=[m,n]$, d be the greatest common divisor of m and n,i.e. $d=(m,n)$. Then $\mathbb{F}_{2^d}=\mathbb{F}_{2^m}\cap\mathbb{F}_{2^n}$, $\mathbb{F}_{2^l}=\langle\mathbb{F}_{2^m},\mathbb{F}_{2^n}\rangle$, i.e. $\mathbb{F}_{2^l}$ is generated by $\mathbb{F}_{2^n}$ and $\mathbb{F}_{2^m}$.

Lemma 3. Let $f(x)$ and $g(x)$ be two irreducible polynomials of degrees m and n respectively and $(m,n)=1$. Then

1) $f*g$ is irreducible.

2) Suppose $\alpha$ is a root of $f(x)$, $\beta$ is a root of $g(x)$. Then for $\lambda\in\mathbb{F}_{2^m}$, $\mu\in\mathbb{F}_{2^n}$, we have

$$Tr_{2^m}(\lambda\cdot\alpha^t)Tr_{2^n}(\mu\cdot\beta^t)=Tr_{2^{m\cdot n}}(\lambda\mu(\alpha\beta)^t),\ t=0,1,2,\dots.$$

Theorem 1. Suppose the characteristic polynomials $p_1(x),p_2(x),\dots,p_k(x)$ and $g(x)$ of $LSR_1,LSR_2,\dots,LSR_k$ and LSR are irreducible of degrees $m_1$, $m_2,\dots,m_k$ and n respectively where $m_1,\dots m_k$ and n are relatively prime in pairs and greater than 1. Suppose $\underline{a}_1, \underline{a}_2, \ldots, \underline{a}_k$ and $\underline{b}$ are output sequences of $LSR_1, LSR_2, \ldots, LSR_k$ and LSR respectively. Then the GMS $\underline{u}$ obtained from $\underline{a}_1, \underline{a}_2, \ldots, \underline{a}_k$, $\underline{b}$ and the scrambling function $\gamma$ has

$$F(x) = \prod_{\substack{j=0 \\ 0 \leqslant i_1 < i_2 < \ldots < i_j \leqslant k}}^{k} (p_{i_1} * p_{i_2} * \ldots * p_{i_j} * g) \tag{3}$$

as its minimum polynomial where $p_0(x)=1$ and $1*g=g$ by convention. Denote the degree of $F(x)$ by $N$, then

$$N = n(m_1+1)(m_2+1)\ldots(m_k+1). \tag{4}$$

Proof. For every k-dimensional vector $\vec{a}=(a_1, a_2, \ldots, a_k) \in \mathbb{F}_2^k$, we construct a monomial as follows. If $a_{i_1}=a_{i_2}=\ldots a_{i_j}=1$, and all other components are 0, then let $\vec{a}$ correspond to the monomial $p_{\vec{a}}=a_{i_1} \cdot a_{i_2} \cdot \ldots \cdot a_{i_j}$. The weight $w(\vec{a})$ of $\vec{a}$ is the number of 1's among $a_1, a_2, \ldots, a_k$, i.e. $w(\vec{a})=\sum_{i=1}^{k} a_i$. We arrange the elements of $\mathbb{F}_2^k$ such that $\vec{a}$ proceeds $\vec{b}$ iff $w(\vec{a}) \leqslant w(\vec{b})$ and arrange the corresponding monomials and function values of $\gamma$ in the same manner. Denote the monomials and function values of $\gamma$ by $p_0, p_1, \ldots, p_{2^k-1}$ and $\rho_0, \rho_1, \ldots \rho_{2^k-1}$ respectively. Then

$$u_t = \bar{a}_{1t}\bar{a}_{2t}\ldots\bar{a}_{kt}b_{t+\rho_0} + a_{1t}\bar{a}_{2t}\ldots\bar{a}_{kt}b_{t+\rho_1} + \bar{a}_{1t}a_{2t}\bar{a}_{3t}\ldots\bar{a}_{kt}b_{t+\rho_2} + \ldots + a_{1t}a_{2t}\ldots a_{kt}b_{t+\rho_{2^k-1}},$$

where $\bar{a}_{it}=a_{it}+1$, $i=1,2,\ldots,k$. Substituting $\bar{a}_{it}=a_{it}+1$ into $u_t$, we find that the coefficient of $b_{t+\rho_j}$ in $u_t$ is of the form

$$\sum_{l=j}^{2^k-1} c_{jl} \cdot p_l(t),$$

where $c_{jj}=1$ and $p_l(t)=p_l(a_{1t}, \ldots, a_{kt})$. Putting $c_{jl}=0$ if $l<j$, we may write

$$u_t = \sum_{j=0}^{2^k-1} \Big(\sum_{l=j} c_{jl} \cdot p_l(t)\Big) b_{t+\rho_j} = \sum_{l=0}^{2^k-1} \Big(\sum_{j=0}^{2^k-1} c_{jl} \cdot b_{t+\rho_j}\Big) p_l(t) =$$

$$= \sum_{l=0}^{2^k-1} b'_{\tau_l t}\, p_l(t) \tag{5}$$

where

$$b'_{\tau_l t} = \sum_{j=0}^{2^k-1} c_{jl} \cdot b_{t+\rho_j}, \quad l=0,1,2,\ldots,2^k-1. \tag{6}$$

Put $\underline{b}_i=(b_{i-1}, b_i, \ldots, b_{i+t}, \ldots)$, $i=1,\ldots,n$ and $\underline{b}'_{\tau_l}=(b'_{\tau_l 0}, b'_{\tau_l 1}, \ldots, b'_{\tau_l t}, \ldots)$, $l=0,1,2,\ldots,2^k-1$. Since $g(x)$ is an irreducible polynomial with degree n and $\underline{b} \in G(g)$, $\underline{b}_1, \underline{b}_2, \ldots, \underline{b}_n$ form a basis of $G(g)$, thus $\underline{b}_{\rho_0}$, $\underline{b}_{\rho_1}, \ldots, \underline{b}_{\rho_{2^k-1}}$ $(0 \leqslant \rho_j \leqslant n-1)$ are linearly independent. From (6), we have

$$(\underline{b}'_{\tau_0}, \underline{b}'_{\tau_1}, \ldots, \underline{b}'_{\tau_{2^k-1}}) = (\underline{b}_{\rho_0}, \underline{b}_{\rho_1}, \ldots, \underline{b}_{\rho_{2^k-1}})C$$

where

$$C=(c_{jl}),\ c_{jj}=1, c_{jl}=0,\ \text{if } l<j \tag{7}$$

therefore $\underline{b}'_{\tau_0}, \underline{b}'_{\tau_1}, \ldots, \underline{b}'_{\tau_{2^k-1}}$ are also linearly independent sequences and g(x) is their minimum polynomial. Let $\beta$ be a root of g(x), from Corollary 1, for every l there is a uniquely determined non-zero element $\mu_l \in \mathbb{F}_{2^n}$ such that

$$b'_{\tau_l t} = Tr_{2^n}(\mu_l \beta^t).$$

Let $\alpha_i$ be a root of $P_i(x)$, i=1,2,...,k, again from Corollary 1 of Lemma 1, for every i, there is a uniquely determined non-zero element $\lambda_i \in F_{2^{m_i}}$ such that

$$a_{it} = Tr_{2^{m_i}}(\lambda_i \alpha_i^t),\ t=0,1,2,\ldots;\ i=1,2,\ldots,k.$$

Now we can calculate the general term $u_t$ of the GMS $\underline{u}$ by using the above root expressions of the sequences $\underline{b}'_{\tau_l}$ and $\underline{a}_i$. We have

$$u_t = \sum_{l=0}^{2^k-1} p_l(t) b'_{\tau_l t} = \sum_{l=0}^{2^k-1} a_{i_1 t} a_{i_2 t} \cdots a_{i_{s(l)} t} \cdot b'_{\tau_l t}$$

where s(l) = degree of $p_l$. Then, By Lemma 3,

$$u_t = \sum_{l=0}^{2^k-1} Tr(\lambda_{i_1} \cdot \alpha_{i_1}^t) Tr(\lambda_{i_2} \cdot \alpha_{i_2}^t) \ldots Tr(\lambda_{i_{s(l)}} \alpha_{i_{s(l)}}^t) Tr(\mu_l \beta^t)$$

$$= \sum_{l=0}^{2^k-1} Tr(\lambda_{i_1} \lambda_{i_2} \cdots \lambda_{i_{s(l)}} \mu_l (\alpha_{i_1} \alpha_{i_2} \cdots \alpha_{i_{s(l)}} \beta)^t)$$

where $\alpha_{i_1} \alpha_{i_2} \ldots \alpha_{i_{s(l)}} \beta$ is a root of the irreducible polynomial $p_{i_1} * p_{i_2} * \ldots * p_{i_{s(l)}} * g$ of degree $m_{i_1} . m_{i_2} \ldots m_{i_{s(l)}} . n$. Therefre, by Corollary 1, (3) is the minimum polynomial of $\underline{u}$.And it follows that the degree of F(x) is (4).

Note that from Theorem 1, it follows that the minimum polynomial of the GMS $\underline{u}$ is independent from the scrambling function $\gamma$ and the complexity of GMS is increased considerably.

For characteristic polynomials with multiple roots, we need some results of [2].

Let $\underline{a}=(a_0, a_1, \ldots)$ and $\underline{b}=(b_0, b_1, \ldots)$ be two arbitrary binary sequences, we define the product $\underline{a}.\underline{b}$ of $\underline{a}$ and $\underline{b}$ to be $\underline{a}.\underline{b}=(a_0 b_0, a_1 b_1, \ldots)$. For two vector spaces G(f),G(g), the product G(f).G(g) of G(f) and G(g) is defined to be the vector space generated by all products $\underline{a}.\underline{b}$, where $\underline{a} \in G(f)$ and $\underline{b} \in G(g)$.

Lemma 4. Let

$$s^{(k)} = \left( \binom{k}{k}, \binom{k+1}{k}, \ldots, \binom{k+t}{k}, \ldots \right).$$

then $s^{(0)},\dots,s^{(e-1)}$ form a basis of the vector space $G((x+1)^e)$.
For two arbitrary positive integers $e_1$ and $e_2$, write

$$e_1-1=\sum_{\nu} j_\nu 2^\nu, \quad j_\nu=0 \text{ or } 1,$$

$$e_2-1=\sum_{\nu} k_\nu 2^\nu, \quad k_\nu=0 \text{ or } 1.$$

Let $\lambda$ be the smallest nonnegative integer such that $j_\nu+k_\nu<2$ for all $\nu\geqslant\lambda$, then Zierler and Mills [2] defined

$$e_1 \vee e_2 = 2^\lambda + \sum_{\nu\geqslant\lambda} (j_\nu+k_\nu)2^\nu .$$

Lemma 5 (Zieler, Mills).

$$G((x+1)^{e_1})\, G((x+1)^{e_2})=G((x+1)^{e_1 \vee e_2}).$$

We have

Theorem 2: Let the k+1 polynomials $p_1(x)^{e_1}, p_2(x)^{e_2},\dots,p_k(x)^{e_k}$ and $g(x)^e$ be characteristic polynomials of $LSR_1,\dots,LSR_k$ and LSR respectively, where $p_1(x),\dots,p_k(x),g(x)$ are irreducible of degrees $m_1,m_2,\dots,m_k$ and n. Assume $m_1,m_2,\dots,m_k$ and n are relatively prime in pairs. Let the sequences $\underline{a}_1,\dots,\underline{a}_k$ and $\underline{b}$ are output sequences of these k+1 linear shift registers respectively. Then the GMS $\underline{u}$ generated by $\underline{a}_1,\dots,\underline{a}_k$ and $\underline{b}$ has the characteristic polynomial

$$F(x)=\prod_{\substack{j=0\\ 0\leqslant i_1<i_2<\dots<i_j\leqslant k}}^{k}(p_{i_1}*\dots*p_{i_j}*g)^{e_{i_1}\vee\dots\vee e_{i_j}\vee e}$$

Next, let's consider the period of GMS. At first, we have the following two lemmas.

Lemma 6. Let f(x), g(x) be two irreducible polynomials over $\mathbb{F}_2$ of degrees m,n respectively, and (m,n)=1. Then

$$p(f*g)=p(f)p(g),$$

where p(f) denotes the period of f(x).

Lemma 7. Suppose that f(x) and g(x) are two polynomials over $\mathbb{F}_2$ with (f,g)=1. Then $p(f.g)=[p(f),p(g)]$.

From Lemmas 6 and 7 we deduce immediately

Theorem 3. Suppose that $f_1(x),\dots,f_k(x)$ and g(x) are irreducible over $\mathbb{F}_2$ and the degrees of these polynomials are relatively prime in pairs. Then the period $p(\underline{u})$ is $p(f_1)\dots p(f_k)p(g)$.

## 3. The translation equivalence properties of GMS's

Throughout this section we suppose that $p_1(x),\dots p_k(x)$ and g(x) are irreducible and their degrees $m_1, m_2, \ldots, m_k$ and n are relatively prime in pairs.

Theorem 4. Let $\underline{a}_i$ and $\underline{a}_i'$ are two non-zero output sequences of $LSR_i$ which are translates of each other, $i=1,2,\ldots,k$. And let $\underline{b}$ and $\underline{b}'$ are two output sequences of LSR which are also translates of each other. Then for a given scrambling function $\gamma$, the GMS $\underline{u}$ obtained from $\underline{a},\ldots,\underline{a}_k,\underline{b}$ and the GMS $\underline{u}'$ obtained from $\underline{a}_1',\ldots,\underline{a}_k',\underline{b}'$ are translates of each other.

Proof. From the sequences $\underline{a}_1,\ldots\underline{a}_k$, we get the sequence

$$\gamma(A) = (\gamma(A_0),\ \gamma(A_1),\ldots)$$

where $\gamma(A_t)=\gamma(A_{1t},a_{2t},\ldots,a_{kt})$. The same, we get

$$\gamma(A') = (\gamma(A_0'),\ \gamma(A_1'),\ldots),$$

where $\gamma(A_t')=\gamma(a_{1t}',a_{2t}',\ldots,a_{kt}')$. Then $u_t=b_{t+\gamma(A_t)}$, $u_t'=b_t'{}_{+\gamma(A_t')}$.

Since $\underline{a}_i$ and $\underline{a}_i'$ are translates of each other, there exists $\tau_i$, $0\leqslant\tau_i\leqslant p(\underline{a}_i)$ such that $a_{it}'=a_{i(t+\tau_i)}$, $i=1,2,\ldots,k$. Since $\underline{b}$ and $\underline{b}'$ are translates of each other, there exists an integer $s$, $0\leqslant s\leqslant p(\underline{b})$, such that $b_t'=b_{t+s}$. Since $p(\underline{a}_i)\,|\,2^{m_i}-1$, $i=1,2,\ldots,k$, $p(\underline{b})\,|\,2^n-1$, and $m_1,\ldots m_k$ and n are relatively prime in pairs, $p(\underline{a}_1),\ldots,p(\underline{a}_k)$ and $p(\underline{b})$ are also relatively prime in pairs. By Chinese Remainder Theorem the following simultaneous congruences

$$\begin{cases} x\equiv\tau_1 & (\mathrm{mod}\ p(\underline{a}_1))\\ x\equiv\tau_2 & (\mathrm{mod}\ p(\underline{a}_2))\\ \quad\vdots & \\ x\equiv\tau_k & (\mathrm{mod}\ p(\underline{a}_k))\\ x\equiv s & (\mathrm{mod}\ p(\underline{b}))\end{cases}$$

have a solution $x\in\mathbb{Z}$ which is unique mod $p(\underline{a}_1)\ldots p(\underline{a}_k)p(\underline{b})$. It follows that $u_t'=u_{t+x}$ for all t. This proves that $\underline{u}$ and $\underline{u}'$ are translates of each other.

Corollary 2. For a given scrambling function $\gamma$, if the characteristic polynomials of the k+1 linear shift registers $LSR_1,\ldots.LSR_k$ and LSR are primitive polynomials whose degrees are relatively prime in pairs then the GMS's obtained from any non-zero initial states are all translates of each other.

Lemma 8. If

$$\sum_{i=0}^{2^k-1} d_i p_i=0,\ d_i\in\mathbb{F}_2, \tag{8}$$

then $d_i=0$ for all i.

Theorem 5. For different scrambling functions $\gamma$ and $\gamma'$, the GMS's $\underline{u}$ and $\underline{u}'$ obtained from the non-zero output sequences $\underline{a}_1,\underline{a}_2,\ldots,\underline{a}_k$, $\underline{b}$ of the k+1 linear shift registers $LSR_1,\ldots,LSR_k$, LSR are translates of each other iff there exist two fixed integers M and M' such that for all

$(a_1,a_2,\ldots,a_k)\in F_2^{\,k}$, we have

$$\gamma'(a_1,a_2,\ldots,a_k)=\gamma(a_1,a_2,\ldots,a_k)+M \text{ or } \gamma(a_1,a_2,\ldots,a_k)+M'$$

where $0\leqslant |M|,|M'|\leqslant n-1$ and $M+M'\equiv 0 \pmod{p(\underline{b})}$.

Proof. We follow the notation of the proof of Theorem 1. For a given $\gamma$, we have (5) and (6). Substituting (6) into (5), we obtain

$$u_t=(b_{\rho_0+t},\ b_{\rho_1+t},\ldots,b_{\rho_{2^k-1}+t})C\,(p_0(t),p_1(t),\ldots,p_{2^k-1}(t))'$$

where C is the matrix (7), thus

$$\underline{u}=(\underline{b}_{\rho_0},\underline{b}_{\rho_1},\ldots,\underline{b}_{\rho_{2^k-1}})\ C\ (p_0,p_1,\ldots,p_{2^k-1})'$$

where ' denotes the transpose of a matrix. Similarly, for $\gamma'$, we have

$$\underline{u}'=(\underline{b}_{\rho_0'},\underline{b}_{\rho_1'},\ldots,\underline{b}_{\rho_{2^k-1}'})\ C\ (p_0,p_1,\ldots,p_{2^k-1})'$$

Let

$$\rho_j'=\rho_j+\delta_j,\ -(n-1)\leqslant \delta_j\leqslant n-1,\ j=1,2,\ldots,2^k-1.$$

Denote the left translate operator by L, i.e. $L(a_0,a_1,\ldots)=(a_1,a_2,\ldots)$, then

$$\underline{u}'=(L^{\delta_0}\underline{b}_{\rho_0},L^{\delta_1}\underline{b}_{\rho_1},\ldots,L^{\delta_{2^k-1}}\underline{b}_{\rho_{2^k-1}})\ C\ (p_0,p_1,\ldots,p_{2^k-1})'$$

The sequences $\underline{u}$ and $\underline{u}'$ are translates of each other iff there exists an integer M such that $\underline{u}'=L^M\underline{u}$, i.e.

$$\begin{aligned}&(L^{\delta_0}\underline{b}_{\rho_0},L^{\delta_1}\underline{b}_{\rho_1},\ldots,L^{\delta_{2^k-1}}\underline{b}_{\rho_{2^k-1}})\ C\ (p_0,p_1,\ldots,p_{2^k-1})'=\\ &=(L^M\underline{b}_{\rho_0},L^M\underline{b}_{\rho_1},\ldots,L^M\underline{b}_{\rho_{2^k-1}})\ C\ (p_0,p_1,\ldots,p_{2^k-1})'\end{aligned}\qquad (9)$$

By Lemma 8 and C being invertible, (9) holds iff

$$(L^{\delta_0}\underline{b}_{\rho_0},\ldots,L^{\delta_{2^k-1}}\underline{b}_{\rho_{2^k-1}})=(L^M\underline{b}_{\rho_0},\ldots,L^M\underline{b}_{\rho_{2^k-1}})\qquad (10)$$

Clearly (10) holds iff the following simultaneous congruences have a solution M:

$$M\equiv\delta_i \pmod{p(\underline{b})}\qquad i=0,1,\ldots,2^k-1$$

Without loss of generality, suppose that $\delta_0,\delta_1,\ldots,\delta_i$ are non-negative and $\delta_{i+1},\ldots,\delta_{2^k-1}$ are negative, then

$$\delta_0=\delta_1=\ldots=\delta_i=\delta,\quad \delta_{i+1}=\ldots=\delta_{2^k-1}=\delta'$$

and

$$\delta\equiv\delta' \pmod{p(\underline{b})}.$$

Taking $M=\delta$, $M'=-\delta'$, the proof is complete.

Corollary 2. In Theorem 5, if the characteristic polynomial g(x) of LSR is primitive, then $M=M'$, $0\leqslant|M|\leqslant n-1$.

## References


[1] S.M.Jennings, Multiplexed Sequences:Some Properties of the Minimum Polynomial. Lecture Notes in Computer Science, No.149,Springer-Verlag, 1983, 189-206.

[2] N. Zierler and W.H.Mills, Products of Linear Recurring Sequences. J. of Algebra 27(1973), 147-157.

# A NOTE ON SEQUENCES GENERATED BY CLOCK CONTROLLED SHIFT REGISTERS*

Bernard Smeets
Department of Computer Engineering
University of Lund
P.O. Box 118, S-221 00 Lund, SWEDEN

**Summary** - In this paper the linear feedback shift registers are determined that can generate the output sequence of two types of clock controlled shift registers suggested by P. Nyffeler. For one type of clock control sufficient conditions are given which guarantee that maximum linear complexity is obtained. Furthermore, it is shown that the randomness properties for sequences of maximal linear complexity depend on clocking procedure.

## 1. Introduction.

Pseudo random sequences generated by linear feedback shift registers are used in various crypto systems as running key generators. In general several linear feedback shift registers are used to produce the final pseudo random sequence. Since such a sequence is periodic, it can be generated by one single linear feedback shift register of finite length. The length of shortest linear feedback shift register that is able to produce the output sequence of a configuration is referred to as the linear complexity of the sequence. If the linear complexity of some periodic sequence is L, then 2L consecutive symbols will be sufficient to determine both the linear feedback and the initial state of a linear feedback shift register that can generate the sequence [1]. As a consequence, a configuration of linear feedback shift registers must be such that the generated sequences do have a large linear complexity.

This paper deals with two types of clock controlled shift registers, suggested by P. Nyffeler [2]. First the linear feedback shift registers are determined that can generate the output sequence of the clock controlled shift registers. For one configuration of clock control sufficient conditions are given which guarantee that maximal linear complexity is obtained. In the sequel of this paper $(a_n)$ will denote a linear recurring sequence over GF(q) with period $T_a$ whose minimal polynomial $f_a$ is irreducible over GF(q), has degree

---

* This work was supported in part by the National Swedish Board for Technical Development under grants 81-3323 and 83-4364 at the University of Lund.

$m \geq 1$, and satisfies $f_a(0) \neq 0$. Furthermore, $(b_n)$ will denote a periodic sequence over GF(q) with period $T_b$. Throughout the paper it is assumed that $(a_n)$ and $(b_n)$ are generated by the linear feedback shift registers LFSRa and LFSRb respectively. It is also assumed that neither $(a_n)$ nor $(b_n)$ equals the null-sequence.

## 2. Cascade Clock Control

Consider the configuration of two shift registers as given in Fig. 1. The clock of the first shift register, LFSRa, is controlled by the sequence generated by the second shift register, LFSRb. At time instant $n>0$ LFSRb is clocked once and LFSRa is clocked $c(b_{n-1})$ times, where c is some function: $GF(q) \rightarrow \{0,\ldots,T_a-1\}$. To avoid a trivial situation, it is assumed that c(x) is not zero for all x in GF(q). Note that the function c may be part of the key information in a crypto system.

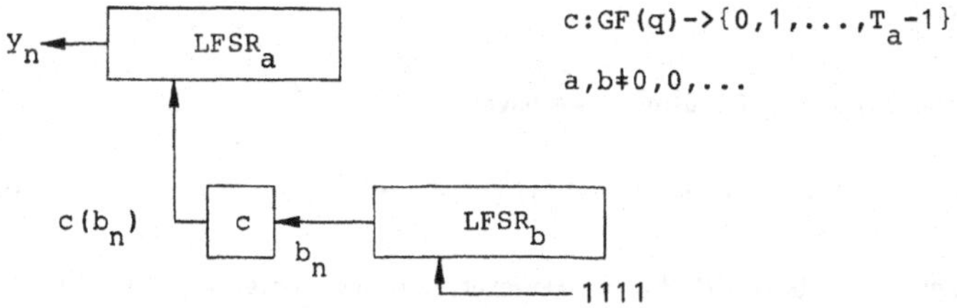


Fig. 1 Cascade Clock Control with two shift registers.

The sequence $(y_n)$ obtained at the output is

$$y_n = a_{s(n)}, \quad \text{where} \quad s(n) = \sum_{k=0}^{n-1} c(b_k), \quad n=0,1,2,\ldots \tag{1}$$

Let $T_b$ denote the period of $(b_n)$. Furthermore, let $S=s(T_b)$, i.e., the number of clock pulses generated in one period of $(b_n)$.

Theorem 1. The sequence $(y_n)$ generated by the cascade clock control configuration of LFSRa and LFSRb has a minimal polynomial $f^*(x)$ such that

$$f^*(x) \mid f^{(S)}(x^{T_b}), \tag{2}$$

where $f^{(k)}$ denotes the minimal polynomial of the k-decimated sequence of $(a_n)$, i.e., $(a_{kn})$.

Proof Let k and l be integers and let $k>0$. Consider now the sequence $(a_{kn+l})$, i.e., the l-th phase shift of $(a_{kn})$. It is easy to see that

$$h_{k,l}(x):=f^{(k)}(x)\sum_{n=0}^{\infty} a_{nk+l}x^n \in GF(q)[x] \quad \text{where} \quad \deg h_{k,l} < \deg f^k \tag{3}$$

Consider the formal power series $y(x)$ associated with the sequence $(y_n)$, defined by $y(x)=\sum_{n=0}^{\infty} y_n x^n$. From (1) we have

$$y(x)=\sum_{n=0}^{\infty} y_n x^n=\sum_{n=0}^{\infty} a_{s(n)}x^n=\sum_{n=0}^{\infty}\sum_{m=0}^{T_b-1} a_{s(m)+nS}x^{m+nT_b}=$$

$$=\sum_{m=0}^{T_b-1} x^m \sum_{n=0}^{\infty} a_{s(m)+nS}x^{nT_b}. \tag{4}$$

Multiplying $y(x)$ with $f^{(S)}(x^{T_b})$ and using (3) and (4) gives us

$$f^{(S)}(x^{T_b})y(x)=\sum_{m=0}^{T_b-1} x^m h_{S,s(m)}(x^{T_b}):=h(x) \in GF(q)[x]$$

From (4) and $\deg x^m < T_b$, for $0 \le m < T_b$, we have

$$\deg h(x) \le (T_b-1) + T_b(\deg f^{(S)}(x) -1) < T_b \deg f^{(S)}(x) \tag{5}$$

This implies that $y(x)=h(x)/f^{(S)}(x^{T_b})$. However, we also have $y(x)=h^*(x)/f^*(x)$, $\deg h^* < \deg f^*$, where $f^*(x)$ is the minimal polynomial for $(y_n)$. The theorem follows from the minimality of $f^*$.

Under favourable conditions it can be shown that the polynomial given in (2) is the minimal polynomial of $(y_n)$. Specializing a theorem by Serret on irreducible polynomials, see [3], we obtain the following result:

Theorem 2. Suppose $f^{(S)}(x)$ has degree $d$ and has order $T_{a,S}$. Suppose also that

(i) all prime factors of $T_b \ge 2$ divide $T_{a,S}$ but not $(q^d-1)/T_{a,S}$,

(ii) $q^d \equiv 1 \bmod 4$ if $T_b \equiv 0 \bmod 4$,

then $f^{(S)}(x^{T_b})$ is prime over $GF(q)$. Hence, it is the minimal polynomial of $(y_n)$. Furthermore it has degree $T_b d$ and has order $T_b T_{a,S}$.

When $f(x)$ is a maximum-length polynomial we have the following interesting special case of Theorem 2.

Corollary 1. If $f(x)$ is a maximum-length polynomial of degree $m \geq 1$,

(i) $\gcd(S,q^m-1)=1$,

(ii) all prime factors of $T_b$ divide $T$ and

(iii) if the hypothesis (ii) in Theorem 2 is satisfied,

then $f^{(S)}(x^{T_b})$ is the minimal polynomial of $(y_n)$.

Proof. We only need to show that condition (i) in Theorem 2 is satisfied. If $f(x)$ is a maximum-length polynomial of degree $m \geq 1$, then $f(x)$ has period $T=q^m-1$. From $\gcd(S,q^m-1)=1$ it follows that $T_{a,S}=T$. Together with the hypothesis that all the prime factors $p$ of $T_b$ divide $T$ and $p \nmid 1$, this shows that the condition (i) in Theorem 2 is satisfied.

For some special instances of the binary case this corollary coincide with results given in [4] and [5]. An other result of Theorem 2 is the following corollary:

Corollary 2. Let $p$, an odd prime, divide $2^n-1$ for some positive integer $n$. If the order of 2 mod $p^k$ equals $e$ for $k=2,\ldots,d$, where $e$ is the order of 2 mod $p$, but $p^{d+1} \nmid 2^e-1$, then $p^d$ divides $2^n-1$.

Proof. Consider first the case $n=n'$=order of 2 mod $p$. Assume that $2^n-1=p^cQ$, with $p \nmid Q$ and $1 \leq c < d$. Let $e$ be the order of 2 mod $p^c$, $e=\mathrm{ord}_2 p^c$, and correspondingly $e_1=\mathrm{ord}_2 Q$. Note that $\mathrm{lcm}(e,e_1)=n$. Since $\gcd(p,Q)=1$ we have $A:=\mathrm{ord}_2(p^cQ)^2= \mathrm{lcm}(\mathrm{ord}_2 p^{2c},\mathrm{ord}_2 Q^2)$. If $2c \leq d$, then $A \leq \mathrm{lcm}(e,e_1Q) \leq nQ$. If $2c>d$, then $A \leq \mathrm{lcm}(ep^{2c-d},e_1Q) \leq nQp^{2c-d}$. Consider now the cascade clock control of two maximum length shift registers of length $n$. Theorem 2 implies that the minimal polynomial $f$ of the output sequence is prime over GF(2), is of degree $B:=n(2^n-1)$ and has period $(p^cQ)^2$. However we just have shown that $\deg f=A<B$, hence $c>d$. Finally, let $n>n'$. Note that $2^{n'}-1 \mid 2^n-1$ iff $n' \mid n$ and $n'=\mathrm{ord}_2 p \mid n$ because $2^n=1$ mod $p$. This proves that $p^d \mid 2^{n'}-1 \mid 2^n-1$.

Note: this result can be obtained also by using only partial results on which Theorem 2 is based, [3].

## 3. Clock Controlled Sampling

Consider the configuration of two linear feedback shift registers as shown in Fig. 2. The output of the first register LFSRa is sampled under control of the outputs of the second register LFSRb and a mapping $g$ from GF(q) onto GF(2). If $g(b_n)=1$ then the output symbol of LFSRa is loaded in cell D and it will become the new output y-symbol. Otherwise the new output y-symbol equals the previous y-symbol. It will be assumed that $g$ is not the zero-map, i.e., not all elements of GF(q) are mapped to only 0.

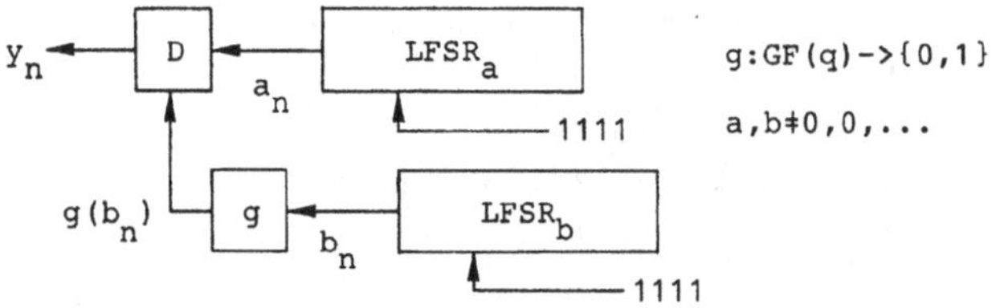


Fig. 2 Clock controlled sampling.

The sequence $(y_n)$ obtained at the output is

$$y_n = a_{s(n)}, \quad \text{where} \quad s(n) = \max_{\substack{0 \le k \le n \\ g(b_k)=1}} k, \quad n=0,1,2,\ldots \tag{6}$$

where g is a mapping as explained above. Furthermore, assume that $b_0$ is such that $g(b_0)=1$. This restriction assures that the first output symbol in $(y_n)$ is $a_0$ instead of the initial state of the memory cell D.

Theorem 3. The sequence $(y_n)$ generated by the clock controlled sampling configuration of LFSRa and LFSRb has a minimal polynomial $f^*$ such that

$$f^*(x) \mid f^{(T_b)}(x^{T_b}). \tag{7}$$

Proof Imitate the proof of Theorem 1 with $T_b$ instead of S and use the fact that $s(nT_b+m)=nT_b+s(m)$.

For the binary case this result is connected with a result given in [2]. Let a be a zero of f(x), then it is easily shown that a is also a zero of (7). Thus f(x) divides $f^{(T_b)}(x^{T_b})$, hence it is much harder to guarantee that (7) is the minimal polynomial of $(y_n)$.

## 4. Randomness aspects

Besides the linear complexity of the generated sequences, their statistical properties are of importance. Particularly, it is desirable that the symbols in the sequence do not depend (too much) on the preceding symbols. If for a sequence x the average conditional entropies $H(X_n), H(X_n|X_{n-1}), H(X_n|X_{n-1},X_{n-2}),\ldots,H(X_n|X_{n-1}..X_{n-m})$ form a rapid decreasing function then there is a strong dependence between a symbol and the symbols preceding it. From Theorem 2 it is clear that, as far as the linear complexity of the generated sequence is concerned, the clock function in the first type of clock control only plays a secondary roll. Though different clock functions give rise to different output sequences, the same linear complexity may be obtained. For example, if we take the maximum-length polynomial $f(x)=x^5+x^2+1$ over GF(2) and $b=1/(x^5+x^3+1)$, then the clock functions $c_0$ and $c_1$, defined as $c_0(0)=0$, $c_0(1)=1$ and $c_1(0)=1$, $c_1(1)=2$, will result in two different sequences which have the same linear complexity L=155. However, the randomness properties of the two sequences (will generally) differ. This is illustrated by Fig. 3 which shows how the conditional entropies $H(X_n), H(X_n|X_{n-1}), H(X_n|X_{n-1},X_{n-2}),\ldots,H(X_n|X_{n-1}..X_{n-10})$ differ for the two different clock functions in the previous example.

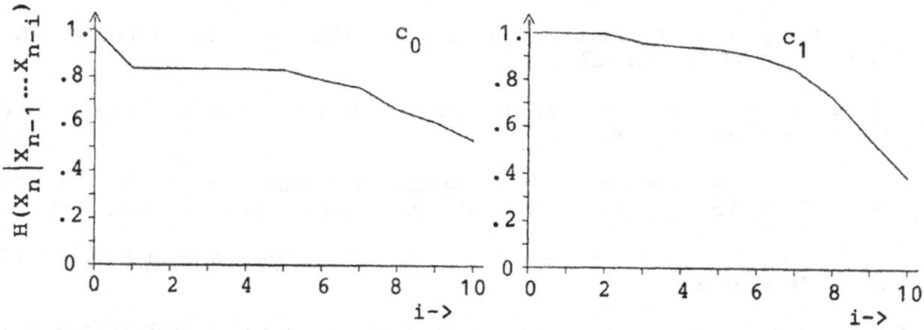


Fig. 3 The average conditional entropies $H(X_n),\ldots,H(X_n|X_{n-1}..X_{n-m})$ of the output symbols using two different clock functions $c_0$ and $c_1$

The symbol dependence observed when clocking is done according to $c_0$ is due to the fact that LFSRa stands still for almost half of the time. As a result of this observation one has to choose the clock function not only with respect to the linear complexity of the sequence but also the randomness properties have to be taken into account.

In the case of clock controlled sampling a symbol in the output stream may also be a repetition. This happens when no new symbol is loaded into the D element. Such repetitions can be avoided when one increases the number of instances in which a new symbol is loaded into D. However this causes the output sequence to become more identical to the sequence generated by LFSRa.

## 5. Conclusion

It has been shown that under certain well defined conditions we can guarantee a high linear complexity for the sequences produced by the cascade clock control configuration. The random properties of these sequences depend on the method of clocking. Furthermore, for the clock controlled sampling configuration it is much harder to guarantee a high linear complexity and (or) good random properties.

**Acknowledgement**

Thanks are due to Tore Herlestam for introducing me into this field and for the many stimulating discussions.

**References**

[1] J.L. Massey, "Shift-Register Synthesis and BCH Decoding", IEEE Trans. on Inf. Th., IT-15, Jan. 1969, pp. 122-127.

[2] P. Nyffeler, "Binäre Automaten und ihre Linearen Rekursionen," Ph.D dissertation, University of Bern, Switzerland, 1975.

[3] R. Lidl and H. Niederreiter, "Encyclopedia of Mathematics and its Applications, Finite Fields, Vol.20, Addison-Wesley Publishing Company, Reading, Mass., 1983.

[4] T. Beth and F.C. Piper, "The stop-and-go generator", Proceedings of EUROCRYPT 84 (Paris, 1984), to appear.

[5] W.G. Chambers and S.M. Jennings, "Linear Equivalence of Certain BRM Shift-Register Sequences," Electr. Letters, Vol. 20, Nov. 1984, pp. 1018-1019.

# USING ALGORITHMS AS KEYS IN STREAM CIPHERS

Neal R. Wagner[1]
Paul S. Putter
Marianne R. Cain

Drexel University
Mathematics and Computer Science
Philadelphia, PA 19104 USA

ABSTRACT.

This paper discusses the use of an arbitrary bit-sequence generating algorithm as the cryptographic key for a stream cipher. Emphasis is placed on methods for combining stream generators into more complex ones, with and without randomization. Threshold schemes give a generalization of many combination techniques.

## 1. INTRODUCTION.

Some years ago Chaitin [Cha66] [Cha69] [Cha75] and Kolmogorov [Kol65] gave a remarkable strong definition of a random bit sequence: a random sequence of length $n$ requires an algorithm nearly of length $n$ to generate it. Martin-Löf [Mar66] suggested that infinite random sequences should withstand all recursively enumerable statistical tests, and then proved that these sequences satisfy the Chaitin-Kolmogorov definition. Such a sequence is said to have no *succinct representation.* In general, it is an undecidable problem to find the shortest algorithm that will generate a given sequence, and even finding a succinct representation, assuming one exists, is believed to be an intractable problem.

Interesting weaker definitions of pseudo-random sequences have recently been proposed [Yao82] [Blu84] [Ko84], and this is now an active research area. See [Kra84] for a survey.

In cryptography one wants to generate a long pseudo-random bit sequence from a succinct secret key. It is a short step to think of using an arbitrary bit generating algorithm (= succinct representation) as a "key" for cryptographic use. This idea goes against the conventional practice that the cryptographic algorithm itself should not be secret, only the particular key used by the algorithm.

[1]Research supported in part by NSF grant DCR-8403350 and by a Research Scholar award from Drexel University.

## 2. ALGORITHMS AS CRYPTOGRAPHIC KEYS.

We propose a keyspace consisting of *all possible* algorithms for generating a bit stream. (By definition, the algorithm must not execute indefinitely at some point without producing a bit.) We want an arbitrarily long bit stream, so if the algorithm halts, repeat the initial sequence indefinitely. In practice we do not want the algorithm to be too long, but we place no upper bound on its length. Similarly, we favor algorithms that produce $n$ bits in $O(n)$ time, but there is no such requirement. At the CRYPTO 84 meeting, in a slightly different context, it was argued that the keyspace was not really infinite, since one could always place a bound on the key size. In practice an opponent must choose a bound that is not ridiculous, and then he always faces the possibility that the size of the key exceeds this bound.

We would like to list several advantages of using algorithms as keys.

- Since the key can be an arbitrarily complex algorithm, one can never be certain that a given key has been discovered, no matter how much plaintext-ciphertext has been matched up using some algorithm. (The actual key might say, "After the $10000000^{th}$ bit, use this other algorithm.")
- There is no bound on the size of the key or on the number of keys -- there are infinitely many possible keys.
- This method immediately adapts to the best current technology for generating secure bit streams.
- One can adjust the key length and key complexity to the desired level of security.
- This contains every other stream cipher based on xor with a pseudo- random sequence as a special case.

We now come to the practicalities of choosing a key (= algorithm). We do not want to choose a "random" algorithm. In fact we do not know any reasonable way to make such a choice. Besides, a random choice might be unacceptably inefficient or it might not be at all secure. Note that the opponent does not necessarily know what level is "unacceptable." Knuth [Knu81, p. 4] nicely illustrates the dangers of using a "random" algorithm for a pseudo-random number generator.

In fact it is an undecidable problem to tell whether a candidate for a key is actually an algorithm, i.e., whether it does not execute indefinitely at some point without generating any more bits. Notice that this is more of a problem for the opponent attempting cryptanalysis than for the person generating the key. The opponent cannot with certainty eliminate such candidate algorithms, while the person generating the key has no such problem.

Instead of a random choice, we propose starting with "prime" bit stream generators that seem strong (Section 3.1) and propose combining them in ways that seem strong (Sections 3.2 and 3.3). Section 3.3 also includes randomization techniques as well as combination methods. It is important that the notation allow the specification of an arbitrary algorithm, so that the opponent cannot rule any out.

## 3. CASCADES.

For high security in conventional cryptography, it is natural to think of combinations of drastically different cryptosystems -- perhaps a composition of block ciphers, or the exclusive or of stream ciphers, or some other combination. We will refer to such combinations as *cascades*. With one model there is a proof that the cascade of two ciphers is at least as hard to break as either individually [Eve84]. We will be focusing on stream ciphers and on ways of combining and enhancing them.

### 3.1 BASIC PSEUDO-RANDOM BIT-STREAMS.

Pseudo-random bit sequences are the "prime parts" from which one might build up strong stream ciphers. Two or more such sequences can then be combined in various ways as described in Sections 3.2 and 3.3 below.

There has been a great deal of work recently on appropriate definitions of pseudo-random sequences and on means for constructing cryptographically secure examples [Blu84] [Sha83] [Yao82]. From our point of view, one should just have a repertory of families of pseudo-random streams -- to be augmented as new ones become available.

### 3.2 CASCADES WITH NO EXPANSION.

This section presents methods of combining or enhancing bit-stream ciphers without any randomization or expansion. We will use notation for figures similar to that in [Riv83]. In particular $R$ stands for a true random sequence, $P$ for a pseudo-random sequence, and $B$ for a source bit-stream being modified.

(a) *Exclusive or.* This is the most common method for producing cascades of bit-stream ciphers.

(b) *Bitwise addition, with carry.*

(c) *Pseudo-random deletions.* Here the output of one pseudo-random stream is used to delete bits from another stream. For example, $P$ = "01010101 ..." would delete every other bit. Even simple alternating deletions was mentioned as a possible strong method for preventing cryptanalysis of a string given by the expansion of an algebraic number [Kan84].

(d) *Pseudo-random alternation between streams.* Use the output of one stream to select from $n$ streams. (See Figure 1.)

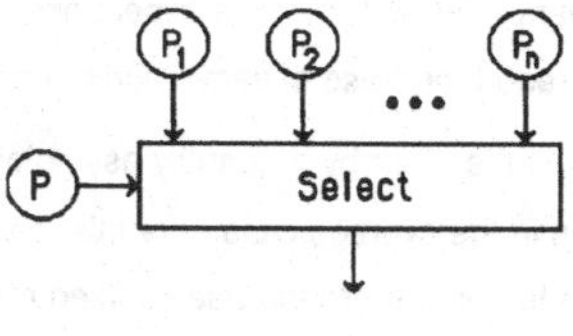


Figure 1.

As a special case, if $n = 2$ and $P$ = "01010101 ...", then this just gives alternation between the two bit streams $P_1$ and $P_2$. If $n = 2$ and $P$ starts with 10000000 0's followed by all 1's, this method just switches from $P_1$ to $P_2$ after 10000000 bits.

(e) *Pseudo-random selection from a buffer.* This scheme is similar to the previous one and is inspired by [Knu81, p. 32].

### 3.3 CASCADES WITH RANDOMIZATION AND EXPANSION.

(a) *Pseudo-random interspersing of random bits* . This simple randomization method can be used at any stage of the encryption process. See Figure 2, and for terminology refer to [Riv83] and the beginning of Section 3.2. This will expand the bit stream *B* by about a factor of two.

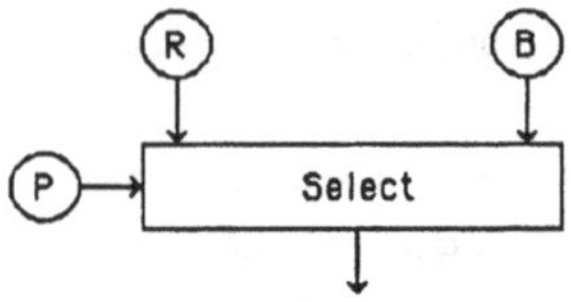


Figure 2.

(b) *Random interspersing of random bits* . This is a technique from [Riv83], shown in Figure 3. It also has an expansion of about two.

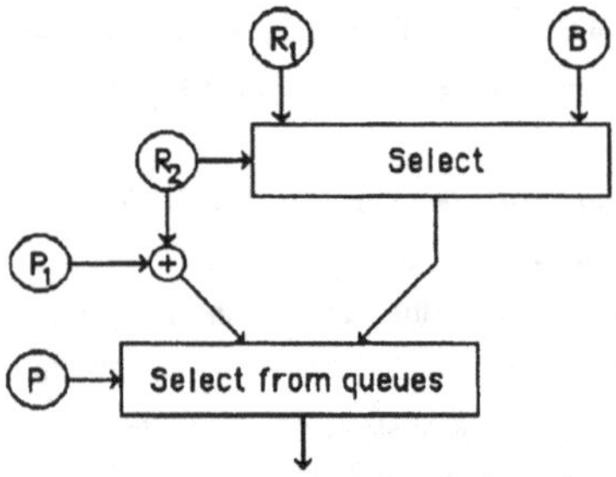


Figure 3.

Here the final selection based on the pseudo-random sequence *P* is just concatenation in [Riv83]. If *P* is the alternating sequence "01010101 ...", then we would get concatenation by alternating bits. If an arbitrary pseudo-random stream is used for *P*, we expect one of the streams selected to get ahead of the other, so buffers will be needed for these streams. On the average, after *n* bits of a random stream, either 0's or 1's will be ahead of the other by a quantity asymptotic to $\sqrt{n}$, so there is no upper bound on the necessary buffer size even in the average case. For this reason we might want to use a stream *P* in which the excess of 0's or 1's is never more than some fixed number which we could use as our buffer size.

(c) *Block-oriented randomization in the stream setting.* One can translate the block-oriented methods of [Riv83] by replacing a block encryption step with the exclusive or of a pseudo-random bit stream, and by replacing concatenation with selection based on a pseudo-random bit stream *P*. Six of the translated schemes in [Riv83] are special cases of Figure 4.

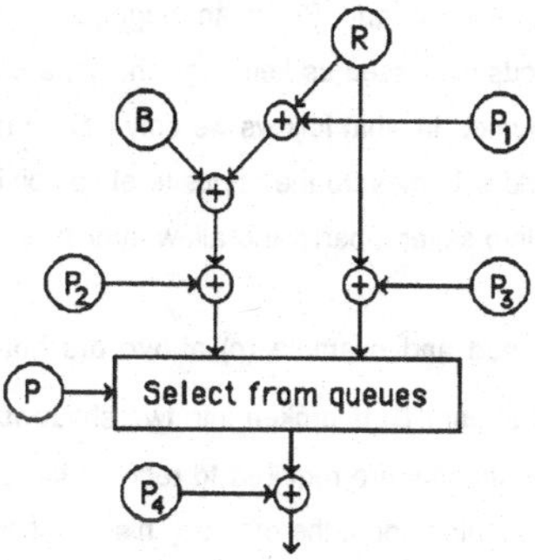


Figure 4.

Four of these special cases are obtained by deleting three out of four of the $P_i$'s. One might also use two, three, or all four of the $P_i$'s. All such schemes have an expansion factor of two.

Suppose an opponent can obtain these individual selected streams. This would be the case for example if $P_4$ were missing and $P$ were simple alternation. The opponent could then take the exclusive or of the two streams and obtain $B \oplus P_1 \oplus P_2 \oplus P_3$. So we might as well use an xor of the streams with no randomization. In the block cipher setting, these techniques do enhance security even with some simple form of concatenation.

The provably secure but impractical *Rip Van Winkel* cipher [Mas85] is obtained as a very special case of Figure 4 by deleting all four of the $P_i$'s and by letting $P$ start with an enormous number of 1's, followed by alternating 0's and 1's.

(d) *Asmuth-Blakley scheme.* In the stream setting, the Asmuth-Blakley scheme for combining two cryptosystems [Asm81] takes the form of Figure 5.

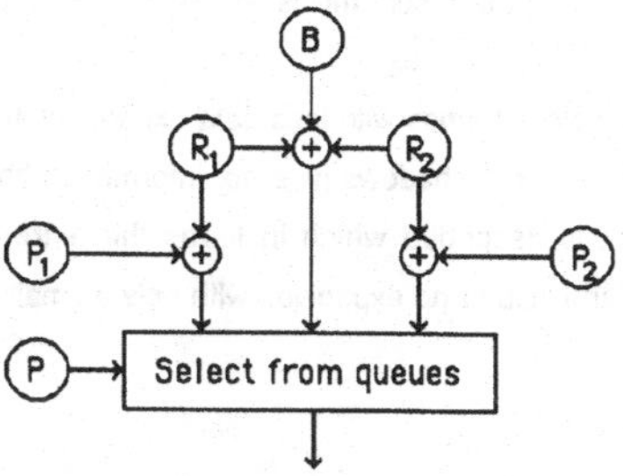


Figure 5.

The output will have an expansion factor of three. The selector stream $P$ is a stream of ternary digits. As before, if an opponent can untangle the three selected streams then he can take the exclusive or of them to obtain $P_1 \oplus B \oplus P_2$. So again one might as well take an xor of the three streams.

(e) *Threshold schemes.* Rivest and Sherman suggested using threshold schemes in randomization [Riv83]. The methods discussed as items (c) and (d) above are just special cases of a single more general threshold scheme. In what follows we only have a need for the special case of a $(k,k)$ threshold scheme. Threshold schemes do the opposite of combining several streams into one. They allow one to split a stream into several parts and allow later recombination and recovery of the original stream.

For example, the one-time pad and example (c) above are both essentially (2,2) threshold schemes in which the source bit-stream $B$ is broken into two shadows: $R$ and $R \oplus B$, for some random stream $R$. Both shadow streams are required to recover the source, and an opponent who learns one stream still has no information about the other. (This threshold scheme provides *Shannon perfect security* [Bla81].) Most of the methods of (c) involve encrypting one or the other of these shadows, or of encrypting the concatenation of the two shadows.

Similarly example (d) above breaks $B$ into three shadows: $R_1$, $R_2$, and $R_1 \oplus B \oplus R_2$. This is a (3,3) threshold scheme in which all three shadow streams are necessary and sufficient to recover the source $B$. (Here again, knowing any two of the streams gives no information about the third.) Asmuth and Blakley encrypt (in block mode) $R_1$ and $R_2$, though it would also make sense to encrypt any two or all three of these shadows.

Now suppose we have a $(k,k)$ threshold scheme. An implementation that is a generalization of the above examples employs $k$-1 random streams and the xor of these with the message stream for the $k^{th}$ stream. Alternatively one could use another $(k,k)$ threshold scheme, such as, for example, Shamir's Langrange interpolation threshold scheme [Sha79]. With both these methods, any $k$-1 out of the $k$ streams give no information about the source stream, and again one has Shannon perfect security up to threshold $k$. The first has an expansion factor of $k$ and the second somewhat greater.

We would normally expect to encrypt one or more of these $k$ shadow streams. Even if an opponent can decrypt all but one of the encrypted shadows, he would still have no information at all about the original stream. Intuitively, this scheme is at least as strong as any of the component encryption schemes used.

There also exist $(k,k)$ threshold schemes with less data expansion, though without at least $k$-fold expansion we can no longer say that $k$-1 shadows give *no* information about the source. In [Bla84] a spectrum of threshold schemes is described which includes the extreme special cases of $k$-fold expansion with perfect security, and little or no expansion with only a small measure of security.

REFERENCES.


[Aho74] A. V. Aho, J. E. Hopcroft, and J. D. Ullman, "Design and Analysis of Computer Algorithms," Addison-Wesley, 1974.

[Asm81] C. G. Asmuth, and G. R. Blakley, "An efficient algorithm for constructing a cryptosystem which is harder to crack than two other cryptosystems," *Comps. and Maths. with Applications* 7 (1981), pp. 447-450.

[Bla79] G. R. Blakley, "Safeguarding cryptographic keys," *Proc. NCC* , Vol. 48, AFIPS Press, 1979, pp. 313-317.

[Bla81] G. R. Blakley, and L. Swanson, "Security proofs for information protection systems," *Proceedings of the 1981 Symposium on Security and Privacy* , IEEE Computer Society, 1982, pp. 75-88.

[Bla84] G. R. Blakley, and C. Meadows, "Security of ramp schemes," *Proceedings of Crypto 84* , Springer-Verlag, New York (1984).

[Blu84] M. Blum, and S. Micali, "How to generate cryptographically strong sequences of pseudo-random bits," *SIAM J. Computing* 13, 4 (Nov. 1984), pp. 850-864.

[Cha66] G. J. Chaitin, "On the length of programs for computing finite binary sequences," *Journal of the ACM* 13 (1966), pp.. 547-569.

[Cha69] G. J. Chaitin, "On the length of programs for computing finite binary sequences: statistical considerations," *Journal of the ACM* 16 (1969), pp. 145-159.

[Cha75] G. J. Chaitin, "A theory of program size formally identical to information theory," *Journal of the ACM* 22 (1975), pp. 329-340.

[Eve84] S. Even, and O. Goldreich, "On the power of cascade ciphers," *ACM Transactions on Computer Systems* 3, 2 (1985), pp. 108-116.

[Kan84] R. Kannan, A. K. Lenstra, and L. Lovasz, "Polynomial factorization and nonrandomness of bits of algebraic and some transcendental numbers," *ACM Symposium on the Theory of Computing* , 1984, pp. 191-200.

[Knu81] D. Knuth, *The Art of Computer Programming: Seminumerical Algorithms* , 2nd Edition, Addison-Wesley, 1981.

[Ko84] K. Ko, "A definition of infinite pseudo-random sequences," manuscript.

[Kol65] A. N. Kolmogorov, "Three approaches to the quantitative definition of information," *Prob. of Inform. Transmission* 1,1 (1965), pp. 1-7.

[Kra84] E. Kranakis, "Theoretical aspects of the security of public key cryptography," *Technical Report 331* , Dept of Computer Science, Yale Univ., Sept. 1984.

[Mar66] P. Martin-Löf, "On the definition of random sequences," *Inform. and Control* 9 (1966), pp. 602-619.

[Mas85] J. L. Massey, and I. Ingemarson, "Toward a practical, computationally-secure cipher," presentation at Eurocrypt 85.

[Riv83] R. L. Rivest, and A. T. Sherman, "Randomized encryption techniques," *Advances in Cryptology: Proceedings of Crypto 82* , ed. by D. Chaum, et al., Plenum, 1983, pp. 145-163.

[Sha79] A. Shamir, "How to share a secret," *Communications of the ACM* 22, 11 (Nov. 1979), pp. 612-613.

[Sha83] A. Shamir, "On the generation of cryptographically strong pseudo-random sequences," *ACM Transactions on Computer Systems* 1,1 (Feb. 1983), pp. 38-44.

[Yao82] A. C. Yao, "Theory and applications of trapdoor functions," *Proc. 23rd IEEE Symp. on Found. of Computer Science* , 1982, pp. 80-91.

# ON THE LINEAR COMPLEXITY OF COMBINED SHIFT REGISTER SEQUENCES.

Lennart Brynielsson
Fst/TSA
Box 80001
S-104 50 STOCKHOLM SWEDEN

Many proposed keystream generators consist of a number of binary maximum length shift registers combined by a nonlinear binary function. The registers guarantee a long period and the nonlinear function destroys the linearity i.e. it gives the output sequence a large linear complexity <1>, (linear equivalent <2>). In order to avoid correlation attacks the function should also be correlation immune <3> i.e. the output sequence should be statistically independent of the various inputs. There is however a trade off between the linear complexity and the order of correlation immunity, since it is not easy to achieve both properties. The reason for this is that in the binary field GF(2) there are too few functions. As an example the only correlation immune function of two variables is linear.

In the field $GF(2^e)$ the situation is different. For instance, the polynomial function $x+y+3xy+2(x^2y+xy^2)+x^2y^2$ in GF(4) is both nonlinear and correlation immune. In order to valuate such a function one must be able to calculate its linear complexity. That is the purpose of this paper. We shall show the following result stated here for two variables.

THEOREM: Let x and y be two sequences in $GF(2^e)$ given by maximum length shift registers of lengths m and n which are relatively prime and greater than three. If they are combined by means of a polynomial function the linear complexity L of the resulting sequence is given by

$$L\left(\sum A_{ij} x^i y^j\right) = \sum_{A_{ij} \neq 0} m^{\|i\|_n \|j\|} \qquad A_{ij} \in GF(2^e)$$

where $\|i\|$ is the number of ones in the binary representation of i. This result is general since all functions in a finite field are polynomial functions <1>. We shall also sketch a generalization to $GF(p^e)$ for p>2.

Example

If the correlation immune polynomial mentioned above is used to combine two registers in GF(4) of length 4 and 5 then the linear complexity is 4+5+20+20+20+20. In fact the polynomial implements the function "x plus y mod 4". A more striking example is obtained if "x plus y mod 16" in GF(16) is written as a polynomial. It turns out to be correlation immune and it contains many nonlinear terms. If GF(16) is implemented as $GF(2)(t)/(t^4+t+1)$ and two registers of length 17 and 19 are combined, the linear complexity is 1670090.

Preliminaries

We shall use the following results which have been proved more generally by among others Selmer <4>, Herlestam <1>, Zierler and Mills <5>.

Lemma: Consider two sequences from two linear feedback registers whose feedback polynomials have simple roots $a_i$ and $b_j$ which are all different. The sum of the sequences will have a feedback polynomial the roots of which constitute the union $\{a_i, b_j\}$. Moreover, if all root pair products $a_i b_j$ are different then the product sequence will have a feedback polynomial with roots $a_i b_j$. This can be seen from the fact that the output n-th term from such sequences can be written as a linear combination of the n-th powers of the roots of the feedback polynomial <6>.

Proof of the theorem

We work in $K=GF(2^e)$. Let the sequence $x=(x_i)$ be generated by a linear shift register with maximum length feedback polynomial f of degree m. This implies that if a denotes a root of f then the extension field $K(a) = GF(2^{em})$ consists of the elements

$0, a, a^2, \ldots, a^{2^{em}-1} = 1$. The polynomial f has the following roots

$$a \quad a^{2^e} \quad a^{2^{2e}} \quad \ldots\ldots \quad a^{2^{(m-1)e}}$$

Now consider the sequence $x^2 = (x_i^{\,2})$. Squaring is an automorphism in fields of characteristic two and therefore this sequence must be obtained if you square the coefficients of f. The roots will also be squared. Repeating this procedure gives that the m roots of the polynomial which generates $x^{2^k}$ are

$$a^{2^k} \quad a^{2^{e+k}} \quad \ldots\ldots \quad a^{2^{(m-1)e+k}} \qquad k=0,\ 1,\ \ldots,\ e-1$$

Thus the roots are of the form a raised to different powers of two: $2^i$, $i=0,1,\ldots me-1$. Consequently, if you multiply a number of different roots then their exponents will add and it is possible to deduce from the resulting exponent which roots that were used as factors. Different factors give different products.

Now consider the sequence $x^n$ where $0 < n < 2^e$. The exponent n can be written as a sum of powers of two and the sequence can be looked upon as a product of the corresponding sequences $x^{2^k}$ which have been described above. The root products are different and we can use the lemma of Selmer <4>. We have now proved:

Theorem: Let the sequence x in $GF(2^e)$ be given by a maximum length polynomial of degree m. Then a polynomial sequence has the linear complexity

$$L\left(\sum_i A_i x^i\right) = \sum_{A_i \neq 0} m^{\|i\|} \qquad A_i \in GF(2^e)$$

We note also that the root products do not belong to K since K consists of the elements $0,\ a^r,\ a^{2r}, \ldots\ldots\ a^{(2^e-1)r}$ where $r=(2^{em}-1)/(2^e-1)$ and these powers are obtained when all roots belonging to one $x^n$ - sequence are multiplied together.

Consider now two sequences x and y over $K=GF(2^e)$ given by maximal length polynomials with degrees m and n which are supposed to be relatively prime. The common splitting field of those polynomials is $GF(2^{emn})$. We denote the primitive roots a and b. Both K(a) and K(b) are subfields and $K(a) \cap K(b) = K$ since the intersection consists of those elements in $GF(2^{emn})$ which remain fixed under the automorphisms $t \rightarrow t^{2^{em}}$ and $t \rightarrow t^{2^{en}}$. Therefore they are also fixed under the automorphism $t \rightarrow t^{2^{e\gcd(m,n)}} = t^{2^e}$ which implies that they belong to $K = GF(2^e)$.

When a term $x^k y^l$ is formed we obtain root products of the type $a^i b^j$ where $a^i$ originates from $x^k$ and similarly $b^j$ from $y^l$. Again we must show that different factors give rise to different products. If $a^i b^j = a^{i'} b^{j'}$ then it follows that $a^{(i-i')} \in K$. That this is impossible when $m \geq 4$ can be seen as follows. Arrange for an element in $K(a) = GF(2^{em})$ the binary representation of the exponent of a in a exm-matrix. Then for elements of K each row will consist entirely of either zeros or ones whereas for elements which are root products there will be at most a single one in each row. For $m \geq 4$ it is impossible for the sum of a "K type" and a "root product type" exponent to yield another "root product type"; there will be too many ones left.

The case $GF(p^e)$ when $p>2$

Similar results are also valid when the characteristic is greater than two i.e. when $K=GF(p^e)$. The difference in the deduction when $p>2$ concerns the roots corresponding to $x^k$ for $1<k<p$. Herlestam has shown <7> that all $C(m+k-1,k)$ possible root products are present. By means of automorphisms it can be shown that the polynomial corresponding to $x^{kp^j}$ has the same number of roots, all of the form $a^i$ where i in the p-ary number system has only one single nonzero digit. The linear complexity of a power $x^n$, $0<n<p^e$, can now be written:

$$L(x^n) = \prod_{i=0}^{e-1} \binom{m+n_i-1}{n_i}$$

where $n_0, n_1, \ldots n_{e-1}$ denote the p-ary digits. This expression is the generalisation of $m^{\|i\|}$ when $p>2$. The condition greater than three should be replaced by greater than p+1. In all other respects the proofs and theorems are similar.

References

<1> T. Herlestam, "On the Complexity of Functions of Linear Shift Register Sequences", IEEE 1982, Les Arcs, France.

<2> E.J. Groth, "Generation of Binary Sequences with Controllable Complexity", IEEE Trans. on Inf. Th. It-17 1971.

<3>. T. Siegenthaler, "Correlation Immunity of Nonlinear Combining Functions for Cryptographic Applications." IEEE Trans. on Inf. Th. It-30 1984.

<4> E.S. Selmer, "Linear Recurrence Relations over Finite Fields", Dept of Math., Univ. of Bergen, Norway, 1966.

<5> N. Zierler and W.H. Mills, "Products of Linear Recurring Sequences", J. Algebra, 27, 1973.

<6> T. Beth, "Stream Ciphers", Proceedings of Secure Digit Comm. C.I.S.M. Udine 1982.

<7> T. Herlestam, private communication, to be published.

# ANALYSIS OF A NONLINEAR FEEDFORWARD LOGIC FOR BINARY SEQUENCE GENERATORS

J. Bernasconi and C.G. Günther
Brown Boveri Research Center
CH-5405 Baden, Switzerland

A new type of nonlinear feedforward logic for binary sequence generators is proposed, i.e. a logic that combines the stages of a linear feedback shift register (LFSR) in a nonlinear way. The sequences generated are analyzed with respect to their transient and ultimately periodic behavior. They are shown to have a balanced zero-one distribution, and a lower bound on their linear complexity is derived which grows exponentially with the length of the LFSR.

Binary sequences with good randomness properties play an important role in cipher systems [1]. Usually, such sequences are generated by a finite state machine and are therefore not truly random. A common measure for the unpredictability of a pseudorandom binary sequence is its <u>linear complexity</u> L, defined as the length of the shortest linear feedback shift register (LFSR) that can generate the sequence. A high linear complexity is an important necessary requirement for cryptographic applications, and corresponding generators therefore have to be nonlinear.

In the case of a nonlinear feedforward logic that combines the stages of a single LFSR, Key [2] has shown how the linear complexity can be determined. If the order of the feedforward function is larger than two, however, the procedure becomes very involved and in general only yields upper bounds. In this paper, we shall show that a <u>lower</u> bound on the linear complexity can be obtained if the feedforward function satisfies certain requirements.

A special type of logic that produces such feedforward functions is shown in Figure 1. It is applied to an $\ell$-stage m-LFSR (i.e. an LFSR generating a sequence $\{u_t\}$ of maximal period $2^\ell-1$) and contains the following elements:

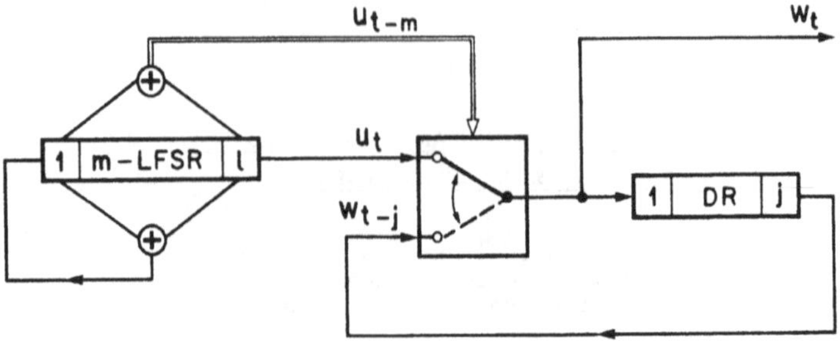


FIGURE 1
The nonlinear binary sequence generator.

- a delay logic which generates a cyclic shift $u_{t-m}$ of $u_t$. (Such a logic may be based on the shift-and-add property of m-sequences [3]);

- a delay register DR of length j, with j relatively prime to $2^{\ell}-1$;

- a switch, controlled by $u_{t-m}$, which connects either $u_t$ (if $u_{t-m}=0$) or $w_{t-j}$ (if $u_{t-m} = 1$) to its output.

With the connections as shown in Figure 1, the output sequence $\{w_t\}$ of the generator satisfies the recursion

$$w_t = (1 \oplus u_{t-m})u_t \oplus u_{t-m}\, w_{t-j} \quad , \qquad t \geq 0 \quad , \tag{1}$$

with initial conditions,

$$w_t = r_{-t-1} \quad , \qquad -j \leq t \leq -1 \quad , \tag{2}$$

where $\{r_t\}_{t=0}^{j-1}$ denotes the initial content of the delay register DR.

A detailed analysis of the properties of the sequence $\{w_t\}$ will be presented in a more extended paper [4]. Here we restrict ourselves to a brief summary of our main results.

We first note that the generator is selfsynchronizing in the sense that for t larger than some transient time $t_E < \ell j$, the solution $\{w_t\}$ of Eq. (1) becomes periodic and independent of the initial conditions $\{r_t\}$. If the period $T = 2^\ell - 1$ of the m-sequence $\{u_t\}$ is prime and larger than 3, then $\{w_t\}$ also has period T.

For our further analysis we now assume that the two delays m and j are related by

$$m = kj \quad , \quad k \leq \ell - 1 \quad . \tag{3}$$

Then the (unique) periodic solution to Eq.(1) is explicitly given by

$$\begin{aligned} w_t = u_t \oplus u_{t-kj}(u_t \oplus u_{t-j}) \oplus u_{t-kj}\, u_{t-(k+1)j}(u_{t-j} \oplus u_{t-2j}) \\ \oplus \dots \oplus u_{t-kj}\, u_{t-(k+1)j} \cdots u_{t-(2k-1)j}(u_{t-(k-1)j} \oplus 1) \quad . \end{aligned} \tag{4}$$

Through Eq. (4), the output sequence $\{w_t\}$ of our generator is expressed in terms of the m-sequence $\{u_t\}$ via a nonlinear function of order k+1. We observe that the highest order term of this function is a single product of k+1 equally spaced shifts of $u_t$,

$$u_{t-(k-1)j}\, u_{t-kj} \cdots u_{t-(2k-1)j} \quad . \tag{5}$$

It is this specific property that enables us to derive a lower bound on the linear complexity of the sequence $\{w_t\}$ :

Theorem 1: Let f denote a nonlinear function combining the cyclic shifts of an m-sequence $\{u_t\}$ of period $2^\ell - 1$, and let the highest order term of f be a product of the form $u_t\, u_{t+j} \cdots u_{t+(n-1)j}$ , with $n \leq \ell$ and $(j, 2^\ell - 1) = 1$. Then the linear complexity L of the sequence defined through f is bounded from below by $L \geq \binom{\ell}{n}$.

It follows that the linear complexity $L_w$ of the sequence $\{w_t\}$ represented by Eq. (4) is bounded from below by

$$L_w \geq \binom{\ell}{k+1} \quad , \quad k \leq \ell - 1 \quad . \tag{6}$$

For a given $\ell$, this bound is optimal if $k+1 = [\ell/2]$. It then becomes

$$L_W \geq \binom{\ell}{[\ell/2]} \sim \sqrt{\frac{2}{\pi\ell}}\, 2^{\ell} \quad , \qquad \ell >> 1 \quad , \tag{7}$$

which is of the same order of magnitude as Key's corresponding upper bound [2],

$$L_W \leq \sum_{i=1}^{[\ell/2]} \binom{\ell}{i} \sim \frac{1}{2}\, 2^{\ell} \quad , \qquad \ell >> 1 \quad . \tag{8}$$

The proof of Theorem 1 is given in Ref. [4], and we note that essentially the same result has been derived independently by R. Rueppel [5]. Recently, we also became aware of a paper by Kumar and Scholtz [6] where a closely related theorem is used to establish a lower bound on the maximum-achievable linear complexity in a family of bent-function sequences.

The proof is based on a result due to Key [2] which can be stated as follows. Let $\alpha$ be a primitive element of $GF(2^{\ell})$, and let $\{s_t\}$ be a binary sequence of period $T = 2^{\ell}-1$ whose elements are represented in the form

$$s_t = \bigoplus_{h=1}^{\ell} \bigoplus_{x \varepsilon H_h^T} \gamma_x\, \alpha^{tx} \quad , \qquad \gamma_x \;\varepsilon\; GF(2^{\ell}) \quad , \tag{9}$$

where $H_h^T$ denotes the set of integers in $\{0,1,\ldots,T-1\}$ with Hamming weight h. Then the linear complexity L of $\{s_t\}$ is equal to the number of nonvanishing coefficients $\gamma_x$.

Now Theorem 1 is concerned with sequences

$$s_t = \prod_{\kappa=0}^{n-1} u_{t+\kappa j} \; + \text{lower order terms} \quad , \tag{10}$$

where $\{u_t\}$ is an m-sequence of period $2^{\ell}-1$ and therefore has the representation [7]

$$u_t = \bigoplus_{i=0}^{\ell-1} \gamma^{2^i}\, \alpha^{t2^i} \quad , \qquad \gamma \;\varepsilon\; GF(2^{\ell}) \quad , \tag{11}$$

with $\alpha$ a primitive root of the characteristic polynomial of $\{u_t\}$. In general, the determination of the expansion coefficients $\gamma_x$ for $s_t$, obtained by inserting Eq. (11) into Eq. (10), is prohibitively complex. Those coefficients $\gamma_x$, however, for which the Hamming weight of x is maximal (i.e. equal to n), all originate exclusively from the highest order term in Eq. (10) and can be expressed explicitly as Vandermonde determinants. If $n \leq \ell$ and $(j, 2^\ell - 1) = 1$, none of these $\binom{n}{\ell}$ coefficients vanishes, so that the linear complexity L of $\{s_t\}$ is at least $\binom{n}{\ell}$.

Let us finally summarize some results on the statistical properties of the sequence $\{w_t\}$ generated by our nonlinear generator (Eq. (4)). The fraction of ones, $P\{w_t=1\}$, is given by

$$P\{w_t=1\} = \frac{1}{2}\left(1 + \frac{2^{\ell-k}+1}{2^\ell - 1}\right) \quad , \qquad k \leq \ell-1 \quad , \tag{12}$$

so that for large values of $\ell$ and k the balance between zeros and ones in $\{w_t\}$ is almost ideal. The autocorrelation function $C_w(\tau)$, however, exhibits peaks (of exponentially decreasing magnitude) at $\tau = j, 2j, \ldots$ These peaks are due to the special structure of our generator (j is the length of the delay register DR, see Figure 1). In addition, the probability that $w_t$ coincides with $u_t$ is close to 3/4, and thus deviates considerably from the ideal value of 1/2.

To overcome these leakage problems ,and to eliminate the peaks in the autocorrelation function, the simple generator of Figure 1 obviously has to be modified. It turns out that the structure allows for a variety of corresponding modifications which leave the lower bound on the linear complexity unchanged, and which moreover introduce a convenient additional key multiplicity [4].

## REFERENCES

[1] H. Beker and F. Piper, Cipher Systems. London: Northwood Books, 1982.
S.W. Golomb, Shift register sequences. Revised edition, Laguna Hills, California: Aegean Park Press, 1982.

[2] E.L. Key, "An analysis of the structure and complexity of nonlinear binary sequence generators", IEEE Trans.Inform.Theory, vol. IT-22, pp. 732-736, Nov. 1976.

[3] S.H. Tsao, "Generation of delayed replicas of maximal-length linear binary sequences", Proc. IEEE, vol. 111, pp. 1803-1806, Nov. 1964.

[4] J. Bernasconi and C.G. Günther, "Analysis of a nonlinear feed-forward logic for binary sequence generators", submitted to IEEE Trans.Inform.Theory.

[5] R.A. Rueppel, New approaches to stream ciphers. Ph. D. Thesis, ETH-Zürich, 1984.

[6] P.V. Kumar and R.A. Scholtz, "Bounds on the linear span of bent sequences", IEEE Trans.Inform.Theory, vol. IT-29, pp. 854-862, Nov. 1983.

[7] N. Zierler, "Linear recurring sequences", J.Soc.Indust.Appl.Math., vol. 7, pp. 31-48, March 1959.

# Linear Complexity and Random Sequences

Rainer A. Rueppel
Swiss Federal Institute of Technology
8092 Zurich/Switzerland
currently: CMRR, University of California, San Diego
La Jolla, CA 92093/U.S.A.

Abstract:

The problem of characterizing the randomness of finite sequences arises in cryptographic applications. The idea of randomness clearly reflects the difficulty of predicting the next digit of a sequence from all the previous ones. The approach taken in this paper is to measure the (linear) unpredictability of a sequence (finite or periodic) by the length of the shortest linear feedback shift register (LFSR) that is able to generate the given sequence. This length is often referred to in the literature as the linear complexity of the sequence. It is shown that the expected linear complexity of a sequence of n independent and uniformly distributed binary random variables is very close to n/2 and, that the variance of the linear complexity is virtually independent of the sequence length, i.e. is virtually a constant! For the practically interesting case of periodically repeating a finite truly random sequence of length $2^m$ or $2^m-1$, it is shown that the linear complexity is close to the period length.

## Linear Complexity and Random Sequences

Stream ciphers utilize deterministically generated "random" sequences to encipher the message stream. Since the running key generator is a finite state machine, the key stream necessarily is (ultimately) periodic. Thus the best one can hope for is to make the first period of a periodic key stream resemble the output of a binary symmetric source (BSS). A BSS is a device which puts out with equal probability a zero or a one independently of the previous output bits, or in other words, a BSS realizes a fair coin tossing experiment. (Note that we have tacitly assumed the sequences under investigation to be defined over GF(2)). The period of the key stream necessarily is a finite quantity. Thus we are confronted with the problem of characterizing the randomness of a finite sequence. But how can this be done in light of the fact that every finite output sequence of a BSS is equally likely? It seems difficult to define adequately the concept of randomness (in a mathematical sense) for finite sequences. Still, nearly everyone would agree that something like a "typical" output sequence of a BSS exists. A finite coin tossing sequence, for example, would "typically" exhibit a balanced distribution of single bits, pairs, triples, etc. of bits, and long runs of one symbol would be very rare. This in contrast to infinite coin tossing sequences, where local non-randomness is sure to occur. D.E. Knuth (Knut 81) discusses various concepts of randomness for infinite sequences and gives a short description of how randomness of a finite sequence could be defined. By the above typicality-argument, one is led naturally to the criterion of distribution properties. A finite sequence of length T may be called "random" if every binary k-tuple for all k smaller than some upperbound (e.g. logT) appears about equally often. The "randomness postulates" of S. Golomb (Golo 67) based on this definition have gained widespread popularity (especially in the cryptographic community). Golomb proposed the following three requirements to measure the randomness of a periodic binary sequence. First, the disparity between zeros and ones within one period of the sequence does not exceed 1. Second, in every period, $(1/2^i)$th of the total number of runs has length i, as long as there are at least 2 runs of length i. Third, the periodic autocorrelation function is two-valued. Every sequence which satisfied these three randomness requirements was called by Golomb a pseudo-noise (PN) sequence. But although

Golomb called his requirements "randomness postulates", they do not define a general measure of randomness for finite sequences. These "randomness postulates" rather describe almost exclusively the sequences which have a primitive minimal polynomial (since they have maximum possible period, they are also called maximum-length sequences or m-sequences). But this means that the so-called PN-sequences are highly predictable, if L denotes the degree of the primitive minimal polynomial of the PN-sequence under investigation, then only 2L bits of the sequence suffice to specify completely the remainder of the period of length $2^L-1$. Clearly the idea of randomness also reflects the impossibility of predicting the next digit of a sequence from all the previous ones. An interesting approach to a definition of randomness of finite sequences based on this concept of unpredictability was taken by R. Solomonov (Solo 64) and A. Kolmogorov (Kolm 65). They chararacterized the "patternlessness" of a finite sequence by the length of the shortest Turing machine program that could generate the sequence. Patternlessness may be equated with unpredictability or randomness. This concept was further developed by P. Martin-Loef (Mart 66). A different approach to evaluating the complexity of finite sequences was given by A. Lempel and J. Ziv (Lemp 76). Instead of an abstract model of computation such as a Turing machine one could directly use a linear feedback shift register (LFSR) model and measure the (linear) unpredictability of a sequence (finite or periodic) by the length of the shortest LFSR which is able to generate the given sequence. This approach is particularly appealing since there exists an efficient synthesis procedure (the Berlekamp-Massey LFSR synthesis algorithm (Mass 69)) for finding the shortest LFSR which generates a given sequence. This length is also referred to as the linear complexity associated to the sequence. The following sequence obtained by the author in 31 trials with a fair swiss coin may serve as an illustration for the concept of linear complexity as measure of randomness (or linear unpredictability).

$$\tilde{s} = (1000111101000011011110100010100)^{\infty} \qquad (1)$$

In Fig. 1, we compare the dynamic behaviour of the linear complexity of the periodically repeated swiss coin sequence (1) to that of a PN-sequence of period 31. $\Lambda(s^n)$ denotes the linear complexity of the first n digit subsequence of $\tilde{s}$.

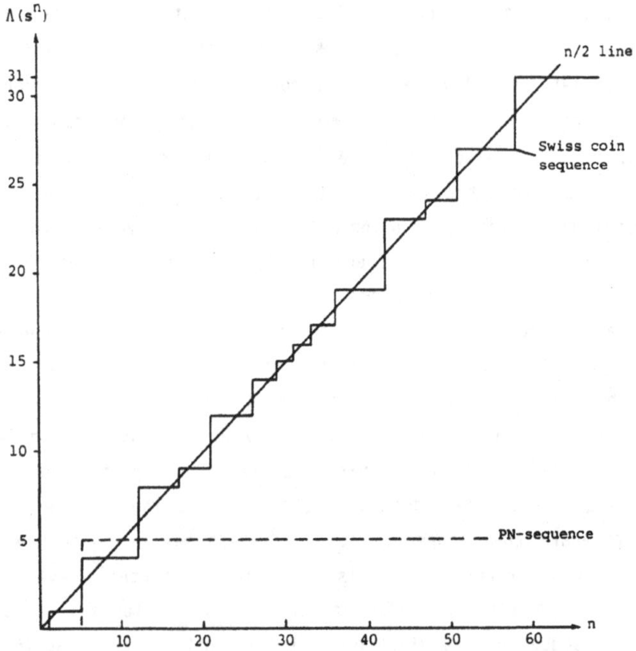


Fig. 1. Linear complexity profiles of the swiss coin sequence (1) and the PN-sequence generated by $<5,1+D^2+D^5>$ and initial state [0,0,0,0,1]

The linear complexity of the swiss coin sequence (1) grows approximately as n/2, where n denotes the number of processed bits, and stops at 31 which is the period of the sequence (1). Thus only the circulating shift register of length L = 31 is able to generate the swiss coin sequence. Conversely, the so-called PN-sequence of period 31 has a linear complexity of only 5 and is highly predictable. But note, a high linear complexity alone does not guarantee good randomness properties. As an example consider the sequence built by 30 consecutive 0's and an appended 1 which is periodically repeated. This sequence can also only be generated by the circulating shift register of length 31, but does not exhibit any randomness properties whatsoever. This could be seen in the associated linear complexity profile, in which the linear complexity remains at 0 until the 1 appears at the 31st position which causes the linear complexity to jump from 0 to 31 in one swoop. Consequently, we expect a "typical" random sequence to have associated a "typical" linear complexity profile closely following the n/2 line.

Let $s^n = s_0, s_1, \ldots, s_{n-1}$ denote a sequence of n independent and uniformly distributed binary random variables, and let $\Lambda(s^n)$ be the associated linear complexity. Our primary interest is in $N_n(L)$, the number of sequences of length n with linear complexity $\Lambda(s^n) = L$. Consider the basic recursion from $\Lambda(s^{n-1})$ to $\Lambda(s^n)$. The difference between the nth binary random variable $s_{n-1}$ and the nth digit generated by the minimal-length LFSR which is able to generate $s^{n-1}$ is called the next discrepancy $\delta_{n-1}$. If the LFSR of length $\Lambda(s^{n-1})$ which generates $s^{n-1}$ also generates $s^n$, then $\delta_{n-1} = 0$ and the linear complexity does not change. Conversely, if the LFSR of length $\Lambda(s^{n-1})$ which generates $s^{n-1}$ fails to generate $s^n$, then $\delta_{n-1} = 1$ and the linear complexity increases when $\Lambda(s^{n-1})$ is smaller than n/2. The recursion describing the length change is basic to the LFSR-synthesis procedure (Mass 69):

$$\delta_{n-1} = 0 \qquad \Lambda(s^n) = \Lambda(s^{n-1}) \tag{2a}$$

$$\delta_{n-1} = 1 \qquad \begin{cases} \Lambda(s^n) = \Lambda(s^{n-1}) & \text{if } \Lambda(s^{n-1}) \geq \frac{n}{2} \\ \Lambda(s^n) = n - \Lambda(s^{n-1}) & \text{if } \Lambda(s^{n-1}) < \frac{n}{2} . \end{cases} \tag{2b}$$

Note that the linear complexity does not change (regardless of the value of the discrepancy) when $\Lambda(s^{n-1}) \geq \frac{n}{2}$. It is illuminating to represent graphically the linear complexity recursion (2) (see Fig. 2. )

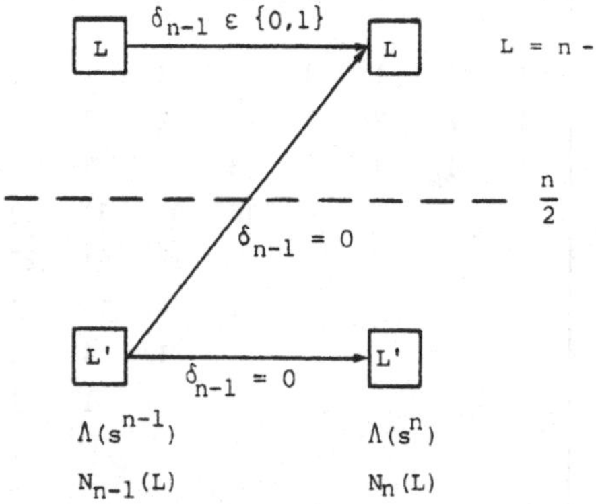


Fig. 2. Graphical illustration of the linear complexity growth process

From the diagram in Fig. 2, we may now directly read off the recursion for $N_n(L)$. If $\Lambda(s^{n-1}) = L' < \frac{n}{2}$, then $N_n(L') = N_{n-1}(L')$ since only one choice for $s_{n-1}$ causes $\delta_{n-1} = 0$. The second choice for $s_{n-1}$ causes $\delta_{n-1} = 1$ and thus transfers $N_{n-1}(L')$ sequences to the new complexity $L = n-L'$. If $\Lambda(s^{n-1}) = L > \frac{n}{2}$, then $\Lambda(s^n) = L$ (irrespective of $\delta_{n-1}$) and $2N_{n-1}(L)$ sequences contribute to $N_n(L)$. The only exception to the sketched process in Fig. 2 occurs when n is even and $L = \frac{n}{2}$. In this case no path from $\Lambda(s_{n-1}) = L' < \frac{n}{2}$ may lead to $\Lambda(s^n) = L = \frac{n}{2}$, since $L = \frac{n}{2} = n-L'$ would require $L' = \frac{n}{2}$ which contradicts the assumption. We can now write the recursion for $N_n(L)$, the number of sequences of length n with linear complexity N, as

$$N_n(L) = \begin{cases} 2N_{n-1}(L) + N_{n-1}(n-L) & n \geqslant L > \frac{n}{2} \quad (3a) \\ 2N_{n-1}(L) & L = \frac{n}{2} \quad (3b) \\ N_{n-1}(L) & \frac{n}{2} > L \geqslant 0 \,. \quad (3c) \end{cases}$$

The initial conditions for the recursion (3) are $N_1(0) = N_1(1) = 1$. At any length n the total number of sequences is $2^n$. In table 1, the values of $N_n(L)$ are listed for all positive $n \leqslant 10$.

| L \ n | 1 | 2 | 3 | 4 | 5 | 6 | 7 | 8 | 9 | 10 |
|---|---|---|---|---|---|---|---|---|---|---|
| 0 | 1 | 1 | 1 | 1 | 1 | 1 | 1 | 1 | 1 | 1 |
| 1 | 1 | 2 | 2 | 2 | 2 | 2 | 2 | 2 | 2 | 2 |
| 2 | | 1 | 4 | 8 | 8 | 8 | 8 | 8 | 8 | 8 |
| 3 | | | 1 | 4 | 16 | 32 | 32 | 32 | 32 | 32 |
| 4 | | | | 1 | 4 | 16 | 64 | 128 | 128 | 128 |
| 5 | | | | | 1 | 4 | 16 | 64 | 256 | 512 |
| 6 | | | | | | 1 | 4 | 16 | 64 | 256 |
| 7 | | | | | | | 1 | 4 | 16 | 64 |
| 8 | | | | | | | | 1 | 4 | 16 |
| 9 | | | | | | | | | 1 | 4 |
| 10 | | | | | | | | | | 1 |

Table 1. Values of $N_n(L)$ for n = 1, ..., 10

The general form of $N_n(L)$ is easily guessed from table 1.

$$N_n(L) = \begin{cases} 2^{\min\{2n-2L,2L-1\}} & n \geq L > 0 \qquad (4a) \\ 1 & n > L = 0 \qquad (4b) \end{cases}$$

To show that this solution is correct, we first prove that the solution satisfies the recursion (3) for all $n > 1$.

Suppose $n \geq L > n/2$, then $N_n(L) = 2^{2n-2L}$, $N_{n-1}(L) = 2^{2n-2-2L}$ and $N_{n-1}(n-L) = 2^{2n-2L-1}$, since $n \leq 2L$ implies $2(n-L) < n-1$. These values satisfy recursion (3a) for all $n > 1$, as can be seen by substitution.

Suppose $L = n/2$, then $N_n(L) = 2^{2L-1}$ and $N_{n-1}(L) = 2^{2L-2}$, which satisfy recursion (3b) for all even $n > 1$.

Suppose $n/2 > L > 0$, then $N_n(L) = N_{n-1}(L) = 2^{2L-1}$ and the recursion (3c) is trivially satisfied for all $n > 1$.

By taking into account the initial conditions $N_1(0) = N_1(1) = 1$ the solution (4) is seen to yield the correct values for $n = 2$. Thus (4) is the solution to the recursion (3). We summarize the result in the following proposition.

<u>Proposition</u> 1. Distribution of $N_n(L)$

The number $N_n(L)$ of binary sequences $s^n = s_0, s_1, \ldots, s_{n-1}$ of length $n$ having linear complexity exactly $L$ is

$$N_n(L) = \begin{cases} 2^{\min\{2n-2L,2L-1\}} & n \geq L > 0 \\ 1 & n > L = 0 \end{cases} .$$

The form of $N_n(L)$ for the general case of q-ary sequences may be found in (Gust 76) where the objective of that author was to evaluate the performance of the Berlekamp-Massey LFSR synthesis algorithm. Our interest is in characterizing a "typical" random sequence by means of the associated linear complexity. Proposition 1 tells us that the vast majority of the possible binary sequences of length n will have linear complexity close to n/2. A quantity of independent interest, related to $N_n(L)$, is the number of semi-infinite sequences of linear complexity L or less, which we denote by $N_L$. For finite L > 0, Proposition 1. gives $N_\infty(L) = 2^{2L-1}$. Thus

$$N_L = 1 + \sum_{j=1}^{L} 2^{2j-1} \tag{5}$$

where the added 1 accounts for the allzero sequence, which has linear complexity L = 0. Evaluating the finite geometric series (5) yields

$$N_L = \frac{2}{3}\, 2^{2L} + \frac{1}{3}\,. \tag{6}$$

When we consider the tree corresponding to the set of all binary semi-infinite sequences, then at depth 2L every sequence of linear complexity L or less is characterized by the fact that the associated LFSR which may produce the sequence is unique. Hence the significance of (6) is that almost exactly 2/3 of all sequences of length 2L may be generated with an LFSR of length L or less. Both proposition 1. and the above argument on $N_L$ suggest that any sequence of n randomly selected binary digits will "typically" have a linear complexity close to n/2. To obtain a precise characterization, we may compute the expected linear complexity of a sequence $s^n$ of n independent binary random variables $s_0, s_1, \ldots, s_{n-1}$ (as emitted from a BSS).

$$E[\Lambda(s^n)] = \sum_{b^n} \Lambda(b^n) \quad P(b^n) \tag{7}$$

where $b^n$ denotes a particular realization of the coin tossing sequence $s^n$. Since each $b^n$ is equally likely, the probability $P(s^n = b^n)$ is $2^{-n}$. Therefore

$$E[\Lambda(s^n)] = 2^{-n} \sum_{b^n} \Lambda(b^n) = 2^{-n} L^*(n) \tag{8}$$

where we have introduced the symbol $L^*(n)$ for $2^n\, E[\Lambda(s^n)]$. The set of all $b^n$ may be subdivided into equivalence classes according to the associated linear complexity. Thus we may rewrite the sum $L^*(n)$ in (8) as

$$L^*(n) = \sum_{L=1}^{n} \sum_{\{b^n:\Lambda(b^n)=L\}} L \;. \tag{9}$$

The Lth equivalent class is easily identified to contain $N_n(L)$ elements. Thus

$$L^*(n) = \sum_{L=1}^{n} L\, N_n(L) \;. \tag{10}$$

Replacing $N_n(L)$ by the solution given in proposition 1, we obtain

$$L^*(n) = \sum_{L=1}^{n} L 2^{\min\{2n-2L,2L-1\}} \tag{11}$$

which may be subdivided into two sums according to the dominance of 2n-2L or 2L-1, which results in

$$L^*(n) = \sum_{L=1}^{\lfloor n/2 \rfloor} L 2^{2L-1} + \sum_{L=\lceil \frac{n+1}{2} \rceil} L 2^{2n-2L} \;. \tag{12}$$

It is now possible to obtain a closed form expression for the finite sum in (12) by applying standard analytical methods. We illustrate the principle by evaluating

$$\sum_{j=1}^{m} j 2^{2j-1} \;. \tag{13}$$

First, we introduce a dummy variable I raised to the (j-1)st power,

$$\sum_{j=1}^{m} j\, I^{j-1}\, 2^{2j-1} \;.$$

Now we integrate the sum with respect to I,

$$\sum_{j=1}^{m} I^j 2^{2j-1} \quad .$$

This is an ordinary geometric series whose sum is given by

$$2I \frac{I^m 2^{2m} - 1}{I\ 2^2\ -1} \quad .$$

Differentiating this sum and setting I = 1, we obtain as the closed form solution for (13)

$$\sum_{j=1}^{m} j2^{2j-1} = \frac{(m+1)}{3}\ 2^{2m+1} - \frac{2}{9}\ (2^{2m+1} - 1) \ . \tag{14}$$

Because of the floor- and ceiling-functions in (12), it is convenient to distinguish between even and odd n. Let $L_e^*(n)$ and $L_0^*(n)$ denote the function $L^*(n)$ evaluated at even n and at odd n, respectively. Then by applying the standard techniques, as explained in the derivation of (14), to the individual sums in (12), we obtain for even n

$$L_e^*(n) = \{2^n (\frac{n}{3} - \frac{2}{9} + \frac{2}{9} 2^{-n})\} + \{2^n (\frac{n}{6} + \frac{4}{9} - 2^{-n} (\frac{n}{3} + \frac{4}{9}))\} \tag{15}$$

where the brackets {} enclose the values of the two distinct sums in (20).

In the case of odd n, we similarly obtain

$$L_0^*(n) = \{2^n (\frac{n}{6} - \frac{5}{18} + \frac{2}{9} 2^{-n})\} + \{2^n (\frac{n}{3} + \frac{5}{9} - 2^{-n} (\frac{n}{3} + \frac{4}{9}))\} \ . \tag{16}$$

Now it is straightforward to combine (8), (15) and (16) to obtain the desired expected linear complexity $E[\Lambda(s^n)]$. We summarize the result in the following proposition.

<u>Proposition 2.</u> $E[\Lambda(s^n)]$

The expected linear complexity of a sequence $s^n = s_0, s_1, \ldots, s_{n-1}$ of n independent and uniformly distributed binary random variables is given by

$$E[\Lambda(s^n)] = \frac{n}{2} + \frac{4+R_2(n)}{18} - 2^{-n}\left(\frac{n}{3}+\frac{2}{9}\right) \tag{17}$$

where $R_2(n)$ denotes the remainder when n is divided by 2.

Proposition 2. confirms our suspicion that the linear complexity of a randomly selected sequence $s^n$ can be expected close to n/2. Nevertheless, it is surprising how very close to half the sequence length that the expected linear complexity actually lies. For large values of n,

$$E[\Lambda(s^n)] \cong \frac{n}{2} + \frac{4+R_2(n)}{18} \qquad n \gg 1 \tag{18}$$

which differs from n/2 by only an offset of 2/9 in the case of even n or 5/18 in the case of odd n. Besides the expectation, the variance of the linear complexity is a second key parameter suited for characterizing "typical" random sequences. The variance is defined as

$$\begin{aligned} Var[\Lambda(s^n)] &= E\left[\{\Lambda(s^n) - E[\Lambda(s^n)]\}^2\right] \\ &= E[\Lambda^2(s^n)] - E[\Lambda(s^n)]^2 \quad . \end{aligned} \tag{19}$$

Following the same approach as for the derivation of $E[\Lambda(s^n)]$, the second moment $E[\Lambda^2(s^n)]$ is found to be (compare 12)

$$L^{2*}(n) = E[\Lambda^2(s^n)]\, 2^n = \sum_{L=1}^{\lfloor n/2 \rfloor} L^2\, 2^{2L-1} + \sum_{L=\lceil \frac{n+1}{2} \rceil}^{n} L^2\, 2^{2n-2L} \tag{20}$$

We apply again the standard technique of integration and differentation of the finite sums in (20) to obtain a closed form expression for $L^{2*}(n)$.

For analytical convenience, let $L_e^{2*}(n)$ and $L_o^{*2}(n)$ denote the function $L^{2*}(n)$ evaluated at even and odd n, respectively. We indicate the two distinct sums in (20) by enclosing them with brackets {}. In the case of even n, we obtain

$$L_e^{2*}(n) = \{2^{n+1}(\frac{1}{12}n^2 - \frac{1}{9}n + \frac{5}{27}) - \frac{10}{27}\}$$
$$+ \{2^n(\frac{1}{12}n^2 + \frac{4}{9}n + \frac{20}{27}) - (\frac{1}{3}n^2 + \frac{8}{9}n + \frac{20}{27})\} \quad . \qquad (21)$$

In the case of odd n, we obtain

$$L_o^{2*}(n) = \{2^n(\frac{1}{12}n^2 - \frac{5}{18}n + \frac{41}{108}) - \frac{10}{27}\}$$
$$+ \{2^n(\frac{1}{6}n^2 + \frac{5}{9}n + \frac{41}{54}) - (\frac{1}{3}n^2 + \frac{8}{9}n + \frac{20}{27}\} \quad . \qquad (22)$$

Now it is straightforward to combine (20), (21), and (22) to obtain the desired closed form expression for the second moment of the linear complexity for all positive n:

$$E[\Lambda^2(s^n)] = \frac{1}{4}n^2 + \frac{4+R_2(n)}{18} + \frac{40+R_2(n)}{36}$$
$$- 2^{-n}(\frac{1}{3}n^2 + \frac{8}{9}n + \frac{10}{9}) \qquad (23)$$

where $R_2(n)$ denotes the remainder when n is divided by 2. Finally, the first moment of the linear complexity (as shown in proposition 2.) together with the second moment as displayed in (23), allow the calculation of $Var[\Lambda(s^n)]$, via (19). We summarize the result in the following proposition.

Proposition 3. $Var[\Lambda(s^n)]$

The variance of the linear complexity of a sequence $s^n = s_0, s_1, \ldots, s_{n-1}$ of n independent and uniformly distributed binary random variables is given by

$$Var[\Lambda(s^n)] = \frac{86}{81} - 2^{-n}\left(\frac{14-R_2(n)}{27}n + \frac{82-2R_2(n)}{81}\right) - 2^{-2n}\left(\frac{1}{9}n^2 + \frac{4}{27}n + \frac{4}{81}\right) \tag{24}$$

where $R_2(n)$ denotes the remainder when n is divided by 2. Moreover,

$$\lim_{n\to\infty} Var[\Lambda(s^n)] = \frac{86}{81} . \tag{25}$$

The variance is a measure of spread. If the variance is small then large deviations of the random variable under consideration from its mean are improbable. One might have expected that the spread of the linear complexity grows with increasing length n of the investigated sequence. Note that $\Lambda(s^n)$ may assume more and more values with increasing n. The interesting implication of proposition 3. is that the spread of the linear complexity $\Lambda(s^n)$ is virtually independent of the sequence length n. Regardless of how many sequence bits are processed, the fraction of sequences centered around the mean is virtually constant. We may make these intuitive statements more precise by invoking Chebyshev's inequality (Fell 68), which implies that, for any $k > 0$, the probability that the linear complexity of a random sequence $s^n$ differs by an amount larger or equal than k from its mean is bounded from above by the variance of the linear complexity divided by $k^2$. Thus, for all n,

$$P\{\left|\Lambda(s^n) - E[\Lambda(s^n)]\right| \geq k\} \leq \frac{Var[\Lambda(s^n)]}{k^2} . \tag{26}$$

Suppose $k = 10$, then, for sufficiently large n, Chebychev's inequality provides a bound of $(86/81)10^{-2} = 0.0106$. Consequently, at least 99 % of all random sequences $s^n$ have a linear complexity within the range $(n/2) \pm 10$. This is a surprisingly sharp characterization of random sequences by means of their associated linear complexity. Moreover, Chebychev's inequality is known to yield fairly loose bounds in individual applications because of its universality, so we may expect an even closer scattering of the linear complexities around the mean.

A different approach which could help to characterize random sequences is to consider the growth process of the linear complexity as a special kind of random walk. In this interpretation, $\Lambda(s^n)$ gives the "position" of the "particle" at time n. We may define the n/2-line as the "origin" of the "particle", since at any time the expected location of the "particle" is about n/2 (compare proposition 2). Typically the "particle" would depart from the n/2-line to some position below the n/2-line, then jump above the n/2-line and walk back to the n/2 line. Fig. 3 illustrates such a typical section of the linear complexity profile of a binary sequence.

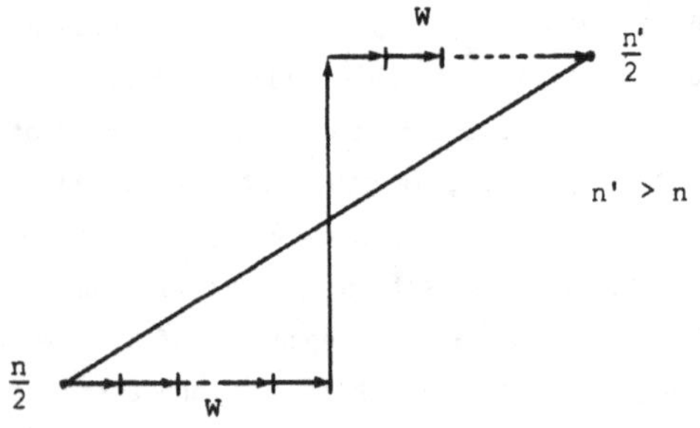


Fig. 3. A typical random walk segment of $\Lambda(s^n)$

Compare also the linear complexity profile of the swiss coin sequence (1) depicted in Fig. 1. The recursion (2) describing the growth of linear complexity forces $\Lambda(s^n)$ to retain its value, whenever that value is greater than n/2, until $\Lambda(s^{n'}) = n'/2$. From this point on, a change in linear complexity could occur at every step. In case of such a change, the jump of $\Lambda(s^n)$ is symmetrical with respect to the n/2-line, i.e. the "particle" $\Lambda(s^n)$ jumps from L to (n+1)-L. Without loss of essential generality, assume that $\Lambda(s^n) = n/2$. (Note that every nonzero sequence crosses at least once the n/2-line). Then the next jump will occur at time n+k, that is, after k time units, if

$$\delta_n = \delta_{n+1} = \ldots = \delta_{n+k-2} = 0 \; ; \; \delta_{n+k-1} = 1 \tag{27}$$

causing the new linear complexity to be

$$\Lambda(s^{n+k}) = (n+k) - \Lambda(s^n) \quad . \tag{28}$$

By the fact that the $s_i$ are independent and fair coin tosses, the probability that the event (27) occurs is $2^{-k}$. Let W be the random variable denoting the number of time units until the next length change occurs, given that at time n $\Lambda(s^n) = n/2$. The above observations then imply

$$E[W] = \sum_{k=1}^{\infty} k\, 2^{-k} = \sum_{k=0}^{\infty} 2^{-k} = 2 \quad . \tag{29}$$

Thus, for the "particle" $\Lambda(s^n)$, the average return time to the origin (the n/2-line) will be $2E[W] = 4$; and the average jump height will be $E[\Delta L] = E[W]$, since $\Delta L = (n + W - (n/2)) - (n/2) = W$. The results obtained from the random walk interpretation of the linear complexity profile are summarized in the following proposition, where we have also generalized to an arbitrary starting point $\Lambda(s^n) = L$ to cover all possible sequences.

Proposition 4. Random walk setup

If $\underset{\sim}{s} = s_0, s_1, \ldots$ denotes a sequence of independent and uniformly distributed binary random variables and if $\Lambda(s^n) = L$, then the average number of sequence bits that have to be processed until the next length change occurs is given by

$$E[W|\Lambda(s^n) = L] = \begin{cases} 2 & \text{if } L \leqslant \frac{n}{2} \\ 2+2L-n & \text{if } L > \frac{n}{2} \end{cases} \quad . \tag{30}$$

Moreover, the average length change is

$$E[\Delta L|\Lambda(s^n) = L] = \begin{cases} 2 & \text{if } L \geqslant \frac{n}{2} \\ n-2L+2 & \text{if } L < \frac{n}{2} \end{cases} \quad . \tag{31}$$

The import of proposition 4. is that it provides information about the details of the linear complexity profile of random sequences.

Proposition 4. tells us that the linear complexity profile of a random sequence will look like an irregular staircase with an average step length of 4 time units and an average step height of 2 linear complexity units. A good illustration of this "typical" growth process is given by the linear complexity profile of the swiss coin sequence depicted in Fig. 1.

The various characterizations of binary random sequences by means of the associated linear complexity (as described in proposition 1. - 4. ) might now suggest that we have only to put a "channel" of sufficient size around the n/2-line to separate the random looking sequences from the nonrandom looking sequences. But obviously enough, the probability that a random sequence $\Lambda(s^n)$ will leave this fictitious channel at least once goes to 1 as n goes to infinity. It is not even true that the sequences whose linear complexity profile stays very close to the n/2 line will always exhibit good statistical properties. An interesting example is provided by the sequence $\tilde{y}$ whose terms are defined as

$$y_j = \begin{cases} 1 & \text{if } j = 2^n-1 \qquad n=0,1,2\ldots \\ 0 & \text{otherwise.} \end{cases} \tag{32}$$

The sequence $\tilde{y}$ is highly "nonrandom", yet it has a linear complexity profile following the n/2-line as closely as is possible at least for $n \leq 127$ (and we conjecture for all n) (see Fig. 4). This conjecture was recently proven to be true by Zong-duo Dai (Dai 85).

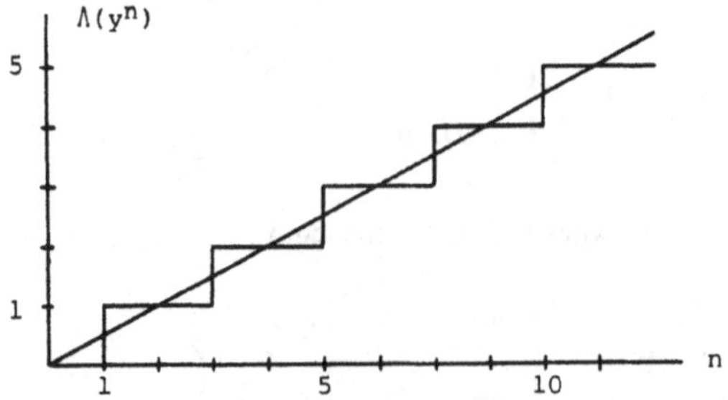


Fig. 4. The perfect staircase profile associated to the sequence (32)

This example suggests that too regular linear complexity profiles are incompatible with the randomness properties of the associated sequences. But note that the sequence $\tilde{y}$ as defined in (32) is not the only sequence with this perfect staircase profile. Whenever $\Lambda(s^n) > \frac{n}{2}$ then, independent of the choice for $y_n$, $\Lambda(y^{n+1})$ will be equal to $\Lambda(y^n)$. This indicates that there exist in fact many sequences which have associated the perfect staircase profil shown in Fig. 4. And undoubtedly, there will be some among them with good statistical properties. But remember that the perfect staircase profil would indeed pass randomness tests based on the expectation of linear complexity (proposition 2. and 3. ), but it never would pass a randomness test based on the random walk setup (proposition 4. ). Hence with the knowledge acquired so far on the linear complexity profile of random sequences, we would not accept as "random" a sequence with such a regular profile as that shown in Fig. 4.

From the practical standpoint in good stream cipher design, one important question remains to be answered. A deterministically generated key stream must necessarily be (ultimately) periodic. Thus, the question of what the linear complexity profile of a periodically repeated random bit string will look like is of considerable practical interest. Let $z^T = z_0, z_1, \ldots, z_{T-1}$ denote the first period of the semi-infinite sequence $\tilde{z}$, and assume $z^T$ to be selected according to a fair coin tossing experiment. Then from the preceding analysis we may immediately deduce that $E[\Lambda(\tilde{z})]$ is at least T/2, since that result holds for the finite random sequence $z^T$. On the other hand $z^T$ could be put into a pure cycling shift register of length T to produce $\tilde{z}$. Thus $\tilde{z}$ certainly satisfies the recursion $z_{T+j} = z_j$, which implies that $E[\Lambda(\tilde{z})]$ is at most T. But how likely is it that $\tilde{z}$ satisfies a linear recursion of order lower than T? And how would the linear complexity profile change from that point on where the first bits of $z^T$ are repeated? Intuitively, one would expect the linear complexity to grow to close to the period length T, since the recursion which produces the second half of $z^T$ from the first half is unlikely to have any similarities to the recursion that produces the first half of $z^T$ from the second half (which is required by the periodic repetition). Now let $Z^*(D)$ denote the polynomial associated with the first period $z^T$ of $\tilde{z}$. Then

$$Z(D) = \frac{Z^*(D)}{1+D^T} \qquad (33)$$

$Z^*(D)$ may be interpreted as the polynomial associated with the initial state of a circulating shift register. The question of the expected linear complexity of $\tilde{z}$ now corresponds to asking for the expected degree m of the denominator polynomial in (33) after reduction by $\gcd(Z^*(D), 1+D^T)$. To every choice of $Z^*(D)$, there is a unique partial fraction expansion

$$Z(D) = \sum_{i=1}^{n} \sum_{k=1}^{m_i} \frac{P_{ik}(D)}{[C_i(D)]^k} \tag{34}$$

where $C_i(D)$, $i=1,..,n$, are the irreducible factors of $1 + D^T$ and $m_i$, $i = 1,...,n$ are their multiplicities, and where $\deg(P_{ik}(D)) < \deg(C_i(D))$. Suppose now that the binary coefficients of the numerator polynomials $P_{ik}(D)$ are chosen independently from a uniform distribution. This induces a uniform probability distribution over the set of possible initial periods $z^T$, (or equivalently, over the set of possible $Z^*(D)$), since there exists a unique correspondence between initial periods $Z^*(D)$ and the choice of numerator polynomials in the partial fraction expansion (34). But a uniform probability measure over all $z^T$ implies that each digit $z_j$, $j=0,...,T-1$, is an independent and uniformly distributed binary random variable. We conclude that the expected linear complexity of z may equivalently be computed as the expected degree of the minimal polynomial of $\tilde{z}$ given that all coefficients of the numerator polynomials $P_{ik}(D)$ are chosen independently from a uniform distribution. Unfortunately, there appears to be no simple solution to this problem since the irreducible factors $C_i(D)$ of $1+D^T$, as well as their multiplicities strongly depend on the value of T. We will demonstrate the solution for 2 extreme cases thereby obtaining results of some significance for the general case. Suppose first that T is equal to $2^n-1$ with n a prime. Then the partial fraction expansion (34) takes on the special form

$$Z(D) = \frac{Z^*(D)}{1+D^{2^n-1}} = \frac{A}{1+D} + \sum_{i=1}^{M} \frac{P_i(D)}{C_i(D)} \tag{35}$$

where each $C_i(D)$ has prime degree n, and thus the number of such factors is $M = (2^n-2)/n$. When we randomly select A and the coefficients of $P_i(D)$, $i=1,...,M$, then the probability that A and $P_i(D)$ are zero is $2^{-1}$ and $2^{-n}$, respectively. Therefore

$$P_k = P(\Lambda(\tilde{z}) = 2^n - 1 - kn) = P(\Lambda(\tilde{z}) = 2^n - 2 - kn)$$
$$= \frac{1}{2}\binom{M}{k} (1-2^{-n})^{M-k} (2^{-n})^k .$$

We obtain for large prime n and small k

$$P_k \approx \frac{1}{2k!n^k} e^{-\frac{1}{n}} \tag{37}$$

By considering the two choices of $2^n$-1 and $2^n$-2 for the linear complexity we may provide a rough lowerbound on the expected linear complexity of $\tilde{z}$,

$$E[\Lambda(\tilde{z})] \geq (2^n-1)P_o + (2^n-2)P_o$$
$$\gtrsim e^{-\frac{1}{n}} (2^n - \frac{3}{2}) \tag{38}$$

The significance of the bound (38) lies in the fact that, as n increases, it approaches the period T, thereby showing that the linear complexity of z can be expected to be very close to the period length for all prime n. A much better estimate of the actual $E[\Lambda(\tilde{z})]$ may be obtained when more than just the two largest choices for $\Lambda(\tilde{z})$, with their corresponding probabilities $P_k$ as computed in (37) are taken into account. When T is chosen odd, then the minimal polynomial of $\tilde{z}$ does not contain any repeated factors (which is equivalent to saying that the minimal polynomial of $\tilde{z}$ has only simple roots). The other extreme may be found when the period length T is chosen to be a power of 2, i.e. T = $2^n$. Then there exists only one root, namely 1, which occurs with multiplicity $2^n$, and

$$Z(D) = \frac{Z^*(D)}{1+D^{2^n}} = \frac{Z^*(D)}{(1+D)^{2^n}} . \tag{39}$$

Then the partial fraction expansion (34) takes on the special form

$$Z(D) = \sum_{i=1}^{2^n} \frac{A_i}{(1+D)^i} . \tag{40}$$

When all the binary coefficients $A_i$ are drawn independently from a uniform distribution, then half the sequences $\tilde{z}$ will have linear complexity $2^n$, one forth of the $\tilde{z}$ will have linear complexity $2^n-1$, one eighth will have $\Lambda(\tilde{z}) = 2^n-2$, and so on. Thus the probability distribution induced on $\Lambda(\tilde{z})$ is given by

$$P(\Lambda(\tilde{z}) = L) = 2^{L-2^n-1} \qquad L = 1,\ldots,2^n \tag{41}$$

With the help of this probability distribution, it is now easy to compute the expected linear complexity

$$E[\Lambda(\tilde{z})] = \sum_{L=1}^{2^n} L \cdot 2^{L-2^n-1} = 2^{-2^n-1} \sum_{L=1}^{2^n} L2^L \quad . \tag{42}$$

Invoking the integration/differentiation technique for sums (as demonstrated in the derivation of ( 14 ))results in

$$E[\Lambda(\tilde{z})] = 2^n - 1 + 2^{-2^n} \quad .$$

This result is summarized in the following proposition.

<u>Proposition 5.</u> Periodic repetition of random sequence

> If the semi-infinite sequence $\tilde{z}$ is generated by periodically repeating a sequence $z^T = z_0,\ldots,z_{T-1}$ of T independent and uniformly distributed binary random variables, i.e. $\tilde{z} = z^T, z^T, \ldots$, and if $T = 2^n$, then the expected linear complexity of $\tilde{z}$ is
>
> $$E[\Lambda(\tilde{z})] = 2^n - 1 + 2^{-2^n} \quad . \tag{43}$$

The two investigated cases of periodically repeating a finite sequence of random bits are extreme in the sense that, for a period $T = 2^n-1$, the minimal polynomial of $\tilde{z}$ is sure to contain only simple roots whose number then equals the linear complexity of $\tilde{z}$, and, for a period $T = 2^n$, the minimal polynomial of $\tilde{z}$ is sure to contain only one root whose multiplicity then equals the linear complexity of $\tilde{z}$. For both choices of the period we were able to show that the expected linear complexity is almost equal to the period length.

Recapitulating, we may say that the linear complexity of a sequence provides a good measure of its unpredictability, expecially when the growth process of the linear complexity with respect to the number of considered sequence bits (which was termed the linear complexity profile) is taken into account. For true random sequences of length n, the expected linear complexity was shown to be about n/2. Moreover, the vast majority of these sequences were shown to have associated a linear complexity very close to n/2. The dynamic characterization of random sequences by means of linear complexity results in an average linear complexity increase of 2 after an average number of 4 considered sequence digits. When a random sequence of length $T = 2^n$ ($n \geq 0$) or $T = 2^n-1$ (n prime) T is periodically repeated, then the expected linear complexity is close to the period length T and the associated linear complexity profile is not distinguishable from the linear complexity profile of a true random sequence up to T digits. Heuristic arguments suggest that the expected linear complexity will in general be close to the period length T and that in fact the associated linear complexity profile will not be distinguishable from the linear complexity profile of a true random sequence even up to 2T digits. (Compare also the swiss coin sequence example displayed in Fig. 4.1.). we conclude that a good random sequence generator should have linear complexity close to the period length, and also a linear complexity profile which follows closely, but "irregularly", the n/2-line (where n denotes the number of sequence digits) thereby exhibiting average step lengths and step heights of 4 and 2, respectively.

References:


Dai 85 Zong-duo Dai, "Proof of Rueppel's Linear Complexity Conjecture", submitted for publication in IEEE Trans. on Info. Th.

Fell 68 W. Feller, "An Introduction to Probability Theory and its Applications", Vol. 1, John Wiley, 1968.

Golo 67 S.W. Golomb, "Shift Register Sequences", Holden-Day, San Francisco, Calif., 1967.

Knut 81 D.E. Knuth, "The Art of Computer Programming, Vol. 2: Seminumberical Algorithms", Addison-Wesley, 1981.

Kolm 65 A.N. Kolmogorov, "Three Approaches to the Quantitative Definition of Information", Probl. Inform. Transmission, Vol. 1, 1965.

Lemp 76 A. Lempel, J. Ziv, "On the Complexity of Finite Sequences", IEEE Trans. on Info. Theory, IT-22, Jan. 1976.

Mart 66 P. Martin-Loef, "The Definition of Random Sequences", Information and Control, Vol. 9, 602-619, 1966.

Mass 69 J.L. Massey, "Shift-Register Synthesis and BCH Decoding", IEEE Trans. on Info. Theory, Vol. IT-15, Jan. 1969.

Solo 64 R.J.Solomonov, "A Formal Theory of Inductive Inference", Part I, Inform. Control 7, 1964.

# SECTION V

# CRYPTOGRAPHIC SYSTEMS AND APPLICATIONS

# ENGINEERING SECURE INFORMATION SYSTEMS

Donald W Davies, Data Security Consultant, UK
Wyn L Price, National Physical Laboratory, UK

## Abstract

This paper gives a brief survey of the authors' experience in designing and assessing systems for the secure processing and transmission of information in electronic media. It considers the range of encipherment algorithms currently available in the civil field for use in protecting financial transactions and the like. As a consequence of using encipherment, key management must be properly engineered and the right physical environment provided for the various sensitive functions. Finally some of the management aspects of secure systems are addressed.

## 1 The Background and Objectives

Information systems affect the lives of all of us; they are used by national and local government, by banks, by industry and commerce, they are even penetrating into the home. For many of these applications security is essential - without it they cannot function in an acceptable way. Security has many aspects; in this paper we shall be particularly concerned with two of them, privacy and integrity. Privacy is the property of preventing unauthorised parties discovering the content of messages or files. Integrity is the property of preventing undiscovered alteration of messages or files by unauthorised parties; it is often impossible to prevent alteration because of the widely dispersed and exposed nature of the system, so detection of alteration is essential. Depending on the application, these two facets of data security have greater or less significance; for example, integrity is absolutely vital to electronic funds transfer, whilst secrecy may only be a desirable quality in this context. On the other hand, personal records must normally be kept secret according to the legislation of many countries, and, indeed, this property is demanded by the public.

Security is a property of the whole system, whether the system be a widespread data communication network or a local data processing installation. It is not something that can properly be added after the system has been designed - that method leads to higher cost, less security and a less convenient system.

The threats to which information systems are prone cover a wide range of possibilities. Within a computer system unauthorised users may try to gain access to facilities or files which are forbidden territory. Perhaps the most common activity of this kind is "browsing", but other, more deliberate, attempts to gain unauthorised access may have more serious implications. In a communication system serving computers the possibilities are many; a simple passive line tap, easily placed in position in, for example, a junction room, can yield vast quantities of information to the tapper. More dangerous to the legitimate system user is the active line tapper; in this case the information is read from the line, altered and then retransmitted. Unless specific countermeasures are taken, such interference may well go undetected, with serious consequences.

This paper will cover some aspects of the design of secure systems that seem to figure prominently in our experience.

Usually, the system designers have already decided what they want the system to do, but their ideas about security are vague. The first task is to help them to analyse their feeling about potential threats to security and to evaluate the seriousness of each type of threat. They must also estimate how much risk arises from each type of threat. This work must be done in close cooperation with those who understand the threats and risks in currently operating systems that are being replaced or in analogous sytems. They may not be able to point out all the new threats that teleprocessing and a greater level of automation bring in their train, so the process must be a joint exercise between system specialist and security expert.

Formal methods of risk analysis can help, but their apparent precision is an illusion. They should be used as just one contribution to the analytic process. The intuition of those who know the application well should be drawn upon to discover the real priorities for the work.

Cost constraints are related to the number of people, terminals, transactions, files, target response times, etc. These should be estimated early, to avoid expending a lot of effort and finding the cost of attaining the desired level of security is prohibitive. Cost/benefit analysis is another formal approach with some usefulness, but the benefit of security is so hard to quantify that there is rarely a trade-off of any real significance.

At the end of this process, there should be a general idea of what has to be protected and against what level of threat. The level of assumed threat should be set high, not only because it is difficult to measure, but also because a few successful attacks on the system could lead to a concentration of effort to break it again that will be hard to protect against by enhancements.

## 2 Algorithms

We find four types of algorithm used in protection schemes. Classical cryptography gives us cipher algorithms (symmetric, with secret keys), authentication algorithms and one-way functions. These are closely related and are more or less interchangeable, but there are specialised algorithms to do each task more efficiently than adaptions of the other types of algorithm.

Stream ciphers of the Vernam type are still widely used, but block ciphers seem to be more adaptable to a range of applications (including the encipherment of streams of data). It is interesting to speculate whether this is a permanent change of direction.

The other class of algorithm comprises public key encipherment and digital signature. Algorithms for these purposes tend to be more elegant and systematic. It is possible that they are more brittle - it seems that they do not bend under stress but break completely. Designs of public key algorithm usually receive massive public scrutiny, leading in some cases to successful cryptanalytic attack.

There are important uses for both hardware and software implementations, both for classical and public key systems, depending on the relative importance of development time, cost, adaptability and performance. There is no absolute reason that a software implementation must be less secure than hardware. Both need some physical protection; without it, software is the most vulnerable thing imaginable.

The famous Data Encryption Standard (DES) appears designed for hardware and difficult to perform in a conventional processor, but software implementations can be very useful, even reasonably fast. A design for a software-oriented algorithm is unlikely to produce a result like the DES, but there is as yet no sign of a software-oriented standard algorithm being put forward. W E Madryga [1] has published a neat algorithm with adjustable block and key size that works on 16 bit microprocessors. Custom-designed algorithms can be kept confidential and thus avoid the intense interest that DES has received. There are arguments for and against using a standard.

In choosing an encipherment algorithm it is well to bear in mind possible difficulties which may arise in the exportability of equipment incorporating the algorithm, whether it be expressed in hardware or software.

## 3 Key Management

The biggest problem of key management is the secure distribution of secret keys (or, in public key systems, of authentic keys). A lot of good principles and techniques have been published [2]. Faced with a practical problem, we usually have to design a key management scheme to match it. It would be nice to have a single standard, but this seems unlikely because of the many factors which influence the design, such as:

the number of places where keys are needed (stations),
processing power at each station,
physical security where key is to be processed or stored,
cost, capacity and reliability of the communications paths,
communication protocols and layers at which the key is used,
centralised or distributed control of system,
level of effort for trustworthy operation.

Faced with the enormous variety of system requirements, computer technology has pushed this variety out of hardware into software. OSI has pushed it up the layers where much of it will emerge at layer 7 (work is well in progress on preparing a security addendum to International Standard 7498 on OSI architecture). Cryptography pushes it out of the cipher and into key management. There is a strict practical limit to standardisation.

## 4 Physical Protection

We have seen how encipherment and related applications, such as authentication, can contribute to the security of information processing systems. However, it is a delusion to believe that steps of this kind are all that is necessary to produce a secure system. Access to cryptographic functions, to keys and to sensitive plaintext must all be strictly controlled. Inevitably this demands some degree of physical protection.

As part of our work we have sometimes been asked to review systems where encipherment is used to protect sensitive data, even double encipherment for the more important parameters; at the same time the calls on the encipherment function are not controlled and the relevant keys are held in plaintext in the application program. The security of such a system is illusory.

Physical protection is not obtained without cost, and it is therefore desirable to limit the extent of the protected area. For this reason we may restrict protection to master keys in a system with a layered key hierarchy; data keys may be held enciphered in general unprotected storage. Use of the data keys may be controlled, for example by a system of tags, enciphered along with the keys, which determine the functions they are permitted to carry out [3].

A secure system may contain mainframes and satellite terminals, with a sophisticated security hierarchy; such a system is exemplified by the IBM design described by Ehrsam et al [4]. Here we have a cryptographic facility at the host which manages key generation, handles key distribution to the terminals and allows encryption of host files and exchange of encrypted files between hosts. Terminals have a minimal secure facility, which protects the cryptographic function and the locally relevant keys.

Inevitably, the establishment of the highest level key at a terminal implies a physical visit to allow entry of the key; transport from the host (or other key generation location) may be via secure stationery or within a special key transport module. The latter may be programmed to issue keys once only and/or to respond to key requests only if a password is correctly presented; a system of this kind was designed for the Clearing Houses Automated Payments System, operated by the London Clearing Banks. Once the highest level key is installed, subordinate keys may be sent over the appropriate communication medium under its protection. This principle of a physical visit for the highest level key applies also to communicating parties of any kind, not just to terminals, and is therefore extensible to systems other than those where the host directly controls a number of terminals. In the case of peer entities, one may be allocated the role of key generation and the other be prepared to receive keys.

The foregoing remarks apply to the transport of secret keys for use in a symmetric cryptosystem. Where public key cryptography is in use, the requirement is different. Here it is essential that public keys be known reliably by all communicating parties; it is the integrity of the key rather than the secrecy that matters. One method of achieving this is to establish a key register which supplies keys on demand, signed by the secret key of the register. There are a number of safeguards that must be built in to such a system, but it should be workable in practice. The entire security of the system depends critically on the secrecy of the secret key of the register; if this is compromised, then false key certificates may be generated. Here, therefore, is another instance of a requirement for high strength physical protection.

As already suggested, cost of physical protection is not inconsiderable; for example, it is quite possible that the cost of a secure terminal may be three or more times greater than that of a similar terminal without physical security; where many terminals are involved, the additional cost may be very substantial. However, economy on physical security is indeed false economy, since it may put in jeopardy the integrity of a complete system.

## 5 Organisation

Design, programming, manufacture, installation and operation of a secure system depends on people. Such people have special knowledge of the system which may make it easier for them to break it; inevitably some people must be trusted, but the number of people in a position of special trust, able to compromise the secure system seriously, must be strictly limited. On the other hand, the operations available to individuals must also be limited, so that the more sensitive actions cannot be authorised without cooperation by appropriate officers. The responsibilities of specially trusted officers should be to different elements in the management structure, so that their different loyalties make it less likely that they will cooperate in fraud.

As far as possible, the design of the secure system should call for as little human operator intervention as possible. Encipherment keys should be generated by random or pseudo-random processes, master key transport should be in secure modules with password protection, data keys should be transmitted under encipherment with master keys, the schedule of key change should be automatically controlled (using a secure schedule).

Maintenance of security equipment presents a special problem. It is obviously undesirable that maintenance staff shall have access to equipment with keys that are still valid installed; even keys that are no longer valid should not be disclosed. This requires that capability to destroy keys must be provided, this to be invoked before handing over equipment for maintenance. In an extreme case, for highest security, the cryptographic function and storage of critical keys can be inside an enclosure which is not intended to be opened for repair; replacement of the whole unit is the only level of maintenance allowed. The over-riding principle must be that, where there is a conflict between the interests of security and of convenient maintenance, those of security must prevail.

An important component in any security design is the monitoring of secure operations. An audit trail of operations should be maintained in such a way that its integrity is at least as great as that of the system which it is monitoring. The existence of the audit trail need not be concealed; knowledge of its existence can act as an effective deterrent against attempted fraud.

## 5 Conclusions

In this short paper we have tried to give advice based on our experience to those who are faced with the task of creating secure systems. In conclusion we would underline those issues which we consider particularly important.

It is of prime importance to ensure that security aspects are taken into account from the outset in system design; any attempt to add security features to an established system is fraught with danger and may be costly to implement. Any system should be seen as a complete whole; piecemeal approaches are as dangerous as attempts at patching existing systems.

Choice of algorithm should be tailored to the particular requirement, bearing in mind the processing power available at the various locations, the availability of specialised implementations of algorithms, and, most important, the complexity of the key management system that the choice of algorithm implies.

Provision of comprehensive encipherment and/or authentication facilities, with a secure key management system, can be completely nullified unless the control of access to cryptographic operations and parameters is made secure. This implies a provision of physical security at those points where it is needed, but, because of cost considerations, at no other points, together with strict control of user access to cryptographic operations.

Management of secure systems demands careful allocation of privileges to systems personnel, with a requirement for cooperation between authorised individuals for the most sensitive operations. Where equipment needs maintenance, steps must be taken to avoid disclosure of sensitive parameters to the maintenance staff. System logging and monitoring is an important function that should be given close attention.

This catalogue of advice may appear daunting to the potential secure system designer, but, provided that attention is given to the relevant aspects of system design, it should be feasible to produce secure systems for almost any application. On the other hand there is always a trade-off between level of security attained and other considerations, such as cost and convenience of operation or maintenance.

## References

1 Madryga, W E. A high performance encryption algorithm. Proc. IFIP/Sec'84, Toronto, September 1984, pp. 367-380.

2 Price, W L. Key management for data encipherment. Proc. IFIP/Sec '83, Stockholm, May 1983, pp. 205 - 215.

3 Jones, R W. Some techniques for handling encipherment keys. ICL Technical Journal, 3, 2, November 1982, pp. 174 - 188.

4 Ehrsam, W F, Matyas, S M, Meyer, C H & Tuchman, W L. A cryptographic key management scheme for implementing the Data Encryption Standard. IBM Systems Journal, 17, May 1978, pp. 106-125.

# THE CHIPCARD - AN IDENTIFICATION CARD WITH CRYPTOGRAPHIC PROTECTION

Dr. Thomas Krivachy
Siemens AG
D-8000 München 70

## 1 Identification Cards

### 1.1 Card technologies with machine-readable data

Plastic cards for identification purposes (ID-cards) have been in use for over 50 years, while cards with machine-readable data have been available for about 20 years. Figure 1 shows card technologies commonly employed today. Most widespread are cards with magnetic stripe. Holographic cards are used e.g. as prepaid cards for public telephones, laser cards for mass storage applications.

| | Card technologies | | | |
|---|---|---|---|---|
| | magnetic stripe | holo-graphic | laser | chip |
| Memory today (bits) | 500/180/500 | 20..200 | $0,1..1.10^6$ | 0,2.. 16K |
| Capacities tomorrow (bits) | 500/180/500 | 20..200 | $0,1..80.10^6$ | 0,2.. 64K |
| Alterable memory | yes | no | no | yes |
| Protected memory | no | no | (yes) | yes |
| Logic functions in the card | no | no | no | yes |
| ISO standards existing | yes | no | no | (yes) |

Figure 1 Card technologies

Chipcards have existed for about 5 years. They are one type of identification cards with machine readable data and they are characterized by one or more chips embedded in the 0.76 mm thick card material.

## 1.2 Chipcards

Either non-volatile memory chips or chips with logic functions (e.g. microprocessors) can be embedded in the card. If non-volatile memory chips are embedded then the card can be used like as a magnetic stripe card. If chips with logic functions are embedded, a new kind of card is obtained, that is, one with processing capabilities or intelligence. This characteristic was chiefly responsible for the name coined in the USA, where chip cards are also called "smart cards".

Since chips with logic functions and non-volatile memory can be embedded, it is possible to subdivide the overall memory capacity into sub-areas of differing access. The data stored in the chipcard can therefore be protected with a variety of access methods. In the main, we distinguish between the following sub-areas of the memory:

- Free memory area: All the information which does not need protection from reading, erasing or altering is stored here. This sub-area has similar features as magnetic stripes.
- Protected memory area: To gain access to this sub-area the user has to enter a password. This password may be a four-digit PIN (Personal Identification Number), a multi-digit system password or, at some future date, even a finger-print or speech recognition. Access to this area is not possible before the right password is entered. After entering the right password the data can be read out. The data read out can be altered or erased too, depending on the application.
- Secret memory area: The data stored in this area can be neither read out nor erased nor altered. Secret data can only be written in at certain phases in the manufacturing process. Data to be checked or to be processed during the application is read in and only the result is read out. Regarding applications which are very sensitive, this secret area surely provides the most important and significant advantage over other card technologies. A PIN, a system password, a program, a secret algorithm or the key to this algorithm can be stored here. Further, incorrect entries of a password can be counted internally by chipcard logic functions and, as soon as a certain number in succession is exceeded, the chip is disabled so that any further attempt to access will fail.

ID-cards and the magnetic stripe have additionally been standardized internationally. The ISO (International Organization for Standardization) also has a Working Group for chipcards with contacts, and a corresponding resolution on a Draft International Standard is scheduled this very year.

Figure 2 shows the location of contacts according ISO DP 7816/2 and the areas of an ID-card which are already standardized, the magnetic tracks and the embossing area. It is of greatest importance for the standardized ID-card that the contacts and the magnetic tracks are not adversely affected under any circumstances by an error on the part of the user.

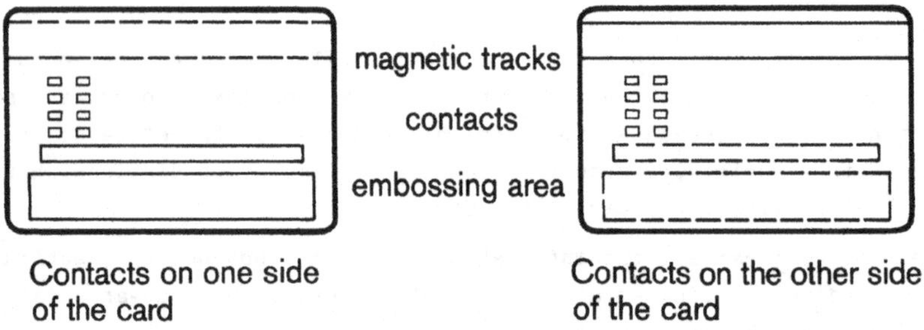


Figure 2 Location of the contacts according ISO DP 7816/2

According to ISO DIS 7816/1, Physical Characteristics, chipcards must work correctly after some specific mechanical tests, e.g. after bending. This in turn restricts the size of the chip which is to embedded. According to the experiences known today chips with a size of about 20 $mm^2$ located between the two rows of contacts fullfil these bending tests.

## 1.3 Encryption ICs

There are already several semiconductor manufacturers who supply encryption ICs for installation in terminals or computers. However, chips with common encryption algorithms known today such as DEA and RSA are out of question for standardized chipcards because they still require too large an area and therefore probably do not satisfy the mechanical test conditions after embedding in the card.

For these reasons and others, it is more appropriate to use special encryption algorithms matched to the chipcard and being programmed in the memory of the chip. Essentially, this requires the algorithm to be of maximum possible reliability, while still allowing the chip to be embedded in a standardized chipcard. Depending on the application, both symmetrical and asymmetrical encryption algorithms may be needed for chipcards.

The difficulties associated with key management and key distribution have to be considered as well as other security aspects of that application when the actual encryption algorithm is being fixed. The chipcard of the future will be used not only in hierarchically organized systems but also in "all-in-all systems". Besides, the chipcard is going to be employed not only by a scarcely changing, limited group of users on specific terminals, but also by a considerably fluctuating and practically unlimited group of subscribers (of the order of 100 million) throughout the world on different terminals fitted to the same application.

## 2 ID-to-end cryptographic protection

Cryptographic protection is implying here both the encryption and decryption of the transmitted data as well as the authentication of the transmitted data in a communication network. Only the encryption procedure will be explained below as an example.

### 2.1 Survey

The possibility of storing the algorithm and the key in the secret memory area of a chipcard offers the user a degree of mobility and the issuer a degree of security previously unknown in systems with cryptographic protected data: mobile ID-to-end encryption is available now in addition to fixed end-to-end encryption.

End-to-end encryption using ID-cards is in use since years. Data is transmitted between the card and the terminal, but the encryption is done outside of the card, i.e. usually in the terminal (Fig. 3).

Using the chipcard with its logic functions specified for cryptographic protection the following new modes are basically possible:

- ID-to-end encryption in dialog mode: Data is transmitted to and encrypted in the chipcard and then transmitted in dialog mode between the chipcard and the other end of the communication, e.g. a host (Fig. 4).

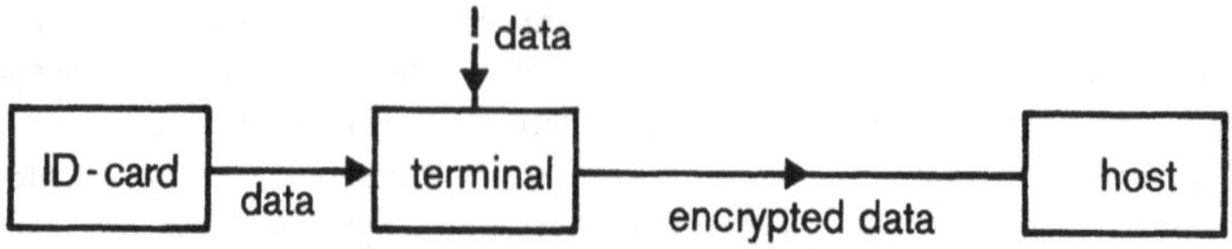


Figure 3 End-to-end encryption

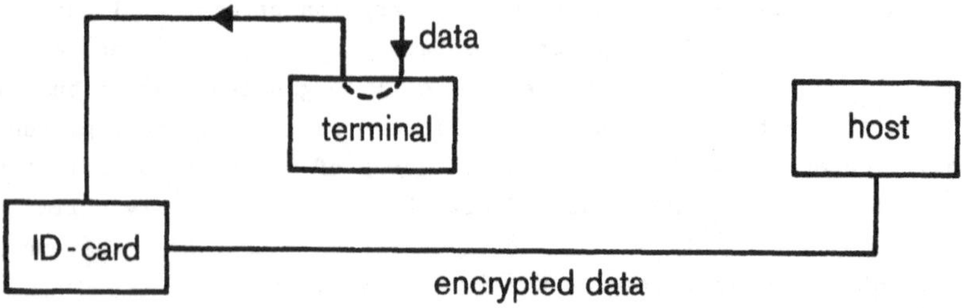


Figure 4 ID-to-end encryption in dialog mode

- ID-to-end encryption with buffer storage: Data transmitted to and encrypted in the chipcard is buffered in a terminal.After a certain time delay the data is transmitted from the terminal to the host (Fig.5).

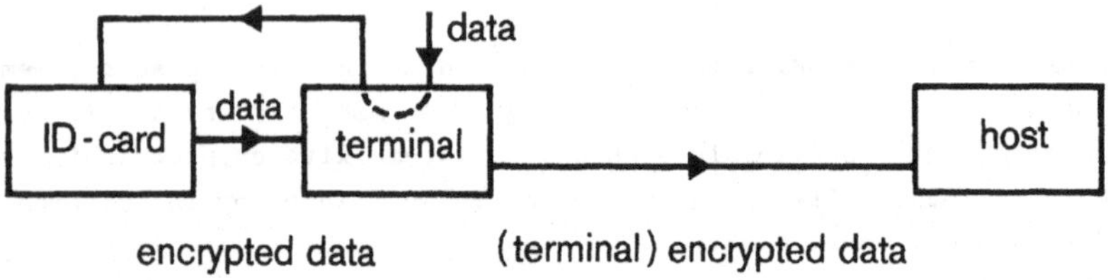


Figure 5 ID-to end encrpytion with buffer storage

Regarding the technical side of transmission,ID-to-end encryption in dialog mode is similar to end-to-end encryption /1/, but here again the advantages of the chipcard make new system and security concepts possible.

## 2.2 ID-to-end encryption with buffer storage

The entire system consists at least of an identification card (ID-card) with cryptographic protection, i.e. a chipcard, a terminal for buffering the messages received from the chipcard, and the other end of the communication, e.g. a host. This mode is suitable for all applications where, on various grounds, on-line dialog with a host is not always wanted every time when the chipcard is used. In a terminal which generally offers free access to several different persons, it is necessary to provide cryptographic protection so that the original data in the terminal buffer can be protected from unauthorized manipulation. We have tried to confine the description of this mode to fundamentals, omitting further subviding such as whether and on what transmission link the messages are encrypted or authenticated, whether use is made of one or two algorithms, and whether the algorithms are symmetrical or asymmetrical, secret or commonly known.

In the example in Fig. 6 it is assumed that there are two different algorithms: The algorithm f is stored in the chipcard and is used for data encryption between the chipcard and terminal. The algorithm g is used for encrypting the data between the terminal and the host. Further it is assumed that the host knows the algorithm f and the key KC stored in the chipcard as well as the algorithm g and the key KT stored in the terminal

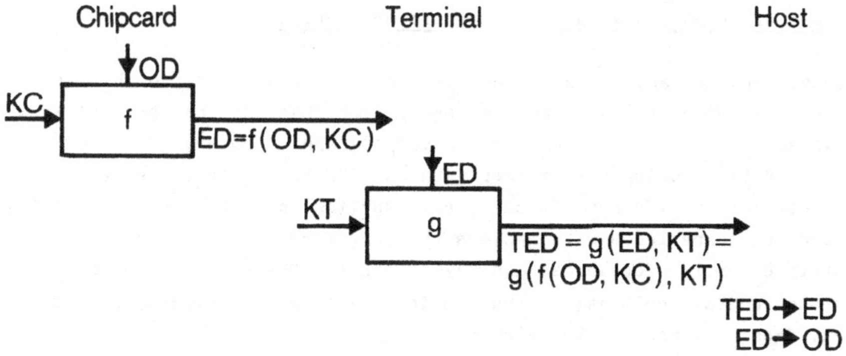


Figure 6 ID-to end encryption with buffer storage

Conventional dialog between terminal and host is conducted by encrypting the data stored in the terminal and read either from chipcards with cryptographic protection or from any type of card without cryptographic protection. This is done using the algorithm and the key stored in the terminal.

Using chipcards with cryptographic protection the data generated in the terminal (no matter whether sums of money or messages) is transmitted in the simplest case as original data OD in plain text from the terminal to the chipcard. Data transmitted to the chipcard can now be processed in the card itself as the encryption algorithm f and the key chip KC are stored in the "smart card". The original data OD is encrypted in the chip card and the output is send as encrypted data ED to the terminal. The encrypted data can now be stored securely in the terminal as the terminal doesn't know the decryption procedure for ED to obtain OD. Usually the terminal stores the encrypted data ED received from one or more chipcards over a certain time as mentioned before and then transmits it as terminal encrypted data TED to the host, using the terminal algorithm g and the key terminal KT.

The terminal encrypted data TED is decrypted in the host with the procedure required for the algorithm g and the key KT to obtain the encrypted data ED. At the next step the data ED is converted to the original data OD,i.e. in plain text, in an analog procedure.

## 3 Use of chipcards with cryptographic protection

Postal services and banks are particularly interested in the chipcard /2-4/. For some applications, the security mechanisms incorporated in the chip are already sufficient, and no cryptographic protection is needed, e.g. for telephoning with a prepaid card /5/. For others, e.g. for access to interactive videotex or for message service and retrieval, it has been found from experience with hackers that cryptographic protection is absolutely essential for access and maybe even for the transmitted data. Further postal applications include in a variety of services, e.g. teletex, facsimile and mobile telephones.

Interactive videotex homebanking and POS (Point Of Sales) are additional public applications for which an ID-card with cryptographic protection is needed. The credit card organizations, alerted by losses due to the abuse of magnetic-stripe cards, are also very much interested in embedding chips in their normal magnetic-stripe credit cards /6/.

In addition to these public applications (some of which have already been tested or are being tested in several countries) there are also certain private uses for identification cards with or without cryptographic protection, e.g. access to equipment (as a substitute for keylock switches), data base access, and for private text, data, image and voice communication systems.

## 4 Outlook

Today's chipcard already offers numerous advantages to user and issuer alike. As technology advances, we shall see chips with more efficient encryption algorithms and larger memory capacities with the small chip areas required for standardized chipcards.

A new generation of chipcards will be the chipcard cryptomodule which will contain keyboard, display and power supply. The PIN will be entered straight into this cryptomodule and will not be transmitted in plain text from the terminal keyboard to the chipcard. However the acceptance of a cryptomodule as a substitute of a chipcard has to be tested:Cryptomodules might be rigid whereas chipcards can be bent.

In order to obtain real information on the risks associated with the various system and security concepts, and on the degree of acceptance by users and issuers, it will be necessary to carry out field tests with the means available today, so that theoretical considerations for future, better systems can be developed on the basis of practical experience.

References:

/1/ Norbert Ryska, Siegfried Herda: Kryptographische Verfahren in der Datenverarbeitung, Springer Verlag 1980

/2/ Eberhard Schröther, Zeitschrift für das Post- und Fernmeldewesen, (1983), H.2, S. 28-31

/3/ Gerd Tenzer, Zeitschrift für das Post- und Fernmeldewesen (1985), H.2, S. 16-19

/4/ Industriemagazin, (1985), Februar, S. 116-119

/5/ Max Ludwig, telcom report 7, (1984), H.2, S. 151-154

/6/ Business Week, (1984), Oct. 15, pp. 112-114

# ENCRYPTION

## Needs, Requirements and Solutions in Banking Networks

U. Rimensberger
Union Bank Switzerland
8021 Zurich

## 1. INTRODUCTION

### 1.1 Union Bank of Switzerland

Union Bank of Switzerland (UBS) with its head office in Zurich, is the leading Swiss bank with total assets of 131 Billion Swiss Francs (1984). There are over 240 branches distributed in Switzerland and 40 more branches are located in the mayor international finance centers.

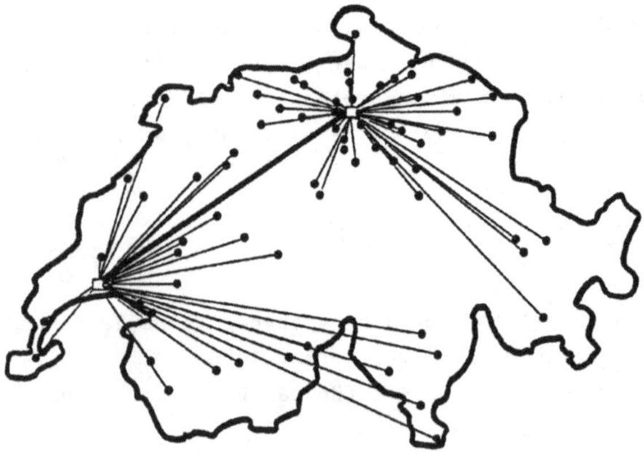

To interconnect all this branches with the main EDP-centers UBS operates a sophisticated, complex online network with some 1200 leased lines within Switzerland. For the international connections, the private worldwide network "UBINET" has been installed.

To meet the steadily growing communication needs, UBS finds itself very often in the role of a pioneer, as for example in the field of security: to prevent computer fraud UBS spends over 10% of its annual EDP-expenditures for security and has protected all data lines by enciphering units from the early beginning.

## 1.2 Security Hazards in Banking Applications

Banks have always been concerned about information security. Their needs exceed the requirements of most other users and go much further than the prescriptions of data privacy laws.

The first point is to protect the transmitted information in online banking networks, because customer related data is transmitted.

The second much more complex area is that of "open networks" like "Videotex". They literally open the computer to everybody and hackers as well as criminals have uncontrolled access if no security measurements have been taken. The most important point in such networks is the authentication, privacy is only the second aspect.

## 2. APPLICATION OF ENCRYPTION TECHNIQUES IN CLOSED NETWORKS

### 2.1 Requirements

The application of hardware encryption units in closed networks (i.e. private online terminal networks) on a link enciphering principle is already well known and relatively simple to implement because:

- both ends are under same control
- hardware is commercially available
- there is a wide experience from military networks

Protection of banking terminal networks links to automatic teller machines (ATM's) etc. against unauthorized access (passive wire tapper), message interception and alteration (active wire tapper) is possible on a maximum level of security with hardware link enciphering units.

According to my experience in such projects, some typical evaluation criterias are (in order of importance)

- implications on the existing networks (throughput, delay)
- investment and operating costs
- flexibility
- key management
- reliability of hardware
- qualified and experienced supplier

and seldom or never the cryptological solution!

## 2.2 UBS Solution

The operational online network "ABACUS" of UBS which is used for all banking transaction comprises actually 27 hosts Sperry 1100/80, over 370 Nixdorf branch computers and some 5700 work stations. The network consists of over 1'000 leased lines all with 9,6 kbps.

Together with this project we prepared a "concept for security in data transmission" as a general guideline. This concept was based on the analysis of the data content, the security hazards and the possible implication to the bank. The concept including all expected expenditures than had to be approved by the top managment.

The following request for proposal and evaluation resulted in a solution with hardware encryption units of which we have now over 1200 units installed.

Today not only the terminal network is enciphered but also the interhost network (with 2 Mbps links) and the facsimile network

# 3. OPEN NETWORKS

## 3.1 General Aspects

Via "open networks" a bank communicates with a large undefined group of users. The most common way to communicate with "third parties" until now was - the ordinary mail.

Using mail, all security aspects seem to be covered: the envelope guarantees privacy, the signature authenticity and by the help of (public) signature registers, authorization. Obviousely the security is not very high, nevertheless the legal requirements are all fullfilled.

New electronic transfer systems have to guarantee much higher security before they are accepted. The main reason is the lack of legal practis and the burden of evidence. Cryptographic systems will be the solution.

### 3.2 Videotex (Prestel, Bildschirmtext...)

Videotex is of great interest for banks because of it's potential for home banking. The customer not only has the possibility to acces data bases, he even will execute transactions on his account. That requires at least a secure authentication procedure. The PIN (personal identification number) may be used as identification, but it must never be transmitted in clear over the telephone line. Otherwise a wire tapper may recognize the PIN and use it for its own purposes. Cryptographic means are demanded.

Solutions are discussed, whereby the so called "intelligent credit card" (with the encapsulated microprocessor and cryptographic unit for authentication) seems to be the most promising.

Because Videotex is already introduced in many countries, there is now the last chance to promote a standard for authentication. Therefore users and user groups have to force the necessary activities with high priority. Experts in cryptologie have to find and publish easy to implement solutions and public organisation like CEPT (PTT's) and/or ISO have to standarize them. If a standard is not found within short time, many different implementations will take place.

### 3.3 Electronic Funds Transfer

If the funds transfer between banks, the so called "Clearing" is done electronically (EFTS) over networks with many users. That means practically open networks, the security aspects are of vital importance. Privacy of course is one point of concern including traffic flow security, but authentication and electronic signatures are much more important.

In Switzerland for example over 100 Billions Swiss Francs are transfered per day. Therefore in the new project SIC, which stands for "Swiss Interbank Clearing" the security concept was a key issue. Together with the manufacturer GRETAG we found a solution which covers all of the following requirements:

A) for the message originator:
- to identify the destinator
- to be able to prove the delivery

B) for the destinator:

- to identify the originator
- to authenticate (verify) the message contents
- to be able to prove the receipt

To fullfill this requirements a complex and sophisticated procedure had to be found with electronic signatures and electronically signed receipts.

For the involved banks the transmission overhead and the necessity for long term storage of the messages and the receipts with all electronic signatures imply high investment.

But it is true also here: one has to pay for security

# THE ROLE OF ENCIPHERMENT SERVICES IN DISTRIBUTED SYSTEMS

R.W. Jones and M.S.J. Baxter
ICL Defence Systems, Defence Technology Centre,
Lovelace Road, Bracknell, Berks RG12 4SN, England

The Open System Interconnection standard (ref 1) describes a model for communication among application processes at different computer installations (formalised as "open systems"). Possible ancilliary services provide security such as: user authentication, data privacy, data authentication, access control, protection against forgery and repudiation. Work is going on at present in standards committees to produce a security appendix to the OSI model. OSI security services and protocols should then follow.

This paper describes how an encipherment service and key distribution service may be incorporated into an end system and discusses possible key distribution protocols.

In figure 1, A, B and KDC are open systems in the OSI sense. Each operates as far as the outside world is concerned as if it had an entity for each of the OSI communication layers. In each case the section named 'communication services' represents those entities.

At each open system there is a "key distribution service" and an "enciphering service". These two together provide the encipherment services which are the subject of this paper. The functions which the key distribution service should provide are discussed in ref. 2. They may be summarised as key generation, key delivery and key acceptance. The functions provided by the enciphering service are encipherment and decipherment and the associated manipulation of keys. In the design we are considering here the enciphering service recognises keys of different types. The type of a key is shown by tag bits which are enciphered with it, using the ideas described in ref. 3.

The enciphering service and the key distribution service are usable by the communication services. In practice the intention is that they be directly usable by a communication entity at least as low (in terms of layers) as that whose data will be enciphered. Higher layer entities wishing to use them address them as if they were remote services and the service which uses them directly routes the messages appropriately, removing protocol headers as necessary. The services, their users, and the functions they perform are summarised in figure 2 which lists the following cases.

Application entities use the communication services (the normal use to pass messages to remote entities).

The key distribution service uses the communication services (when requested to distribute a key).

The communication services use the enciphering service to encipher and decipher messages which are sent and received on behalf of applications.

Application entities use the enciphering service to encipher and decipher data held locally.

The key distribution service uses the enciphering service to encipher and decipher keys and associated data during key distribution. The encipherment needs of key distribution protocols have caused us to modify the ideas described in ref. 3. During distribution keys are accompanied by data . To simplify matters we allow the key and the data to be enciphered by the same "key encryption key". Such data is accompanied by a tag to distinguish it from a key and to signal to the enciphering service that it may be output in plain text form. Data enciphered by a "data encryption key" has no appended tag in its enciphered form.

The communication services use the key distribution service to generate and distribute a key when asked to establish a secure connection.

Application entities may use the key distribution service in order to generate a key for local use or to establish a common key with remote entities.

A key at an open system, except when it is in the local store of the enciphering service, is itself enciphered. A hierarchy of key enciphering keys is possible but there must be some key or keys enciphered directly by a master key for that open system. The master key is held in plain text form in the store of the enciphering service. When a key is delivered to another open system it must be re-enciphered by the master key of the receiving open system. In large networks it may be impractical for every open system to know the master key of every other open system with which it needs to communicate. A special open system is then created which has been called (among other names) a Key Distribution Centre (KDC)(see ref 4). A KDC can send and receive keys securely to and from each open system either because it knows its master key or because it shares with it another key enciphering key (KEK) for this purpose. Thus when the key distribution service at A in figure 1 wishes to send a key to its counterpart at B it does so with the help of the KDC.

Key generation, being a sensitive operation, may be another function of the KDC. In a very large community it is likely that there will be more than one KDC and they themselves will form either a network or a hierarchy in their ability to pass keys to each other, using shared KEK's.

We now discuss a number of key distribution protocols which we have considered. At the time of writing we have not yet picked a definite protocol.

Figure 3 shows a protocol which is, in essence, that of ref. 4 with improvements (the time stamp) suggested by several commentors. A wishes to establish a common key with B. To do so A sends a message to KDC enciphered by KA, a key known only to A and KDC. The message contains B's identity and a time stamp, DT. KDC generates a key and returns to A the key, a new time stamp, B's identity and a package, P, for A to send on to B, all enciphered by KA. The package consists of the same key and time stamp, and A's identity, all enciphered by KB (known to B but not A). A sends this message to B, who is assured that the key has been generated by the KDC at time DT, and is to be used also only by A. Messages 4 and 5 assure B that the correspondent knows KS and therefore is A. The time stamp eliminates the threat that the correspondent is a false A who has discovered the plain text form of an old KS. However, if B is unable to go ahead with the connection within the agreed timing window, the timestamp will render the key unusable, and A must go back to phase 1.

Figure 4 shows a protocol we have devised which differs from the previous one for three reasons.

First, it seems worthwhile to eliminate the threat of a malefactor replaying an old KS whose plain text form he has discovered and to do so without the need for synchronised clocks for time stamping.

Second, it is better (on grounds of security and efficiency), to apply to the KDC for a session key only when both A and B are ready to proceed.

For these two reasons A does not ask the KDC to generate KS. Instead A generates a random number, R, sends it to B and is convinced when he receives it back, encrypted by KA in message 4, that the KS which accompanies it has been generated by the KDC in reply to B's request, triggered by the original message from A. R is sent with each message as a transaction code.

Finally, the messages contain extra fields caused by the environment in which they are exchanged. In figure 1 we can see that the key distribution services which exchange the keys are not the eventual users. Thus : "Buser" is the identity of the eventual user (often the communication service at B); "Kref" is a reference number invented by B which is to identify the key and which will be told to Buser and related by Buser to its opposite number at A; "tag" tells B the kind of key (e.g. KEK or DEK) which A wants. In message 2, B asks the KDC for a key of type 'tag', to be sent to A. R and Kref are sent to the KDC so that it may include them in the package to be sent on to A, enciphered by KA. The identity A tells KDC to use KA which it holds. I is invented by KDC and included in the package sent on to A. The fact that A can send back I's plain text form in message 5 assures B of A's identity (although B knows that an impersonator without knowledge of KA cannot understand subsequent messages). S and S+1 are sequence numbers to preserve the integrity of the chain of messages between B and the KDC.

Figure 5 illustrates the messages which are exchanged when attempting to establish a transport connection. Assuming that encryption is done in that layer we are interested in integrating the key distribution protocol with the connection protocol. Figure 5 shows that A and B each contribute a value (A ref and B ref) to identify themselves and the particular connection. They may also be used to identify the distributed key.

With this in mind figure 6 illustrates a protocol which combines the connection and key distribution protocols. An additional difference from figure 4 is that the KDC does not pass A's version of KS back to B so that B may send it on to A. It keeps it for A to retrieve as shown in messages 5 and 6, another way of eliminating the "Packaged Key replay" threat. If the KDC has functions extra to the generation and distribution of keys, such as recording who used which keys and when, this method becomes more attractive since the KDC has the information needed in any case. In figure 6 as compared with figure 4, there are other small points of difference which may be adjusted in deciding on a definite protocol. It is assumed that the tag of the key is implicit in figure 6. Aref and Bref in figure 6 together correspond to both R and Kref in figure 4. If they are too easy to guess an extra randomising value may be needed. Similarly R might serve as a reference to the key in figure 4.

## References

1. International Standard ISO/IS 7498. Information processing systems - open systems interconnection - basic reference model.

2. Jones, R.W.: "User functions for the generation and distribution of encipherment keys", ICL Tech. J, 1984, 4(2), 146-158.

3. Jones, R.W.: "Some techniques for handling encipherment keys, ICL Tech. J, 1982, 3(2), 175-188.

4. Needham, R.M. and Schroeder, M.D.: "Using encryption for authentication in large networks of computers". Communications of the ACM, December 1978.

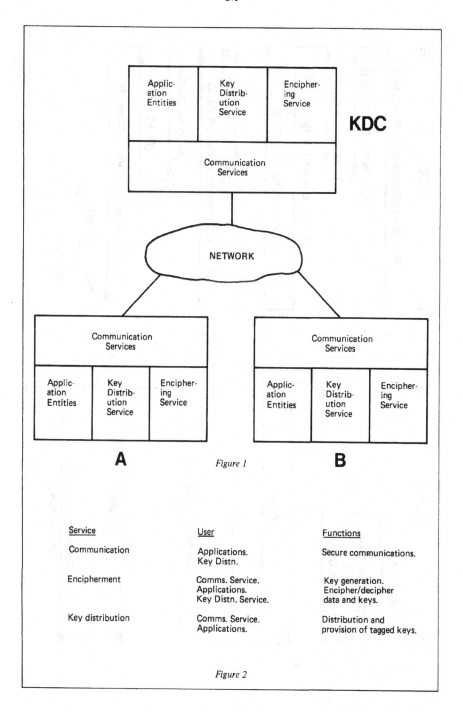

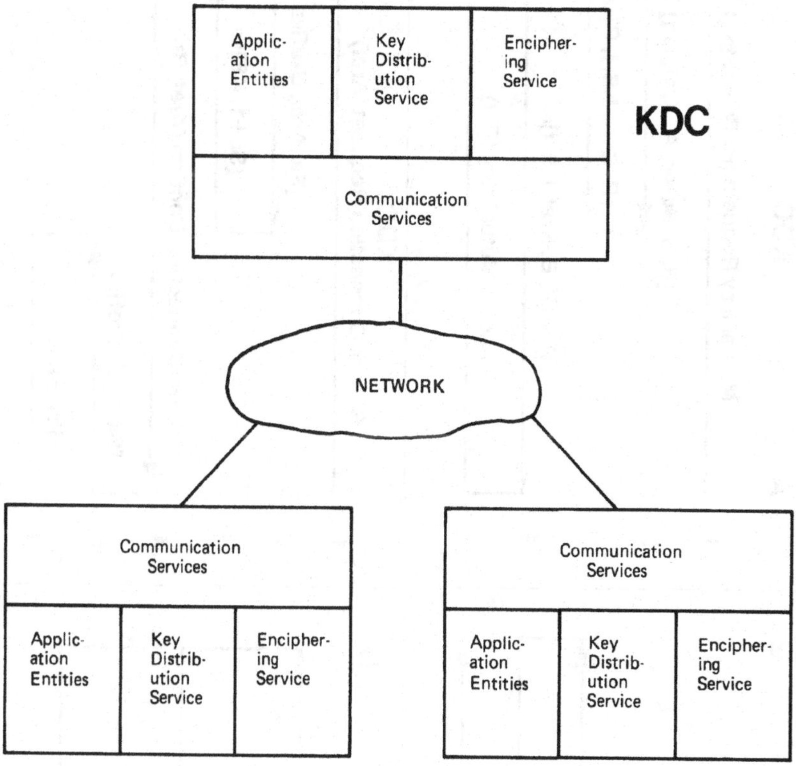


*Figure 1*

| Service | User | Functions |
|---|---|---|
| Communication | Applications.<br>Key Distn. | Secure communications. |
| Encipherment | Comms. Service.<br>Applications.<br>Key Distn. Service. | Key generation.<br>Encipher/decipher<br>data and keys. |
| Key distribution | Comms. Service.<br>Applications. | Distribution and<br>provision of tagged keys. |

*Figure 2*

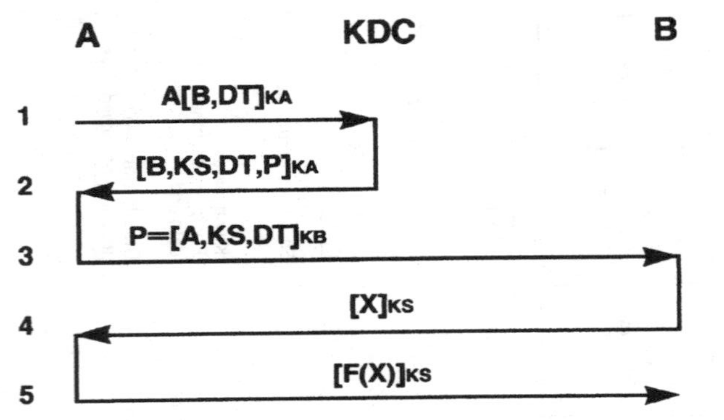


*Fig 3*

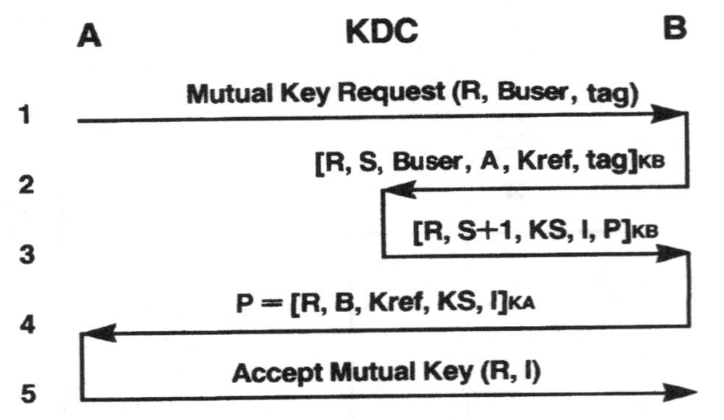


*Fig 4*

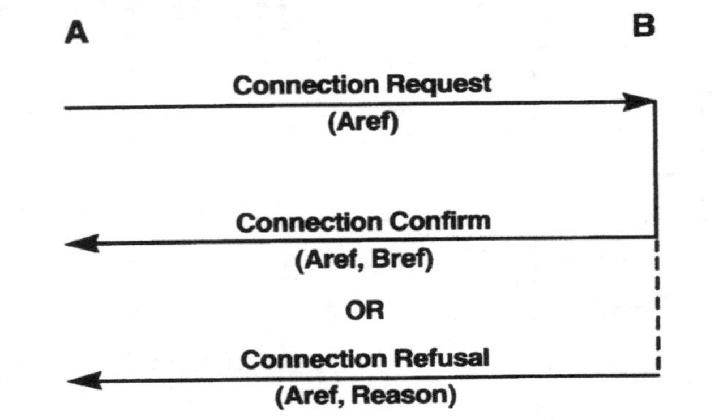


*Fig 5*

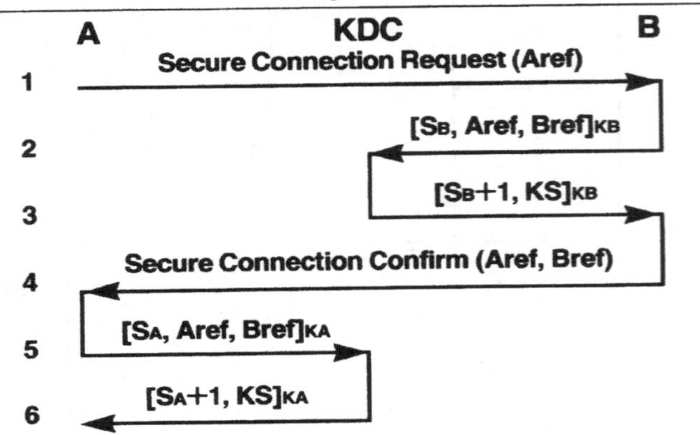


*Fig 6*

# MODELING OF ENCRYPTION TECHNIQUES FOR SECRECY AND PRIVACY IN MULTI-USER NETWORKS

G.B. Agnew
Computer Communications Networks Group
University of Waterloo
Waterloo, Ontario, Canada
N2L 3G1

Much of the present literature on computer security deals with cryptographic methods and cryptanalytic attacks. Most of these systems are based on dedicated communication links or single computer systems. In this study, we examine some aspects of incorporating cryptographic methods into multi-user systems by exploiting the underlying network structure.

A multi-user network provides the physical and procedural facilities to establish and operate a communication path between any two or more users. Here, we define a user as the smallest uniquely identifiable entity in the network (later we will distinguish between users and groups of users which are multiplexed into a larger entity). We also define an association as a communication path established between any subgroup of the set of users. (To simplify our analysis, we will only consider associations between two users, one designated the source (S), and the other the destination (D).)

A broadcast channel is a common communication channel where messages are 'heard' by all users. To use the broadcast channel yet preserve the separation of messages into their respective associations, some form of addressing must be performed. In networks in which the associations are not determined apriori (e.g., Time Division Multiplexing), messages will usually consist of two parts; the data portion of the message and the header portion which uniquely defines the association (see Fig. 1).

The nature of broadcast channel also aids the attacker in his job. In a purely passive attack (passive wiretap), the attacker has access to all of the channel messages. The presence of header information allows him to selectively intercept messages. Even if the data portion of the message is obscured, the existence of an association may provide sufficient information to the attacker (traffic analysis). In active attacks (active wiretap), the attacker may try to systematically insert, delete or modify messages.

If the physical portion of the network cannot be protected from active or passive attacks, then cryptographic techniques (encryption) must be used to thwart the attacker. Encryption methods are divided into two classes, i) one-key (symmetric) encryption techniques where the encryption and decryption functions are closely related and one cannot be exposed without compromising the other, and, ii) two-key (public key) encryption techniques where separate encryption, decryption functions are used. At present (and in the foreseeable future), two-key systems are very restricted in throughput. Hybrid systems are generally used where two-key methods are used to exchange the keys which are used in higher throughput one-key systems. In our approach, we will assume that such a mechanism exists to exchange keys which will be used to encipher data for transmission on the high bandwidth channel. The actual encryption may be of two forms; stream encryption where message bits are combined with a stream of enciphering bits and, block encryption where messages are divided into blocks (generally fixed size) which are then enciphered as a unit. We will not distinguish any further between these methods, but our examples will only consider fixed block size encryption methods such as the National Bureau of Standards Data Encryption Standard (DES) algorithm which operates on 64 bit blocks with a 56 bit key.

In the network environment, we consider two levels of protection that encryption can provide: i) Secrecy where messages from one association are completely isolated from external observers and all other network users (this requires a secret encryption function unique to each association) and, a less stringent form of protection, ii) Privacy where messages are only protected from external observers (i.e., a common encryption function could be used by all associations).

## Systems using Multiple Encryption Functions

In the absence of apriori information such as known ciphertext or chosen plaintext, the passive wiretapper is forced to use cryptanalytic methods to recover the content of messages. In block encryption methods, the cryptanalytic strength lies in the difficulty of removing the uncertainty of the enciphering key H(K). This usually involves the accumulation of sufficient quantities of text enciphered under one key to recover that key [3], [5].

We now examine some properties of systems which have one or more enciphering keys.

Let $\underline{K}$ be the ensemble of network keys $\underline{K} = \{K_1, K_2, \ldots, K_N\}$. The uncertainty associated with this ensemble is [5],

$$H(\underline{K}) = H(K_1, K_2, \ldots, K_N)$$

$$= H(K_1) + H(K_2|K_1) + H(K_3|K_1, K_2) + \ldots.$$

if all of the keys are independent and identically distributed (iid) and $H(K)$ is the average uncertainty of a key, then

$$H(\underline{K}) = N * H(K)$$

We note in passing that this does not suggest that the key ensemble could be replaced by an equivalent key of size $N * k$, where k is the size of one key. This would result in a privacy only system. We can see this in another way if we examine the effect of successfully cryptanalysis on part of the ensemble. Let $\hat{}H(\underline{K})$ be the normalized change in system uncertainty when a key $K_i$ is recovered. In an N key ensemble

$$\hat{}H(\underline{K}) = \frac{N * H(K) - (N-1) * H(K)}{N * H(K)}$$

$$= \frac{1}{N}$$

This shows that the impact to the network caused by disclosure of cryptanalytic recovery of a key can be reduced by increasing the number of keys. Ideally, each association would have a unique key. This of course introduces other problems as discussed in [4].

Despite our ability to increase the ensemble uncertainty $H(\underline{K})$, we are still constrained to an individual key uncertainty of $H(K)$. In the next section, we consider ways of increasing the apparent or observed key uncertainty $H(K')$, that is, the key uncertainty as observed by the passive wiretapper.

The passive wiretapper's observation of the communication channel is modeled as shown in Fig. 3. Here a random plaintext message M is selected from the set of all messages of length m. This message is then enciphered by all functions $Y_i = E_i(M)$ where enciphering function i is determined by key $K_i$ which is selected at random for each box from the set of all keys of length k. The channel output $Y_i$ is then selected at random from the N enciphering functions as indicated by the output switch position. This operation simulates the random message arrival process in a multi-user network.

In terms of the channel observation, we define a message to be of class c, $c \varepsilon C = \{1, 2, \ldots, N\}$, if it is enciphered under key $K_c$. By our model, the apparent key uncertainty is equal to the joint uncertainty of the key K and the message class C.

$$H(K') = H(K,C)$$
$$= H(K|C) + H(C)$$

If the keys are chosen independently of the class of the message, then

$$H(K') = H(K) + H(C)$$

If the attacker knows the switch position, then $H(C) = 0$ and there is no gain over the individual key uncertainty. On the other hand, if the switch position can be hidden and is equally likely among the N classes then,

$$H(C) = \log_2 N \text{ bits}$$

and

$$H(K') = K(K) = \log_2 N \text{ bits}$$

This is shown in Fig. 4 for a system with $H(K) = 56$ bits.

Thus, we can increase the observed uncertainty of an individual key by (at most) $\log_2 N$ bits by obscuring the message class information.

Let us now consider the case where messages can be enciphered by the source user in such a way that they can be uniquely identified and recovered by the destination user (this is code division multiple access (CDMA)). As we have mentioned previously, an association is identified by its source and destination. If we associate a separate enciphering function with each association, then the uncertainty of the message class is the joint uncertainty of the source S and destination D.

$$H(C) = H(S,D)$$
$$= H(S) + H(D|S)$$

If the selection of source and destination is independent and identically distributed among U users, then

$$H(C) = H(S) + H(D)$$
$$= 2\log_2 U$$

(In reality, there would only be U * (U-1) possible associations, but we will approximate this by $U^2$.)

This indicates we can hope to gain $2\log_2 U$ bits of uncertainty, but, as we shall see, will not be possible.

## Effects of Network Scheduling

There are two broad classes of network access methods: i) random access techniques and ii) conflict free (fully scheduled) techniques. In random access techniques (such as CSMA and CSMA/CD), a user wishing to transmit a message waits until the channel is silent, then begins transmitting. This technique leads to loss of transmission bandwidth due to message collisions when two or more users try to transmit at the same time. To make better use of the bandwidth available on the channel, scheduling techniques such as token passing are used to eliminate contention among the users [6].

These differences also have an effect on the level of system security. This can be seen in the following way: if the attacker can observe the scheduling mechanism (this could be done by observing the token passing or simply counting modulo the number of users in the system), then the attacker can observe the message source thus removing $\log_2 U$ bits of uncertainty (i.e., there will always be the equivalent of $\log_2 U$ bits of information in the scheduling scheme if the system is capable of resolving all contention among U users). Recall that

$$H(C) = H(S) + H(D|S) \leq 2\log_2 U \text{ bits}$$

If the scheduling information is available to the attacker, then $H(S) = 0$, that is scheduling information is equivalent to knowing the message source. We now have the condition that

$$H(C) = H(D|S)$$

which can only reach $\log_2 U$ bits if the destination is independent of the source. This indicates that the deterministic properties of the scheduling which are used to improve the performance of the network, also help the attacker gain information.

In random access systems, the lack of scheduling information should improve the gain in observed key uncertainty, that is, we should be able to gain $H(C) = \log_2 U$ bits. In an ideal network, this would be possible, unfortunately, it can be shown that, if we allow analog attacks on the network, the source information can still be recovered (see [7]).

In the above discussion, we have shown that a gain in the apparent key uncertainty can be realized if the destination user is independent of the source. We shall examine this condition with respect to the network protocol structure. In the International Standards Organization's (ISO) model for Open Systems Interconnection (OSI), seven layers of protocol for networks have been defined [8]. The uppermost layers contain protocols which deal with individual users. At the lowest level (Physical layer), we deal with network transceivers (TCVRs) as an identifiable entity.

The protocols are structured such that several layers of multiplexing can exist between the user levels and the physical level. Thus many users may be associated with one TCVR. The throughput requirements and nature of messages of the two levels may also be quite different. Consider the case where we have a number of terminals connected to one TCVR. In most cases, the individual terminal throughput requirements will be relatively small. In addition, associations at the terminal level tend to exist for comparatively long periods (this will permit us to set up protocols to generate and exchange keys on a per association basis). At the physical level, the throughput requirements are much higher due to the concentration effect of the terminal traffic. We also note, that consecutive TCVR messages may have different destination (e.g., terminals may be associated with hosts connected to different TCVRs). Thus, multplexing above the physical layer may produce the desirable effect (cryptographically), of making the destination TCVR independent (from message to message) of the source.

The network structure also divides the protection which can be provided at each layer. For user secrecy, encryption must be applied where the user is an identifiable entity, that is, at the upper protocol layers (end-to-end encryption). Encryption at the physical layer can be used to provide privacy and prevent traffic analysis.

If encryption is performed at the upper layers on a per association basis, then the data portion of the messages passed to the physical layer will already be enciphered. This implies that the physical level encryption is required to protect only $\log_2 U$ bits of information. For example, if the system has $U = 256$ users, the physical layer requires a minimum of 8 bits of class uncertainty. In practice, this could be provided by a single key using the Data Encryption Standard.

In the next section, we look at some of the benefits and problems of implementing a CDMA system at the physical level.

## Implementation of Code Division Multiple Access

As discussed previously, in a multi-user, random access system, we must dedicate some portion of the message to address information. This requires at least $\lceil \log_2 N \rceil$ bits of header information to uniquely identify a destination in an N transceiver system. If the messages are M bits in length, there are $2^M$ possible messages. We define a message as being a valid or meaningful message for a particular transceiver if the first $j = \lceil \log_2 N \rceil$ bits match a bit pattern unique to that transceiver (address). Thus there are $2^{M-j}$ valid messages for each transceiver (the message space is partitioned into $2^j$ non-overlapping sets of messages). We observe that any M bit string will be a valid message for at most one transceiver (in the absence of channel errors). We define address aliasing as the condition where a message is valid message for two or more transceivers (i.e., the message space partitions are overlapping).

In a system with headers as described above, an attacker can always generate a message which appears valid to a particular user simply by attaching that users address to the beginning of an (m-j) bit string. We shall call this type of attack a spoofing attack on a selected transceiver. If $j > \lceil \log_2 N \rceil$, then some strings will not be valid messages for any transceiver.

We define the spoofing probability $P_{sp}$ as the probability of a random message being valid for at least one transceiver. In this case

$$P_{sp} = N/2^j$$

To provide protection from traffic analysis and spoofing attacks, the system can incorporate header encryption as discussed previously. To preserve the ability to address individual transceivers, we must again allocate some portion of the message to identification (at least $\lceil \log_2 N \rceil$ bits). There are two basic methods by which we can achieve this addressing, i) we could use one transform common to all transceiver and use the transceiver's address in the header, or, ii) we could define a unique transform for each transceiver and require the deciphered message to match a bit pattern in the header. In the first system, the enciphering transform defines a specific one-to-one mapping of the ciphertext space into the message space. Thus, if the message space is divided into non-overlapping partitions, then the ciphertext space will be similarly partitioned.

Without knowledge of the encryption transform, the attacker can do no better than try a random message to spoof the system so,

$$P_{sp} = N/2^j$$

as for the unenciphered case. In the second case though, the use of multiple enciphering functions produces a different effect. The probability of a random message being valid for one transceiver is $2^{-j}$. If we assume that our enciphering functions are independent, then the probability of spoofing is equal to

$$P_{sp} = 1 - \Pr(\text{a random message is not a valid message for any of the N transceivers})$$

$$= 1 - (1 - 1/2^j)^N$$

Which is strictly less than $N/2^j$ for $N > 1$. Thus, using multiple enciphering functions can improve the resistance of the system to random spoofing attacks. But, multiple enciphering functions have other effects. If we now consider the probability of address aliasing, we can define

$$\Pr(\text{address aliasing})$$

$$= \Pr(\text{message is valid for at least one other TCVR} \mid \text{it is a valid message for one})$$

$$= 1 - (1 - 1/2^j)^{N-1}$$

that is, it is directly related to the spoofing probability. This implies that if we try to isolate data passed at the physical layer by using multiple enciphering functions, we can improve the immunity to spoofing attacks but we also increase the probability of address aliasing occurring. (Even though we cannot provide user isolation at the physical level, we might use multiple enciphering functions to separate groups of users on the same network.)

The above result indicates that to reduce the probability of aliasing and simultaneously reduce the probability of an attacker generating false messages, we should ensure that the header sequence is large with respect to the number of users, i.e., $j > \log_2 N$ bits.

## Remarks

The incorporation of cryptographic techniques into a multi-user network is a very complex problem. In this study, we have analysed a few of these problems and have provided some guidelines for implementation. We show that, both from a user isolation (secrecy) and system protection point of view, maximizing the number of system enciphering functions is desirable. If we are constrained to a fixed size for individual encryption keys, we can increase the apparent key uncertainty as observed by the attacker by an amount equal to the uncertainty of a message's destination. We have also shown that the way in which we implement a code division multiple access scheme will affect the ability of the attacker to generate false messages and the probability of the system itself to generate meaningful messages for more than one transceiver.

## Bibliography

1. V. Voydock, S. Kent, 'Security Mechanisms in High-Level Network Protocols', Computing Surveys, Vol. 15, pp. 135-171, June 1983.

2. National Bureau of Standards, 'Data Encryption Standard', FIPS PUB 46, Washington, D.C., Jan. 1977.

3. M.E. Hellman, 'A Cryptanalytic Time-Memory Tradeoff', IEEE Trans. on Info. Theory, IT-26, pp. 401-406, July 1980.

4. G. Agnew, 'Secrecy and Privacy in a Local Area Network Environment', Proceeding of EUROCRYPT '84, Paris, Apr. 1984.

5. C.E. Shannon, 'Communication Theory of Secrecy Systems', Bell System Technical Journal, Vol. 28, pp. 656-715, Oct. 1949.

6. J. Mark, J. Field, J. Wong, T. Todd, J. McMullan, G. Agnew, 'WELNET, A High Performance Local Area Communication Network', Computer Communications Networks Group, University of Waterloo, Report E-114, May 1983.

7. G. Agnew, 'Encryption in a Multi-user Network' Computer Communications Networks Group, Report CCNG E-124, University of Waterloo, Dec.1984.

8. H. Zimmerman, 'OSI reference model - The ISO Model of Architecture for Open Systems Interconnection, IEEE Trans. on Comm., COM-28, pp. 425-432, Apr. 1980.

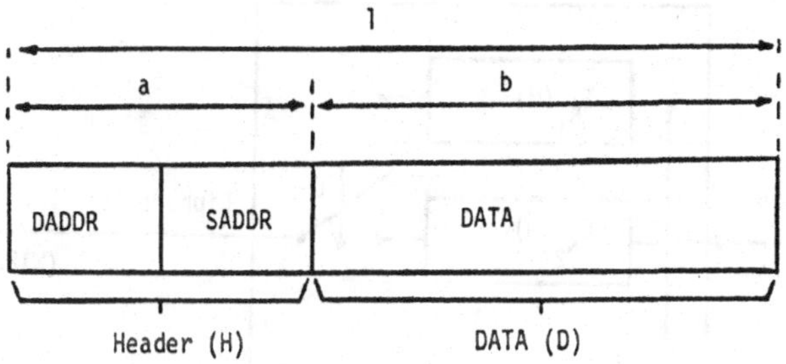


Fig. 1 Message Format

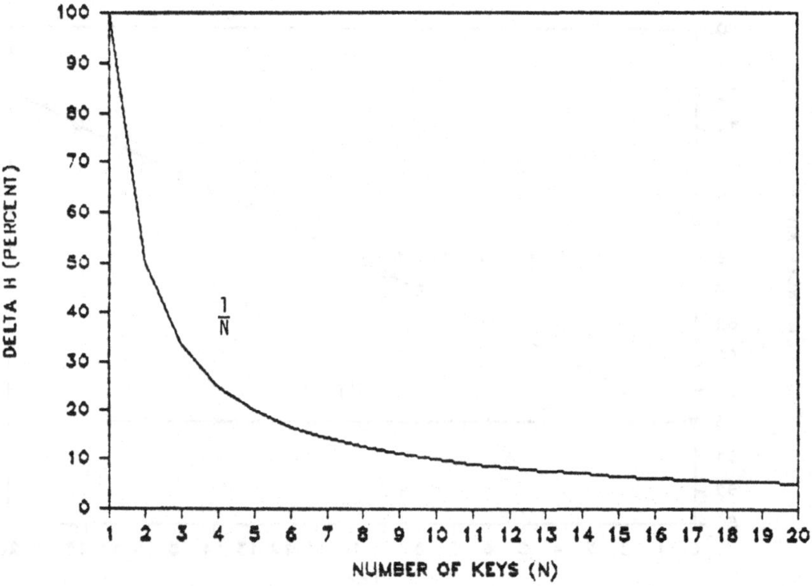


Fig. 2 Relative Change in System Uncertainty

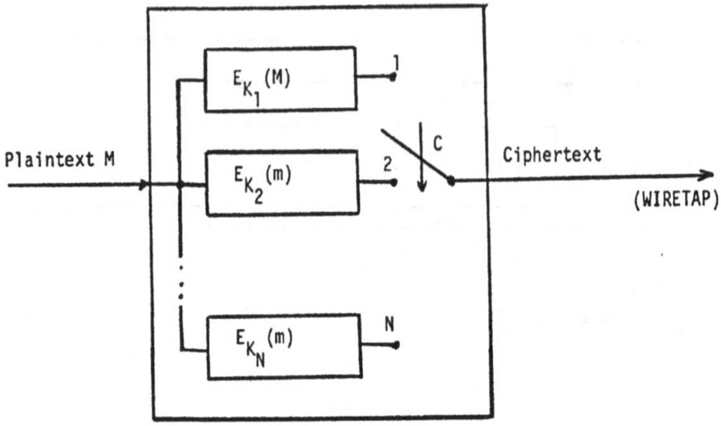


Fig. 3 Channel Model as Observed By Attacker

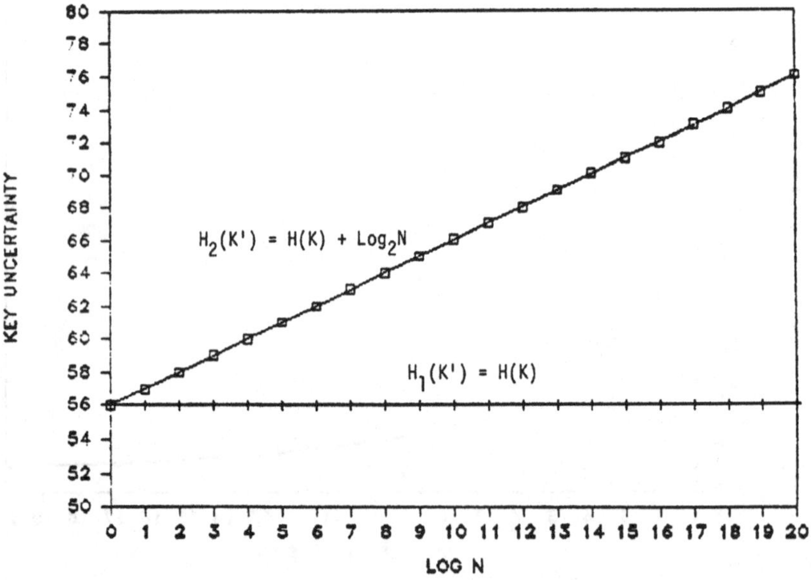


Fig. 4 Comparison of Observed Key Uncertainty with and without Header Encryption

# FULL ENCRYPTION IN A PERSONAL COMPUTER SYSTEM

Robert L. Bradey and Ian G. Graham
ERACOM PTY. LTD.
26 Greg Chappell Drive, Burleigh Heads,
Queensland 4220, AUSTRALIA

Full security in a personal computer system necessitates the provision of both hardware and software to incorporate full cryptographic services. In the IBM PC system, and its equivalents, this involved the design and construction of a hardware module to install onto the system bus as well as the development of appropriate ROM based and diskette based system software. Overall design parameters were set to make cryptographic security services "transparent" to the normal end-user. This meant that the operating system had to be enhanced to incorporate both interface routines for the high-speed hardware as well as higher level "driver" interfaces. Key management design played a major part in the overall integration of cryptography into this type of operating system. A multi-level key management scheme proved to be necessary to enable simple (and transparent) system level key management while user-level key management was provided as an option for total secure network integration the hardware module and software routines were enhanced to incorporate support for an optional data communications facility. Additional software was created to provide a secure network node based on the personal computer system.

## Design Criteria

Three main security objectives, as specified by the U.S. National Bureau of Standards (1), were paramount throughout the design and implementation phases. They were:

a) Confidentiality of personal, proprietary, or otherwise sensitive data handled by the system.

b) Integrity and accuracy of data and the processes that handle the data.

c) Availability of systems and the data or services they support.

The major security problem with the design of the current generation of personal computers is the lack of built-in hardware facilities that are taken for granted in large ADP systems. Without these facilities it is difficult to isolate the determined user or his application program from the sensitive, security related, system functions.

The hardware facilities most needed to implement total security in a system include (1):

a) multiple processor states for complete separation of users and system processes.

b) priveleged instructions to limit access to certain restricted functions.

c) memory and data protection features to prevent unauthorised access to sensitive areas.

These hardware facilities are designed to restrict and control unauthorised access routes within a computer system. Figure 1 highlights the many access routes available to the skilled or experienced user of a personal computer system. Only by designing security features that complement and enhance the personal computer hardware and operating system environment can full security be offered in the personal computer system.

For this reason it was decided to address the problem of providing a complete solution for full encryption in a personal computer system by offering a hardware and PROM software package for basic disk encryption and decryption, which also included full encryption for the operating system and proprietary software. Additional hardware options could be added to the basic board which when coupled with appropriate software modules could provide advanced key management and communications facilities.

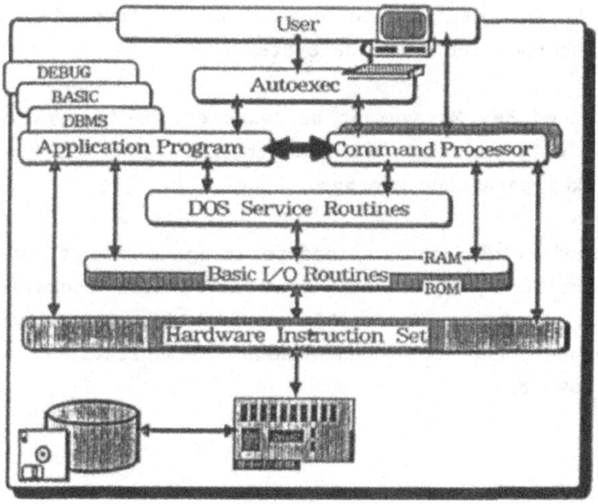


Figure 1. Personal Computer Access Routes ((1)).

The principle features of this PC Encryptor were to be:

* A high speed cryptographic processor to provide Electronic Code Book (ECB) encryption for random access block disk data, Chain Block Cipher (CBC) encryption for file and message authentication, and Byte Cipher Feedback (BCF) for serial data.

* A PROM on the basic board to contain routines that automatically encrypt data written onto fixed disks and diskettes for secure SYSTEM INDEPENDENT operation.

* A distribution diskette providing routines and System Drivers that enable the user to further enhance the security options

available.

* A "SETKEY" utility that communicates with the program drivers to assign drivers different keys to provide a simple key management procedure to protect individual disk(ette)s or individual files within the system. All root directories must remain encrypted with the system key for overall user transparency.

* A "CRYPDISK" utility to enable non encrypted disk(ette)s to be incorporated into the system.

* An advanced Key Management hardware option to provide storage for 256 different keys with additional 256 x 8 bytes of associated key parameter storage.

* A Communications option incorporating a dual channel serial communications controller, with associated operating system driver interfaces, to enable support for asynchronous, byte synchronous and bit synchronous communications at speeds up to 9600 bps.

## Hardware Design Implementation

The encryption design requirements of the PC Encryptor called for a high speed cryptographic processor to embrace both Electronic Code Book (ECB) for block disk data and Byte Cipher Feedback encryption for serially communicated data. From the possible byte or multi-byte encryption algorithms, it was decided to implement the US National Bureau of Standards Data Encryption Standard (DES, (2)) because of its wide acceptance, particularly in banking industry and EFT networks.

To cater for the required modes of operation (as well offering Byte Chain Feedback mode), and because it was the fastest DES processor available (1770 kbytes/s) the A.M.D. AmZ8068 Cipher Processor ((3)) was chosen. Previous experience with this cipher processor meant that implementation would be easier and would also permit the DES based PC Encryptor to be compatible with other existing networking security products. This would give the added advantage of permitting installation of a totally secure network.

This cipher processor provided some other very useful features:

(a) The provision of separate Master, Encryption and Decryption keys within the DES processor. This allowed for encrypted keys to be stored in the key memory, and then be decrypted within the DES processor before use. It also provided for separate encryption and decryption keys to be used for received and transmitted data strings.

(b) The provision of a separate key entry path into the DES processor to help maintain the integrity of the key data. This meant that the key data pathway was inaccessible from the PC data bus, thus prohibiting any PC programs from reading these keys.

(c) The provision of two separate data enty paths into the DES processor that allowed for data "pipelining" of information through the DES processor, permitting data to be read from the DES processor while new data is simultaneously written into the DES processor.

The PC bus DMA capability was utilised to permit maximum data throughput via the PC Encryptor. If the PC configuration precluded the utilisation of DMA channels, a switch option would permit the DES processor to be accessed as a standard direct I/O peripheral on the PC data bus.

## Installation Key

A unique hardware key was incorporated into the basic PC Encryptor design. All keys loaded into the DES processor via the normal key entry port are folded with this hardware key in a proprietary manner. The key was chosen to be 32 bytes in length, so that each key in a contiguous block of four keys could be folded with a different pattern depending on its position in the group.

The hardware key would normally be randomly selected and so would be unique for each board. This of course would ensure that each personal computer had individual protection against transfer of diskette data. If required, the same hardware key could be provided for fixed installations wanting diskette transfer between specified personal computers.

## Key and Parameter Storage Option

The PC Encryptor board was designed for the optional inclusion of battery backed up storage (CMOS static RAM) for 256 separate keys available to user programs. Additionally it was decided to include 256 x 8 bytes of associated Key Parameter Memory to permit the implementation of advanced key management systems. Keys can be loaded into the DES processor directly from the key storage for greater security, or can be loaded from the PC processor to enable key verification.

This memory had to be disconnectable from the battery, which would result in the immediate destruction of all keys when the mains power is turned off to the unit. Facilities were provided for incorporation of appropriate "tamper proofing".

## Communications Option

To enable the personal computer to be properly installed as a secure node within a communications network, additional hardware could be optionally incorporated onto the PC Encryptor board. The communications processor selected was the AmZ8530 Serial Communications Controller (SCC, (4)), or its equivalents.

The 8530 SCC supports two independent full duplex interface channels in asynchronous, byte synchronous and bit synchronous (HDLC/SDLC) communications modes, and thus offers the greatest flexibility for different protocol handling.

The PC Encryptor implementation supported one full asynchronous/synchronous modem channel capable of 9600 bps. This channel was terminated in a full V.24/V.28/RS-232C specification 25 Pin D-type connector. The second channel interface was implemented as an asynchronous interface operating at speeds up to 9600 bps and was terminated in a 9 Pin D-type connector.

## Software Design Implementation For Disk Encryption

There are a number of ways to intercept disk access so that data can be encrypted or decrypted as it goes to or from disk(ette)s in a personal computer system. However, most of the methods suffer from the ability to be bypassed either deliberately or accidentally (Figure 1). The way that was chosen for this implementation of disk encryption is similar to that introduced by the IBM PC-DOS operating system for trapping fixed disk I/O.

The IBM fixed disk controller is contained in ROM (either on the main board or on the controller board). Possible ROM modules are searched for during the power-up test sequence and control is passed to each valid ROM module in turn. At this point, the fixed disk controller saves the initial diskette I/O software interrupt vector and inserts a vector into its own controller. Thus, anytime a disk I/O software interrupt is made, it goes to the fixed disk controller first. The controller can then decide whether it is for the fixed disk or floppy diskettes. If the latter, then it passes control on to the saved diskette I/O vector.

The PC Encryptor board was implemented to operate in the same way, in that it will save the vectors contained in the diskette I/O and IPL (Initial Program Load or "bootstrap loader") software interrupt locations and insert vectors into its own on-board controller. Thus the initial system loading sequence can be intercepted to provide encrypted or unencrypted system loading alternatives, as well as an option to encrypt disk(ette)s. If the encrypted system operation is selected, then all disk(ette)s I/O would be intercepted and all data disk(ette)s (and decrypted after the write is complete). Similarly all data read from the disk(ette)s would be decrypted after being read.

## Basic Disk Encryption

Basic disk(ette) encryption was implemented using a key that is a combination of 8 bytes stored in the controller PROM and 8 bytes of a unique hardware key contained in a separate fusible link ROM on the board. This basic disk(ette) encryption did not depend on any system or disk format and could be used to provide basic security for any PC operating system that used the above described ROM BIOS procedures.

To extend disk encryption, an extension to the controller must be incorporated into the main system memory by installing a memory resident module or an installable device driver. Either method automatically makes this extension "operating system dependent". Consequently to operate such a system in a personal computer required the cryptographic drivers to be configured into the operating system.

## Extend Disk Encryption

To provide different keys for different disk(ette) drives required RAM and more intelligence than could be practicable provided in the basic controller. Three associated cryptographic drivers were therefore supplied on a diskette to extend the facilities of the PC Encryptor. These drivers then had to be configured into the operating system by the user. This was a simple process for the PC-DOS, MS-DOS operating systems; achieved by including a supplied file contraining pointers to the driver routines in the standard configuration file (CONFIG SYS).

Four possible modes of disk encryption, assigned on a Physical Drive basis, were deemed to be necessary for full encryption in a personal computer system. They were:

(a) System Key - This was the basic disk encryption using the default system hardware key, intended for encryption of the whole disk(ette).

(b) User Key - In this mode the description parts of the disk(ette), i. e. the boot record, the File Allocation Tables and the directory were encrypted with the System Key. The files in the data area were encrypted with the User Key specified at the time. The User Key must be specified by a "SETKEY" utility, and folded with the on-board hardware key before being used.

(c) Absolute Key - This mode leaves the boot record and file allocation table in plain text, while all files are encrypted under an absolute key, which is not folded with the hardware system key.

(d) Read Only, Unencrypted - This mode provided the ability to read unencrypted distribution software diskettes, but inhibited writing to the diskette by generating a Write Protect error.

The driver to support these three modes was implemented to permit user applications to select a desired mode in the same fashion as the supplied "SETKEY" utility.

## Implementation of Communications Facilities

The hardware housing of the standard personal computer, coupled with the physical board dimensions defined for a PC Encryptor board, meant that any practical implementation of dual communications channels was restricted to one 25 Pin and on 9 Pin connector. This was viewed to be not a restriction, since only one full RS-232C communications interface would be required for a personal computer to operate in most networks. The 9 Pin connector was implemented as an asynchronous interface only since it was envisaged that it would be only used to provide a special purpose terminal interface. Such a terminal could be a PIN Pad attached to a PC based POS cash register, or alternatively could be an access control terminal for secure key management

## Summary

The incorporation of a PROM based hardware encryption/decryption module directly onto the PC system bus has enabled complete security facilities to be offered within a personal computer system. This method introduced data encryption security and protection, not only for user programs and data stored on disks, but also for proprietary software packages and, uniquely, for the operating system itself. By fully incorporating security into the personal computer system at the right level, operation becomes user "transparent" while at the same time offering complete privacy of file content and protection against theft. All personal computer data can be "locked" to one PC or a group of PCs. Since one PC is often shared by many people in an organisation, a facility has been provided for each user to enter their own key to protect their particular programs and data stored on the shared personal computer.

The Key Management/Storage option permits system designers and security managers to develop Key Management Schemes based around the safe storage, retrieval and indentification of 256 keys kept in the actual PC Encryptor module. Similarly the Data Communications option enables network designers to create computer networks based upon secure PC work stations. The PC Encryptor was provided with all the basic hardware and software device drivers necessary to incorporate system software to emulate a programmable data line encryptor and thus operate as a secure node in an encrypted communications network.

References


(1) " Security of Personal Computer Systems: A Management Guide", National Bureau of Standards, Washington, D.C., NBS Spec. Pub.

(2) "Data Encryption Standard", National Bureau of Standards, Washington, D.C., FIPS Pub. 46 (Jan., 1977).

(3) "AmZ8068 Data Ciperhing Processor", Product Profile MMC-1017, Product Descr. AMPUB-128 and Product Spec. AMZ-237, Advanced Micro Devices Inc., U.S.A. (Apr., 1981).

(4) "AmZ8030/AmZ8530 Serial Communications Controller Technical Manual", AIZ2135, Advanced Micro Devices Inc., (Apr., 1982)

(5) "Disk Operating System", Personal Computer Series, International Business Machines, (Jan., 1983).

(6) "Technical Reference Manual", Personal Computer Series, International Business Machines, (Jan., 1983).

## Showing Credentials Without Identification

### *Signatures Transferred Between Unconditionally Unlinkable Pseudonyms*

David Chaum
Center for Mathematics and Computer Science (CWI)
Kruislaan 413, 1098 SJ Amsterdam, The Netherlands

### EXTENDED SUMMARY

It is becoming increasingly easy and common for organizations to routinely exchange data on individuals. Because each individual provides most organizations essentially the same uniquely identifying information, such as social security number, or name, age and place of birth, the records held by one organization on an individual are readily matched or linked with those held by other organizations. Thus, organizations are capable of exchanging information about individuals whenever and to whatever extent they choose. Clearly some such transfers of information are quite useful and beneficial to society. The problems stem from the inability of anyone, particularly the individuals whose data is involved, to control or even effectively monitor such transfers. These problems were not present in completely paper based systems, where the transfer of information about an individual was only through credential documents issued to the individual by one organization and shown by the individual to other organizations.

Cryptographic protocols that give individuals the ability to effectively control and monitor transfers in completely computer based systems, are presented. The essential idea is that an individual will be known to each organization by a different *pseudonym*, and that the individual will retain the exclusive ability to link the pseudonyms and transform digitally singed statements or *credentials* made about one pseudonym into credentials about the individual's other pseudonyms. Thus the individual regains control over inter-organizational transfers.

### The Basic Credential System

The essential concept can be seen by analogy to carbon-lined window envelopes. First, you would make up your pseudonyms at random and write them on a plain slip of paper. When you want to get a credential from an organization, you put the slip of paper in a carbon-lined envelope with a window exposing only the part of the slip bearing the pseudonym you will use with that organization. Upon receiving the envelope from you, the organization makes a special signature in a repeating pattern across the outside of the envelope. The kind of signature pattern indicates the kind of credential the issuing organization decides to give based on the pseudonym they see through the window; the signature pattern serves as the credential. When you get the envelope back from the issuing organization, you verify the signature pattern. Before showing the credential to an organization, you place the slip in an envelope with a window position exposing only the pseudonym you use with that organization and some of the adjacent credential signature pattern. The receiving organization verifies the pseudonym and credential signature pattern recognizable through the window. This approach naturally allows a variety of credentials to be obtained and shown.

You need not show all of your credentials to every organization: you can restrict that which is revealed to only what is necessary. Because of the way the signature patterns repeat across the slip, a recognizable part of every signature pattern appears adjacent to each pseudonym. In providing an envelope to an organization, though, you can limit the view through the window so that only necessary signatures are visible. The credentials visible could simply be limited by blacking out parts of the window, but more flexible restriction is possible in actual systems. You could transform a credential representing your income, for instance, into a more restricted credential indicating only that your income falls within some range. An even more powerful kind of restriction allows an organization only to verify that you hold a combination of credentials meeting some requirement, without revealing anything to the organization about which sufficient combination you actually hold.

An organization can ensure that no individual is able to transact with it under more than one pseudonym. One way an individual could attempt to use more than one pseudonym with an organization is to use different pseudonyms on the same slip of paper. This is prevented by a standard division of the slip into zones, such that each zone is assigned to a particular organization; an envelope is accepted by an organization only if the window exposes the organization's zone, bearing a single indelibly written pseudonym. A second way of attempting to use more than one pseudonym per organization is to use more than one slip. This is prevented by the establishment of an "is-a-person" organization that limits each person to at most one is-a-person signature. Other organizations only accept envelopes with this signature recognizable through the window. This is-a-person organization might ensure that it issues no more than one signature per person by taking a thumbprint and checking before giving a signature that the print is not already on file. The collection of thumbprints poses little danger to individuals, since the is-a-person organization cannot link the prints with anything. The pseudonyms used by individuals are untraceable, in the sense that envelopes give no clue, apart from the signatures shown, about the other randomly chosen pseudonyms they contain. It is important to note that the actual cryptographic protocols provide unconditional untraceability using digital blind signatures on numbers.

## Credential Clearinghouses

When individuals have similar relationships with many organizations, there is often need for the centralized control provided by a *credential clearinghouse,* an organization that develops credential information about individuals' relationships with its member organizations and provides this information to these organizations. In current practice, clearinghouse functions are performed by such major organizations as credit bureaus, bank associations, insurance industry associations, national criminal information systems, and tax authorities.

For concreteness, consider how a credit clearinghouse might control the use of consumer credit using an extended form of the credential system. The clearinghouse gives you a number of *enabling* credentials that in effect say "This person is authorized for $100 worth of credit. If no resolution credential is returned to us within a year, we will assume that the individual has not repaid." You could provide one such credential to a shop, which then gives you credit worth up to $100. When you settle your account with the shop some time later, they give you the corresponding *resolution* credential, which you ultimately return to the clearinghouse. An important property of this approach is that the clearinghouse and shops cannot link the credentials; the clearinghouse with the cooperation of all the shops cannot learn which shop you went to, any more than the shop can learn your pseudonym with the clearinghouse, since the enabling and resolution credentials are unconditionally untraceable.

Security against abuse by individuals requires that the enabling credential be prevented from being shown to more than one shop. Otherwise someone could obtain too much credit from a single enabling credential. Similarly, it would not be possible to show a single resolution credential more than once to the clearinghouse, since otherwise someone could convince the clearinghouse that more debt had been repaid than was in fact repaid.

If individuals change pseudonyms periodically, they cannot be linked to obsolete information. Pseudonyms might be changed on a yearly basis. The initial information associated with new pseudonyms would be provided through the transfer of credentials from previous pseudonyms. The changeovers might be staggered to allow time for completion of pending business.

## Conclusions

The techniques presented allow powerful, readily extensible, and flexible arrangements for exchange of information between organizations about individuals. They protect against abuses by individuals, while providing unconditional security against linking of pseudonyms.

## Reference

(1) Chaum, D., "Security without Identification: Transaction Systems to make Big Brother Obsolete" *Communications of the ACM*, 28, 10, (October 1985), 1030-1044. © 1985 by the Association for Computing Machinery. Excerpted by permission.

# NETWORKS WITHOUT USER OBSERVABILITY -- DESIGN OPTIONS

Andreas Pfitzmann, Michael Waidner
Institut für Informatik IV, Universität Karlsruhe, Postfach 6380,
D 7500 Karlsruhe 1, West Germany

## ABSTRACT

In usual communication networks, the network operator or an intruder could easily observe when, how much and with whom the users communicate (traffic analysis), even if the users employ end-to-end encryption. When ISDNs are used for almost everything, this becomes a severe threat. Therefore, we summarize basic concepts to keep the recipient and sender or at least their relationship unobservable, consider some possible implementations and necessary hierarchical extensions, and propose some suitable performance and reliability enhancements.

## 0 Motivation

Public and private networks have a growing importance for our daily life. We use them for telephony, telegraphy, television, videotex, radio and in the near future we will use them for video telephony, electronic mail, ordering and receiving of newspapers, home banking, etc.
All these services will be integrated in a so called Integrated Services Digital Network (ISDN). If such a network is built as planned e.g. by the german PTT and operated on a "transmission on demand basis" even for the classical broadcast services TV and radio, great parts of the life of any user could easily be observed by the PTT or by an intruder.
Eavesdropping can be foiled by link-by-link encryption [Bara_64], but this does not foil attackers at the stations (e.g. via Trojan Horses).
There are some well known measures how the users themselves can decrease their observability. The content of a message can be sufficiently hidden by end-to-end encryption. However, an attacker can still see who sends how many messages to whom and at what time (traffic analysis). To hide this information, too, they can use public network stations (e.g. telephone boxes) instead of private ones. This will prevent observation but is very uncomfortable for the users (e.g. who would watch TV in a video telephone box?). If they use private network stations, they can only try to hide their behaviour by making their network stations do more things than necessary at other times than necessary. For example a user can order a whole newspaper or several newspapers instead of a single article, and he can do so at any time before he wants to read them.

This is an easy but expensive measure and not suitable for services like telephony.

So the only way to decrease user observability in a comfortable and cheap fashion seems to be to design a network for anonymity and not to try to realize anonymity afterwards.
The standard requirements on an ISDN, i.e. high performance and reliability, have to be met, too.

In the following chapters we will describe the existing proposals for anonymous networks in a systematic way and some options how they can be adapted to meet the stringent requirements on performance and reliability.

## 1 Basic concepts for anonymous networks

### 1.1 A closer look at anonymity

What we would like to realize is absolute anonymity against every possible attacker. But an attacker can control all network stations, all lines, and even the communication partner and so absolute anonymity is theoretically impossible. Therefore we need reasonable models of possible attackers.

There are several possible attackers: the administration, foreign states, companies, one's neighbours and communication partners. During the design of an anonymous network these possible attackers have to be translated into terms of stations and lines. A station is always under control of its owner and might be under control of everybody who has had access to it so far, e.g. its manufacturer, because he might have installed a Trojan Horse [PoKl_78, Thom_84]. Trojan Horses are a serious problem in stations with high complexity, e.g. switching centers. In simple user stations they can be detected more easily (if this is tried). Lines are assumed to be owned by the PTT. Normally they can easily be observed by the PTT or an eavesdropper, but by physical measures such an attack can be made much more difficult.

Given a model of the attacker we have to define what we want to keep hidden from him. A strong possibility is to keep the sender and the recipient of a message secret. A weaker possibility is to keep only their relationship secret, i.e. sending and receiving of physical messages is observable, but it is infeasable for an attacker to link the physical message sent by the sender and the physical message received by the recipient.

### 1.2 Recipient anonymity

Receiving a message can be made completely anonymous to the network by delivering the message to all stations (broadcast). If the message has an intended recipient, a so called addressee, it has to contain an attribute by which he and nobody else can recognize it as addressed to him. This attribute is called an implicit address in contrast to an explicit address, which describes a place in the network.

Implicit addresses can be distinguished according to their visibility, i.e. whether they can be tested for equality or not. An implicit address is called invisible, if it is only visible to its addressee and is called visible otherwise [Waid_85]. Invisible implicit addresses can be realized with a public key cryptosystem. A message is addressed by encrypting it (or a part of it) with a public key of the addressee. Each station decrypts all messages with each of its private keys and uses the message redundancy to decide which messages are addressed to it.
Conversely, if you have any invisible addressing scheme, you can do public key distribution: If you want to communicate a n bit key to your partner, choose n messages randomly, and address them to your partner if the corresponding key bit is 1, and address them not to your partner otherwise. Send these n messages in one explicitly addressed message to your partner.

Visible implicit addresses can be realized much easier: Users choose arbitrary names for themselves, which can then be prefixed to messages.

Another criterion to distinguish implicit addresses is their distribution. An implicit address is called public, if it is known to every user (like telephone numbers today) and private if the sender got it secretly from the addressee either outside the network or as a return address or by a generating algorithm the sender and the addressee agreed upon [FaLa_75, Karg_77].
Public addresses should not be realized by visible implicit addresses to avoid the linkability of the visible public address of a message and the addressed user.

Private addresses can be realized by visible addresses but then each of them should be used only once.

### 1.3 Unlinkability of sender and recipient

This form of anonymity can be realized by a special network station, a so called MIX, which collects a number of messages from the senders, changes their encodings and forwards the messages to the recipients in a different order.
This measure hides the relation between sender and recipient of a message from everybody but the MIX. By using more than one MIX to forward a message from the sender to the recipient, the measure hides the relation from every attacker in the network who doesn't control all the MIXes [Chau_81].

### 1.4 Sender anonymity

A powerful scheme for sender anonymity is superposing sending which is published in [Cha3_85, Cha8_85] and is called DC-net (dining cryptographers net) there.
Each user station generates at least one keybit for each message bit and sends each keybit to exactly one other user station over a secure channel. To send one bit every user station adds modulo 2 (superposes) all generated and received keybits and its message bit if there is one. The sums are sent over the network and added up modulo 2. The result is distributed to all user stations. The result is the sum of all sent message bits, because every keybit was added twice. Therefore the scheme realizes a multi-access channel with collisions. For its efficient use a medium access protocol [Tane_81] preserving anonymity is needed. Two of them are mentioned in [Cha3_85].
If an attacker controls all lines and some of the user stations, he gets no information about the sender of a message among the other users, as long as their key graph, i.e. the graph with the users as nodes and the keys as edges, is connected.
Superposing sending requires the exchange of a tremendous amount of randomly chosen keys. To reduce costs, pseudorandomly generated keys can be used instead, reducing information-theoretic [Sha1_49] to complexity-theoretic security.

The expensive generation, distribution and superposing of keys (and messages) of the concept of superposing sending can be avoided, if the network is designed for preventing attackers from physically observing all lines connecting a user with the rest of the world.
A simple and efficient way to do so is to connect the user stations by rings, which are in wide use for local area networks. If an anonymous medium access protocol is used, a user station is only observable if its two neighbour stations collude or the lines are tapped. The latter attack can be prevented by an appropriate cable run [Pfi1_83, Pfit_84]. Possible medium access protocols are slotted ring with sender remove and token ring, both with exhaustive service [Höck_85, HöPf_85].

## 2 Performance

The two main performance characteristics of networks are throughput and transfer delay. Their importance depends on the services the network should offer. Throughput and delay are less critical for services like electronic mail, only throughput is critical for services like file transfer, only delay for services like telephony and both are critical for video telephony.

### 2.1 Some remarks on the basic concepts for anonymous networks

Analyzing the performance of the concepts of chapter 1 must go along with considering how they would be implemented physically.

In local areas with a few hundred stations the performance of a ring network implemented as a physical ring is about as good as or even better than that of an equally expensive usual star or bus network [Bürl_84, Bürl_85, Mann_85]. However, performance and reliability of ring networks with more than 10000 stations become inacceptable.

In [Cha3_85] David Chaum suggests implementing superposing sending on a physical ring network. Each message bit requires two circulations around the ring: in the first round the user bits are successively superposed by the users, in the second round the resulting bit is broadcasted.
This implementation seems quite efficient, because under the assumption of uniformly distributed traffic it increases the average expenditure of transmission only by a factor of four compared with a traditional ring access protocol in which the recipient removes the message from the ring, whereas on a star or tree network the factor is the number of stations. But the amount of transmission on each line, i.e. the required bandwidth, is the same for all implementations, so implementations on stars or trees might still be better if their delay time is shorter. The nodes of such networks can be less complex than normal switching centers and constructed in a way that the overall delay in the network is only proportional to the logarithm of the number of stations whereas in ring networks it is always proportional to the number of stations [Pfi1_85].
As throughput and reliability of any network based on superposing sending can't be greater than that of a ring network, these networks can't be built with more than 10000 stations either.

In the MIX network, several factors are to be considered: How many and which stations act as MIXes and how many MIXes are used per message?
As expenditure of transmission of a message grows quadratically with the number of MIXes chosen for it, this number must not be too large. Especially not all stations can be chosen as MIXes for all messages.
To guarantee short delay for time critical services the throughput of a station that acts as MIX must be very high because it must always have enough messages to mix. These lots of messages must be decrypted and rearranged and forwarded. So a MIX must be extremely powerful and complex, and therefore there can only be a limited number of MIXes in the network.
If the MIX network is implemented using some user stations of an existing physical network as MIXes, each message must pass the physical network several times which adds additional delay to that occuring in the MIXes. But using the switching centers of the physical network as MIXes can not be recommended either, because the probability that they collude is too great (and the assumption that they are independent becomes altogether absurd in states with a telecommunication monopoly like the FRG).

## 2.2 Hierarchical networks

As mentioned above networks which provide sender and recipient anonymity cannot be built for that number of stations an ISDN would have. To achieve high performance, it seems reasonable to divide the network stations statically or dynamically into groups which perform one of the schemes of paragraph 1.4 and to support the possible groupings by a physical structure.

The simplest form of such a structure is the switched/broadcast network (SBNS), which has two levels, broadcast networks based on rings or superposing sending at the lower level and an arbitrary switched network as backbone [Pfit_83, Pfil_83, Pfit_84, Pfit_85, Pfil_85]. If the scheme of superposing sending is used, the SBNS can easily be generalized to a tree network. The partitioning into local broadcast networks can then be made variable by changing the depth of the backbone network [Pfil_85].

### 2.3 Channel switching

So far only networks based on slotted rings with exhaustive service are suitable for services that require a continuous stream of information with short delay (channel switching), because once a station is allowed to use a slot, it can use this slot again and again as a channel.

The MIX network is inappropriate for such services, because of the delay during the transport of each message, and the networks based on the concept of superposing sending, because the basic medium access protocols don't guarantee exhaustive service.
New possibilities of increasing the performance of these network can be achieved by giving up one requirement on anonymity that seems unreasonable for channel switching services anyway: the requirement that the relationship between different messages of the same connection is hidden [Pfil_85].

In a network based on superposing sending, channels can then be switched as in normal broadcast networks.

In a MIX network in its pure form the delay results essentially from the fact, that every MIX has to await all bits of a long packet, before it can decrypt it and send the first bit to the next MIX. This can be avoided, if a single message is used for setting up a connection and giving each MIX a key of a fast private key system used as a stream cipher. These private keys are used to encrypt the following messages of the initiated connection just as the public keys in the normal MIX network [Pfil_85].

In a hierarchical network, channels are switched by concatenating channels of the different levels of the hierarchy.

## 3 Fault tolerance

So far, all networks are serial systems in the sense of reliability: all MIXes of a chosen sequence of MIXes, all stations of a ring, and all stations taking part in superposing sending must work correctly. To fulfil the high reliability requirements on an ISDN, each scheme must be extended to include some fault-tolerance mechanisms. These mechanisms can work end-to-end, i.e. the sender retransmits a message if it doesn't receive an acknowledgement after a certain amount of time. Even if the sender chooses a different encoding of the message for each retransmission, the retransmitted messages can enable statistical attacks in some networks. Moreover, the performance of such mechanisms in terms of average transfer delay, variance of transfer delay, or usable throughput can be unsatisfactory. Therefore, it seems worthwhile to use mechanisms which avoid end-to-end retransmission wherever possible.

### 3.1 MIX network

If every MIX in a sequence of chosen MIXes can bypass the next MIX, a failure of one MIX (or more, as long as no two consecutive MIXes break down) can be tolerated. To bypass one MIX, its predecessor must not only get the message part for it but also for its successor. If it receives both message parts and this is done for every MIX, the length of the whole message grows exponentially. To avoid this exponential growth, the sender of a message chooses a different key (e.g. of a fast private key system) for each MIX. Together with its message part each MIX must get its key, that of its successor, and the addresses of the next two MIXes, all together encrypted with its own public key.

Let $A_1,\ldots,A_n$ be the sequence of addresses and $e_1,\ldots,e_n$ be the sequence of public keys of the chosen MIXes $M_1,\ldots,M_n$, $A_{n+1}$ the address of the addressee $M_{n+1}:=A$ and $e_A$ his public key, $k_1,\ldots,k_n$ the chosen sequence of keys, and $N_i$ the message that $M_i$ shall receive. The messages $N_i$ are formed according to the following scheme, starting from the message content N that A shall receive:

$$N_{n+1} = e_A(N)$$
$$N_n = e_n(k_n, A_{n+1}), k_n(N_{n+1})$$
$$N_i = e_i(k_i, A_{i+1}, k_{i+1}, A_{i+2}), k_i(N_{i+1}) \qquad i=1,\ldots,n-1$$

So $M_i$ can get $N_{i+1}$ and $N_{i+2}$ out of $N_i$, but as long as at least two consecutive MIXes are not controlled by the attacker, the scheme is as secure as the original scheme [Pfi1_85].
The scheme can easily be modified to tolerate the failure of d consecutive MIXes instead of one for every fixed number d.

### 3.2 Other networks

The ring network can be made fault tolerant by using a braided ring and special protocols [Mann_85]. A quantitative examination of the reliability improvement is given there.

Some remarks on the DC-net and the hierarchical anonymous networks can be found in [Pfi1_85].

## 4 Concluding remarks

The previous three chapters dealt with the design of a network with high performance and reliability which allows its users to send and to receive anonymously.
If using the network isn't free of charge the charges must either be paid anonymously with each use of the network (e.g. by anonymous numbered accounts [Pfit_84, Pfi1_83] or digital banknotes [Cha4_85,Cha8_85]), which seems rather troublesome, or measured anonymously (e.g. by safeguarded counters at user stations [Pfit_84, Pfi1_83]), or paid by flat rates.
As mentioned in the motivation, the content of a message can be hidden by using end-to-end encryption.

The initially mentioned services like electronic mail, ordering of newspapers or home banking can be implemented by higher protocols upon such a network.
If identification is required instead of anonymity, the well known authentication schemes can be used. Otherwise it is necessary to implement the services in a way which preserves the anonymity of the network. This must be proved in addition to proofs that the implementation fulfils its normal specification, e.g. security against fraud [WaPf_85].

It should be mentioned that many communication services where users nowadays have to identify themselves can be used in an anonymous way in the future, if there is a protocol that allows people to act under several pseudonyms and to transform documents that carry one of these pseudonyms into documents carrying another of their own pseudonyms, in a secure and anonymous way [Cha1_84, Cha2_85, Cha8_85].

## Acknowledgements

We are grateful to David Chaum for sending us his drafts and for stimulating discussions and to Klaus Echtle and Birgit Pfitzmann for a lot of useful comments and discussions.

## Literature

Bara_64 Paul Baran: On Distributed Communications: IX. Security, Secrecy, and Tamper-Free Considerations; Memorandum RM-3765-PR, Aug. 1964, The Rand Corporation, Santa Monica, California

Bürl_84 Gabriele Bürle: Leistungsvergleich von Sternnetz und Schieberegister-Ringnetz; Studienarbeit, Univ. Karlsruhe, 1984

Bürl_85 Gabriele Bürle: Leistungsbewertung von Vermittlungs-/Verteilnetzen; Diplomarbeit, Univ. Karlsruhe, Mai 1985

Chau_81 David Chaum: Untraceable Electronic Mail, Return Addresses, and Digital Pseudonyms; CACM Vol. 24, Nu. 2, Feb. 1981, pp. 84..88

Cha1_84 David Chaum: A New Paradigm for Individuals in the Information Age; Proc. of the 1984 Symp. on Security and Privacy, IEEE, Apr. 1984, Oakland, California, pp. 99..103

Cha2_85 David Chaum: Showing Credentials Without Identification. Signatures Transferred Between Unconditionally Unlinkable Pseudonyms; Eurocrypt 85, Draft, received May 13, 1985;

Cha3_85 David Chaum: The Dining Cryptographers Problem. Unconditional Sender Anonymity; Draft, received May 13, 1985;

Cha4_85 David Chaum: Privacy Protected Payments. Unconditional Payer and/or Payee Anonymity; Draft, received May 13, 1985;

Cha8_85 David Chaum: Security Without Identification: Transaction Systems to Make Big Brother Obsolete; CACM Vol. 28, Nu. 10, Oct. 1985, pp. 1030..1044

FaLa_75 David J. Farber, Kenneth C. Larson: Network Security Via Dynamic Process Renaming; Fourth Data Communications Symp., Oct. 1975, Quebec City, Canada, pp. 8-13..8-18

Höck_85 Gunter Höckel: Untersuchung der Datenschutzeigenschaften von Ringzugriffsmechanismen; Diplomarbeit, Univ. Karlsruhe, Aug.1985

HöPf_85 Gunter Höckel, Andreas Pfitzmann: Untersuchung der Datenschutzeigenschaften von Ringzugriffsmechanismen; 1. GI-Fachtagung "Datenschutz und Datensicherung", Okt. 1985, München, IFB Band 113, Springer-Verlag, Heidelberg, pp. 113..127

Karg_77 Paul A. Karger: Non-Discretionary Access Control for Decentralized Computing Systems; Master Thesis, MIT, Laboratory for Computer Science, May 1977, Report MIT/LCS/TR-179

Mann_85 Andreas Mann: Fehlertoleranz und Datenschutz in Ringnetzen; Diplomarbeit, Univ. Karlsruhe, Okt. 1985

Pfit_83 Andreas Pfitzmann: Ein Vermittlungs-/Verteilnetz zur Erhöhung des Datenschutzes in Bildschirmtext-ähnlichen Neuen Medien; 13. Jahrestagung der GI, Okt. 1983, Univ. Hamburg, IFB Band 73, Springer-Verlag Heidelberg, pp. 411..418

Pfit_84 Andreas Pfitzmann: A switched/broadcast ISDN to decrease user observability; 1984 Intern. Zurich Seminar on Digital Communications, March 1984, Zurich, Switzerland, Swiss Federal Inst. of Tech., Proc. IEEE Cat. No. 84CH1998-4 pp. 183..190

Pfit_85 Andreas Pfitzmann: Technischer Datenschutz in diensteintegrierenden Digitalnetzen - Problemanalyse, Lösungsansätze und eine angepaßte Systemstruktur; 1. GI-Fachtagung "Datenschutz und Datensicherung", Okt. 1985, München, IFB Band 113, Springer-Verlag, Heidelberg, pp. 96..112

Pfi1_83 A. Pfitzmann: Ein dienstintegriertes digitales Vermittlungs-/ Verteilnetz zur Erhöhung des Datenschutzes; Fak. f. Inform., Univ. Karlsruhe, Interner Bericht 18/83, Dez. 1983

Pfi1_85 Andreas Pfitzmann: How to implement ISDNs without user observability - Some remarks; Fak. f. Inform., Univ. Karlsruhe, Interner Bericht 14/85, 1985

PoKl_78 G. J. Popek, C. S. Kline: Issues in Kernel Design; Operating Systems, An Advanced Course, Ed. by R. Bayer et. al.; LNCS 60, 1978; Springer-Verlag, Heidelberg, pp. 209..227

Sha1_49 C. E. Shannon: Communication Theory of Secrecy Systems; Bell Syst. Tech. J., Vol. 28, No. 4, Oct. 1949, pp. 656..715

Tane_81 Andrew S. Tanenbaum: Computer Networks; Prentice-Hall, Englewood Cliffs, N. J., 1981

Thom_84 Ken Thompson: Reflections on Trusting Trust; CACM, Vol. 27, No. 8, Aug. 1984, pp. 761..763

Waid_85 Michael Waidner: Datenschutz und Betrugssicherheit garantierende Kommunikationsnetze. Systematisierung der Datenschutzmaßnahmen und Ansätze zur Verifikation der Betrugssicherheit; Diplomarbeit, Fak. f. Inform., Univ. Karlsruhe, Interner Bericht 19/85, Aug. 1985

WaPf_85 Michael Waidner, Andreas Pfitzmann: Betrugssicherheit trotz Anonymität. Abrechnung und Geldtransfer in Netzen; 1. GI-Fachtagung "Datenschutz und Datensicherung", Okt. 1985, München, IFB Band 113, Springer-Verlag, Heidelberg, pp. 128..141; Revised version appears in DuD, "Datenschutz und Datensicherung, Informationsrecht, Kommunikationssysteme", Vieweg Verlag, Wiesbaden

# THE VERIFIABILITY OF TWO-PARTY PROTOCOLS

Ronald V. Book[1] and Friedrich Otto[2]
[1]Department of Mathematics,
University of California,
Santa Barbara, CA 93106 / USA

[2]Fachbereich Informatik,
Universität Kaiserslautern,
6750 Kaiserslautern / West Germany

Public key encryption as used in network communication has been investigated extensively. The main advantage of the techniques developed in this area is the potential for secure communication. However, while public key systems are often effective in preventing a passive saboteur from deciphering an intercepted message, protocols must be designed to be secure when dealing with saboteurs who can impersonate users or send copies of intercepted messages on the public channel. Dolev and Yao [3] have shown how informal arguments about protocols can lead to erroneous conclusions, and they have developed formal models of two-party protocols, both cascade protocols and name-stamp protocols. Recall that a protocol is a set of rules that specify what operators a pair of users, the sender and the receiver, need to apply in an exchange of messages for the purpose of transmitting a given plaintext message from the sender to the receiver. In terms of their models, Dolev and Yao developed an elegant characterization of cascade protocols that are secure, a characterization with conditions that can be checked by inspection.

The problem that is studied in this paper is that of message authentication in the sense of Diffie and Hellman [2]. How can a user determine whether the messages received are the correct messages that comply with the rules of the protocol used ? The security of a protocol limits the ability to authenticate messages as shown by Dolev and Yao [3]. Our goal is to develop a method for message authentication that allows a user to determine whether the messages he receives actually comply with the protocol and, in this sense, are free of error. This method should be based on properties of the protocol itself, not on the messages exchanged or on the users. Further, the property of security should be retained whenever possible.

We call a protocol sender-verifiable if the sender is able to check whether the reply messages he receives actually comply with the protocol. Thus, if a protocol is sender-verifiable, then the sender can detect whether a saboteur has injected improper messages into the system. Similarly, a protocol is receiver-verifiable if the receiver can check whether the reply messages received comply with the protocol.

The notion of verifiability may also be used as an additional requirement for security. Recall that the power of a potential saboteur (as described by Dolev and Yao [3]) depends on the fact that in an exchange both the sender and the receiver follow the rules of the protocol and apply the specified operators to the messages they receive without checking that the received message itself complies with the protocol. If the user can check whether the messages received comply with the protocol before continuing with the exchange, then he can end the exchange as soon as he detects a message not complying with the protocol, thus restricting the power of a saboteur.

The main results of this paper are simple characterization theorems for two-party protocols that are sender-verifiable (resp., receiver-verifiable). These characterization theorems yield fast algorithms to determine whether a protocol is sender-verifiable or receiver-verifiable.

Our notation is based on that of Dolev and Yao [3].

A cascade protocol has a set of cancellation rules $\{D_X E_X = 1, E_X D_X = 1 \mid X \text{ is a user}\}$. For every operator word $\gamma$, let $\bar{\gamma}$ be the result of applying all possible cancellation rules until there is nothing left to cancel; operator words of the latter type are called irreducible. It turns out that for every operator word $\gamma$ there is a unique irreducible word $\bar{\gamma}$ such that for every plaintext message M, $\gamma(M) = \bar{\gamma}(M)$. Further, any two operator words $\gamma_1$ and $\gamma_2$ are considered to be equivalent if for all plaintext messages M, $\gamma_1(M) = \gamma_2(M)$. Hence, $\gamma_1$ and $\gamma_2$ are equivalent if and only if $\bar{\gamma}_1 = \bar{\gamma}_2$.

Let $P = \{\tilde{\alpha}_i, \tilde{\beta}_j \mid 1 \le i \le t, 1 \le j \le t'\}$ be a two-party cascade protocol where $t' = t$ or $t' = t-1$. For any two distinct users X and Y, let $N_1(X,Y) = \alpha_1(X,Y)$, $N_{2j}(X,Y) = \beta_j(X,Y)N_{2j-1}(X,Y)$, $1 \le j \le t'$, and $N_{2i+1}(X,Y) = \alpha_{i+1}(X,Y)N_{2i}(X,Y)$, $1 \le i \le t-1$.

If user X initiates an exchange with user Y to transmit plaintext message M, the messages exchanged are $N_1(X,Y)(M), N_2(X,Y)(M), \ldots,$

$N_{t+t'}(X,Y)(M)$. We illustrate this exchange as follows:

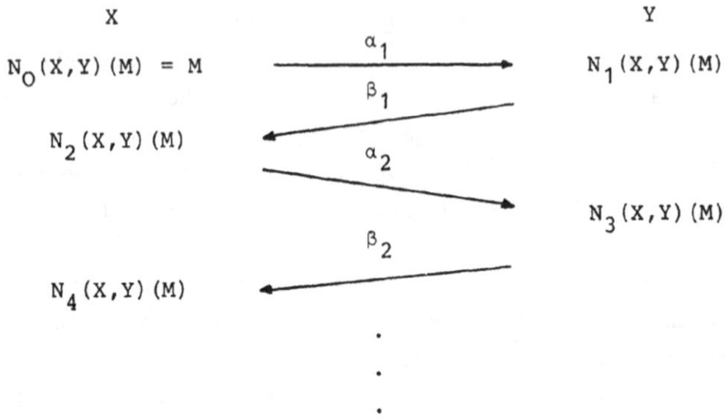


The sender X would like to verify that the receiver Y actually receives the correct message at each stage. Also, the receiver Y would like to verify that the sender X receives the correct replies. If both of these things can be done, then the message authentication problem (in the sense of Diffie and Hellman [2]) can be solved. The definition of verifiability is vague. Clearly, some notion of effective process is desired. Therefore, we restrict our attention to the following simpler notions.

A sequence of pairs $(u_j, v_j)$, $1 \le j \le t'$, with $u_j, v_j \in \{E_X, E_Y, D_X\}^*$ is a *sender-verification sequence for* P if for each j, $1 \le j \le t'$, $\overline{u_j N_{2(j-1)}(X,Y)} = \overline{v_j N_{2j}(X,Y)}$. (Here, $N_0(X,Y)$ is the identity function).

A sequence of pairs $(u_i, v_i)$, $1 \le i < t$, with $u_i, v_i \in \{E_X, E_Y, D_Y\}^*$ is a *receiver-verification sequence for* P if for each i, $1 \le i < t$, $\overline{u_i N_{2i-1}(X,Y)} = \overline{v_i N_{2i+1}(X,Y)}$.

The first result can be stated in the following way.

*Theorem 1*. Let $P = \{\tilde{\alpha}_i, \tilde{\beta}_j\}$ be a two-party cascade protocol.

(a) If P has a sender-verification sequence, then P is sender-verifiable.

(b) If P has a receiver-verification sequence, then P is receiver-verifiable.

Let us sketch a proof of part (a). Consider the situation where user X initiates an exchange with user Y in order to transmit the plaintext message M. For each $j \ge 1$, X wishes to know if the reply message received is the unique reply that complies with the protocol. It is assumed that the sender X always remembers the last message

$N_{2j-2}(X,Y)(M)$ received. When a new reply message M' is received, X tries to determine whether M' is in fact the message $N_{2j}(X,Y)(M)$ that is expected. If the protocol has a sender-verification sequence, then there exist $u_j$ and $v_j$ in $\{D_X, E_X, E_Y\}^*$ such that $\overline{u_j N_{2j-2}(X,Y)} = \overline{v_j N_{2j}(X,Y)}$ and so $u_j N_{2j-2}(X,Y)(M) = v_j N_{2j}(X,Y)(M)$. If the received message is M', then X can apply $v_j$ to M' and compare $v_j(M')$ with $u_j N_{2j-2}(X,Y)(M)$. Now these two bit streams agree if and only if M' is in fact equal to $N_{2j}(X,Y)(M)$, since the equation $\overline{u_j N_{2j-2}(X,Y)} = \overline{v_j w}$ has the unique irreducible solution $w = N_{2j}(X,Y)$. Thus, X can determine whether the reply message M' received at this stage of the exchange is in fact the unique reply that complies with the protocol.

Thus, we see that in the case of two-party cascade protocols, the existence of verification sequences allow both sender and receiver to determine whether the reply messages received actually comply with the protocol. Now the question of whether or not such sequences exist depends on the protocol itself, not on the choice of users, and so this concept is uniform in the same sense that Dolev and Yao's definition of the protocol is uniform.

We have characterized those two-party cascade protocols that have sender-verification (resp., receiver-verification) sequences. These characterizations are similar to the characterization of security given by Dolev and Yao in the sense that the conditions involve properties of each $\tilde{\alpha}_i$ and $\tilde{\beta}_j$ that can be checked by inspection. We combine the conditions that characterize security with those that characterize the existence of such sequences.

Theorem 2. Let $P = \{\tilde{\alpha}_i, \tilde{\beta}_j \mid 1 \leq i \leq t,\ 1 \leq j \leq t'\}$ be a two-party cascade protocol. Then the following are equivalent:

(a) P is secure and has both a receiver-verification sequence and a sender-verification sequence;

(b) for any two user names X and Y, the following hold:

- (i) $E_X$ or $E_Y$ occurs in the word $\alpha_1(X,Y)$;
- (ii) for every $i \geq 2$, $\alpha_i(X,Y) \in \{E_X, E_Y\}^*$ or $\alpha_i(X,Y) = w_1 E_X w_2 w_3$ with $w_1$, $w_3 \in \{E_Y, D_X\}^*$, $w_2 \in \{E_X, E_Y\}^*$, and $w_3^{-1}$ is a prefix of $\beta_{i-1}(X,Y)$;
- (iii) for every $j \geq 1$, $\beta_j(X,Y) \in \{E_X, E_Y\}^*$ or $\beta_j(X,Y) = w_1 E_Y w_2 w_3$ with $w_1$, $w_3 \in \{E_X, D_Y\}^*$, $w_2 \in \{E_X, E_Y\}^*$, and $w_3^{-1}$ is a prefix of $\alpha_j(X,Y)$.

This development is completely constructive. That is, knowing the existence of a sender-verification sequence for a protocol P allows us to construct such a sequence.

Theorem 3. There is a linear time algorithm that on input a two-party cascade protocol P will halt and output a sender-verification sequence (resp., receiver-verification sequence) for P if such a sequence exists and will halt with output "NO" if such a sequence does not exist.

Now we turn to the study of name-stamp protocols. Let $D = \{D_X \mid X \text{ is a user}\}$ and $E = \{E_X \mid X \text{ is a user}\}$. For each $\gamma \in (D \cup E)^*$, there is a unique irreducible $\gamma^{-1}$ such that $\gamma\gamma^{-1} = \gamma^{-1}\gamma = 1$. In the case of name-stamp protocols, there exist other types of functions, the name-appending, and name-matching functions (see [3]). Let $I = \{i_X \mid X \text{ is a user}\}$, where each $i_X$ is the name-appending function associated with X, and let $J = \{d_X \mid X \text{ is a user}\}$, where each $d_X$ is the name-matching function associated with X. Then every operator word in $(I \cup D \cup E)^*$ has a left inverse and every operator word in $(J \cup D \cup E)^*$ has a right inverse. No nontrivial operator word in $I^*$ has a right inverse and no nontrivial operator word in $J^*$ has a left inverse. These facts lead to certain difficulties when we consider the question of verifiability of name-stamp protocols.

The first problem comes when one tries to extend Theorem 1 to name-stamp protocols. The definition of a verification sequence changes in the sense that for a sender-verification sequence, each $u_j$, $v_j$ is taken from the set $\Gamma_X^*$ where $\Gamma_X = \{D_X, E_X, E_Y, i_X, i_Y, d_X, d_Y\}$, and similarly for a receiver-verification sequence. But more importantly, since there are operator words in $(I \cup J \cup D \cup E)^*$ which do not have left inverses, the argument given in the sketch of the proof of Theorem 1(a) fails since equations of the form $\bar{\gamma} = \overline{\delta w}$ do not necessarily have solutions, let alone unique solutions. In fact, Theorem 1 fails for name-stamp protocols. Therefore we are forced to put an additional constraint on the type of verification sequences used.

We make the following notational convention. If $\gamma \in (D \cup E \cup I \cup J)^*$ has a (two-sided) inverse, then let $\gamma^{-1}$ be the unique irreducible word such that $\gamma\gamma^{-1} = \gamma^{-1}\gamma = 1$. If $\gamma \in (D \cup E \cup I \cup J)^*$ has only a one-sided inverse, either right or left, then let $\gamma^{-1}$ be the unique irreducible word with the appropriate property. Notice that there is no ambiguity introduced.

The following theorem gives a characterization for name-stamp protocols that are sender-verifiable where the verifiability is carried out by a strong sender-verification sequence $\{(u_j, v_j)\}_{j=1}^{t'}$, i.e., each $v_j$ is left-invertible. Thus, this characterization will allow the argument used to prove Theorem 1(a) to carry over to name-stamp protocols.

<u>Theorem 4</u>. Let $P = \{\tilde{\alpha}_i, \tilde{\beta}_j \mid 1 \leq i \leq t, 1 \leq j \leq t'\}$ be a two-party name-stamp protocol, and let X and Y be any two users. Then P has a strong sender-verification sequence $\{(u_j, v_j)\}_{j=1}^{t'}$ if and only if the following conditions hold: for each $j \geq 1$, let $\overline{\beta_j(X,Y)\alpha_j(X,Y)} = w_1 w_2$, $\overline{N_{2j-2}(X,Y)} = w_2^{-1} w_3$, and $\overline{N_{2j}(X,Y)} = w_1 w_3$ where $w_2$ is right-invertible. Let z be the longest common suffix of $w_1$ and $w_2^{-1}$, let $w_1 = f_1 f_2 z$ where $f_1 = 1$ or $f_1$ ends in $D_Y$ and $f_2 \in \Gamma_X^*$, and let $w_2^{-1} = g_1 g_2 z$ where $g_1 \in (D \cup \{E_X\} \cup I)^*$ and $g_2 = 1$ or $g_2$ begins in $E_Y$. Then either

(a) $g_2 = 1$ and $f_1 \in (D \cup \{E_X\})^*$, or

(b) $f_1, f_2 \in (D \cup \{E_X\})^*$ and $g_2 \in (E \cup \{D_X\} \cup I)^*$.

The conditions in Theorem 4 are such that for any name-stamp protocol P one can check in linear time whether P has a strong sender-verification sequence $\{(u_j, v_j)\}_{j=1}^{t'}$. Further, we have the analogue of Theorem 3.

<u>Theorem 5</u>. There is a linear time algorithm that on input a two-party name-stamp protocol P will halt and output a strong sender-verification sequence for P if such a sequence exists and will halt and output "NO" otherwise.

Theorems 4 and 5 are concerned with sender-verifiability. However the notion of receiver-verifiability is essentially isomorphic and the analogous theorems also hold.

The reader may question why we have not stated our characterization theorems in terms of name-stamp protocols that are secure, similar to Theorem 2. Not only is there no known characterization of secure name-stamp protocols of the same type as the characterization of secure cascade protocols given by Dolev and Yao, in fact we have shown that no such characterization can exist [1].

Finally, we consider one other aspect of these models for protocols. The protocols discussed so far can be called <u>symmetric</u> since for every user X, the encryption function composed with the decryption function yields the identity, i.e., $E_X D_X = 1$. By definition of decryption, the decryption function composed with the encryption function yields the identity, i.e., $D_X E_X = 1$. There are valid reasons for considering protocols that are <u>nonsymmetric</u> in the sense that for every user X, $E_X D_X \neq 1$ (while $D_X E_X = 1$). We have developed the entire theory of nonsymmetric protocols in terms of the properties of security and verifiability and have obtained results similar to those reported in this paper.

Acknowledgement

This research was supported in part by the National Science Foundation under Grant DCR83-14977.

References

1. R.V. Book and F. Otto, On the security of name-stamp protocols, Theoret. Comput. Sci. 40 (1985), to appear.
2. W. Diffie and M. Hellman, New directions in cryptography, IEEE Trans. Information Theory IT-22 (1976), 644-654.
3. D. Dolev and A. Yao, On the security of public key protocols, IEEE Trans. Information Theory IT-29 (1983), 198-208. An extended abstract appears in Proc. 22nd IEEE Symp. Foundations of Computer Science (1981), 350-357.

# THE PRACTICE OF AUTHENTICATION*

Gustavus J. Simmons
Applied Mathematics Department
Sandia National Laboratories
Albuquerque, New Mexico 87185

## Introduction

One of the most pervasive problems in military and in commercial communications-like systems is the need to authenticate digital messages; where authentication is interpreted broadly to mean verification both that a message was originated by the purported transmitter and that it has not been altered subsequently, which includes verifying that it is not a repetition of an earlier legitimate but already accepted message. The terminology "message" is a carryover from the origins of the problem in communications systems, but as used here includes resident computer software, data bank information, access requests and passes or passwords, hand-shaking exchanges between terminals and central facilities or between card readers and teller machines, etc.; i.e., digital information exchange over a suspect channel or interface in general. The need to authenticate information presupposes an opponent(s) -- who may in some circumstances be either the transmitter or receiver -- that desires to have unauthentic messages be accepted by the receiver, or by arbiters, as authentic or else to fraudulently attribute to the transmitter messages that he did not send.

Message authentication is commonly -- and inexplicably -- treated as though it were a single, simple function of the message, much like a parity check, for example. The probable explanation for this is that the result of the authentication operation is two valued; i.e., either the message is accepted as authentic or else it is rejected as inauthentic. What makes the authentication of digital messages such a challenging problem though is that there is no single authentication function that can suffice for all, or even for a large fraction, of the real world authentication needs. For example in some cases the message content cannot (by design) be kept secret from the opponent, while in others he is denied this information. Similarly, in some cases the opponent succeeds if he can cause the receiver to accept any fraudulent message, while in others he succeeds only if he can get a specific message (or one of a small set of messages) accepted as authentic.

* This work performed at Sandia National Laboratories supported by the U. S. Department of Energy under contract no. DE-AC04-76DP00789.

In addition, the opponent may either be an outsider with no privileged information or, in a particularly difficult case to deal with, he may be a legitimate receiver misusing insider information provided him so that he can authenticate messages to generate forgeries. Clearly, digital message authentication in circumstances as widely varying as these cannot be expected to be a simple operation. In this paper we shall first derive several theoretical bounds on the quality of authentication that can be achieved for particular authentication channel specifications -- and then exhibit an example system based on the data encryption standard (DES) that seemingly violates these bounds [4]. This apparent contradiction -- arising from the difference between computationally feasible and infeasible problems -- highlights an essential aspect of most practical authentication (or crypto) systems.

## Authentication

In message authentication, there are three essential participants: a transmitter who observes an information source*, such as a coin flip, and wishes to communicate these observations to a remotely located receiver over a publicly exposed, noiseless, communications channel; and a receiver who wishes to not only learn what the transmitter has observed but also to assure himself that the communications (messages) that he receives actually came from the transmitter and that no alterations have been made to them subsequent to the transmitter having sent them. The third participant, the opponent, wishes to deceive the receiver into accepting a message that will misinform him as to the state of the source. He can achieve this end in either of two ways: by impersonating the transmitter and getting the receiver to accept a fraudulent message of his own devising when in fact none has been sent by the transmitter, or else by waiting and intercepting a message sent by the transmitter and substituting some other message that is accepted by the receiver as genuine, but which misinforms him of the state of the source. There are many "side" constraints that must be considered in actual applications of authentication:

---

* Ideally we would call the states of the source "messages" as is the practice in communications theory. However, if we did this we would be forced to introduce terminology to designate the collection of sequences that can be sent through the channel, perhaps "authentication code," paralleling "error detecting and correcting code" from communications theory. Unfortunately, the natural contraction "codeword" already has an accepted meaning in communications theory so that we would either have to coin a new word to designate the particular sequence of symbols sent to convey and authenticate a message -- none of which seem very natural -- or else use the cumbersome term "authentication codeword". The term "authenticator", usually used in the sense of an authentication codeword appended to a message, has too restricted a connotation for the general case. We have opted instead to use the term "message' to designate what is actually transmitted and to tolerate the rather artificial device that the information conveyed by a message is the state of a hypothetical source.

the opponent could, for example, be the receiver attempting to falsely attribute messages to the transmitter that he didn't originate and to convince a third party of the authenticity of these forgeries or the transmitter disavowing authentic messages that he did send -- a problem situation commonly referred to as the customer-broker scenario. In the present discussion we only consider one constraint; i.e., whether the receiver is ignorant of the state of the source observed by the legitimate transmitter (authentication with secrecy) or knowledgeable of it (authentication without secrecy).

The source $\mathcal{S}$ is defined by a probability distribution S on its states; $s_i$. H(S) is the resulting binary entropy of $\mathcal{S}$, i.e., on average this much information must be communicated to the receiver to inform him of the state of the source. If only H(S) bits were communicated, then there would be no possibility of authentication, hence authentication codes -- like error detecting and correcting codes -- depend on the deliberate introduction and use of redundant information in the transmission.

In a common U. S. military authentication protocol both the transmitter and receiver have matched sealed authenticators -- actually a short random sequence of symbols produced and distributed by the National Security Agency. The sealed packets are constructed so as to provide a positive indication (tattle-tale) if they are opened. Each communicant is responsible for the protection of his sealed authenticator and is administratively restrained from opening it until it is needed to authenticate a message. To authenticate a message, the transmitter opens a sealed authenticator, appends the enclosed authentication suffix to the message and then encrypts the resulting extended message. The receiver, upon receiving the cipher would open his matching sealed authenticator and accept the message as genuine if the cipher decrypted to a string of symbols with the proper suffix, and otherwise reject it as inauthentic. If there are r bits of information in the authenticator suffix, an opponent (if he cannot break the "sealing" encryption algorithm) would have only a $2^{-r}$ probability of "guessing" a cipher which would decrypt into a message ending with the unknown (to him) authentication suffix and hence be accepted as authentic by the receiver. This example illustrates the essential point in all authentication schemes -- namely that for a particular choice of authenticator the receiver will accept only a fraction out of the total number of messages possible.

Continuing the parallel between error detecting and correcting codes and authentication codes, let the particular mapping of states of the source into acceptable (authentic) messages determined by a specific choice (of authenticators) by the transmitter and receiver be called an encoding rule; $e_i$. $\mathcal{E}$ is then the set of all available (to the transmitter/receiver) encoding rules. Given $\mathcal{E}$, the transmitter and receiver choose encoding rules according to a probability distribution E, which in turn determines a binary entropy of H(E) as to the average equivocation about the rule being employed. Finally, there is a space $\mathfrak{M}$ consisting of all of the messages that the transmitter can use to communicate states of the source to the receiver. We assume that the transmitter can communicate to the receiver any observation he makes of the source; therefore $|\mathfrak{M}| > |\mathcal{S}|$ where $|\mathcal{S}|$ is interpreted to be the cardinality of states of $\mathcal{S}$ that have nonzero probability of occurrence. The inequality is strict, since as has already been remarked if $|\mathfrak{M}| = |\mathcal{S}|$, all messages would have to be acceptable to the receiver and, hence, no authentication would be possible.

A concise representation of authentication against an opponent impersonating the transmitter is now possible in the form of an $|\mathcal{E}| \times |\mathfrak{M}|$ matrix, **A**. The rows of **A** are indexed by encoding rules and the columns by messages. The entry in $a(e_i, m_j)$ is the element of $\mathcal{S}$ encoded by rule $e_i$ into message $m_j$ if such a source mapping exists under $e_i$ and 0 otherwise. As a consequence of the (reasonable) assumption that the transmitter can communicate any state he observes of the source to the receiver, every element of $\mathcal{S}$ appears in each row of **A** at least once and perhaps several times. Earlier comments imply that each row and column contains at least one 0 entry. We now define another $|\mathcal{E}| \times |\mathfrak{M}|$ matrix **X**, in which

$$\chi(e_i, m_j) = \begin{cases} 1 & \text{if} \quad a(e_i, m_j) \in \mathcal{S} \\ 0 & \text{otherwise} \end{cases} .$$

For example, for $|\mathcal{S}| = 2$, $|\mathfrak{M}| = 4$, the "best" authentication system possible has:

$$\mathbf{A} = \begin{vmatrix} s_1 & s_2 & 0 & 0 \\ s_1 & 0 & s_2 & 0 \\ 0 & s_2 & 0 & s_1 \\ 0 & 0 & s_2 & s_1 \end{vmatrix} \quad \text{and} \quad \mathbf{X} = \begin{vmatrix} 1 & 1 & 0 & 0 \\ 1 & 0 & 1 & 0 \\ 0 & 1 & 0 & 1 \\ 0 & 0 & 1 & 1 \end{vmatrix} .$$

It is now easy to see the relationship of the impersonation "game" to the matrix **X**. If $m_j$ is an acceptable (authentic) message to the receiver when encoding rule $e_i$ has been agreed to by the transmitter and receiver then $\chi(e_i m_j) = 1$ and the opponent has a probability of success of $p = 1$ if he communicates $m_j$ to the receiver. Conversely, whenever $\chi(e_i, m_j) = 0$ he is certain the message will be rejected. It is certainly plausible -- and in fact rigorously true -- that the opponents probability of success in impersonating the transmitter is the value, $v_I$, of the zero sum game whose payoff matrix is **X**.

The matrix representation, **Y**, of authentication against an opponent who waits to observe a message sent by the legitimate transmitter and then substitutes some other message is considerably more complex, since the simple strategies available to him in this case are conditional probabilities; i.e., he observes message $m_j$ and must choose, based on this observation, a message $m_k$ to substitute in its stead. The choices available to the transmitter and receiver are the same as in the impersonation case, namely the choice of an encoding rule $e_i$ and perhaps a choice (by the transmitter) of which message to use to communicate the state of the source, $s_\ell$, if $e_i$ maps $s_\ell$ into two or more messages.

**Y** is a $|\mathcal{E}| \times |\mathfrak{m}|^2$ array whose rows are indexed by $e_i$ and whose columns are indexed by the $|\mathfrak{m}|^2$ pairs $m_j|m_k$; meaning $m_j$ is observed and $m_k$ is substituted. The entries in **Y** are:

$$y^i_{jk} = \begin{cases} 1 & \text{if encoding rule } e_i \text{ is used, and when message } m_k \text{ is substituted for } m_j \text{ the receiver is deceived as to the state of the source*} \\ 0 & \end{cases} .$$

A strategy for the opponent in this case consists of an $|\mathfrak{m}|^2$-tuple $(q_{jk})$ where $\sum_{k=1}^{|\mathfrak{m}|} q_{jk} = 1$, for $1 \le j \le |\mathfrak{m}|$, and $q_{jk}$ is the probability of his substituting message $m_k$ for $m_j$.

Since the opponent has, as a part of his strategy, the option to either impersonate the transmitter before a legitimate message is sent or else to wait and substitute some other message in an attempt to deceive the receiver, the complete authentication "game" is the concatenation of **X** and **Y**, i.e., a rectangular $|\mathcal{E}| \times |\mathfrak{m}|(|\mathfrak{m}| + 1)$ game subject to the strategy constraints mentioned above plus some additional ones having to do with the transmitter's optimal use of his choices (if any) among available messages to communicate an observed state of the source (splitting). Not surprisingly there exist authentication systems in which the optimal strategy for the opponent is either pure impersonation, pure substitution, optional linear combinations of the two, or most interesting -- essential mixing of both as well as examples in which splitting is essential in the transmitter/receiver's optimal strategies. The point of these remarks is that we have shown in earlier papers that an opponent's overall probability of success under an optimal strategy in deceiving the receiver, $P_d$, is at least the value of the game whose payoff matrix is the concatenation of **X** and **Y**, and hence that

$$P_d \ge \max(v_I, v_S)$$

where $v_I$ and $v_S$ are the values of the impersonation game on **X** and of the substitution game on **Y**, respectively. We will not pursue this game theory formulation [1] further here, since the purpose of this paper is to review some "channel bounds" on $P_d$ for the authentication channel in terms of the parameters H(S), H(M) and H(E) and then to exhibit a practical system (based on DES) that appears to violate this

---

* If a common state of the source, $s_\ell$, is mapped into $m_j$ and $m_k$ under $e_i$, then even though $m_k$ would be accepted by the receiver as an authentic message when in fact the transmitter sent $m_j$, he would not be misinformed as to the state of the source and hence $y^i_{jk} = 0$ in this case also.

bound. Of course, the real purpose of the paper is to explain away this apparent contradiction.

## The Authentication Channel Bound

Since they have been derived in full detail elsewhere [2], we only exhibit the principal results on the authentication channel bound that are needed to make this paper self-contained. Theorem 1 states the fundamental authentication channel bound.

Theorem 1 (Authentication Channel Bound)

There is a strategy for the opponent such that

$$\log P_d \geq H(MES) - H(E) - H(M) \tag{1}$$

for any transmitter/receiver strategy, E.

Discussion

$P_d$ is the probability that the receiver is deceived as to the state of the source. H(E) and H(M) are the a priori equivocation about the encoding rule being used by the transmitter and receiver and of the message(s) respectively. H(MES) is the joint uncertainty as to the state of the source, the encoding rule and the resulting message. (1) is only one of many equivalent formulations of the channel bound, but is the form most naturally proven by information theoretic arguments.

The expression (1) shows an interesting, and often valuable (to the transmitter/receiver) difference between the essential equivocation faced by the opponent in attempting to deceive the receiver and that faced by the legitimate receiver in attempting to recover the state of the source from the message. The difference in their tasks arises only when the encoding rule encodes at least one state of the source into two or more acceptable messages. In this case H(MES) when expressed in the form

$$H(MES) = H(E|MS) + H(MS)$$

makes clear that to the opponent, meaningful uncertainty about the encoding rule can exist even though he knows both the state of the source and the message chosen to communicate it. H(E|MS) is essentially the uncertainty (to the opponent) introduced by splitting messages. By meaningful, we mean that this uncertainty can be used by the transmitter/receiver to confound him in choosing a substitute message. The receiver on the other hand doesn't care about which message the transmitter chooses, since he knows the encoding rule and hence will correctly infer the state of the source irrespective of which choice the transmitter made.

Theorem 2 gives eight equivalent expressions to (1) for the case of authentication with secrecy: i.e., the opponent does not know the state of the source observed by the transmitter. This, of course, only matters if the opponent elects to substitute messages rather than to impersonate the transmitter.

Theorem 2

$H(MES) - H(E) - H(M)$ is equivalent to any of the following eight entropy expressions.

| | X | Equivalent Form |
|---|---|---|
| (2) | ES | $H(M\|ES) + H(S) - H(M)$ |
| (3) | MS | $H(E\|MS) - H(E) + H(MS) - H(M)$ |
| | | or |
| (4) | | $H(E\|MS) - H(E) + H(S\|M)$ |
| (5) | ME | $H(E\|M) - H(E)$ |
| | | or |
| (6) | | $H(M\|E) - H(M)$ |
| (7) | S | $H(ME\|S) + H(S) - H(E) - H(M)$ |
| (8) | E | $H(MS\|E) - H(M)$ |
| (9) | M | $H(ES\|M) - H(E)$ |

Proof:

The proof in each case proceeds by splitting the argument in the entropy H(MES) appearing in (1) through conditioning the joint probability on the variable X and then using simple identities to reduce the resulting expressions. The derivation of (2) is typical.

$$H(MES) = H(M|ES) + H(ES)$$

$$= H(M|ES) + H(E|S) + H(S)$$

$$= H(M|ES) + H(E) + H(S)$$

since E and S are independent random variables. Hence

$$H(MES) - H(E) - H(M) = H(M|ES) + H(S) - H(M)$$

as was to be shown, etc.

Eq. (2) says that

$$\log P_d \geq H(S) - H(M) + H(M|ES) \quad .$$

The right-hand term $H(M|ES)$ is the average uncertainty about M given the encoding rule $e_j \in \mathcal{E}$ and state of the source $s_i \in \mathcal{S}$. But there is no uncertainty if there is no splitting, i.e., if there are no choices of messages available to the transmitter to communicate state $s_i$ to the receiver when using encoding rule $e_j$. In this case, and indeed in general,

(10) $$H(S) < H(M)$$

for authentication to be possible at all. We have noted earlier that the inequality

(11) $$|\mathcal{S}| < |\mathcal{M}|$$

had to also hold for authentication to be possible. In view of the similarity of (10) and (11) a natural question is whether one of the inequalities is stronger than the other, i.e, implies the other. The following small example shows that this is not the case.

Consider two sets $\mathbf{A} = (a_1, a_2)$ and $\mathbf{B} = (b_1, b_2, b_3)$ with probability distributions

$$A = (\tfrac{1}{2}, \tfrac{1}{2}) \quad \text{and} \quad B = (\tfrac{7}{8}, \tfrac{1}{16}, \tfrac{1}{16}) \quad ,$$

respectively. Then $H(A) = 1$ and

$$H(B) = \frac{25}{8} - \frac{7}{8}\log 7 \approx \frac{2}{3} \quad .$$

Now let $\mathcal{S} = \mathbf{A}$ and $\mathcal{M} = \mathbf{B}$, so that

$$|\mathcal{S}| < |\mathcal{M}|$$

but

$$H(S) > H(M)$$

showing that (11) doesn't imply (10). Conversely, let $\mathcal{S} = \mathbf{B}$ and $\mathcal{M} = \mathbf{A}$, so that

$$H(S) < H(M)$$

then

$$|\mathcal{S}| > |\mathcal{M}|$$

showing that (10) need not imply (11) either. ▮

What is true is that for authentication to be possible both (10) and (11) must be satisfied; i.e., that there must be more messages than states of the source and the average information content in a message must be at least as large as the average uncertainty it resolves (for the receiver) as to the state of the source. Stated in this way, both conditions are certainly reasonably, the only surprising thing is that they are independent.

Using the results of Theorem 2, it is possible to derive some (generally) weaker but enlightening channel bounds. We first note that the total effective equivocation to the opponent playing the substitution game but without knowledge of the source state, i.e., authentication with secrecy, is no greater than $H(E|M)$ and as remarked earlier, the opponent's total effective equivocation if he knows the source state, i.e., authentication without secrecy, is at most $H(E|MS)$.

<u>Theorem 3</u>

For authentication with secrecy

$$\log P_d \geq -\frac{1}{2} H(E) \tag{12}$$

while for authentication without secrecy

$$\log P_d \geq -\frac{1}{2} \{H(E) - H(MS) + H(M)\} = -\frac{1}{2} \{H(E) - H(S|M)\} \tag{13}$$

<u>Proof.</u>

For authentication with secrecy

$$\log P_d \geq \min\{\log v_I, -H(E|M)\} \tag{14}$$

while for authentication without secrecy

$$\log P_d \geq \min\{\log v_I, -H(E|MS)\} \tag{15}$$

In either (14) or (15) the bounds derived in Theorem 1 and 2 on the value of the impersonation game can be substituted, since the opponent's impersonation strategy is independent of whether he plays substitution with or without secrecy. Replacing the minimum on the right-hand side of the inequality by the average of the two bracketed terms either weakens the inequality if the terms are not identical or leaves it unaffected if they are. Therefore for authentication with secrecy, replacing $v_I$ with the bound (5) in (14) we get

$$\log P_d \geq \frac{1}{2}\{H(E|M) - H(E) - H(E|M)\} = -\frac{1}{2}H(E)$$

and similarly by replacing $v_I$ with the bounds (3) or (4) in (15) we get

$$\log P_d \geq \frac{1}{2}\{H(E|MS) - H(E) + H(MS) - H(M) - H(E|MS)\}$$

$$= -\frac{1}{2}\{H(E) - H(MS) + H(M)\}$$

or

$$\log P_d = \frac{1}{2}\{H(E) - H(S|M)\}$$

as was to be shown.

Corollary

(16) $$P_d \geq \frac{1}{\sqrt{|\mathcal{E}|}}$$

Proof:

(17) $$H(E) \geq \log|\mathcal{E}|$$

with equality if and only if the transmitter/receiver's optimal strategy E is the uniform probability distribution on $\mathcal{E}$. The conclusion follows by substituting (17) into (12).∎

The expression of the channel bound given in (16) is the one which is apparently violated by the DES based authentication scheme described in the next section.

## A "Practical" Authentication Scheme

The source is a "fair" coin flip, i.e., the probability of heads or tails is 1/2. The transmitter/receiver choose to encode (not authenticate) the state "heads" as the sixty-four bit binary string 11...1 and "tails" as 011...1. In other words the redundant information used to authenticate a message is the suffix of 63 1's and only the left-most bit conveys any information about the state of the source. They then encrypt whichever of these strings is indicated by the coin flip using DES and a secret (known only to them) DES key -- which as is well known consists of fifty-six bits of equivocation to an outsider; the opponent. Each choice of a DES key corresponds in this scheme to a choice of an authentication encoding rule. Consequently, $|\mathcal{E}| = 2^{56}$, and (16) says that

$$P_d \geq \frac{1}{\sqrt{|\mathcal{E}|}} = \frac{1}{2^{28}} \approx 3.7 \times 10^{-9}$$

i.e., the transmitter/receiver cannot, even if they use the $2^{56}$ encoding rules optimally, limit the opponent's chances of deceiving the receiver to less than roughly four parts in a billion.

Now consider the "practical" chance that the receiver will be deceived. First, there are $2^{64}$ possible ciphers (messages), only two of which are acceptable for any particular choice of a key (authentication encoding rule). Therefore, if the opponent merely selects a cipher at random and attempts to impersonate the transmitter, his chances of success are $2^{-63}$ or approximately one chance in $10^{19}$ not four in $10^{9}$! The question is, can he do better. As far as impersonating the transmitter is concerned, the answer is essentially no, even if he has unlimited computing power. For each choice of an encoding rule, there are two (out of $2^{64}$) ciphers that will be acceptable as authentic. Assuming that the mapping of $\mathcal{S}$ into $\mathcal{M}$ under DES keys is a random process, this says that the total expected number of acceptable ciphers (over all $2^{56}$ keys) is $\approx 2^{56.9888}$, i.e., $\varepsilon$ close to $2^{57}$. Even if the opponent could restrict himself to choosing a cipher from among this collection, his chances of having a fraudulent message be accepted by the receiver would only be $2^{-56}$ or roughly one chance in $10^{17}$ which is what we meant when we said that the answer was essentially no. The opponent could not do better, nor worse, (in attempting to impersonate the transmitter) than choose a cipher randomly from among the $\approx 2^{57}$ potentially acceptable ciphers, if the transmitter/receiver chose an encoding rule indexed by the $2^{56}$ DES keys using a uniform probability distribution as their strategy.

The argument in the preceding paragraph is not misleading, i.e., the opponent's chances of deceiving the receiver through impersonating the transmitter are no better than stated. On the other hand, the channel bound in (16) applies to all authentication schemes -- hence the apparent contradiction must arise in connection with the opponent's substitution strategy. If the opponent waits to observe a legitimate message (cipher), can he put this information to practical use to deceive the receiver. Even if he doesn't know the state of the source, he knows that the cipher is the result of encrypting either 111...1 or 011...1 with one of the $2^{56}$ DES keys. He also knows that with a probability of essentially one ($\approx 0.996$), there is only one key that maps the observed message into either of these codes, hence, he is faced with a classical "meet in the middle" cryptanalysis of DES. Clearly if he succeeds in identifying the DES key, i.e., the encoding rule being employed by the transmitter receiver, he can encrypt the other binary string and be certain of having it accepted and hence be certain of deceiving the receiver. The point, though, is that in order for him to make use of his observation of a message he must be able to cryptanalyze DES. If he can do this, the expected probability of deceiving the receiver is $\varepsilon$ close to one -- the small deviation being attributable to the exceedingly small chance that two (or more) DES keys might have encoded source states into the same message (cipher). Thus, we have the paradoxical result that the practical system is some eight or nine orders of magnitude more secure than the theoretical limit simply because it is computationally infeasible for the opponent to carry out in practice what he should be able to do in principle. In this respect practical message authentication [3] is closely akin to practical cryptography where security is equated to the computational infeasibility of inverting from arbitrarily much matching cipher text and plaintext pairs to solve for the unknown key -- even though in principle there is more than enough information available to insure a unique solution.

## References


1. G. J. Simmons, "Message Authentication: A Game on Hypergraphs," Proceedings of the 15th Southeastern Conference on Combinatorics, Graph Theory and Computing, Baton Rouge, LA, March 5-8, 1984, pp. 161-192.

2. G. J. Simmons, "Authentication Theory/Coding Theory," Proceedings of Crypto'84, Santa Barbara, CA, August 19-22, 1984, in Advances in Cryptology, Ed. by R. Blakley, Springer-Verlag, Berlin (1985), to appear.

3. G. J. Simmons, "Message Authentication Without Secrecy," in Secure Communications and Asymmetric Cryptosystems, ed. by G. J. Simmons, AAAS Selected Symposia Series, Westview Press, Boulder, CO (1982), pp. 105-139.

4. Data Encryption Standard, FIPS, Pub. 46, National Bureau of Standards, Washington, D.C., January 1977.

# MESSAGE PROTECTION BY SPREAD SPECTRUM MODULATION IN A PACKET VOICE RADIO LINK

M. Kowatsch, B.O. Eichinger, F.J. Seifert
Technische Universität Wien
A-1040 Vienna, Austria

## 1. Introduction

In spread spectrum communication systems the bandwidth of the transmitted signal is far in excess of the information bandwidth itself. The spectrum spreading is controlled by a pseudonoise (PN) code. Knowledge of this code allows authorized receivers to process the arriving signal with a significant gain in signal-to-noise ratio by correlating it with a locally generated reference waveform. The inherent interference suppression capability has been the primary motivation for the development of spread spectrum techniques /1/. The two most common forms of spread spectrum modulation are direct-sequence (DS) and frequency-hopping (FH), the first of which is considered in this paper. In DS systems the carrier is phase-modulated by a PN code with a code rate (chip rate) much higher than the data rate. The term 'chip' is used to distinguish between code and data stream. Although the codes most frequently used are not secure in a cryptographic sense, protection against unauthorized message access is associated with the low power spectral density of the wideband DS signals. This attribute applies even more to systems employing non-repeating spreading codes.

This paper describes a DS system for the transmission of packet voice. The next section presents a brief outline of the system concept. In section 3 the leading aspects for the selection of the PN codes are discussed.

## 2. The System Concept

A block diagram of the system to be considered is shown in Fig. 1. Continuously variable slope delta (CVSD) modulation is used to encode speech signals at 16 kbit/s. The encoder output data stream is split into blocks of 1024 bits. By adding a 14-bit header at the beginning

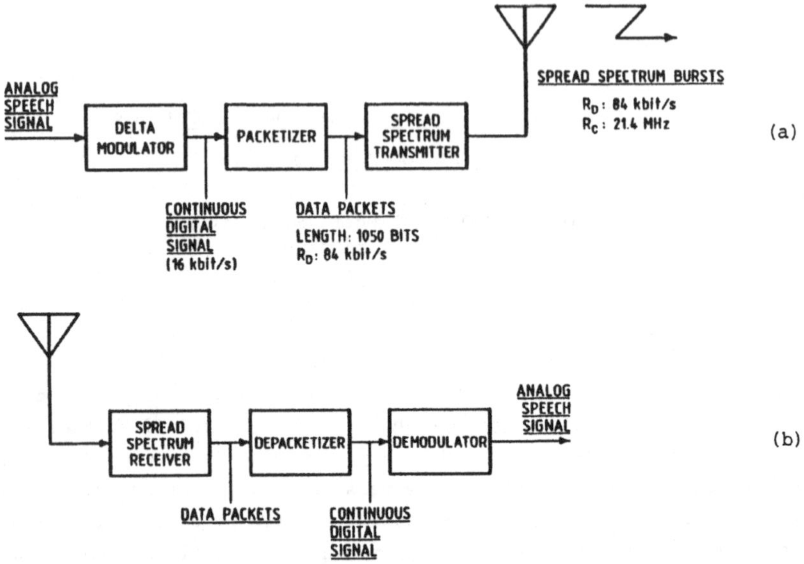


Fig.1: Block diagram of packet voice spread spectrum system
(a) Transmitter
(b) Receiver

and a 12-bit control sequence at the end of each block, data packets with a length of 1050 bits are obtained. These packets are routed to the spread spectrum section and transmitted in bursts at the data rate $R_D$ = 84 kbit/s. For data signalling binary code shift keying (CSK) is employed. That is, ones and zeros of the message are represented by 255-chip PN codes with low crosscorrelation. The resulting chip rate $R_C$ is 21.4 MHz. The spreading code is changed from bit to bit of the data packet. No code is used more than once in any particular burst.

The receiver design is based on the application of surface acoustic wave (SAW) elastic convolvers to programmable matched filtering of the continuously changing PN patterns. The alignment of received signal and local reference is accomplished by means of an 11-bit synchronization preamble preceding each data packet /2/,/3/.

## 3. Spreading Code Selection

Several aspects have to be considered for the selection of the spreading codes. The first is to make it impossible for unintended parties to predict the PN sequences used to encode future data bits based on the observation of past code segments. Furthermore, in the present case, each PN pattern used to encode one bit should be easily time-reversible, as the receiver code chips have to be in reversed order, because of the counterpropagation of the two waveforms in the convolver. Finally, for CSK applications, low crosscorrelation of the PN patterns representing ones and zeros, respectively, is of paramount importance. Thus, a large set of PN codes with bounded crosscorrelation is required. Moreover, a code-generation algorithm which allows direct generation of the time-reversed sequences is desirable.

A code set satisfying these conditions is the so-called large set of Kasami sequences /4/. These codes can be generated by modulo-2 addition of the output sequences of three properly selected linear feedback shift registers (LFSR). Two registers have length n, one has length n/2, the period of the resulting codes being $2^n-1$ for any even n. The number of sequences in the set is given by

$$K = \begin{cases} 2^{n/2}(2^n+1), & n \equiv 2 \bmod 4 \\ 2^{n/2}(2^n+1)-1, & n \equiv 0 \bmod 4 \end{cases} \tag{1}$$

In either case, the maximum value of the periodic crosscorrelation function $\theta$ is

$$\theta_{max} = 1 + 2^{(n+2)/2} \tag{2}$$

Of course, (2) does not directly apply to the present case, where the PN pattern is changed from bit to bit of the data stream. However, it is a bound on the crosscorrelation for any two codes of the set in the zero code shift situation at the data decision instant, where periodic and aperiodic correlation values are equal. Thus, it yields an adequate estimate for CSK performance evaluations.

The principle of Kasami sequence generation is illustrated in Fig.2 for the 255-chip codes (n = 8) employed in the modem discussed in this paper. The three basic registers are represented by the polynomials 435E, 675C and 23F in the table of irreducible polynomials by Peterson and Weldon /5/. According to (1) a total number of 4111 different sequences satisfying (2) is available from all combinations of the relative phases of two or three of the fundamental sequences.

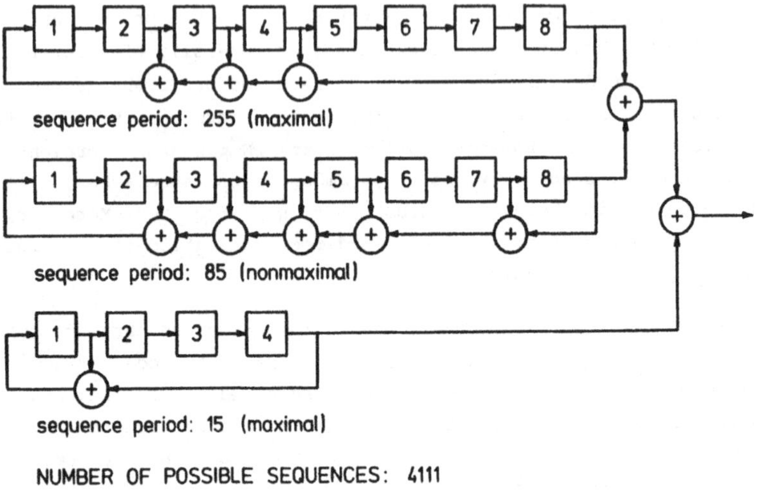


Fig.2: Generation of 255-chip Kasami sequences

The basic unit of the data code generator (Fig.3) is composed of two 8-bit LFSRs and two 4-bit LFSRs. On principle, three registers are required to implement the Kasami sequence generation algorithm, as in Fig.2. Using the two 4-bit registers data modulation is easily accomplished by assigning 7 of the 15 possible initial states for message

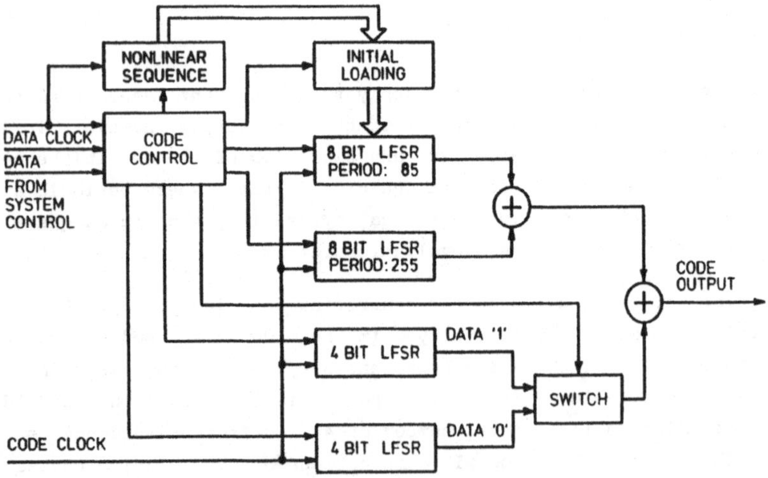


Fig.3: Implementation of code generation and CSK modulation

ones, and 7 for zeros. In order to obtain the large sequence set, the initial state of the 8-bit nonmaximal LFSR with period 85 has to be varied too. This is done under control of a nonlinear code. The applied strategy allows to generate two code sets, each containing 1764 different sequences, for the representation of ones and zeros in the message.

## 4. Results and Conclusion

A breadboard packet voice spread spectrum modem was built and tested on a simulated additive white Gaussian noise channel, measures of performance being the probability of packet loss and the bit error probability within a packet. The experiments indicated that the system can maintain reliable speech communication at receiver input signal-to-noise ratios down to - 10 dB. This is in good agreement with theoretical predictions /6/.

In conclusion, spread spectrum modulation can be used to reduce the power spectral density of radio signals. This facilitates covert communication with low probability of intercept by unintended parties, provided that the transmission bandwidth is sufficiently wider than the information bandwidth. However, with restricted spreading ratios effective protection against unauthorized information access is still feasible. In the case of CSK signalling with continuously changing codes, as discussed in this paper, the eavesdropper has no realistic chance to determine whether a particular received PN pattern represents a message one or a zero.

## References

/1/ R.C.DIXON, Spread Spectrum Systems, 2nd ed., New York: Wiley, 1984.

/2/ M.KOWATSCH, "Synchronization in a Spread Spectrum Communication Modem Based on SAW Convolvers," Proc. 1984 IEEE Military Communications Conference, pp.125-130.

/3/ M.KOWATSCH, "Application of Surface-Acoustic-Wave Technology to Burst-Format Spread-Spectrum Communications," IEE Proc., Vol.131, Pt.F, pp.734-741, Dec.1984.

/4/ D.V.SARWATE and M.B.PURSLEY, "Crosscorrelation Properties of Pseudorandom and Related Sequences," Proc.IEEE, vol.68, pp.593-619, May 1980.

/5/ W.W.PETERSON and E.J.WELDON, Jr., "Error-Correcting Codes," 2nd ed., Cambridge, MA: M.I.T. Press, 1972.

/6/ M.KOWATSCH, "Design of a Convolver-Based Packet Voice Spread Spectrum System," Proc. IEEE 1984 Ultrasonics Symposium, pp.127-131.

## KEYWORDS

# AUTHOR INDEX

Vol. 167: International Symposium on Programming. Proceedings, 1984. Edited by C. Girault and M. Paul. VI, 262 pages. 1984.

Vol. 168: Methods and Tools for Computer Integrated Manufacturing. Edited by R. Dillmann and U. Rembold. XVI, 528 pages. 1984.

Vol. 169: Ch. Ronse, Feedback Shift Registers. II, 1-2, 145 pages. 1984.

Vol. 170: Seventh International Conference on Automated Deduction. Edited by R. E. Shostak. IV, 508 pages. 1984.

Vol. 171: Logic and Machines: Decision Problems and Complexity. Proceedings, 1983. Edited by E. Börger, G. Hasenjaeger and D. Rödding. VI, 456 pages. 1984.

Vol. 172: Automata, Languages and Programming. Proceedings, 1984. Edited by J. Paredaens. VIII, 527 pages. 1984.

Vol. 173: Semantics of Data Types. Proceedings, 1984. Edited by G. Kahn, D.B. MacQueen and G. Plotkin. VI, 391 pages. 1984.

Vol. 174: EUROSAM 84. Proceedings, 1984. Edited by J. Fitch. XI, 396 pages. 1984.

Vol. 175: A. Thayse, P-Functions and Boolean Matrix Factorization. VII, 248 pages. 1984.

Vol. 176: Mathematical Foundations of Computer Science 1984. Proceedings, 1984. Edited by M.P. Chytil and V. Koubek. XI, 581 pages. 1984.

Vol. 177: Programming Languages and Their Definition. Edited by C. B. Jones. XXXII, 254 pages. 1984.

Vol. 178: Readings on Cognitive Ergonomics – Mind and Computers. Proceedings, 1984. Edited by G. C. van der Veer, M. J. Tauber, T. R. G. Green and P. Gorny. VI, 269 pages. 1984.

Vol. 179: V. Pan, How to Multiply Matrices Faster. XI, 212 pages. 1984.

Vol. 180: Ada Software Tools Interfaces. Proceedings, 1983. Edited by P. J. L. Wallis. III, 164 pages. 1984.

Vol. 181: Foundations of Software Technology and Theoretical Computer Science. Proceedings, 1984. Edited by M. Joseph and R. Shyamasundar. VIII, 468 pages. 1984.

Vol. 182: STACS 85. 2nd Annual Symposium on Theoretical Aspects of Computer Science. Proceedings, 1985. Edited by K. Mehlhorn. VII, 374 pages. 1985.

Vol. 183: The Munich Project CIP. Volume I: The Wide Spectrum Language CIP-L. By the CIP Language Group. XI, 275 pages. 1985.

Vol. 184: Local Area Networks: An Advanced Course. Proceedings, 1983. Edited by D. Hutchison, J. Mariani and D. Shepherd. VIII, 497 pages. 1985.

Vol. 185: Mathematical Foundations of Software Development. Proceedings, 1985. Volume 1: Colloquium on Trees in Algebra and Programming (CAAP'85). Edited by H. Ehrig, C. Floyd, M. Nivat and J. Thatcher. XIV, 418 pages. 1985.

Vol. 186: Formal Methods and Software Development. Proceedings, 1985. Volume 2: Colloquium on Software Engineering (CSE). Edited by H. Ehrig, C. Floyd, M. Nivat and J. Thatcher. XIV, 455 pages. 1985.

Vol. 187: F.S. Chaghaghi, Time Series Package (TSPACK). III, 305 pages. 1985.

Vol. 188: Advances in Petri Nets 1984. Edited by G. Rozenberg with the cooperation of H. Genrich and G. Roucairol. VII, 467 pages. 1985.

Vol. 189: M.S. Sherman, Paragon. XI, 376 pages. 1985.

Vol. 190: M.W. Alford, J.P. Ansart, G. Hommel, L. Lamport, B. Liskov, G.P. Mullery and F.B. Schneider, Distributed Systems. Edited by M. Paul and H.J. Siegert. VI, 573 pages. 1985.

Vol. 191: H. Barringer, A Survey of Verification Techniques for Parallel Programs. VI, 115 pages. 1985.

Vol. 192: Automata on Infinite Words. Proceedings, 1984. Edited by M. Nivat and D. Perrin. V, 216 pages.1985.

Vol. 193: Logics of Programs. Proceedings, 1985. Edited by R. Parikh. VI, 424 pages. 1985.

Vol. 194: Automata, Languages and Programming. Proceedings, 1985. Edited by W. Brauer. IX, 520 pages. 1985.

Vol. 195: H.J. Stüttgen, A Hierarchical Associative Processing System. XII, 273 pages. 1985.

Vol. 196: Advances in Cryptology. Proceedings of CRYPTO '84. Edited by G.R. Blakley and D. Chaum. IX, 491 pages.1985.

Vol. 197: Seminar on Concurrency. Proceedings, 1984. Edited by S.D. Brookes, A. W. Roscoe and G. Winskel. X, 523 pages. 1985.

Vol. 198: A. Businger, PORTAL Language Description. VIII, 186 pages. 1985.

Vol. 199: Fundamentals of Computation Theory. Proceedings, 1985. Edited by L. Budach. XII, 533 pages. 1985.

Vol. 200: J.L.A. van de Snepscheut, Trace Theory and VLSI Design. VI, 0-140 pages. 1985.

Vol. 201: Functional Programming Languages and Computer Architecture. Proceedings, 1985. Edited by J.-P. Jouannaud. VI, 413 pages. 1985.

Vol. 202: Rewriting Techniques and Applications. Edited by J.-P. Jouannaud. VI, 441 pages. 1985.

Vol. 203: EUROCAL '85. Proceedings Vol. 1, 1985. Edited by B. Buchberger. V, 233 pages. 1985.

Vol. 204: EUROCAL '85. Proceedings Vol. 2, 1985. Edited by B. F. Caviness. XVI, 650 pages. 1985.

Vol. 205: P. Klint, A Study in String Processing Languages. VIII, 165 pages. 1985.

Vol. 206: Foundations of Software Technology and Theoretical Computer Science. Proceedings, 1985. Edited by S.N. Maheshwari. IX, 522 pages. 1985.

Vol. 207: The Analysis of Concurrent Systems. Proceedings, 1983. Edited by B.T. Denvir, W.T. Harwood, M.I. Jackson and M.J. Wray. VII, 398 pages. 1985.

Vol. 208: Computation Theory. Proceedings, 1984. Edited by A. Skowron. VII, 397 pages. 1985.

Vol. 209: Advances in Cryptology. Proceedings of EUROCRYPT '84. Edited by T. Beth, N. Cot and I. Ingemarsson. VII, 491 pages. 1985.

Vol. 210: STACS 86. Proceedings, 1986. Edited by B. Monien and G. Vidal-Naquet. IX, 368 pages. 1986.

Vol. 211: U. Schöning, Complexity and Structure. V, 99 pages. 1986.

Vol. 212: Interval Mathematics 1985. Proceedings, 1985. Edited by K. Nickel. VI, 227 pages. 1986.

Vol. 213: ESOP 86. Proceedings, 1986. Edited by B. Robinet and R. Wilhelm. VI, 374 pages. 1986.

Vol. 214: CAAP '86. 11th Colloquium on Trees in Algebra and Programming. Proceedings, 1986. Edited by P. Franchi-Zannettacci. VI, 306 pages. 1986.

Vol. 215: Mathematical Methods of Specification and Synthesis of Software Systems '85. Proceedings, 1985. Edited by W. Bibel and K.P. Jantke. 248 pages. 1986.

Vol. 216: Ch. Fernstrom, I. Kruzela, B. Svensson, LUCAS Associative Array Processor: Design, Programming and Application Studies. XII, 323 pages. 1986.

Vol. 217: Programs as Data Objects. Proceedings, 1985. Edited by H. Ganzinger and N.D. Jones. X, 324 pages. 1986.

Vol. 218: Advances in Cryptology – CRYPTO '85. Proceedings, 1985. Edited by H.C. Williams. X, 548 pages. 1986.

Vol. 219: Advances in Cryptology – EUROCRYPT '85. Proceedings, 1985. Edited by F. Pichler. IX, 281 pages. 1986.